Managing Hedge Fund Risk

**FROM THE SEAT OF THE PRACTITIONER –
VIEWS FROM INVESTORS, COUNTERPARTIES,
HEDGE FUNDS AND CONSULTANTS**

Managing Hedge Fund Risk

FROM THE SEAT OF THE PRACTITIONER – VIEWS FROM INVESTORS, COUNTERPARTIES, HEDGE FUNDS AND CONSULTANTS

Edited by Virginia Reynolds Parker

Published by Risk Books, a division of the Risk Waters Group.

Haymarket House
28–29 Haymarket
London SW1Y 4RX
Tel: +44 (0)20 7484 9700
Fax: +44 (0)20 7484 9758
E-mail: books@riskwaters.com
Site: www.riskwaters.com

Every effort has been made to secure the permission of individual copyright
holders for inclusion.

ISBN 1 899 332 78 2

British Library Cataloguing in Publication Data
A catalogue record for this book is available from the British Library

Risk Books Commissioning Editor: Emma Elvy
Desk Editor: Martin Llewellyn

Typeset by Mark Heslington, Scarborough, North Yorkshire

Printed and bound in Great Britain by Bookcraft (Bath) Ltd, Somerset.

Contents

Authors

Mark J. P. Anson is the senior investment officer for Global Equity. Prior to joining CalPERS he held positions as a portfolio manager at OppenheimerFunds Inc, a registered options principal in equity derivatives for Salomon Brothers Inc, and a practising attorney specialising in securities and derivatives regulation. He is the author of two books on derivatives and frequently contributes numerous articles to academic and professional publications on the topics of risk management, derivatives and portfolio management. His articles have appeared in *The Journal of Portfolio Management*, *Journal of Derivatives*, *The Journal of Investing*, *The Journal of Wealth Management*, *The Journal of Alternative Investments*, *Journal of Financial Engineering*, *Derivatives Quarterly* and *Derivatives Week*, as well as numerous financial industry books. He earned his law degree from the Northwestern University School of Law in Chicago where he was the executive/production editor of the *Law Review*, and his Master's and PhD in finance from the Columbia University Graduate School of Business in New York.

A. R. (Rajpal) Arulpragasam currently serves as president of Arktos and Beta Management Limited (BML). Arktos and BML are the onshore and offshore trading managers for Beta Hedge, which is an innovative, market-neutral, US equity hedge fund strategy. He is also the president of ARA Portfolio Management Company, (ARA), that manages portfolios of commodity interests for its investment clients. Prior to this, he directed research and development at a boutique yield-curve arbitrage firm, after which he engaged in private consulting until founding ARA in 1992. He was born in Sri Lanka and brought up in England, then left for the United States in 1970. He received his BS in mathematics from the Massachusetts Institute of Technology and later pursued graduate studies in the field of operations research at Stanford University.

Alex Balfour founded Balfour Capital Ltd, in March 2000. The company is a hedge fund boutique specialising in the Japanese equity market. He has managed and acted as an investment adviser to the Furinkazan Fund, a Japan equity long/short fund. Alex previously worked for Baring Asset Management at its Tokyo operation, where he managed a unit trust as well as pension fund accounts. He has a thorough knowledge of several hundred companies and his fluency in Japanese has been an important asset enabling a much closer relationship with corporate leaders. He is a graduate of Oxford University.

Tanya Styblo Beder is a managing director of Caxton Corporation, an investment management firm located in New York City where she heads the Strategic Quantitative Investments division of the firm. She is also chairman of the board of the International Association of Financial Engineers. She has been on the faculty of the Yale University School of Management for several years and is an appointed fellow of the International Center for Finance at Yale. Previously Ms Beder was president and founding partner of Capital Market Advisors and Capital Market Risk Advisors. She is an author of *Risk Standards for Institutional Investors and Institutional Investment Managers*. She has also written numerous articles in the financial area that have been published by *The Journal of Portfolio Management, Financial Analysts Journal, The Harvard Business Review, Journal of Financial Engineering*, and has also contributed to several books. Her academic work focuses on global capital markets, financial engineering and risk in the financial system. Ms Beder holds a MBA in finance from Harvard University and a BA in mathematics from Yale University. At both universities she received academic awards, including the Anthony D. Stanley award in pure and applied mathematics.

Mike Boren is a principal of Sawtooth Investment Management. Mr Boren has been involved in fixed income arbitrage since 1984. Sawtooth Investment Management is an investment advisor that specialises in global fixed income arbitrage and other relative value and fixed income investment strategies.

Michael A. Boyd, Jr, is the senior founder, managing general partner, chairman and chief investment officer of Forest Investment Management. He is also the sole shareholder of Michael A. Boyd Inc. He chairs the Executive Committee, Investment Policy Committee, and Strategic Development Committee. Mr Boyd was a co-founder in 1992, of the Fund Manager, the General Partner, Forum Capital Markets and other affiliated companies engaged in the financial services business. Forum Capital Markets was merged into First Union in June 2000. Prior to these enterprises, he was an outside contractor and general partner of McMahan Securities Co, LP, a convertible securities broker-dealer. From 1983 to 1988, Mr Boyd was an outside contractor at McMahan & Co, with principal responsibility for overall firm risk management, strategic objectives and management of trading activities. Previous to McMahan & Co, Mr Boyd was the managing partner of Boyd, Upton & Company, a member firm of the New York Stock Exchange and Chicago Board of Options Exchange, which specialised in arbitrage securities. At the firm, Mr. Boyd managed the options trading desk and associated floor brokers, and the firm's stock loan/stock borrow operation. Mr Boyd has more than 30 years of experience in various capacities within the convertible securities, options and arbitrage trading and investment management areas of the securities industry, including Goldman Sachs, Kidder Peabody and Dean Witter Reynolds. He has been a contributing editor to a leading financial publication in his areas of expertise and serves as trustee for several charitable organisations.

Norman Chait joined AIG Global Investment Corporation in 1999. He heads the hedge fund group, which is responsible for AIG's investments with external hedge funds and other liquid alternative assets. He is also portfolio manager for the AIG Diversified Strategies Fund, a Swiss-registered investment fund. He was previously at Banco Santander International, where he managed large portfolios comprised of external managers. He developed the bank's New York based hedge fund research capabilities over four years. He has also spent five years in the Israel Defence Force as a military attorney and graduated from the IDF officers' school. He received his law degree from the Hebrew University of Jerusalem and his MBA from Columbia Business School.

James S. Chanos is president and founder of Kynikos Associates Ltd. The company provides investment management services for both domestic and offshore clients. Through the domestic Ursus Partners fund, as well as Ursus Partners International for international clients, the company provides the investment strategy of profiting from unhedged short selling of overvalued securities. He also manages the fully hedged Beta Hedge and Beta Hedge International funds for domestic and offshore investors. Mr Chanos gained his financial experience as an analyst with Paine Webber, Gilford Securities and Deutsche Bank, where he specialised in finding and evaluating overpriced securities. He is a graduate of Yale University.

A. Paul Chappell is currently the director of both C-View Ltd, the investment advisory business that he founded and Harmer Hyde Investment Ltd. He has previously been a director of Bank of America International Ltd, FX Net Ltd, and Electronic Broking System Ltd where he was at the forefront of developing the system with a number of other leading banks. In 1985 he was hired by Bank of America in London to develop the London Foreign Exchange Trading operations and later was given the responsibility of head of foreign exchange trading for Europe, Middle East, and Africa. He subsequently became responsible for co-ordinating, among other things, the development, structure and customer service of 23 FX Trading operations in all the major global locations. Originally employed as a manager at Hambros Bank in London, he became involved initially in foreign exchange marketing and subsequently went into trading. He began his career with Chemical Bank in London as a trader and then assumed responsibility for FX Spot Trading activities. He gained Part I of his Institute of Bankers Examinations in 1973.

Sam Y. Chung is an assistant professor of finance at the School of Business at Long Island University and is also a research associate at the Center for International Securities and Derivatives Markets (CISDM) at the University of Massachusetts. He has published various articles in journals such as the *Journal of Alternative Investment* along with numerous researches and consulting endeavours in the area of financial risk management and measurement. Professor Chung's current research interests include risk measurement (VAR) and management through derivatives markets, alternative investment (hedge funds, CTAs, managed futures, etc), futures market microstructure, and international banking and finance. Dr Chung received his PhD of finance from the University of Massachusetts, his Master's of finance from Boston College, MBA from Illinois State University and his BA from KyungHee University.

Marcelo Cruz is a director of operational risk at UBS AG, where he is responsible for the development of risk methodology and quantitative analysis. Previously he worked as a derivatives trader for major financial institutions. He has published a range of articles, those most recently published focus on pricing operational risk derivatives, applying extreme value theory and other leading edge quantitative techniques to operational risk. He wrote the first academic quantitative article on operational risk measurement. He holds a PhD in mathematics, a MSc, MBA and BSc in Econometrics.

Jonathan Davies is head of operational risk control at UBS Warburg. He is responsible for the development of the operational risk measurement and risk management process and expanding the application across the other divisions of UBS AG. He also actively represents the bank to regulators and the industry on the development of practices in the field and has recently been appointed as chairman of the ISDA working group on operational risk. Jonathan has had eight years' experience at UBS Warburg in many functions across operations, financial control and business unit control. Prior to his current position he was the global business unit controller for the interest rate derivatives business, managed from London. He has also worked for Bankers Trust and Ernst & Young audit and consulting. He is also a chartered accountant and graduated from the University of Warwick with a BSc in molecular sciences.

Luc Estenne is the director of Partners Advisers SA, a Geneva based family office which provides global hedge fund investment advisory services to a group of privately held investment companies and institutions in Europe. Mr Estenne was previously an officer of Bank Brussels Lambert (BBL) in New York and Brussels, where he was involved in trading proprietary capital. Prior to joining BBL, he held different positions in the Global Technology and Operation group of JP Morgan Brussels. Mr Estenne received his MBA with distinction from the Catholic University of Louvain.

Alexander M. Ineichen is executive director and head of European equity derivatives research for UBS Warburg in London. His current responsibilities include global index research, global index derivatives research and European stock derivatives research as well as research on flow of funds and alternative investment strategies (hedge funds). He holds a federal diploma in economics and business administration from SEBA (School of Economics and Business Administration) in Switzerland and is a CFA (chartered financial analyst). He is a member of the index advisory committee of STOXX, a member of AIMR (Association for Investment Management and Research) and UKSIP (UK Society of Investment Professionals).

Robert A. Jaeger is vice chairman and chief investment officer of Evaluation Associates Capital Markets, which designs, constructs and operates multi-manager hedge fund portfolios for individuals, families and institutions. Prior to this, he was a member of the faculty of Yale University and the University of Massachusetts at Amherst. He holds a BA from Princeton, a BPhil from Oxford and a PhD from Cornell University.

Mary Ann Johnson is the founder of Johnson Custom Strategies, Inc, an independent investment consulting firm. Services include asset allocation, investment program design, manager research and evaluation, cost-effective implementation and ongoing supervision and performance measurement. Ms Johnson spent 10 years on Wall Street in research and corporate finance. In 1979, she joined Rogers, Casey & Barksdale, Inc, a pension fund-consulting firm. As a Principal of RC&B she headed their manager research and selection activities. Ms Johnson custom designed one of the first fund of funds using hedge funds for an institutional level private investment group. She later became President of Tremont Partners, Inc, a specialty consulting firm formed by former employees of Rogers, Casey & Barksdale, Inc, where she remained until she was recruited by Whitehead/Sterling, a private investment company, as the director of Investment Products. She has written numerous articles for *Pensions & Investments* and *Lookout Mountain*, and she has appeared on *The Wall Street Journal Report*. Ms Johnson is a graduate of the University of Redlands in

California and is a frequent speaker for the Institute for International Research and Wealth Management conferences.

Eric Keiter is a principal of MKP Capital Management, LLC, which was founded by Mr Keiter, Patrick McMahon and Chip Perkins. The firm, in New York City, is a private investment management company specialising in relative value fixed income strategies, specifically concentrating on mortgage backed (MBS) and asset backed (ABS) securities. Mr Keiter is responsible for all facets of portfolio and risk management and has been instrumental in the development of the firm's proprietary analytics. Before founding MKP Capital Management, he spent a year and a half as the head mortgage portfolio manager at Fischer Francis Trees & Watts, where he was directly responsible for the management of mortgage-backed assets across portfolios benchmarked to the Mortgage Index, LIBOR and aggregate indices. Prior to Fischer Francis Trees & Watts, Mr. Keiter spent seven years with Salomon Brothers Inc, where he was a vice president in the Mortgage Backed Securities department. Mr Keiter holds a MA in chemistry from Columbia University and a Honors BS in chemistry from the Pennsylvania State University.

Andy Lee is an associate at NetRisk and is responsible for the development of CrystalBox's performance and risk methodologies. Before joining NetRisk, Andy was a senior officer at Askari, a risk management technology firm. His role evolved from risk consulting and research to client implementation, management and support of an enterprise risk management system. He worked extensively in the system testing and validation process and was charged with clarifying and explaining most analytical, operational and repricing issues concerning the technology to both internal and external clients. He received his Master's degree in science, in which he specialised in financial mathematics, from the University of Chicago. His previous educational background includes a BS degree in finance and actuarial science from the Stern School of Business at New York University.

George Martin is currently research director at the Center for International Securities and Derivatives Markets at the University of Massachusetts. He is also a senior associate at TRS Associates, a consulting firm that provides analytical support to financial institutions. He is a frequent speaker on the subject of hedge funds, risk management, structured products and related subjects at industry and academic conferences. He has been published in a wide variety of publications, including the *Journal of Alternative Investments*. Prior to his present position he was a research fellow at the Brookings Institution. He has a BA and a MA from Johns Hopkins University and is currently studying for a doctorate at the University of Paris-Dauphine.

Alastair MacGregor joined Balfour Capital in June 2000. Having graduated from the University of Newcastle, he joined Friends Ivory and Sime, where he assisted in the running of numerous Japanese equity pension funds and retail products. In 2000 he completed the CFA programme, which has provided a solid background and a bridge to applying his analytical skills in an investment context.

Irenee duP. May, Jr is the senior relationship and industry manager for JP Morgan's hedge funds, CTA's and leveraged clients. His responsibilities include the development and execution of JPM strategy to provide managers access to institutional investors and capital markets through debt and structured products as well as direct equity investment. For the past six years, Mr May has significantly expanded business through client acquisition and product development strategies by marketing the firm's product and services across all asset classes. Prior to his involvement in the leverage industry, he was head of global markets and treasurer of the JP Morgan office in Hong Kong and regional head of sales. He has a BA in economics from the University of Virginia and a MBA from the Darden School of Business Administration.

William P. Miller II is a senior vice president and independent risk oversight officer for the Commonfund Group, that provides investment management services for a large number of educational, healthcare and other non-profit organisations. William joined Commonfund in 1996 and is responsible for risk oversight and co-ordinating the risk management activities for Commonfund Group and its subsidiary organisations. In addition, he is responsible for insurance, compliance and internal audit activities.

Marti P. Murray is the founder of Murray Capital Management, Inc. The firm serves as investment adviser to two pooled funds and certain separately managed accounts. The firm focuses on the distressed, transitional high yield, special situation equity and private claims sectors and conducts all primary research in house. Ms Murray serves as president and portfolio manager of Murray Capital. Prior to forming Murray Capital, Ms Murray spent five years at Furman Selz Inc where she was a senior managing director and portfolio manager of ReCap Partners, LP. Previously Ms Murray worked at Oppenheimer & Co, on accounts that invested in the debt and equity securities of troubled companies. Before that, she was an associate at First New York Capital, an investment banking firm for middle market companies engaged in mergers and acquisitions, private placements and venture capital. Before joining New York Capital she worked for Bank of America as a relationship manager for the Bank's Fortune 500 accounts, where her responsibilities included lending into numerous leveraged buyout transactions, leveraged acquisition financing and workout loans. Ms

Murray received an Executive MBA in finance from the Stern School of Business of New York University and a BA in international relations and Chinese from Colgate University.

Murray Nash is a managing director at NetRisk, a firm that provides risk management advice and internet-delivered software products. He leads the Market and Credit Risk group and is responsible for CrystalBox, a web enabled solution for money owners and managers to measure and monitor risk and performance on portfolios of separate and co-mingled investments. Before that, Murray was the head of NetRisk's Advisory group, where he oversaw projects for banks, investment managers, insurance companies, corporations and government agencies on all phases of the risk management process, including developing methodologies for measuring risk over time for credit and investment risks. Prior to joining NetRisk, Mr Nash was senior manager of Askari, Inc, a risk management consulting and technology firm. From 1987 until 1995, he worked for the New Zealand Treasury and for the last three years of that time, he was chief analyst of the Debt Management Office. He also worked in the Social Welfare and Policy Coordination and Development Groups in the New Zealand Treasury. Mr Nash received a Master of Commerce (first class honours) degree in 1987 and a Bachelor's degree in commerce from the University of Auckland.

Erik Norland is vice president and a portfolio strategist at CDC Investment Management Corporation, which he joined as a quantitative analyst in the Global Dynamic Asset Allocation Group (GDAA) and currently works as a portfolio strategist. His primary responsibilities include assisting with portfolio strategy and providing support for the sales and client service staff. Additionally, he contributes actively to the research effort as well as writing articles for financial publications on a variety of topics related to the management of the GDAA funds. Previously, he conducted research for an earlier generation of quantitative models at Bankers Trust. Mr Norland received a MA in statistics from Columbia University and a BA in economics and political science from St. Mary's College of Maryland.

John Michael Pagli, Jr is the managing partner and member of the executive committee of Forest Investment Management and is also the president and a director of the Forest Global Convertible Fund Ltd. He has also served as CEO of one its corporate joint ventures. He is a co-founder and member of the board of directors of Divitiae LLC, a joint venture with Forest Investment Management, and also serves on the board of Greenwich Annuity & Life Insurance (Barbados), a special purpose offshore investment company. He is also a member and past officer of the Association for Corporate Growth. He previously worked for Merrill Lynch Capital Markets. He is a frequent speaker internationally at many alternative investment conferences and is a contributing author on alternative invest-ments and convertible arbitrage to *Hedge Fund Research, Euromoney, Derivatives Strategy* and many other titles. He earned a BSBA degree in finance and international economics from Boston University's School of Management. He earned a MBA in finance and corporate strategy at New York University's Stern School of Business Administration where he was also an adjunct professor of convertible securities.

John Paulson is the president of Paulson & Co, Inc (PCI). He is also the investment manager for Paulson International Ltd and general partner for Paulson Partners LP. Both funds specialise in risk arbitrage. Prior to organ-ising PCI in 1994, John was a general partner of Gruss Partners and a Managing Director in Mergers and Acquisitions at Bear Stearns. He received his Master's degree in Business Administration with high distinc-tion, as a Baker Scholar, from Harvard Business School and graduated *summa cum laude* from New York University.

José M. Quintana is the managing director and co-head of the Global Dynamic Asset Allocation team of CDC Investment Management Corporation. He was previously vice president and head of quantitative research for the strategic asset allocation team in the Global Investment Management Group of Bankers Trust Company. Before that, he was a vice president in the Global Risk Management sector of the Chase Manhattan Bank, responsible for developing and implementing global asset allocation strategies for managing internal and external investment programs. José has also been a vice president of Chase Investors Management Corporation's Indexing and Hedging group. He also served as a staff supervisor for AT&T's Market Analysis and Forecasting Directorate. His research interests are Bayesian forecasting and optimal decision making in the investment management context. He has published articles in both the academic and popular press on topics ranging from dynamic statistical modelling to optimisation algorithms to portfolio management techniques. He has made presentations at the University of Chicago and Duke University as well as several international conferences. He received his PhD in statistics from Warwick University, his Master's in statistics & oper-ations research and his BA in actuary from the Autonomous University of Mexico.

Virginia Reynolds Parker is the founder and president of Parker Global Strategies. Ms Parker has expertise in both traditional and alternative investment strategies, combined with a strong background in currency risk and returns, independent risk measurement and management of multi-manager hedge fund portfolios and principal protection guarantees. She is well known for developing industry-recognised performance benchmarks for foreign exchange and fixed income trading. Her research is widely published and she is a frequent speaker at industry conferences. From 1988 until 1995, Ms Parker was managing director and director of research and risk management at Ferrell Capital Management, where she guided the firm's portfolio structuring, asset allocation strategies, new product development and risk management. While at Ferrell, Ms Parker developed the Ferrell FX Index. She purchased the Index in July 1997. Previously, she was the chief investment officer for a family office. Ms Parker earned an AB in economics and political science from Duke University. She is registered as an Associated Person with the National Futures Association and as a Direct Participation Principal with the NASD.

Graham Rowlands is the global head of prime broker risk management at Lehman Brothers. For the preceding eight years he occupied a senior role in Lehman Brothers' risk management group focusing primarily on market risk. His prior career includes establishing a listed options/futures market-making company as well as a company that provided bespoke risk management software. He has a MSc in computation and BSc (Hons) in civil engineering.

Jane Tisdale is a principal of State Street Global Advisors where she is responsible for product development, client service and new business development across all of the quantitative US active equity investment processes. In addition, she is co-manager of the Mid Cap Strategy and a member of the Long/Short US Equity team. Previously, she served as portfolio manager in SSGAs US structured products group as well as comptroller for the firm. She is a member of the Boston Security Analysts Society and the Association for Investment Management and Research (AIMR). She received a Master's in finance from the Wallace E. Carroll School of Management at Boston College and a BS in finance from Ithaca College

Randolf G. Warsager is managing director of Marketing and Client Services at Parker Global Strategies. PGS constructs customised multi-manager hedge fund portfolios for institutions and conducts ongoing risk management and oversight. The firm also sponsors onshore and offshore hedge funds. Prior to joining PGS, Mr Warsager was vice president of Institutional Marketing at the New York Mercantile Exchange from 1997 until 1999. At the Exchange he developed an educational programme on hedge funds and managed futures for investors in the US, Canada and Europe. He also held the position of vice president of Marketing at the Exchange, overseeing Product Marketing, Corporate Communication and Statistics. He is a member of the Advisory Board of the Center for International Securities and Derivatives Markets at the University of

Massachusetts and the Board of Directors of the Foundation for Managed Derivatives Research, which provides grants for original research on the use of derivatives in investment products. Mr Warsager co-authored an article on commodity investment vehicles in the *Journal of Alternative Investments* and has written articles on managed futures and energy-based investment products. He received his undergraduate degree from New York University in psychology and philosophy.

D. Sykes Wilford is the chief investment officer and member of the board of CDC Investment Management Corporation. He was formerly the chief investment officer of Bankers Trust's Private Bank and managing director of Bankers Trust's Global Investment Management. He has also held the position of managing director of Chase Manhattan Bank NA as global component executive for the Portfolio Strategies Group. He has directed Chase's Global Commodity Risk Management and European Index Linked Derivative Products businesses and was director of the Chase Europe Development Institute. He has been an economist with the Federal Reserve Bank of New York, and chief international fixed-income strategist for Drexel Burnham Lambert. His research interests are monetary economics and international finance and his articles have appeared in many research journals including the *American Economic Review* and the *Journal of Finance*. He has also authored and edited several books, ranging from economic policy in developing countries to *Managing Financial Risk*. He has been a visiting faculty member at several universities, including New York University, Pace University in New York, L'Université de Saint-Louis in Brussels, and the University of New Orleans; he presently holds a visiting professorship at City University of London. He received his PhD in economics from Tulane University in New Orleans, a Master's in economics from Vanderbilt University and a BS in economics from the University of Tennessee.

The Diversity and Commonality of Risk

Virginia Reynolds Parker and Randolf G. Warsager

Parker Global Strategies LLC

With each passing year, the topic of hedge fund risk management gains importance. This corresponds with increasing volatility in world markets, complex strategies gaining in popularity, new hedge funds proliferating, and the size of the industry continuing on its steady growth pattern. Marquee names rise and fall. Investors and managers alike know that diligent risk management is essential. Diligence must be reinforced with knowledge about identifying, understanding, controlling and minimising risk. Consequently, recent years have seen an explosion in interest in risk management, and issues of risk management remain (or should remain) high on every investor's list of concerns.

Different risk managers have different concerns, depending on the nature of the portfolios for which they are responsible and the kinds of firms or institutions that employ them. And since risk is linked to a range of other variables – liquidity, transparency and control – a broad view may serve the reader best. These variables are fundamentally related, both to risk management and to one another, and as such they arise at various points throughout these chapters.

Tanya Styblo Beder of Caxton Corporation writes in her chapter that, "It is vital to acknowledge here that not all hedge funds pose the same risks; some are inherently riskier than others. The level of risk also depends upon the risk appetite, risk control discipline and common sense of the hedge fund management. Nevertheless, there are common elements of risk management that define the current practice for hedge funds".

This volume has two objectives. First, we hope that the collection of viewpoints from diverse perspectives will be a valuable and accessible primer on managing hedge fund risk. Second, we hope that, through the treatment of several advanced topics, it provides useful information to experienced risk managers. This is not a theoretical volume – most of the authors are practitioners whose significant expertise in their specific areas helps shine light on the discipline.

Hedge fund risk comes in many forms. In approaching risk, one must address the topic at its various levels: enterprise-wide risk, multi-manager portfolio risk, single manager risk, and instrument risk. Investors, fund of fund managers and hedge fund managers all face multiple kinds and degrees of risk, some of which are shared by their counterparts. That there are many aspects of risk common across strategies is supported by the increase in correlations among hedge fund returns that took place in August 1998 and at other times of severe market stress.

Others kinds of risk are unique to managers, driven by the strategies and tactics they employ. Even within a single strategy, managers can address risk in different ways and at different stages. This volume contains chapters written by hedge fund managers for each of the following strategies: global macro, global fixed income arbitrage, US equity market neutral, merger arbitrage, convertible arbitrage, mortgage arbitrage, distressed securities, short selling, Japanese equity long / short, and currency trading.

INCREASED LEVEL OF SCRUTINY OF HEDGE FUNDS

Financial theory, according to D. Sykes Wilford of CDC Investment Management Corp, tells us that "earning high returns and controlling risk are part of the same process. Yet although sophisticated investors have long known the value of high risk-adjusted returns, it took recent problems at Long Term Capital Management, Tiger, Quantum and other trading operations, to refocus the asset management industry on risk management. Gone are the days when asset management firms differentiated themselves largely on the basis of how much return they could earn. These days, the focus has shifted to risk-adjusted returns . . . what will really differentiate firms are their respective methods of interpreting and applying risk management".

Tanya Styblo Beder of Caxton observes that, in the aftermath of the widely known hedge fund losses during the 1990s, attention has been focused on risk management. "A useful by-product of this spotlight has been an increased focus on greater education, information and market transparency at the highest level of public and private organisations". In her chapter, she examines key aspects of risk management for the large hedge funds discussed in the February 2000 report "Sound Practices for Hedge Fund Managers", which is reprinted in the Appendix of this volume.

The bail out of Long Term Capital Management, the huge US-based hedge fund noted for its secrecy, the magnitude of its failure, and the Nobel Prize-winning laureates among its principals, has precipitated attempts by regulators to require greater disclosure of hedge fund risks. The regulators and the hedge fund industry employ "transparency" as the term for such increased disclosure.

The hedge fund industry continues to be largely unregulated. Until recently, most managers supplied minimal information to investors: monthly returns, maximum losses, and maybe a quarterly letter for investors. Since performance statistics relay very little information about hedge fund risks, the statistics might be considered "opaque". On the other hand, reporting of risk information has commonly occurred just once a quarter. This level of reporting has made gauging interim risk levels difficult at best. Additionally, managers have been able to "window-dress" portfolios for quarter-end reporting, further obscuring the risk picture.

Some hedge fund managers, under pressure from investors and fearing regulatory controls, now provide further information: value-at-risk (VAR) by product, leverage measures, liquidity levels, limited portfolio composition, and performance attribution by asset class. In some cases, managers provide this information on a daily basis. Some managers are willing to discuss portfolio information openly and directly with investors, yet continue to object to displaying the information on a secured website or in a document. And some investors are still quite satisfied with this opaque approach, as they have confidence in the manager.

What is risk?

Risk is generally defined by example rather than articulation of its "essence", perhaps because a universally agreed-upon and succinct definition remains so elusive.

Risk is the potential for loss of control and / or value. Risk may range from the benign to the malignant, from the dormant to the brewing to the exploding. Risk may be expected or it may be a surprise. Most importantly, risk is ever-present.

Robert A. Jaeger, of Evaluation Associates Capital Markets, considers the question of whether there is, in fact, some essential definition of risk to be discovered. He argues that the conventional tendency to equate risk with volatility does not provide a complete picture of risk. In his view, attempts to discover a single measure or number that is the essence of risk are bound to fail, and he points out that this gives rise to an obvious dilemma in risk management: "How can you manage something that you cannot even measure?" He goes on to write, ". . . a proper appreciation of the difficulties of measuring risk actually improves one's ability to manage risk". On a cautionary note Mr Jaeger adds that, "Those who overestimate their ability to measure risk, who have too much confidence in the sophistication of their quantitative tools, are precisely the ones most likely to get into trouble". Recent history provides our evidence. Mr Jaeger writes that his simple definition of risk "would be something like 'expected pain', which would combine a rough measure of the likelihood of various unfavourable outcomes with a rough measure of how unfavourable those outcomes are. This simple definition at least captures the fact that risk judgments depend on two elements: the likelihood of various painful outcomes, and the level of pain associated with those outcomes. Think of the difference between AM radio and FM radio. AM radio works by modulating the amplitude of the signal, FM radio works by modulating the frequency of the signal. Risk combines frequency with amplitude. But this definition is, of course, an idealised over-simplification, since in most real-life situations we have no real hope of measuring either the probabilities or the level of pain. Investment situations give us the opportunity to measure standard deviations, value-at-risk, and all sorts of other numbers, but that is not the same as measuring risk".

Mark Anson, of Global Equity, for the California Public Employee Retirement System, writes in his chapter that, "The hedge fund industry has received tremendous attention over the past decade as an alternative investment class to hedge traditional portfolio returns. However, as a new investment class, there are new risks that require consideration. [There are] five risk factors associated with hedge fund investments that must be considered *in addition to the market exposures received*". [Our emphasis]. Mr Anson defines and discusses these risk factors – process risk, mapping risk, event risk, data risk, and performance measurement risk – and recommends that they be carefully considered by investors. I emphasise his words because he makes the point that these risks are *above and beyond* market risk. Market risk gets most of the attention, but these other risk factors can be insidious.

Mr Anson concludes that "these five factors do not diminish the value of hedge fund investments, but are useful for developing realistic expectations with respect to the value added of hedge funds in a diversified portfolio".

William P. Miller of Commonfund, who has written widely on risk, writes that, "At heart, investors tend to think of risk as the possibility of a decline in the market prices or net asset value of their investments, and this is certainly the easiest definition for a complex condition. To give us a better handle on the chance of decline, professional investors have defined risk in terms of the volatility we can track in an investment's performance record. We then get further help from the science of statistics, which gives us a convenient marker for the range of volatility as related to the stock's net price change in the standard deviation. Statistical analysis also gives us a benchmark for a security's volatility in relation to the overall stock market in its beta".

Luc Estenne of Partners Advisors writes that, "Risk is the exposure to uncertain change. It can be seen as the combination of the probability of a negative event happening and the loss associated with the occurrence of this negative event".

Just as the general concept of risk needs a clarification of definition, so do specific types of risk. Marcelo Cruz and Jonathan Davies of UBS Warburg write that, "Operational risk has earned considerable attention [in the mid-1990s] in the wake of huge losses that took place at investment banks such as Barings and Daiwa. Yet, the fact is there is no agreed industry definition of operational risk". In their chapter, Cruz and Davies evaluate various definitions and discuss how to manage operational risk.

WHAT IS RISK MANAGEMENT?

D. Sykes Wilford of CDC writes, "Even the exact definition of risk management is nebulous, the term being frequently used in different firms to mean different things. Many, if not most, institutions now employ very sophisticated models to evaluate the risks of their portfolios. In fact, many even have a department called 'risk management'". He goes on to observe that, "Ironically, while the term 'risk management' implies action, the departments that use VAR models and scenario tests to provide very important services to the firm actually do very little by way of *managing risk*. Rather, they *measure risk*".

He continues, "Managing risk is more than just measuring the degree of risk inherent in portfolios that have already been put into place: it entails using certain risk measures to allocate risk optimally among different assets, while using other types of risk measures to monitor exposures and make refinements. There is, unfortunately, no one single risk allocation process that can be applied to all types of investment strategies".

TRANSPARENCY AS A FACTOR IN RISK

The hedge fund industry has come to recognise that transparency can add great value to the risk measurement and management process. At the same time, in the absence of meaningful liquidity and control at the portfolio and instrument levels, the benefits of complete transparency cannot be fully realised. If investors are without a level of liquidity that corresponds to the degree of transparency, they are prevented from responding to time-sensitive portfolio information.

Can there ever be too much transparency? There are several kinds of transparency and many ways that the information can be used. So, whether there is too much transparency depends on who is looking. An investor whose goal is simply to benefit from the diversification of hedge fund styles may lack the training and systems necessary to evaluate massive amounts of daily data. Nonetheless, this investor may benefit from somebody else doing it on their behalf. Fund of fund managers and manager of managers are often in a position to assess such information.

There are two opposing views on the value of complete transparency, but the trend in the industry is toward increased disclosure. Greater disclosure may take various forms for an investor, from informal conversations with the hedge fund managers about current activity to obtaining a download of every transaction, which is then evaluated for risk by an expert on the investor's behalf. The level of information provided depends on the manager, the strategy and style of investing, as well as the degree to which the manager employs short selling. These factors can all influence the manager's view.

The concept of benign transparency has emerged as a compromise between full and partial disclosure of position information. What makes this transparency benign, rather than malignant? Why don't managers simply divulge their positions on a daily basis? Two arguments emerge. First, that investors lack the skills to evaluate even benign information, meaning that more information, such as position information, would either overwhelm or provide false comfort. Second, that position information in the wrong hands hurts both manager and investor, since the dealer community would be able to trade against this information, potentially causing losses.

So, does transparency really help investors? Some investors do have the skills to understand and evaluate a portfolio of positions. Others outsource this process to professional risk managers. Either way, complete *daily* transparency of manager positions makes the job of analysing risk more complicated, while increasing its utility. More importantly, this kind of transparency facilitates the analysis of a *portfolio* of hedge fund investments.

William P. Miller of Commonfund writes, "When you have limited information about what is held in a partnership, your due diligence and monitoring can be expanded to acquire greater comfort with that investment. But then, the fund can change very fast. Within hours, some hedge funds can switch their entire strategy in pursuit of a new opportunity... transparency [is] one of the keys to risk management".

Few hedge fund investors allocate to one hedge fund only. Usually, investors build multi-manager portfolios, seeking diversification. Without daily transparency and the appropriate knowledge and infrastructure, risk analysis of a multi-manager portfolio is still something of a guessing game. In some fund of funds, when an attempt is made to avoid the impact of a single manager blow-up, inadequate transparency results in too much diversification, often resulting in lacklustre performance. Only complete transparency can allow the investor or their manager of managers to create a well diversified portfolio, and to compare actual and expected asset diversification and risk on a daily basis.

On the threat of transparency resulting in confidential position information reaching the market place, one may argue that the dealer community poses a far greater risk to the hedge fund managers than an investor does. If hedge funds know who their investors are, they can determine whether the investors are likely to use position information improperly. Confidentiality agreements bind investors and managers of managers to maintaining secrecy relating to hedge fund investments. Investors, or their manager of managers, should be able to hedge against risks in the portfolio or multi-manager portfolio, but should be limited to hedging versus position-taking or front-running.

LIQUIDITY AS A FACTOR IN RISK

Liquidity issues are a concern at several levels, as with so many aspects of risk. Redemption policies are a general guide to the kind of fund liquidity and they are predictable, at least in principle. When crises arise, redemption becomes a slave to liquidity at the instrument level. Some investors prefer to target only funds with a high degree of liquidity, while others are quite willing to assume liquidity risk in pursuit of a specific investment strategy. Irenee duP. May, of JP Morgan, observes that, "In recent years it appears that liquidity risk is more likely to cause a fund a problem than the other risks taken in the portfolio". Liquidity risk is discussed by several of the contributors to this volume.

What is liquidity?

Liquidity is one of the most complex concepts in hedge fund and fund of funds investment. The considerations listed below help to create an understanding of the different meanings of liquidity. A bottom-up approach to its definition makes the most sense, starting with the liquidity of hedge fund instruments and ending with the direct impact on the investor.

Hedge fund manager considerations
Instrument liquidity
If we ranked all traded instruments from most to least liquid, we might start with US government Treasury bills and end with over-the-counter (OTC) derivatives on emerging market securities. When global markets experience shifting fundamentals or market shocks, investors often take a "flight-to-quality", and spreads widen. For a small market, such as an emerging market, this is akin to someone yelling "fire!" in a crowded theatre – the rush to the door leaves few unscathed.

Redemption liquidity
A realistic relationship must exist between the liquidity of the instruments in a portfolio and the redemption provisions agreed to by a hedge fund manager for an orderly redemption. An additional consideration is the size of the hedge fund manager. Larger managers, even those trading highly liquid strategies, find that the sheer size of their assets under management limits flexibility to shift a portfolio quickly to the more liquid end of the spectrum without causing a market scare. At the same time, many investors avoid smaller managers, simply because of size. These are often excellent managers who have good flexibility in turning positions without impacting markets.

Financing liquidity

Hedge fund managers frequently require financing for leveraged trading, for strategies such as fixed income and mortgage arbitrage. Prime brokers may have the right to pull financing lines at any time, forcing a liquidation of the portfolio. Prime brokers may choose to withdraw financing at a particularly bad time for portfolio liquidation.

Fund of fund manager considerations
Risk management liquidity

Investors hire fund of funds managers to provide professional oversight of investments and allocations. In the traditional fund of funds structure, the fund of funds manager purchases shares in third-party hedge funds. A fund of fund manager may decide to reduce risk in a portfolio by changing an allocation to a manager. Redemption notice periods, however, can limit the usefulness of this professional oversight. The purpose of redemption notice periods is to allow the underlying hedge fund manager to perform an orderly liquidation of assets but, in some instances, real-time risk management might better serve the interests of investors. Some manager of managers use managed account fund structures, which enable real-time liquidity and proactive management of the risk profile of a portfolio. This can be accomplished by subscriptions and redemptions, providing daily liquidity for risk management purposes. Additionally, manager of managers can proactively manage risk by instructing a manager to reduce positions or by adjusting the portfolio through a risk overlay.

Liquidity mismatches

Fund of funds managers need to consider the underlying manager redemption procedures before establishing their own. Liquidity mismatches occur when a fund of funds manager offers more frequent liquidity than its underlying hedge fund managers. This sometimes causes the "rush to the door", because investors know that if they do not get out first, they may be left with the fund's illiquid assets, while the more fleet of foot have secured the cash. Occasionally, fund of fund managers have suspended redemptions to address the liquidity mismatch.

Writing from the standpoint of an insurance company with proprietary hedge fund investments, Norman Chait of AIG Global Investment Corp cites a potential example of a liquidity mismatch. "Certain US convertible arbitrage managers do offer monthly liquidity to clients. But unless the managers use limited leverage, or stick with investment grade issues, this could create an asset-liability mismatch. Convertible arbitrage entails the purchase of a convertible bond and the concurrent short sale of the correct ratio of equity of the same issuer. While there are many ways to make money in this strategy (price appreciation of the bonds, positive carry coupon clipping, volatility trading, etc), in most instances the convertible bond is traded less frequently than the equity hedge. Moreover, some convertible arbitrage managers will lever up their investments six to ten times, and will purchase over 20% of some issues."

He continues, "it is clear that it will take some time to unwind positions. One leading US manager with a focus on non-investment grade convertible bonds admitted it would take her up to six months to liquidate the majority of her portfolio. Nevertheless, the fund offers monthly liquidity to investors. Thus, in the event that most investors wanted to exit the fund at the same time, this would have a severe price impact if the manager were to honour redemptions. In a similar instance in 1998, another manager limited the amount of capital that could exit the fund in a given calendar quarter. Redemption requests were pro-rated, so that while the fund offered quarterly liquidity, it took most investors up to a year to get their money back. A large portion of the portfolio was invested in Regulation D convertibles, which tend to become extremely illiquid in times of market stress".

LEVERAGE AS A FACTOR IN RISK

Understanding leverage is a necessary part of understanding risk. It is a concept, however, that is often misapplied. Discomfort with the leverage of a portfolio reflects a concern for portfolio volatility risk and, for those strategies depending heavily on leverage to generate returns, a concern about the availability of financing.

Unfortunately, the most common leverage measurements derive from balance sheet leverage concepts. Corporate leverage calculations have value as a relative measure between companies in the same industry sector, although as a stand-alone measure they provide little meaningful information about the financial risk of a specific company. The corporate world focuses more on cash flow, and considers EBITDA (earnings before interest, taxes, depreciation and amortisations) ratios as more indicative of financial risk. In the hedge fund world, the most common measures of leverage are gross leverage and net leverage. Gross leverage is: (longs + absolute value of shorts)/portfolio equity. Net leverage is: (longs + shorts)/portfolio equity. While these ratios have value as relative measures between hedge funds trading the same strategies, as stand-alone measures they provide little insight. Other tools must be used to analyse the true risk of leverage in a hedge fund – the volatility and financing risks.

The concepts of VAR and leverage overlap in their common concern for measuring portfolio volatility risk. Several methods exist for assessing the level of volatility risk in a portfolio, depending on the strategy. For strategies with little non-systematic risk, such as those well-suited to VAR analysis, the units of VAR divided by the portfolio equity provide an excellent measure of volatility risk in a portfolio. For these strategies, VAR is superior to other leverage measures. For example, consider two accounts with US$1 million of portfolio equity each, where Portfolio A has US$500,000 of 30-year US Treasuries and Portfolio B has US$3 million of US Treasuries bills that mature in one week. Using the standard definition of hedge fund leverage, Portfolio A has only 0.5% leverage, while Portfolio B has 300% leverage. And yet, Portfolio A has much more capital at risk than Portfolio B. This is because US Treasury bills maturing in one week have a very short duration, or low volatility, compared to the 30-year Treasury bond.

The more appropriate measure of risk for this type of portfolio is VAR. A good example of a situation where VAR appropriately measures leverage is fixed income arbitrage strategies, particularly as related to higher quality bonds.

What does a leverage ratio based on VAR divided by portfolio equity really tell us about a fixed income arbitrage strategy that includes little non-systematic risk? Since VAR is *not* a good measure of non-systematic risk and tail risk, this leverage ratio gives us a very good measure of what per-centage of portfolio equity is at risk in normal markets, because, in this instance, the portfolio has little non-systematic risk. But it tells us little about the portfolio equity at risk under extreme or catastrophic circum-stances. What happens, for instance, when Russia defaults on its debt, and yield curves and bond spreads suffer extreme volatility? What happens when asset liquidity dries up and when financing availability dissipates? Stress-testing and scenario analysis provide additional insight into the potential downside risk to such a portfolio.

Leverage calculations provide limited value in the analysis of the true risk of a hedge fund. Ultimately, managers and investors need to drill down to the imperfect art of volatility and financing risk analysis to make informed judgments about manager and portfolio risk.

Value-at-risk

VAR measures the systematic risk of portfolio assets (also known as the risk that cannot be diversified away) and creates a standard for comparing systematic risk across asset *classes*. VAR calculates the value for the sys-tematic risk of each asset class in a portfolio by referring to an index or a commonly recognised proxy that is representative of its asset class. The index or proxy represents the market, or "system", for the asset class as a whole.

Sam Y. Chung, of Long Island University, describes VAR as "a primary tool for financial risk assessment, has become as commonly used a term in corporate and investment analysis as the Capital Asset Pricing Model (CAPM) or Markowitz portfolio theory. While a variety of VAR definitions exist, VAR is generally defined as an amount lost on a portfolio with a given small probability over a fixed number of days".

"VAR is a single statistical measure of maximum possible portfolio losses. Specifically, it is a measure of losses due to "normal" market movements. Losses greater than the VAR are suffered only with a specified small probability. VAR aggregates all of the risk in a portfolio into a single number suitable for use in the boardroom, reporting to a regulator, or disclosure in an annual report...The major challenge in implementing VAR analysis is the specification of the probability distribution of extreme returns used in the calculation of the VAR estimate. Since VAR estimation, by its nature, is highly dependent on good predictions of uncommon events, or catastrophic risk, any statistical method used for VAR estimation has to have the prediction of tail events as its primary goal."

It is widely felt among risk managers that VAR models should be complemented with other measurement tools, for the reasons listed below.

❏ VAR enables an investor with a portfolio containing US$10 million in market value of the S&P and US$10 million in market value of US government 10-year bonds, to quantify and compare the dollars at risk for an equally probable move in US equities or bonds, such as a 2 standard deviation move in each. In this case, VAR represents a good approximation of total risk, because the majority of the portfolio risk is systematic; that is, they replicate the reference indices and move in tandem with the US equity and bond "systems".

❏ VAR does not measure non-systematic risk, such as specific risk, political risk, event risk or model risk. Generally, the more equity-like the characteristics of a given asset, the less likely VAR is to provide a good approximation of total risk. In other words, the more non-systematic risk an asset has, relative to the index or proxy for its asset class, the less likely VAR is to provide a good approximation of total risk.

❏ VAR also falters in its measurement of tail risk. While VAR represents a good indication of the potential level of portfolio volatility risk under normal market circumstances, it does not reflect extreme or catastrophic market conditions.

❏ Certain hedge fund strategies focus on assets that contain a higher degree of non-systematic risk than others. To manage the portfolio volatility of these strategies, we use different measures and approaches. The non-quantitative methods include diversification of strategy, manager and assets; allocation control; and, enforceable limits on what managers may trade and what concentrations of assets they may hold. Stress-testing, back-testing and scenario analysis reinforce, or substitute for, VAR for certain strategies.

The genius of VAR was the creation of a quantitative method to compare risks across asset classes. For example, prior to its introduction, risk managers could not quantify the risk being taken by a manager trading US$10 million in the S&P Index and US$10 million in US government T-bills with short maturities. Intuitively, they grasped the risk differences, but VAR enabled them to quantify the differences and to properly allocate risk limits and capital costs. Although limited in its strength as a stand-alone risk measure, VAR has significantly improved risk measurement techniques.

THE ROLE OF TECHNOLOGY IN RISK MANAGEMENT

Technology plays an increasingly important role in risk management. As institutional and individual investors use the Internet to keep track of their investments, electronic forms of information become a valuable currency. The hedge fund industry has used technology to make progress in response to this investor-led desire for greater transparency. Technology enables a sophisticated investor to:

❏ gather hedge fund position data from both the manager and its prime broker and counterparties;
❏ reconcile these positions independently, including cash positions;
❏ analyse the risk of the reconciled positions using value-at-risk, stress-testing, correlation analysis, concentration analysis;
❏ calculate a daily (or real-time) NAV, incorporating estimated fees and expenses;
❏ report NAV and risk information via the web in a customised and client-friendly format; and
❏ provide position information via the web, as needed.

This is a very comprehensive level of risk measurement, usually followed by those investors trained in risk management oversight. Present technology is fast, efficient and considerably less expensive than a decade ago. As the hedge fund industry becomes increasingly institutionalised, we are likely to see farther strides in the standardisation of risk reporting, performance reporting, and portfolio information reporting. Over the long term, careful due diligence and sufficient risk measurement tools, along with skilled judgment, will drive successful risk allocation.

HIGHLIGHTS OF THE CHAPTERS
Part I. Perspectives from the Investors
Norman Chait, AIG Global Investment Corporation, "Risk Management: A Practical Approach to Managing a Portfolio of Hedge Funds for a Large Insurance Company"
Norman Chait discusses the philosophical and practical aspects of risk management for hedge fund portfolios. He gives the reader some insights into what is required in order to develop a "consistent, rigorous and comprehensive risk management system".

He discusses liquidity, leverage, and the evaluation of market risk in the portfolio, as well as qualitative issues in managing risk.

Mark J. P. Anson, California Public Employees Retirement System, "Hedge Fund Risk Management for Institutions"
Mark Anson writes from the standpoint of a public pension fund about the need for institutional investors to carefully consider the risks that accompany hedge fund investing, as this area is new to many institutions. He describes five risk factors of hedge fund investing that deserve attention: process risk, mapping risk, event risk, data risk and performance measurement risk.

Luc Estenne, Partners Advisors, "Risk Management Issues for the Family Office"
Luc Estenne writes about the investment needs and objectives of a typical family office, including wealth preservation and wealth transfer issues, and describes the asymmetrical sensitivity to loss with regards to profits that governs family office allocations to hedge funds.

William P. Miller, Commonfund, "Risk Management Issues for Endowments and Foundations"
William Miller emphasises the importance of risk management "working in every part of the investment management process, at every step of the investment continuum..."

Robert A. Jaeger, Evaluation Associates Capital Markets, "Risk: Defining it, Measuring it and Managing it"
Robert Jaeger considers the meaning of risk and discusses the key elements in risk analysis. He reminds the reader that risk and risk management are complicated, and notes that he is chronically suspicious of the idea that risk can be reduced to a single number.

Virginia Reynolds Parker, Parker Global Strategies LLC, "The Critical Path to Effective Hedge Fund Risk Management: Control, Transparency and Risk and Performance Measurement"
Virginia Reynolds Parker writes that risk management is both an art and a science. Numbers alone do not tell the story. The process of managing risk is "most effective when the trading manager has control over the many facets of the programme, along with transparency. With an open, controlled and transparent process, the trading manager may independently confirm portfolio information." Ms Parker adds that while "risk management does not create positive performance, nor does it prevent losses, the discipline of independent, skilled risk management oversight provides a sophisticated approach to hedge fund investing that works to serve the best interest of investors over time". She also reviews the important conclusions of the Group of Thirty study, "Derivative Practices and Principles

for Dealers and End Users", which aimed to establish "best practices" in the use of derivative instruments.

Part II. Perspectives from the Counterparties
Irenee duP. May, JP Morgan, "From a Dealer's Perspective"
Irenee May writes from the point of view of a creditor, and emphasises how important it is to recognise that each fund is different and requires individual assessment, so the creditor can decide whether to participate in the transaction. He describes the process of risk management as a constantly changing balance between factors, and not at all static and linear. The ultimate challenge for the creditor, he says, is to stay flexible enough to allow for the constant dynamic process. "This requires a degree of art amidst the science." (This chapter represents Irenee May's views, and not those of JP Morgan.)

Susan Webb, CDC Capital Markets, "Risk Management of Hedge Funds"
Writing from the standpoint of a structurer and enhancer, Ms Webb says it is essential to understand the liquidity of the underlying fund or trust investments that are being protected. She describes the variety of methods used to arrive at a complete understanding of the risk as it relates to both the fund and the structure being implemented. She includes a sample deal summary and term sheet.

Graham Rowlands, Lehman Brothers, "From the Practitioner's Perspective as a Prime Broker"
Mr Rowlands focuses on the credit, market and legal risk issues that face prime brokers. His "risk overview" discusses the dominant risk factors for portfolios of primarily linear and non-linear assets and how they differ, and he provides an extensive list of types of risk.

Marcelo Cruz and Jonathan Davies, UBS Warburg, "Operational Risk"
Marcelo Cruz and Jonathan Davies write that an important risk is missing from product pricing when a transaction is priced solely in terms of market and credit risks. "This can produce devastating consequences for a bank, and asset manager or a hedge fund." The authors believe that it might only be a matter of time until the presentation of good operational risk standards becomes the standard in marketing to investors.

Part III. Perspectives from the Hedge Fund Managers
D. Sykes Wilford, Erik Norland and José M. Quintana, CDC Investment Management Corps, "Risk Management for the Asset Management Firm"
The authors write that there will undoubtedly be more crises in the future. Some of the risk management techniques that will be used then may exist already. It is important for risk managers to try to keep one step ahead, by

researching and refining risk models. They believe that transparency is likely to become important for investors, and that the Internet is increasingly being used as a tool to provide fast access to portfolio allocations and risk estimates.

Tanya Styblo Beder, Caxton Corporation, "Sound Practices for Hedge Funds"

Tanya Beder describes the concepts and conclusions that underlie "Sound Practices for Hedge Fund Managers", a February 2000 report developed by several large hedge funds, including Caxton Corporation, in the wake of the Long Term Capital Management bail out. She discusses the common elements of risk management for hedge funds and the key ingredients for a successful risk function. Ms Beder recommends the document as an excellent starting point for a fund to perform a self-evaluation of its risk management practices.

Mike Boren, Sawtooth Investment Management LLC, "Risk Management for Hedge Fund Strategies"

Writing from the point of view of a global fixed-income relative value investors, Mike Boren notes that these strategies differ from other methodologies in that they involve significant amounts of leverage. Leverage on a large scale introduces certain unique risks – which he goes on to discuss – for which even the professional investor may not be prepared.

Jane Tisdale, State Street Global Advisors, "Risk Management for Hedge Fund Strategies: US Equity Market Neutral"

Jane Tisdale describes the kinds of risks investors can face in selecting market neutral managers and brings some clarity to the meaning of market neutral. She discusses some misconceptions about this style and also considers issues associated with the investment process, implementation and aspects of the management firm itself.

Alex Balfour and Alastair MacGregor, Balfour Capital Limited, "Long/Short Japanese Equities"

The authors view risk control as more of an art than a science. They believe that the ultimate form of risk management is both quantitative and qualitative. It should have "strict statistical parameters, but should also take into account potential scenarios that cannot be measured by history alone". This chapter has two parts, focusing first on what the authors consider to be the principal risks of investing in Japanese equities and second, on the tools they used to assess risk both on quantitative and qualitative bases.

John Paulson, Paulson & Co Inc, "The 'Risk' in Risk Arbitrage"
John Paulson opens by quoting a 40 year veteran of risk arbitrage: "Risk arbitrage is not about making money, it's about not losing money". To avoid losses, one must understand, evaluate and manage risk. Mr Paulson discusses the macro and micro-risks of this strategy and examines the elements of risk management that must be practised if the goal of delivering non-correlated, low volatility returns is to be achieved.

John Michael Pagli, Jr Forest Investment Management LLC; Forest Global Convertible Fund Ltd, "Convertible Arbitrage"
Writing about this relative value, risk-controlled strategy, John Pagli gives an overview of convertible securities theory and a synopsis of convertible hedging theory. He then describes the 10 elements of risk that must be navigated, including the interplay of liquidity an investor psychology and the attendant impacts on broad financial markets. The other risks are strategy-specific, some of which are exacerbated by overall market risk. He argues that risk which cannot be properly managed should be avoided.

Eric Keiter, MKP Capital Management LLC, "Mortgage Strategies"
Eric Keiter discusses the utilisation of models in mortgage backed securities (MBS) strategies. He argues that models are just the starting point and are not enough to analyse risk, as they "can never truly represent reality". He writes that the risk management process in MBS strategies enables managers to measure and set limits on portfolio exposures to changes in interest rates, credit spreads, prepayments and volatility.

Marti P. Murray, Murray Capital Management Inc, "Risk Management for a Distressed Securities Portfolio"
Ms Murray points out that the way to begin the risk management process in distressed securities investing is to carefully do your homework. Investment decisions should be subject to a rigorous analytical process that clearly identifies both the potential rewards and risks. Third party research should always be supplemented with independent analysis. She discusses managing risk of the overall portfolio and managing the risk of market dislocations.

A. R. Arulpragasam and James S. Chanos, Arktos LLC, "Short Selling: A Unique Set of Risks"
The authors write that short selling is a viable investment strategy, especially at this stage of the long term bull market in US equities. Short selling faces many of the same risks as the long side, with the addition of many risks unique to the short side, the most prominent of which is borrowing risk. They discuss ways in which risks that present themselves on the short side can be effectively managed.

A. Paul Chappell, C-View Ltd, "Risk Management for Hedge Fund Strategies – Foreign Exchange"

Mr Chappell describes the types of risk facing currency managers, including market risk, liquidity risk, regulatory risk and – usually by deferral – credit and delivery risk. He discusses the issues related to each of these and highlights some of the techniques used to address them. Mr Chappell also examines the different approaches to VAR. He concludes by writing, "As more FX transactions move to an electronic base, and execution is done via the internet, the opportunity exists for risk management to move closer to real time".

Part IV. Perspectives from the consultants

Mary Ann Johnson, Johnson Custom Strategies, Inc, "Incorporating Hedge Fund Risk into the Design Parameters of a Traditional Investment Programme"

Ms Johnson writes that hedge funds present a series of difficult analytical problems for those who are responsible for integrating them into a more traditional investment programme. It is important to ensure that the objective of the hedge fund allocation is clearly defined at the onset, and that expectations regarding return potential and risk characteristics are both clearly understood and realistic. She goes on to discuss the customisation of an investment programme and the analysis of risk.

George Martin and Sam Y. Chung, University of Massachusetts and TRS Associates; Long Island University, "Risk Management for Hedge Funds and CTAs: VAR Versus Span Margin"

The authors examine the relationship between VAR measures and margin constraints that seek to limit the quantity of capital allocated to a particular position or positions. In particular, they investigate the relationship between generic parametric and non-parametric VAR measures and a set of futures margins set by various derivatives exchanges. They develop a number of results, including some rules of thumb, that should be of value to some risk managers.

Murray Nash and Andy Lee, NetRisk, "Enterprise Risk Management for Hedge Funds: An Applied Perspective"

The authors take a step back and look at a different level of risk to the other contributors to this book. They are concerned with the questions of managing risk at the entity level. They deal with questions about the issues and practical questions involved in bringing together decentralised and disparate information to support a consolidated view and consistent decision-making across the entity, without unduly compromising the individual manager's accountability.

Part I

Perspectives from the Investors

1

Risk Management: A Practical Approach to Managing a Portfolio of Hedge Funds for a Large Insurance Company

Norman Chait, CFA

AIG Global Investment Corporation

Today's multinational insurance companies are allocating capital to externally managed hedge funds. The major issues encountered every day by investment professionals who allocate to hedge funds on behalf of large insurance companies relate to the specific challenge of managing a large pool of capital within the context of such companies.

In this chapter, I will address risk management in the above context. First, I will focus on what I believe to be the principles of sound risk management. Then I will explore the more practical aspects gathering, aggregating and interpreting risk management data both at manager and "fund of funds" portfolio level.

I will focus on the substantive issues and, in particular, the risks inherent to the various investments and trading strategies under evaluation. I will not be discussing other important issues, such as operational risk or key man risk, in depth. This is because key man risk, for instance, is a Pandora's Box of personal and personnel issues, including (although not limited to) bloated ego risk, excessive greed syndrome and the effect of not uncommon personal events, eg, the impact of a manager's divorce on her portfolio management.

It is important to note that while certain aspects of the management process pertain strictly to insurance company matters, a similar approach can also be applied to the management of other pools of capital, regardless of size or investor type. It is strongly recommended that one performs regular and consistent operations reviews of one's major holdings, as well as keeping abreast of industry information.

Finally, where possible, I avoid technical jargon and excessive use of Greek letters.

RISK MANAGEMENT – OVERALL PHILOSOPHY

Sound risk management harbours quantitative and qualitative aspects, plus a dose of common sense. In attempting to evaluate where the current and future portfolio risks are, the approach should be proactive rather than reactive. Analysis of historical data is only part of the process: while one may apply lessons learned from the past in developing strategy, it is almost certain that risk factors not encountered before will emerge. Therefore, it is insufficient just to interview hedge fund managers about these issues; one should follow the markets actively and be open to inputs from all sources.

The major issues to focus on are liquidity, leverage and counterparty risk.

Liquidity: Before entering, be sure of your exit!

A thorough understanding of liquidity is perhaps the key factor when it comes to designing any risk management system or approach. Prior to investing, one should have a clear idea of when and under what circumstances the investment ought to be harvested. Many people – and especially hedge fund managers – forget that the main purpose of investing is to generate a cash-on-cash return over some period of time – ie, real money rather than a percentage statistic. In other words, what goes in should come out.

In addition, one should evaluate the possibility of harvesting the investment under adverse market conditions. *It is important to ensure that the underlying assets in a particular hedge fund are liquid enough to fulfil all obligations to investors.* All hedge funds prospectuses contain terms giving the investment manager the right to suspend the payment of redemption proceeds to investors in a number of loosely defined scenarios, regardless of the general liquidity terms offered. The following theoretical example best demonstrates this.

Example 1

Manager X has created a hedge fund that has only two investments in it. One investment is a private unsecured loan that is not callable for the first year, where the borrower may elect to distribute cash or in-kind payments. The second investment is an unlisted private convertible bond that may be converted into the equity of the company at a 15% discount to market value at the time of conversion. This may only be done after an initial lock-up period of six months. In order to raise capital to participate in these enthralling opportunities, the manager sets up a hedge fund vehicle that offers monthly liquidity, without any initial lock-up period. The reality is that this liquidity provision is meaningless, because its execution cannot be enforced in the first months of the new fund's existence.

Therefore, in Example 1, there is no asset-liability match. The next level is to determine the impact of forced liquidations in various market scenarios.

While this is difficult to determine on an absolute basis, one can do so in relative terms. Therefore, in Example 2, let us compare two hedged equity managers.

Example 2

The first manager manages US$1 billion in large cap US equities. The second manager manages US$200 million in mid-to-small cap US equities. Assuming current market conditions, one could ask both managers how long it would take them to liquidate 75% of their portfolio without a price impact. For this purpose, the assumption is that they cannot trade more than 20% of the six-month average daily trading volume of each security, as this would create downward price pressure. It is possible and often the case that the large cap manager is able to liquidate in less time, despite having more assets under management.

As a related rule of thumb, if a manager claims it will take 25–30 business days to liquidate the majority of her portfolio, she should not offer monthly liquidity to clients.

But what is more interesting than the answer to this "75/20" question is how long it takes the manager to answer it. Many have never focused on this issue. If a manager is unaware of the liquidity traits of portfolio investments, this should raise a red flag.

One should try to understand the underlying liquidity of each of the asset classes that hedge fund managers typically invest in. This is more difficult to ascertain for over-the-counter securities such as convertible bonds, mortgage-backed securities and high-yield debt. However, one can gauge the relative liquidity of these securities by talking periodically to investment professionals both on the buy side and the sell side, and by gleaning insights from sell-side publications on these asset classes.

Liquidity: practical experience

Certain US convertible arbitrage managers do offer monthly liquidity to clients. But unless the managers use limited leverage or stick with investment grade issues, this could create an asset-liability mismatch. Convertible arbitrage entails the purchase of a convertible bond and the concurrent short sale of the correct ratio of equity of the same issuer. While there are many ways to make money in this strategy (price appreciation of the bonds, positive carry coupon clipping, volatility trading, etc), in most instances the convertible bond is traded less frequently than the equity hedge. Moreover, some convertible arbitrage managers will lever up their investments six to ten times, and will purchase over 20% of some issues.

In cases where managers are running a large balance sheet way in excess of their capital base, it is clear that it will take some time to unwind positions. One leading US manager with a focus on non-investment grade convertible bonds admitted that it would take her up to six months to liquidate the majority of her portfolio. Nevertheless, the fund offered monthly liquidity to investors. Thus, in the event that most investors wanted to exit the fund at the same time, this would have a severely negative price impact should the manager honour redemptions. In a similar instance in 1998, another manager limited the amount of capital that could exit the fund in a given calendar quarter. Redemption requests were pro-rated and, while the fund offered quarterly liquidity, it took most investors up to a year to get their money back. A large portion of the portfolio was invested in Regulation D convertibles, which tend to become extremely illiquid in times of market stress.

Another issue to examine is the proportion of the manager's assets from any individual investor. If, for example, a hedge fund has 50% of its capital from a single investor who can sell along the same lines as everyone else in the portfolio, this could potentially impact investment results on account of the execution slippage caused by liquidating half the portfolio. It is therefore important to determine the diversification of the investor base. Moreover, it is preferable not to exceed 10% of the assets of a fund because, if an exit is necessary, it can then be effected without impacting the manager's entire portfolio.

Leverage: ROA beats ROE

Leverage is not always undesirable and, when used prudently, can be a useful way to enhance returns. For example, a significant portion of US families run levered investment portfolios because they have mortgages on their houses. But in these cases, there is usually sufficient collateral backing the loan, which can be seized in the event of default. Also, among businesses, there is usually sufficient cash to service both interest and principal debt payments.

The above principles should apply to any levered asset class. In hedge fund land, the problem arises when an excessive amount of leverage is used. For a given strategy, if two managers are able to generate similar returns, the manager who uses less leverage is preferable. One should look for return on assets (ROA) rather than returns on equity (ROE). According to the classic Du Pont analysis, the difference between ROA and ROE is financial leverage.

Let's take a step back and examine hedge fund managers for what they advertise themselves to be. While there are many efforts to try to institutionalise the business, hedge funds are still considered a talent pool rather than an asset class, and the managers therefore promote themselves as the best and the brightest. With the global financial markets as dynamic and diverse now as ever, talented investment managers should be able to discover enough attractive investment opportunities without having to over-lever their balance sheets.

For each hedge fund asset class, one can determine maximum leverage boundaries. As a rule of thumb, regardless of strategy, the net exposure (long minus short) should be lower than 100% of investor capital. The higher the gross leverage (long plus short), the lower the net exposure should be.

Counterparty risk: do not operate on a business plan that puts you at the mercy of others

Counterparties include both debt and equity claims against a manager's portfolio. It is essential to determine whether the hedge fund manager really understands the nature of all these counterparties, and how they will behave in times of stress. Moreover, one should always ask what steps the manager has taken to mitigate and diversify counterparty risk. A hedge fund is a business and should be run as such; it is not just about sitting in a room and picking stocks or trading spreads.

Debt holders

These include Prime Brokers, who provide financial leverage and stock loan to hedge funds. They have policies pertaining to how much each type of hedge fund can borrow, and the margins they are willing to provide. Managers should be fully aware of the notice period given for changes in lending policies or margin requirements. One should also examine the hedge fund manager's knowledge of the intricacies of the stock loan markets. It is useful to know how often the manager is subject to stock loan recalls (which force her to cover a short position at an inopportune time), and whether she has multiple sources of stock loan. Established hedge funds have their own internal policies regarding contractual arrangements with debt counterparties. Funds that employ more than Regulation T leverage (2:1) should demonstrate expertise in documentation of over-the-counter derivative contracts such as swaps.

Equity holders

These are the investors in the fund. Unstable "hot money" investors who want to sell can often affect the remaining shareholders if their actions cause the manager to liquidate attractive positions at unattractive prices. Therefore, it is important for the investor to evaluate both how well the manager knows her clients and whether the client base is sufficiently diversified. This is less important if the fund offers tougher liquidity provisions, such as a limit to how much of the fund can be sold in any given quarter.

LIQUIDITY, LEVERAGE AND COUNTERPARTY RISK ARE ALL INTER-RELATED

While it is important to understand each of these risks separately, liquidity, leverage and counterparty risk are inter-related and cannot be viewed in isolation. The Long-Term Capital Management (LTCM) crisis in the autumn of 1998 best illustrates this. There were many fixed-income arbitrage hedge funds that were affected. They also ran highly levered portfolios – often with similar trades to LTCM. When LTCM had to liquidate, these hedge funds found that they were unable to sell positions at attractive prices. Liquidity evaporated and counterparties became nervous. Investors put in redemptions and, critically, some lenders either increased their margin requirements or refused to roll over short-term loans.

The end result was that a number of funds other than LTCM either suffered double-digit losses or had to close down. Most significantly, this all happened at a time of relative global prosperity, evidenced by the fact that all the US Federal Reserve had to do to effect a full recovery was to inject some liquidity into the system by relaxing short-term rates. Those managers who had properly managed their liquidity, leverage and counter-party risks not only survived 1998 intact, but enjoyed excellent 1999 performance, because the number of players in the arbitrage markets decreased.

RISK MANAGEMENT PROCESS

Now we move from the theoretical to the practical aspects of risk management for hedge fund portfolios. These can be divided into three primary stages:

1. data collection;
2. interpretation of data collected at the manager or strategy level; and
3. data aggregation and interpretation at the portfolio level.

Data collection

Contrary to common belief, it is not too difficult to obtain relevant risk management information from hedge fund managers. The key is to know what information to obtain, and how to integrate it into one's own risk management systems. Here are some pieces of information one can usually obtain from managers:

❏ assets under management, including monthly client inflows and outflows;
❏ monthly profit and loss (P&L), with some level of attribution analysis;
❏ gross and net exposures;
❏ sector exposure, or, in the case of multi-strategy arbitrage or event-driven managers, breakdown of long and short dollars by asset class;
❏ for equity managers, details of the top 10 or 20 longs, and the percentage of long market value they comprise (individual shorts are generally not disclosed in writing);
❏ breakdown of the long portfolio by market capitalisation, (eg, percentage of companies in the portfolio with market caps of over US$10 billion, US$1–10 billion, and under US$1 billion);

❏ percentage exposure to foreign securities; and

❏ options and futures hedges.

It is not necessary to have full disclosure of a manager's entire portfolio. The utility of analysing whole portfolios is limited relative to the time spent doing so. It is better to receive the necessary information in aggregated form. Some managers will allow their prime brokers to provide clients with the relevant statistics – however, this practice is still not widespread. Below are some of the guiding principles used in determining what risk management information to obtain and how to go about doing so.

❏ Try to understand the major exposures a manager has, and what the key factors are that keep her up at night.

❏ Do not ask managers for intricate trade secrets. They are irrelevant to the risk management process. Rather, one should be able to build a sound risk management platform based on non-confidential information. Moreover, the biggest secret sometimes is that there are no secrets. It is no use grilling managers on issues they may be unwilling to disclose when they may be more than comfortable discussing other more important matters.

❏ Disclosure of individual positions is not important unless the manager runs a concentrated portfolio. However, most equity managers provide a top ten long list, which is helpful in tracking portfolio turnover and idea overlap amongst managers.

❏ If a manager is reluctant to provide certain information that her peers do provide, it does not hurt to remind her of this fact.

❏ One should always explain to managers why the information is needed and how it will be used.

❏ Try to automate the process as much as possible. Often, managers provide sufficient information on their web sites or in monthly fax updates. If not, then it is best to deal with someone in the organisation other than the investment manager, where possible. This could be the Chief Operating Officer or Director of Investor Relations. Discussions with the manager should focus on substantive investment issues. Managers are extremely responsive to focused questions based on previously collected risk management data and portfolio holdings information.

Risk management – evaluation at the individual manager level

Once the information is collected as outlined above, one may perform periodic variance analysis on each fund. Any significant variations provide a reason to speak with the investment manager directly. Indeed, the following factors may raise an eyebrow.

❏ A large influx of capital into the fund that makes it exceed the capacity level at which the manager had previously said she would feel comfortable. (Note how managers see things differently once they have raised a lot of capital – the discussion usually moves from the benefits of nimbleness to the virtues of economies of scale!)

❑ A significant increase in gross leverage (longs plus shorts). This should also be viewed in conjunction with capital outflows.

❑ An increase of net exposure to a level in excess of previously determined net long limit. This is a common occurrence with equity managers who cannot find sufficient short ideas, but who do not want to sell their longs in order to avoid a short-term taxable event.

❑ A large shift in sector or asset class allocation, especially where this is not indicative of the manager's style.

❑ For convertible and fixed income arbitrage managers, an increase in leverage when credit spreads are narrowing.

❑ Special openings either in mid-month or mid-quarter for those funds that only have quarterly openings. While these are sometimes due to truly attractive investment opportunities, one should still, when they occur, take note of the fund's current financial position (high gross leverage and so on.

Risk management in the portfolio context

In managing a large portfolio of hedge funds, one cannot evaluate each hedge fund in isolation. Therefore, when evaluating prospective investments, the following two key questions should be asked.

1. Does the manager meet the quality test? If not, it probably is not worth pursuing the investment, even if it is in an asset class where one would like to increase exposure.

2. If "yes" is the answer to the first question, how does the manager fit within the portfolio context? While many managers may present themselves as the best thing in the investment world since the discovery of the tulip bulb, the reality is that many are really executing the same strategies as their colleagues across the street. Often, two fund managers may share a summer rental in the Hamptons[1] and their investment ideas at the same time. In some cases, an investment professional may have crossed the street to start up a new shop, having been dissatisfied with the terms offered by her former employer. If one invested in both the old fund and the start-up founded by the renegade former employee, the chances are that no real strategy diversification would be achieved (while key man and operational risks may either be enhanced or diminished).

Therefore, *it is crucial to ensure efficient diversification at the strategy level.* To put it simply, one should invest with a lot of talented managers who all do different things.

Once a prospective manager has passed both tests, then one should determine the appropriate size of the investment by considering the following aspects.

1. The manager's total assets. Typically, one should not exceed 10% of the assets of a fund, because having more than this may make it more difficult to exit.
2. The maximum size limit for each individual investment. Depending on the size of the overall hedge fund portfolio (or fund of funds), a single manager should not exceed 5-10% of total portfolio assets. The larger the portfolio, the smaller the position size should be, leading to a more diverse portfolio.
3. Optimal and maximum exposure to each asset class. It is not necessary to determine minimum exposures to any asset class. Accordingly, one should not invest in a particular asset class, however attractive, if there are no good managers. Rather, a maximum asset class exposure level should be determined. The next step is to aggregate long and net exposures by asset class to see if these boundaries are exceeded. As many managers are able to shift assets between strategies, one should monitor exposure levels on a monthly basis. This is very important in helping to decide where to place the incremental dollar.

The idea is to add one's exposure to each major asset class on a gross and net dollar basis. Therefore, if manager Z accounts for 5% of the fund of funds portfolio and has 150% long dollar and 100% short dollar exposure to merger arbitrage, then assume, on a portfolio basis, that the manager adds 7.5% gross long merger arbitrage exposure and 2.5% net merger arbitrage exposure. If the manager also has 50% of investor assets long in convertibles and 40% short, then assume this adds 2.5% gross long and 0.50% net exposure to convertibles on a portfolio basis. One can add up these exposures on a dollar basis for each fund, and then aggregate the data from all the funds at the portfolio level.

The important distinction to make here is that actual assets allocated to each asset class are counted, regardless of how the manager is classified. This is because both multi-strategy arbitrage and event-driven managers invest in merger arbitrage, and both macro-oriented and equity-hedged managers invest in stocks. It seems that in today's investment climate, the three major areas where a large portfolio may easily become over-exposed are fundamental equities, merger arbitrage and convertible arbitrage. Smaller portfolios may also become over-exposed to distressed debt, statistical arbitrage, fixed income arbitrage, trend-following CTAs, volatility traders and emerging markets.

Let us illustrate how one may determine maximum exposure to the three larger asset classes.

Equities

This area focuses only on fundamental stock pickers, whether hedged or long only, and not on other strategies that may use equities – eg, short-term trading or systematic statistical equity arbitrage. (Assume at this stage that the latter two asset classes have little market exposure – they will be accounted for later on.)

The fundamental equity book should first be examined in isolation. The investor should determine a comfort level with regards to maximum gross and maximum net exposure. By determining this on a portfolio basis, one can use a limited number of long-biased managers (often without having to pay a performance fee) if they are offset by more hedged players who will bring the aggregate net equity exposure to the desired level. As a rule of thumb, the aggregate gross leverage should not exceed 150% of the assets of the managers that invest in this asset class. Funds with gross leverage in excess of this level often tend to be too volatile, and may test margin requirements. Net exposure should be well below 100%. There is no point in giving up 20% of the performance in the form of an incentive fee for a levered long-only portfolio. A comfortable range net exposure level is between 35% and 65%, depending on how much market exposure one is willing to tolerate.

One may further fine-tune this to determine maximum geographic or sector limits, but this entails a lot more data collection. It is usually better to invest with equity managers who invest in many sectors as opposed to sector specialists. The latter tend to have a net long bias, often fall in love with their sector, and do not hedge sufficiently in times of sector weakness. Generalist managers have the advantage of shifting assets to the more attractive sectors. While it is not always practical to track sectors systematically every month, one can gauge this once every 3–4 months, or on a more random basis. For example, when a number of interesting new technology-related funds knocked on our door recently, I immediately added up the long technology exposure with our existing managers and came to the realisation that the technology exposure was sufficient.

Let us now assume, that one desires a maximum average net exposure of 60% to equity managers. The next stage is to determine how much net exposure to fundamental equity strategies one is willing to accept on an overall portfolio level. If the answer is 20%, then one could only invest up to a third of one's portfolio with managers who invest in this asset class.

One should not forget that this is really a rule of thumb exercise, which does not address issues such as tracking error in hedging or sector bias. However, it does go a level further than just determining that if, for example, one gave US$10 million to Manager X, then she is 10% of a US$100 million fund. The key driver of the system is the tracking of actual portfolio dollar gross and net exposure every month. This allows for the making of informed portfolio management decisions. The following example is indicative.

In April 2000, following the NASDAQ correction, managers became more defensive and their average net exposure dropped by almost 10%. As a result, one could see that there was a potential opportunity to add to some existing hedged equity managers. This triggered analysts to call these managers to get a sense of how they saw opportunities in the coming months. It became clear that most were afraid of the Federal Reserve raising interest rates and would remain defensive through the summer. With one small exception, it was decided not to beef up exposure.

Here, the process is more important than the result. By having the information at hand, one is able to perform timely research that allows for informed portfolio decisions.

Merger arbitrage
The reality today is that most managers invest in the same deals. An effective risk management model therefore assumes that if a well-known large merger breaks, all managers who do invest in merger arbitrage will be in the deal. This limits the marginal utility of adding another merger arbitrage manager to the portfolio over and above a core number, as little additional diversification is achieved.

There are also managers whose main focus is not merger arbitrage but they nevertheless, still invest in the strategy. Therefore, dollar merger arbitrage long and net exposure should be tallied up manager by manager. Assuming that only 10% of a portfolio as counted by investment dollars is invested with pure merger arbitrage managers, total dollars invested in merger arbitrage may amount to over 30% of the fund of funds portfolio assets. This is a function of both leverage and merger arbitrage investments by multi-strategy funds.

From a risk management perspective, the key issue is to decide how much exposure one is prepared to lose on a total portfolio basis if a large deal breaks. As a rule, managers try to limit individual deal break risk to 3% portfolio loss (one can fine-tune this by asking each manager what their risk limit is, and then aggregating this on a weighted basis). In addition, if one does not want to lose more than 1% on a fund of funds portfolio basis, then one must cap the total long dollars allocated to merger arbitrage to no more than 33% of fund of funds assets.

If one wanted the above 33% overall portfolio cap on merger arbitrage, and the weighted average long dollar exposure to merger arbitrage per manager that invested in the asset class was 150%, then one could only allocate 22% of the portfolio to these managers.

Based on the experience of merger arbitrage managers (especially in 1987 and 1989, when many deals broke simultaneously), one cannot rule out four deals breaking at once and causing each manager who has invested in merger arbitrage a 12% loss. All the managers trying to close out the position at the same time may compound this loss.

Convertible arbitrage

The rules here are similar to merger arbitrage, and one should add up one's gross and net dollar exposure to the asset class. For example, if there are only four managers in the portfolio with a 5% weighting each and they are levered 3:1 on the long side, then the portfolio exposure to long convertibles would be 60% of the total capital allocated to all hedge funds. If the managers were short 70 cents for every dollar long, then the net dollar exposure would be 18%.

As a rough rule of thumb, one can assume that half the short exposure is related to the delta hedge of the convertible, while the other half is the premium dollars at risk. The premium is the value of the convertible over and above the sum received if the bond is converted to equity. The premium exists as the convertible bond typically pays an interest coupon in excess of the dividend of the underlying stock. Some managers will disclose the exact delta-premium breakdown upon request. Therefore, in the above example, if convertible premiums were to collapse to zero, the overall fund of funds portfolio could lose 9%. While this is an extreme scenario that is unlikely to occur, it does allow one to place an outer boundary on the maximum portfolio loss.

One could also determine one's maximum desired exposure to convertibles based on either portfolio sensitivity to sharp moves in interest rates, the equity markets, or based on past performance. Convertible arbitrage is a cyclical strategy, which has tended to under-perform every four years or so (1990, 1994 and 1998 are good examples). One should also take heed that this asset class is fairly illiquid, owing in part to the fact that hedged convertible traders comprise such a large part of the market now. There is thus crowded exit risk.

Where possible, one should ask for a portfolio breakdown between European, Asian and US convertibles, because each of these markets has different characteristics. For example, the US market is far more credit sensitive than the European or Japanese markets. Such a breakdown can give one a better understanding of portfolio diversification.

Evaluation of market risk in the portfolio

This can be determined first by examining the net market exposure of all the fundamental stock pickers on a portfolio basis, as described above. Whereas all the other strategies in the portfolio are supposedly market neutral, there is always some long bias, especially in merger arbitrage and other event-driven strategies (even when they are hedged with S&P futures). Therefore, it is essential to estimate the market exposure of these other strategies through qualitative judgement, with the help of historical statistics. One may over-estimate in order to be conservative. So, if net long equity exposure is 20%, a market risk factor of 10% could be added, so that the expected net market exposure of the entire portfolio is 30%. This is not an exact science, but it is a useful exercise all the same.

QUALITATIVE RISK MANAGEMENT ISSUES
The above quantitative analysis provides a platform for understanding manager and portfolio risks, and in so doing allows one to pose informed questions to managers when detecting deviations from the normal state of affairs.

However, quantitative analysis alone is insufficient, meaning qualitative facets must be part of any sound risk management system. Here are a few items to focus on.

Timeliness of replies
When calling a manager to obtain an answer to some factor highlighted by the risk management system, one should note the time and the manner in which these queries are answered.

Understanding the underlying investment philosophy of each manager
This provides a framework for future evaluation of how the managers go about executing their strategies. A sound approach is to write detailed investment reports prior to each new investment and revisit these reports periodically to check whether the managers have deviated from their investment style or mandate.

Evaluation of past mistakes
One should get a sense of whether or not the manager has readily applied lessons learned from the manner in which questions regarding past mistakes are answered. In many cases, managers shrug off these questions. Sometimes, one may ask for examples of losing trades, only to be given situations where the manager did not make or lose money. This is not the same thing. A solid manager should have nothing to hide.

Understanding the process of how managers mark unlisted securities
For unlisted securities, it is important that managers receive quotes from parties who are willing to execute at the prices quoted. For example, there was a situation once where three managers owned a private security. One of the managers marked the security at 75 cents on the dollar, while the other two marked it at 30 cents on the dollar.

Understanding how the portfolio is priced
Does the manager price the portfolio, or does someone else in the organisation do it?

MANAGING RISK WITHIN THE CONTEXT OF A LARGE INSURANCE COMPANY

Fully invested portfolio

Hedged fund investments are generally managed as part of the insurance float. The float is the pool of capital that resides at the insurance company from the time the insurance premiums are collected to the time they are paid out. As insurance underwriting and claim activities occur continuously, this pool of capital is permanent.

The majority of the float is generally invested in investment-grade fixed-income instruments. The other, riskier investments typically constitute a yield enhancement overlay on the bond portfolio. Bonds are sold when hedge fund investments are made and bought back when such investments are sold. Bond positions are not counted as part of the hedge fund portfolio.

As such, *the hedge fund portfolio is always fully invested*. No cash or cash equivalent positions are held. Therefore, in a market downdraft, the portfolio could possibly take a larger hit than a similar portfolio able to raise cash. Therefore, the only way to manage risk is to reduce the size of the portfolio on a dollar basis during risky market periods, or to purchase portfolio insurance. The latter is expensive and should typically be avoided. Therefore, one must be especially vigilant in selecting managers who will protect their portfolios in tough times. It is theoretically possible to be fully invested with managers who have 100% cash positions. One has to rely on the managers to raise cash when necessary, as it is not possible to do so at the portfolio level.

Managing a large pool of capital

For liquidity reasons, it is preferable not to be more than 10% of the total size of each invested fund. This prevents one from investing in smaller funds as investments of under US$10 million do not make a meaningful impact on portfolio returns. As mentioned, a maximum individual position size limit should be applied. As such, the portfolio is more diversified than many smaller portfolios.

The ideal would be to find twenty-five 4% positions that one would never have to sell. Unfortunately, it takes much time and active monitoring to determine whether a manager has the ability to generate consistent returns going forward. Therefore, positions tend to be built up slowly.

Finally, if a position exceeds the maximum position limit, one should consider taking profits to pare it back. An exception to this would be in the event of the particular fund closing to new investment and the insurance companies overall hedge fund allocation being expected to increase. As there are limited times in which one can invest and sell hedge funds, it is difficult to fine-tune portfolio exposures unless the portfolio is more diversified.

Liquidity issues

The underwriting activity of an insurance company is influenced by the degree of liquidity of the investment float. Therefore, one should strive to improve the liquidity terms offered by the hedge funds. In most cases, at least quarterly liquidity should be made available. Less liquid strategies should be deferred to other alternative assets classes, such as a private equity portfolio.

Taxation issues

A major issue encountered is the necessity to reduce corporate interest expense. Thus is it prudent to avoid highly levered strategies, such as fixed-income arbitrage. This also makes sound investment sense, as the highly levered strategies are most susceptible to blow-up risk.

As insurance companies have corporate form, they are less sensitive to issues that affect individual investors, such as capital gains tax. Therefore, where possible, it is not advisable to invest alongside individual investors, on whose behalf the hedge fund manager may try to tax manage the portfolio. Tax management strategies often lead managers to hold to investments for longer than they would have had after-tax returns been less of an issue. This can impact pre-tax performance.

CONCLUSION

This article has spanned the philosophical and practical aspects of risk management for hedge fund portfolios. While this is not rocket science, it is useful to develop a consistent, rigorous and comprehensive risk management system based on hard data provided by managers on a regular basis. A successful system, combined with experience and sound judgement, will allow the portfolio manager to make timely data-driven risk management decisions.

1   A Long Island resort popular with the New York investment community.

2

Hedge Fund Risk Management for Institutions

Mark J. P. Anson

The California Public Employees Retirement System

Institutions have become a driving force in the hedge fund industry. A key issue for institutional investors is the risk control philosophy and risk management systems employed by the hedge fund manager. In this chapter, we consider several issues related to hedge fund investments from an institution's point of view.

Risk management extends beyond the economic risks undertaken by a hedge fund manager. Institutions are sufficiently sophisticated to comprehend and assess the economic exposures received as a result of an investment in a hedge fund. However, there are several considerable risks that an institution should also consider when investing in hedge funds.

Beyond the economic risks of a hedge fund investment, there are five additional risk factors that are of concern to an institution: process risk, mapping risk, event risk, data risk and performance measurement risk. Process risk relates to the "skill-based" style of hedge fund investing. Mapping risk considers the lack of additivity of individual hedge fund risk profiles. Event risk measures the impact of financial turmoil across the hedge fund industry. Data risk considers the biases inherent to hedge fund performance data. Lastly, performance measurement risk exposes the dangers of relying on historical hedge fund performance data.

PROCESS RISK

Most investors prefer a well-defined investment process that describes how an investment manager makes its investments. The articulation and documentation of the process can be just as important as the investment results generated by it. Consider the following language from a hedge fund disclosure document:

> The General Partner makes extensive use of computer technology in both
> the formulation and execution of many investment decisions. Buy and sell

decisions will, in many cases, be made and executed algorithmically according to quantitative trading strategies embodied in analytical computer software running the General Partner's computer facilities or on other computers used to support the Fund's trading activities.

This is a "black box", the algorithmic extension of the hedge fund manager's brainpower. Computer algorithms are developed to quantify the manager's skill or investment insight.

For black box managers, the black box itself is the investment process. It is not that the black boxes are bad investments; hedge fund research indicates that proprietary quantitative trading strategies can be quite successful (see CrossBorder Capital, 1999; Goldman Sachs & Co and Financial Risk Management Ltd, 1999; and Goldman Sachs & Co and Financial Risk Management Ltd, 2000). Rather, the issue is whether good performance results justify the lack of a clear investment process.

A black box is just one example of process versus investment results. The hedge fund industry considers itself to be "skill-based". However, it is very difficult to translate manager skill into a process – especially when the performance of the hedge fund is dependent upon the skill of a specific individual.

Consider another, well-publicised skill-based investment process. In Spring, 2000, the hedge funds headed by George Soros stumbled leading to the departure of Stanley Druckenmiller, the chief investment strategist for Soros Fund Management. *The Wall Street Journal* documented the concentrated skill-based investment style of this hedge fund group:

> For years, [Soros Fund Management] fostered an entrepreneurial culture, with a cadre of employees battling wits to persuade Mr. Druckenmiller to invest.
>
> "[Mr. Druckenmiller] didn't scream, but he could be very tough. It could be three days or three weeks of battling it out until he's convinced, or you're defeated." (*Wall Street Journal*, 2000.)

Mr. Druckenmiller compiled an exceptional track record as the manager of the Soros Quantum Fund. However, the concentration of decision-making authority is not an economic risk, but a process risk.

This is another example of "skill-based" investing. There is no discernible process. Instead, all information is filtered through the brain of one individual. In essence, the institutional investor must trust the judgment of one person.

Institutional investors should accept economic risk but not process risk. A diversified portfolio should have broad exposure to different asset classes, market segments and market sectors. Investors understand the economic risks of those asset classes, segments and sectors, and are willing to bear them. However, investors are generally unwilling to bear risks that are not fundamental to their tactical and strategic asset allocations.

Process risk is not a fundamental risk. It is an idiosyncratic risk of the hedge fund manager's structure and operations. Generally, it is not a risk that investors wish to bear. Nor is it a risk for which they expect to be compensated. Furthermore, how would an investor go about pricing the process risk of a hedge fund manager? It cannot be quantified and it cannot be calibrated. Therefore, there is no way to tell whether an institutional investor is being properly compensated for this risk (see Park and Staum, 1998).[1]

Process risk also raises the ancillary issue of lack of transparency. Skill-based investing is usually opaque. Are the decisions of the key individual quantitatively or qualitatively based? There is no way to really tell.

To summarise, process risk cannot be quantified and it is not a risk that institutional investors are willing to bear. It also raises issues of transparency. Investors want clarity and definition, not opaqueness and amorphousness. The investment process is one of three basic questions that must be documented with every hedge fund manager (see Anson, 2000a).[2]

MAPPING RISK

One problem with hedge fund risk management is that there is no standard platform for measuring risk and no standard format for reporting it. Different hedge funds map risk differently. Consequently, the risks of several hedge fund managers cannot be combined.

A good example of the mapping problem is the work done by Fung and Hsieh (1997) and Liang (1999). Both studies attempt to analyse the returns to hedge funds by applying the factor or style analysis conducted by William Sharpe (1992) with respect to mutual funds. In his 1992 study, Sharpe compared the returns of mutual funds to the returns from financial asset class indices to determine the amount of variation in mutual fund returns explained by asset class returns. His results indicated that up to 90% of mutual fund returns are explained by asset class returns.

Fung and Hsieh apply Sharpe's style analysis to hedge funds. They find that the amount of variation of hedge fund returns that is explained by financial asset class returns is low; R-square measures were less than 25% for almost half of the hedge funds studied. Fung and Hsieh then apply a principal components analysis based on a hedge fund's trading style. They find that five different trading styles (systems/opportunistic, global/macro, value, systems/trend following and distressed) explain about 45% of the cross sectional variation in hedge fund returns.

Liang conducts a style analysis similar to Sharpe and finds R-squares in the range of 20% for hedge funds that invest in foreign exchange to 77% for hedge funds that invest in emerging markets.

The point of these studies is that it is very difficult to map hedge fund returns onto standard asset classes as has been done for mutual funds. One reason is that the hedge fund industry is a diverse and heterogeneous mix.

Consequently, hedge funds require detailed individual examination to assess their risk profiles. Another reason is that hedge funds often invest in derivative instruments that have non-linear payoffs, and non-linear derivative instruments map poorly onto linear asset classes.

Unfortunately, value-at-risk (VAR) measures cannot resolve this issue. VAR is a statistic that measures the likelihood of a loss exceeding a certain threshold dollar amount over a specified time. It is a measure of probability that is dependent upon a manager's time horizon, specified confidence level and asset mix.

Given that hedge fund managers may have different time horizons, confidence levels and asset mixes, VAR measures will vary widely across hedge fund managers. Additionally, different types of hedge fund strategies will have different types of risk exposures.

For instance, equity long/short hedge funds have considerable market risk, but little credit exposure. Conversely, arbitrage hedge funds, such as convertible arbitrage, have a small market exposure but a large credit exposure. This is because arbitrage funds take small market bets but use leverage (sometimes considerable amounts) to magnify the size of the market bets.

Figure 1 plots market risk versus credit risk for several styles of long-only managers. We use a relative scale of 0–5, where 0 represents zero exposure to financial market risk and 5 represents the maximum exposure. The same relative scale is applied with respect to credit risk.

As Figure 1 demonstrates, traditional long-only managers have considerable exposure to market risk but no exposure to credit risk. At one end of the scale are money market cash managers. To avoid "breaking the buck", these managers do not take any credit risk or market risk. At the other end of the scale are growth managers. They take no credit risk, but have considerable exposure to market risk. In between, we find value managers, fixed income managers, and equity index managers.

The graphical analysis changes considerably for hedge fund managers. Figure 2 demonstrates the market versus credit risk exposures for several major styles of hedge funds. Near the zero axis, we find market neutral funds; hedge funds with no market exposure (market neutral) and low leverage. Market neutral funds use limited amounts of leverage because there is no market exposure to leverage or magnify.

Along the Credit Risk axis, we see that the exposure to credit risk increases for merger arbitrage, convertible arbitrage, and fixed income arbitrage. These types of hedge funds extract their value from relative value trades. They trade based on relatively small price discrepancies in the market, but use large amounts of leverage to extract the most value.

Long Term Capital Management (LTCM) of Greenwich, Connecticut is the best-known example of these relative value/arbitrage players. It has been well documented that LTCM used massive amounts of leverage to

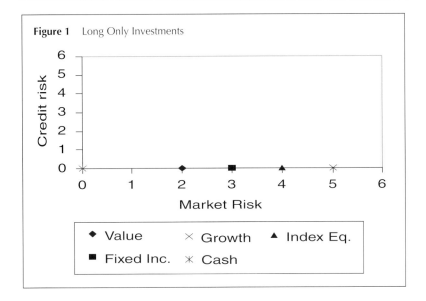

Figure 1 Long Only Investments

extract value from its relatively small market bets. Consequently, it defines the upper boundary for credit exposure.

Last, equity long/short and directional hedge funds have exposure to both credit and market risk (see CrossBorder Capital, 2000 for more detail). Global macro funds tend to make large bets on the direction of certain currencies, or on the movement of growth/momentum stocks. Consequently, they have a large market exposure. By their very nature, long/short equity hedge funds, will have some exposure to the stock market. Also, this type of hedge fund manager uses leverage to increase the value of his long/short positions.

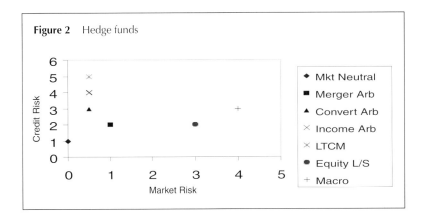

Figure 2 Hedge funds

Two points should be made with respect to Figures 1 and 2. First, hedge fund managers have risk profiles that differ considerably to those of traditional long-only investments. In particular, hedge funds take considerable credit risk in their investment strategies. Consequently, the risk analysis applied to long-only managers is not sufficient for hedge fund managers.

Second, different hedge fund managers have different types of concentrated risk exposure and this cannot simply be added to give a total exposure. Even if they all measured risk in a consistent manner, their risk exposures are sufficiently different that to combine them into one risk statistic would be misleading.

Two solutions to the mapping problem are possible. First, institutions can act as global risk managers. It is the manager's responsibility to generate the excess returns, and the institution's job to manage the risks that arise from that investment. This is a macro-approach to risk management.

Under this solution, the institution loads the hedge fund manager's risk exposures into its risk management system. This solution is advantageous in that the institution controls the mapping of the risk exposures rather than the individual hedge fund managers. The difficulty is acquiring the sufficient performance data from the hedge fund manager in order to map the manager's exposures accurately.

This may be less difficult than it seems. As a starting point, hedge fund managers can be generally classified as those taking market exposure and those taking credit exposure (see Figure 2). Once the primary risk exposure has been identified, this risk can be more finely parsed. If it is a long or short equity hedge fund, for instance, then the institution needs to determine in which market sector or segment the manager invests. The institution can then determine the manager's average net exposure to that market sector or segment. For example, if the equity hedge fund manager is long or short the technology sector, an appropriate measure of the risk for this manager would be his net exposure to a technology index such as the Standard & Poor's Technology Index.

Under the second solution, the institution could ask for each hedge fund manager's investment positions. This is a micro-approach.

Unfortunately, this micro-approach is problematic for two reasons. First, it is unlikely that the hedge fund manager would be willing to reveal his individual investment positions. Hedge fund managers do not usually like disclosing their investment positions, because these tend to be the manager's proprietary data. Most hedge fund managers fear losing their competitive edge should this information be inadvertently disclosed.

Another difficulty is that the institution must aggregate the individual positions across several hedge fund programmes within its risk management system. Collecting and combining these into reportable risk exposures requires a very sophisticated internal risk management system.

There are also pragmatic difficulties of having the hedge fund managers transmit their daily positions to the institution.

One possibility is that the hedge fund managers could report this information to a central prime broker who could use its risk platform to prepare the risk analysis. However, this would require hedge funds to voluntarily report their positions to a central prime broker who may not be the prime broker for the hedge fund. This "hearsay reporting", while a theoretical solution, is, unfortunately, far from a practical solution. Most hedge funds do not wish to report their daily positions to their own and their clients' prime brokers.

The reality is that hedge fund managers do not like to report their individual positions at all, whether to investors or other prime brokers. There is constant debate with hedge fund managers regarding the level or depth of transparency they are willing to provide. This means that pension funds must rely on themselves to be global risk managers.

At Calpers, we conduct our own analysis to ensure that the risks of hedge fund managers do not overlap. Perhaps the greatest danger of investing in hedge funds is selecting hedge fund managers with similar trading styles and market exposures.

Hedge fund managers are selected so that there is no concentration of risk, either side of the event. A significant risk of a hedge fund investment programme is that each vehicle's performance tracks a similar risk profile. This could lead to similar (negative) results during periods of market turbulence – the very problem that hedge funds are expected to alleviate. Before the event, each hedge fund manager is selected so that its investment and risk profile does not mimic or parallel either that of another hedge fund manager or with the Calpers' benchmark portfolio. After the event, the performance of each hedge fund manager is analysed to ensure that it is consistent with the manager's stated investment objective and risk profile, and that the hedge fund maintains a low correlation with Calpers' chosen benchmark.

EVENT RISK
By their very name, hedge funds are supposed to hedge the risk and return profile of a diversified portfolio. Indeed, many, if not most, hedge fund managers claim that their return distributions are "skill-based"; ie, they are not readily identifiable with the returns to financial asset classes (see Fung and Hsieh, 1997, and Liang, 1999). This argument is the source of the additional claim that hedge funds are "total return", or "absolute return" investments for which no benchmark is appropriate (see Anson, 2001, for a more detailed discussion). The lack of an identifiable benchmark for a hedge fund would indicate that the hedge fund returns are independent of financial market returns.

Also, we would expect the returns to hedge funds to be independent of one another. Again, this stems from the skill-based, absolute return claim of the hedge fund managers. If hedge fund returns are truly skill-based, not only should they be independent of the financial markets, but also their returns should be uncorrelated with each other. Benchmarks would therefore be inappropriate.

We put these claims to the test by conducting an event analysis. The third quarter of 1998 saw the following two serious financial events that added considerable turmoil to the financial markets.

❏ In August 1998, the Russian government defaulted on its outstanding treasury bonds. Credit spreads on all types of debt widened significantly relative to US treasury bonds, and liquidity in many debt markets was reduced. It is this type of financial turmoil that hedge funds are expected to hedge. If hedge fund managers truly generate returns through pure skill, such economic events should have very little impact on the distribution of returns from hedge funds.

❏ In September 1998, Long Term Capital Management of Greenwich, Connecticut, one of the best known and largest of the hedge fund managers, almost collapsed. A consortium of commercial and investment banks, acting in consultation with the Federal Reserve Bank of New York and fearing the possible reverberations in the financial markets, injected US$3.6 billion of fresh capital into Long Term Capital. Again, if hedge fund managers derive their returns from pure skill, their returns should be independent of each other, and events such as Long Term Capital should have very little impact on their return distribution.

To start with, we examine the returns to hedge funds in the month of August 1998. Again, if hedge funds' returns are generated independently of the financial markets, we would expect to see their returns unaffected by the Russian bond crisis during that time. Next, we examine the returns to hedge funds in the month of September 1998. If hedge funds offer skill-based returns independent of each other, we should expect to see no impact on their performance from the near demise of Long Term Capital Management.

We use the data from two hedge fund indices: the CSFB/Tremont Hedge Fund Index, and the Hedge Fund Research HFRI Fund Weighted Composite Index. The CSFB/Tremont index has data beginning in January 1994, while the HFRI index has data from January 1990.

We focus on three event months: August 1998 through October 1998. These three months should capture much of the turmoil caused by the Russian bond default and the Long Term Capital near-collapse. We acknowledge that these two events overlap. For instance, the Russian bond debacle undoubtedly caused spill-over effects on Long Term Capital's positions, even though Long Term Capital did not own any Russian Bonds.

While we cannot separate these events, we can observe their impact on the returns to the hedge fund industry.

Table 1 presents the results of our analysis. Using the CSFB/Tremont index, we examine 54 months of data prior to August 1998. This gives us the mean and standard deviation of monthly returns for this index. For the HFRI index, we use 102 months of data prior to August 1998 to calculate the mean and standard deviation of the index. In Table 1, we also calculate the t statistic for both distributions.

As can be seen, the t statistic for both indices is statistically negative at the 1% level for August 1998. Our first conclusion is that hedge funds did not offer significant diversification benefits during this market event, and were, in fact, affected by the same turmoil that impacted the traditional financial markets.

With respect to the near disaster of Long Term Capital Management, neither index shows a significant impact. True, in both indices, the return in September 1998 is below their average return, but this difference is not statistically significant. However, the t statistic for October 1998 is significantly negative for the CSFB/Tremont Index. It could be that the full impact of Long Term Capital Management was not felt until October, as the full extent of the near disaster unfolded. Yet the HFRI index does not indicate any negative impact in either September or October of 1998. Therefore, it appears that the Long Term Capital affair did not have a measurable impact on the returns to the hedge fund industry. This supports the conclusion that hedge fund returns are independent of each other.

Several lessons can be gleaned from this analysis.

1. Many of the mispricing (arbitrage) opportunities that hedge funds attempt to capture can require an investment horizon of several months or more. Additionally, arbitrage strategies generally make the assumption of normal liquidity. However, when that liquidity dried up as a result of the Russian bond default, many mispricing relationships increased instead of decreasing, thus creating large, temporary paper losses. This situation was further exacerbated by margin calls from

Table 1   Event study of hedge fund returns

	Average return	Std. Deviation (t-statistic)	Aug 98 (t-statistic)	Sept 98 (t-statistic)	Oct 98
CSFB/Tremont	1.29%	2.58%	−7.55% (−3.42)*	−2.31% (−1.4)	−4.57% (−2.27)*
HFRI Index	1.42%	1.66%	−8.70% (−6.09)*	0.69% (−0.44)	1.22% (−0.12)

* significant at the 1% level

    prime brokers that forced some hedge fund managers to liquidate their positions and turn paper losses into realised losses.

2. Many lending institutions that provided liquidity to hedge funds were themselves invested in the same markets and under pressure to manage their own risk exposures. These institutions were unable to provide liquidity to the market when hedge fund managers were needing it the most.

3. Hedge fund managers received redemption calls from their investors during this period. This forced hedge fund managers to liquidate positions to fund their customer's redemption requests. Consequently, hedge fund managers were faced with a liquidity mismatch between the investment horizon of their arbitrage strategies and the investment horizon of their investors. This is similar to a mismatch between the duration of an institution's liabilities and assets. Pension funds and banks long ago learned the lessons of immunisation, but hedge fund managers were forced to learn this lesson the hard way in 1998 (see Goldman Sachs & Co and Financial Risk Management Ltd, 2000).[3]

In conclusion, what this event analysis demonstrates is that hedge fund managers are influenced by tumultuous financial market events. An absence of liquidity in the financial markets can have the same impact on hedge fund managers as it does for long only managers. A hedge fund manager may have all of its economic risks appropriately balanced or hedged, only to be caught in a liquidity crisis. This is exacerbated to the extent that a hedge fund manager invests in less liquid financial markets or custom-tailored derivative transactions.

DATA RISK

Much of the desire to invest in hedge funds stems from academic research into the performance of this asset class. Empirical studies carried out with respect to hedge funds demonstrate convincingly that hedge funds are a valuable addition to a diversified portfolio. In summary, they demonstrate that an allocation to hedge funds can increase the overall return to the portfolio while reducing its risk (see Anson, 2000b for a more detailed summary). However, there are several caveats with respect to these studies.

    First, almost all of these studies were conducted during the same, and relatively brief, period of the early to mid-1990s. Given that these studies examined the return behaviour of hedge funds during the same time period, it is not surprising that they find consistent performance. Additionally, the fact that they also find consistently positive performance is a tribute to the lack of financial market turmoil during most of the 1990s.

    However, as the event analysis above indicates, in the latter part of the 1990s (specifically, the third quarter of 1998), hedge funds stumbled badly.

As demonstrated in the previous section, the dual punch of the Russian bond crisis and the Long Term Capital Management disaster were sufficient to send ripple effects throughout the hedge fund industry. Therefore, prior empirical studies must be taken with a pinch of salt. More analysis is required with respect to instances of market turmoil to determine how hedge funds operate during troubled times.

A second reason to be sceptical of hedge fund performance data is the number of inherent biases to be found in hedge fund databases used in most of the research (see Liang, 2000 and Fung and Hsieh, 2000, for a thorough discussion on the subject of data biases). As a reminder, hedge funds are generally organised as private investment vehicles and do not generally disclose their investment activities to the public. Therefore, many hedge funds do not disclose their performance record to a reporting service in the same way that mutual funds do. A complete performance record of every hedge fund is simply unobtainable.

For example, one study of hedge fund performance found that across 16 different hedge fund styles, the highest Sharpe ratio achieved was 1.11 (for merger arbitrage) and the average Sharpe ratio across all hedge funds was 0.36 (see Liang, 1999). However, another recent study across 21 hedge funds styles found Sharpe ratios as high as 3.63 (for relative value) with an average Sharpe ratio across all hedge funds of 2.23 (see Lo, 2000).

These are large differences. Part of the difference might be explained by time periods that overlapped without being synchronised (but this would then indicate the time sensitivity of hedge fund returns). However, the more likely explanation is that the two studies used different databases. Therefore, the different results indicate that some portion of performance depends on the database used in the study.

Furthermore, most of the databases that track hedge fund performance did not come into existence until the early 1990s, the starting period for most of the hedge fund research to date. Consequently, the performance of hedge funds prior to 1990 may be lost forever.

Within this imperfect framework, there are three data biases that can affect the reported performance of hedge funds. The first is survivorship bias. Survivorship bias arises when a database of hedge funds includes only surviving hedge funds, meaning hedge funds that have ceased operations may be excluded from the database. This leads to an upward bias in performance reporting because, presumably, those hedge funds that ceased operations performed poorly. In other words, only well-performing hedge funds survive.

In addition, the database may be biased downwards in risk relative to the universe of all hedge funds, because those hedge funds that ceased operations may have had more volatile returns (the cause for their demise). Survivorship bias is a natural result of the way the hedge fund industry (or any new financial industry) evolved. Databases were not developed until sufficient interest amongst the academic and institutional community rendered such a service necessary. By that time, many hedge funds that had started and failed were never recorded.

Survivorship bias has been documented in the mutual fund industry. One way to measure this bias is to obtain the complete sample set of all funds that operated during a certain period. The average return of all funds operating during that period is compared to the average return generated by the funds in existence at the end of the period. The difference gives us the amount of survivorship bias (see Malkiel, 1995).

The amount of survivorship bias in the hedge fund industry has been estimated at 3% per year (see Fung and Hsieh, 2000a; and Brown, Goetzmann and Ibbotson, 1999). This is the amount of upward bias reflected in the returns reported to a hedge fund database if not corrected for hedge funds that ceased operations. Clearly, this is a very large bias that, if left uncorrected, can provide misleading conclusions about the investment benefits of hedge funds.

Survivorship bias is more important in the hedge fund industry than the mutual fund industry because of the high turnover rate. It has been estimated that the average life of a hedge fund is about three years, and that the yearly attrition rate is greater than 15% (see Edwards and Liew, 1999; and Park, Brown and Goetzmann, 1999). Consequently, hedge funds cease operations with great frequency, and this should be expected to exacerbate the survivorship problem.

A second bias affecting hedge fund performance results is selection bias. Generally, those hedge funds that are performing well have an incentive to report their results to a database in order to attract new investors to the fund. This results in hedge funds included in the database having better performance than those that are excluded because of their (presumably) poor performance.

A process known as "backfilling" further magnifies this selection bias. When a database adds a hedge fund's historical performance to its pool of funds, it "backfills" the hedge fund's performance to the date it began operations. This creates an instant history of hedge fund returns. Because a hedge fund manager holds the option of when to reveal his historical performance, it is reasonable to expect that he will disclose his performance when his results look most favourable. This leads to an upward bias in performance results within the hedge fund database. To eliminate a backfill bias, it has been estimated that the first 12–24 months of reported data should be eliminated from the hedge fund data.

There is a converse to the selection bias. It is also possible that those hedge funds that are very successful have no incentive to report their performance to a database because they have already attracted a sufficient number of investors to their fund. This would lead to a downward bias of hedge fund performance reported by the databases. Nonetheless, selection bias has been documented to add approximately 1.4% to reported hedge fund returns (see Fung and Hsieh, 2000b).

Finally, a third bias exists, called "catastrophe" or "liquidation" bias. This bias arises from the fact that hedge funds that are performing poorly and likely to cease operations stop reporting their performance before they actually close shop. A hedge fund that is performing poorly and is likely to go out of business has no incentive to continue to report its performance. Indeed, the hedge fund probably has greater issues to deal with, such as liquidating positions to fund customer redemptions, rather than reporting its performance.

Catastrophe bias results in an upward bias in returns and a downward bias in risk, because poor performance history is excluded from the data bias. One study attempted to measure this bias by contacting hedge fund managers directly to determine their return performance subsequent to the termination of reporting (see Ackermann, McEnally and Ravenscroft, 1999). This study measures the impact of liquidation bias to be approximately 70 basis points.

As Table 2 demonstrates, the combination of survivorship and selection bias can add up to 4.5% in hedge fund returns before the impact of catastrophe bias is considered. As a consequence, it is safe to say that studies of hedge funds, if not properly discounted for inherent data biases, will inflate the returns to hedge funds.[4]

In summary, there are several biases that are embedded in historical returns to hedge funds. These biases tend to increase the returns to hedge fund performance, which in turn creates a risk of inflated expectations with regard to the performance of hedge funds.

Every hedge fund disclosure document contains the warning: "past performance is no indication of future results". This is all the more apparent when considering the data biases associated with historical hedge fund performance.

PERFORMANCE MEASUREMENT RISK

The Sharpe ratio is the statistic most often used to compare the performance of two investment managers. It is a measure of risk-adjusted returns and it divides the performance of an investment manager in excess of the

Table 2   Biases associated with hedge fund data

Bias	Park, Brown and Goetzmann (1999)	Brown, Goetzmann and Ibbotson (1999)	Fung and Hsieh (2000a)
Survivorship	2.6%	3%	3%
Selection	1.9%	Not estimated	1.4%
Catastrophe	Not estimated	Not estimated	Not estimated
Total	4.5%	3%	4.4%

risk-free rate by the standard deviation of that manager's performance results. Its purpose is to provide a basis for comparing the performance of different managers that may invest in different financial assets.

However, there are some practical difficulties with using a Sharpe ratio analysis to compare hedge fund returns. As previously indicated, many hedge funds use derivatives with non-linear payoff structures as part of their investment plan. These non-linear instruments can lead to misleading Sharpe ratio conclusions.

Many hedge fund managers have investment styles that contain a short option exposure. When a hedge fund manager shorts or sells an option, he collects the option premium. If the option expires worthless, the hedge fund manager pockets the option premium at no cost and can thereby increase his total return.

Short options exposure also helps to boost a manager's Sharpe ratio because the hedge fund manager collects the option premium and deposits it in a cash account with low volatility. The result is high total return with low risk. Portfolio optimisation techniques will tend to over-allocate to these hedge fund managers because of their high total return and Sharpe ratio, and the fact that the risk inherent in short option positions did not manifest itself during the hedge fund manager's short operating history.

This over-allocation process is sometimes referred to as a "short volatility bias" and it is a dangerous trap for unaware investors (see Weisman and Abernathy, 1999). Hedge fund managers using a short volatility strategy can pump up their returns with low risk in the short run because they have yet to experience a "volatility event" during their short history. Selling options is just like selling insurance: premiums continue to be collected and invested in short term cash instruments until some catastrophe hits the financial markets and, as with an insurance policy, the options are exercised.

To the extent that risk-adjusted returns are inflated through the short selling of options, portfolio optimisers will tend to over-allocate to those strategies. Yet, allocating to these hedge fund managers will increase rather than reduce portfolio risk because the portfolio has now increased its exposure to a financial market catastrophe event. The trap is that hedge fund managers can boost their short term risk-adjusted performance through a short volatility strategy, only to increase their exposure to a volatility event.

Consider the following example. A hedge fund manager accepts a US$1,000,000 investment from a pension fund and invests this money in six-month US Treasury bills. In addition, at the beginning of every month, the hedge fund manager sells fairly priced out-of-the-money call options and out-of-the-money put options on the S&P 500 that will expire at the end of the month. The strike prices are chosen to be 2.5 standard deviations away from the current market price.

The sale of an out-of-the-money call option and an out-of-the-money put option is known as a "strangle". Option traders and hedge fund managers use this strategy when they believe that the value of the underlying asset will not move outside a certain range.

The hedge fund manager invests the option premiums received in US treasury bills. The hedge fund manager writes enough of these options to generate a return equal to 1.5 times that of the risk-free rate.

Since a 2.5 standard deviation event occurs only 1% of the time, the manager has a 99% chance of outperforming the risk-free rate in any one month. In other words, it would take a "one in a hundred" type market event to trigger the exercise of the options in any given month. This means that a volatility event is expected roughly once every eight years (100 months divided by 12). A volatility event occurs when the S&P 500 trades outside the 2.5 standard deviation range of the put/call option strangle.

In the meantime, the manager collects the option premiums and produces impressive Sharpe ratios. In addition, a sufficient track record is established that can be fed into an optimiser resulting in the selection of the hedge fund manager. This hedge fund "house of cards" will come tumbling down, however, when the market turns against this short volatility investment strategy. The large short option exposure will result in a large negative cumulative return for the hedge fund manager that will wipe out most of the hedge fund manager's prior gains.

Let us attach some actual numbers to this. For simplicity, we will assume that the US Treasury bill rate stays constant at 6% a year. Using monthly data from 1995–99, we find that the monthly standard deviation of the SPX Index is about 4%. Therefore, a 2.5 standard deviation move up or down means that the SPX would have to increase or decrease by more than 10% in any one month for the put/call option strangle to be exercised against the hedge fund manager.

Option pricing models shows that a 10% out of the money strangle on the SPX would cost about US$7.50 per strangle. Therefore, each month, the hedge fund manager must leverage his invested capital by selling enough strangles so that his return on invested capital is 9% or, 1.5 times the Treasury bill rate of 6%.

As an example, assume that in the first month, the hedge fund manager receives US$1,000,000 from his client. US$1,000,000 invested for one month at 9% would generate an end of period total of $(1,000,000 \times 1.0075) =$ US$1,007,500. The catch is that the manager invests the money in US Treasury bills earning 6%. Therefore, the hedge fund manager must sell enough put/call strangles and take in enough option premiums so as to generate a total return equal to US$1,007,500. The calculation is:

$$(1,000,000 + \text{option premiums}) \times (1 + 0.06/12) = US\$1,007,500$$

The amount of option premiums that must be generated is US$2,487. At an expected cost of US$7.50 per option strangle, the hedge fund manager must sell 331 put/call strangles to generate a return of 9%.

This strategy will work well until a volatility event occurs and the expected loss of capital results. At that point, the SPX will move by more than the 10% limit (2.5 standard deviations) and the strangle will be exercised. Also, as the size of the investment increases, the hedge fund manager must sell more and more options to maintain the 9% return.

We performed a Monte Carlo simulation to determine how long it would take for a volatility event to occur. Running 5,000 simulations, our model estimated that it would take 80 months for the options to be exercised against the hedge fund manager.[5]

Figure 3 demonstrates what happens when the manager employs this strategy. It works fine for the first almost seven years. Then a volatility event occurs and the options are exercised against the portfolio manager. The exercise of the options does not wipe out all of the manager's gains, but it does eliminate a good portion. After the volatility event, the manager is left with an effective annual return of 2.85%, well below that of US Treasury bills.

Table 3 shows the returns and Sharpe ratios generated by the hedge fund

Table 3 Performance statistics for short volatility investment strategy

	Pre-Volatility Event	Post-Volatility Event
Average annual return	9%	2.85%
Excess return	3%	–3.15%
Standard deviation	0.28%	0.28%
Sharpe ratio	10.98	–11.25

Figure 3 Short volatility investment strategy

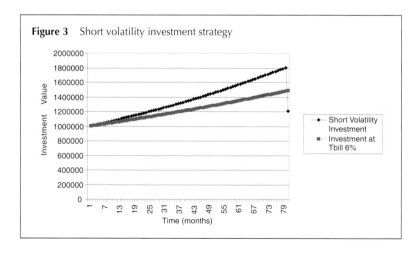

manager before and after the volatility event. As we can see, the hedge fund manager looks like a star before the volatility event, but is unmasked once the event occurs. Unfortunately, before the volatility event is reached, the hedge fund manager can achieve a stellar track record. The low volatility associated with Treasury bill returns allows the hedge fund manager to achieve a large, positive Sharpe ratio before the volatility event occurs.

Clearly, the above example is an extreme one. However, it does highlight the problems associated with the short selling of options. Short volatility positions can increase performance in the short run, but they expose the hedge fund to large downside risk should a volatility event occur.

Unfortunately, there is no simple solution for this problem but there are some practical suggestions. First, hedge fund managers with short track records and high Sharpe ratios should be scrutinised carefully. They may not have experienced a volatility event sufficient to damage their performance history. It is possible that by selecting managers based on their history of risk-adjusted returns may be a negative selection process if their trading history is too short.

Second, we look at the age-old issue with respect to the hedge fund industry: transparency. Just what is the hedge fund manager doing? How is he generating his excess performance? To what extent does he use options (particularly, short options) in his trading strategies? These questions must be asked and answered before investing with a hedge fund manager.

Last, new analytical tools are needed. Risk-adjusted ratios were developed for the linear investment world of traditional long-only investment managers and mutual funds. Additional analysis is needed to account for the non-linear investment strategies employed by many hedge funds.

SUMMARY

The hedge fund industry has received tremendous attention over the past decade as an alternative investment class to hedge traditional portfolio returns. However, as a new investment class, there are new risks that require consideration. In this chapter, we presented five risk factors associated with hedge fund investments that must be considered in addition to the market exposures received. These five factors do not diminish the value of hedge fund investments, but are useful for developing realistic expectations with respect to the value added of hedge funds in a diversified portfolio.

---

1   They demonstrate that idiosyncratic process risks can largely be eliminated through a diversified fund of funds programme. Park and Staum indicate that a portfolio of 15 to 20 hedge funds can eliminate much of the idiosyncratic risk associated with hedge fund investments.

2   The other two questions are: what is the investment objective of the hedge fund, and, what makes the hedge fund manager so smart?

3   See this text for more discussion on the lessons of Long Term Capital Management and the Russian bond default as it related to the hedge fund industry.

4   These biases are not observed in all cases. Ackermann, McEnally and Ravenscroft (1999) found no systematic bias in their hedge fund data. Specifically, their study finds that there are competing forces in survivorship bias: termination bias and self-selection bias. Some funds stop reporting their information because they terminate their operations while other funds stop reporting their performance because they have become so successful that it is no longer in their best interests to publicly report their performance.

5   We estimate our parameters over 60 months from 1995–99. Our simulation indicated that a volatility event could occur as early as the first month and take as long as 237 months. Additionally, we use a conservative estimate that the option is in-the-money by 10 SPX points when exercised.

Bibliography

Ackermann, C., R. McEnally and D. Ravenscroft, 1999, "The Performance of Hedge Funds: Risk, Return, and Incentives", *Journal of Finance*, June.

Anson, M., 2000, "Selecting a Hedge Fund Manager" *The Journal of Wealth Management*, forthcoming, 2000.

Anson, M., 2001, "An Institutional View of the Hedge Fund Industry", *Journal of Investing*, forthcoming, 2001.

Brown, S., W. Goetzmann and R. Ibbotson, 1999, "Offshore Hedge Funds: Survival and Performance, 1989-1995", *Journal of Business* 72.

CrossBorder Capital, 1999, "Choosing Investment Styles to Reduce Risk", *Hedge Fund Research*, October.

CrossBorder Capital, 2000, "TSS(II)-Tactical Style Selection: Integrating Hedge Funds into the Asset Allocation Framework", *Hedge Fund Research*, August, 2000.

Edwards, F., and J. Liew, 1999, "Hedge Funds versus Managed Futures as Asset Classes", *Journal of Derivatives*, Summer.

Fung, W., and D. Hsieh, 1997, "Empirical Characteristics of Dynamic Trading Strategies: The Case of Hedge Funds", *Review of Financial Studies* 10.

Fung, W., and D. Hsieh, 2000a, "Performance Characteristics of Hedge Funds and Commodity Funds: Natural versus Spurious Biases", *Journal of Financial and Quantitative Analysis*.

Fung, W., and D. Hsieh, 2000b, "Hedge Fund Performance Benchmarks: Information Content and Measurement Biases", Working Paper, Fuqua School of Business, Duke University.

Goldman Sachs & Co. and Financial Risk Management Ltd, 1999, "The Hedge Fund "Industry" and Absolute Return Funds", *The Journal of Alternative Investments*, Spring.

Goldman, Sachs & Co. and Financial Risk Management Ltd, 2000, "Hedge Funds Revisited", *Pension and Endowment Forum*.

Liang, B., 1999, "On the Performance of Hedge Funds", *Financial Analysts Journal*, July/August.

Liang, B., 2000, "Hedge Funds: The Living and the Dead", *Journal of Financial and Quantitative Analysis*, September.

Lo. A., 2000, "Risk Management for Hedge Funds: An Introduction and Overview", Working Paper, Sloan School of Management, MIT.

Malkiel, B., 1995, "Returns from Investing in Equity Mutual Funds 1971 to 1991", *Journal of Finance* 50.

Park, J., S. Brown and W. Goetzmann, 1999, "Performance Benchmarks and Survivorship Bias for Hedge Funds and Commodity Trading Advisors", *Hedge Fund News*, August.

Park, K., and J. Staum, 1998, "Fund of Funds Diversification: How Much is Enough?", *The Journal of Alternative Investments*, Winter. "Shake-Up Continues at Soros's Hedge-Fund Empire", *The Wall Street Journal*, May 1, 2000, p. C1.

Sharpe, W., 1992, "Asset Allocation: Management Style and Performance Measure", *Journal of Portfolio Management* 18.

Weisman, A., and J. Abernathy, 2000, "The Danger of Historical Hedge Fund Data", in L. Rahl (ed), *Risk Budgeting: A New Approach to Investing* (London: Risk Books).

3

Risk Management Issues for the Family Office

Luc Estenne

Partners Advisers SA

The risk management issues of a family office should be examined in relation to its subjective definition of risk, which is derived from the family investment preferences and objectives. Accordingly, in this chapter, we will first expose the typical family office preferences and objectives. We will then briefly review the theory of risk quantification and its limits. Finally, we will examine some of the key issues of hedge fund risk qualification that we have identified as hedge fund asset allocator.

THE INVESTMENT PREFERENCES AND OBJECTIVES OF THE FAMILY OFFICE

The typical family group is already rich. Consequently, its investment strategy will be mostly guided by wealth preservation and wealth transfer issues from one generation to the next, as opposed to pure wealth creation objectives. In this context, one would expect the family to have a long-term investment horizon that should govern short term return volatility acceptance and lead to long-only equity investments. Most investment management textbooks reinforce this view.

However, the behavioural reality of family office investment is different. The fact that the majority of global assets allocated to hedge funds comes from private investors and family offices clearly illustrates the specificity of their investment preferences. These preferences, which are fundamentally governed by an asymmetrical sensitivity to loss vis-à-vis profits, govern family office allocation to hedge funds.

Objective one: Avoid large losses
The family office will structure its investments in order to avoid large losses. Because it attaches a high value to capital preservation, it will tend to exclude from its universe of potential investments the high-risk, high-return investment strategies so that it can focus most of its resources on

strategies displaying a higher chance of success. Instead of trying to hit home runs, the family office objective will be to concentrate on return consistency in order to benefit from the returns compounding effect.

Objective two: Protect the downside

Equity markets' performance over the last decade has certainly twisted investors' return expectations and their perception of financial risks. Financial markets do not always move up; bear markets, corrections and crashes do happen. The fear of these disasters and the search for a remedy are central to the family office investment behaviour. In this context, hedge fund allocation is motivated by the capacity of some strategies to absorb financial markets' shocks and to provide substantial downside protection.

Objective three: Search for α or absolute returns

The corollary to the downside protection need for the family office is its search for investments that display asymmetric return profiles like that produced by the best hedge fund strategies. Typically, their performance engine is not β the market index, but rather the α that is extracted from successful short term market timing, equity hedge stock picking, equity market neutral, event driven, relative value or arbitrage relationship.

Objective four: Maximise risk-adjusted returns

Within the framework delimited by the above preferences and objectives, the family office should aim to optimise the risks-adjusted returns related to its investment strategy. The realisation of this objective will be conditioned by its capacity to allocate assets:

❏ to managers who display significant competitive advantage and skills; and
❏ within a structure that secures a commonality of interest between the manager and their investors.

Based on these preferences and objectives, the risk management objective of the family office hedge fund asset allocator will be to:

❏ identify and exclude disaster loss potential;
❏ understand and evaluate the performance engine and attached risks; and
❏ define and implement a coherent portfolio construction process.

RISK QUANTIFICATION IN THE CONTEXT OF HEDGE FUND ALLOCATION

The theory

Risk is the exposure to uncertain change. It can be seen as the combination of the probability of a negative event happening and the loss associated with the occurrence of this negative event. Financial risks are usually split into three main categories: credit risk, market risk and operational risks. The table below shows how these different risk categories are usually structured into sub-components.

Table 1   Categorisation of risk

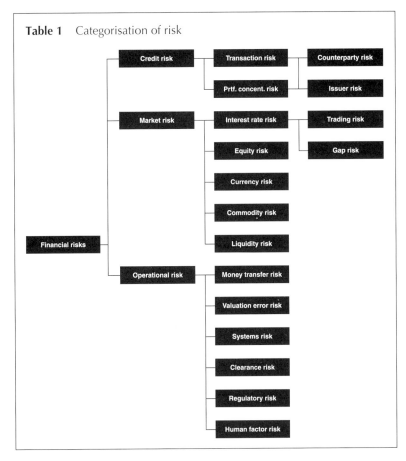

The financial industry measures market risks and credit risks using value-at-risk (VAR) methodology. VAR is defined as the maximum possible loss for a given portfolio within a known confidence interval over a specific time horizon. In their never-ending quest for more quantification, some also measure operational risks using a similar value-at-operational risk methodology.

According to these methodologies, it should be possible to measure the VAR for each hedge fund and each potential combination of hedge fund portfolio. The association of hedge funds portfolio returns to these measures should enable us to construct the optimised portfolio in terms of risk-adjusted returns.

The limitations

It is reassuring to measure what we fear most and human nature is such that the quantification and measure of risk too often translate into an improper sense of comfort and control. Beyond the very large number of system and operational issues that would need to be solved and summarised into a single VAR number to quantify the risks of hedge fund investing, I strongly believe that the value of such an exercise would be very limited. Here are the main reasons.

Market rate distribution

The quantification of risk relies on the definition of a probability distribution of market moves. The precise definition of such distribution is extremely difficult. Typically, most methodologies fail to take skewed distributions into account, and are very imprecise when it comes to extreme market move measurements, ie, when we most need them.

Linear versus non-linear relationships

The relationship between portfolio market value and market change for complex financial instruments is not typically linear. Accordingly, it becomes much more difficult to measure the impact of market moves on the value of such instruments because most calculations neglect the second order or gamma effects. This is usually the case for any instrument with embedded optionality, or convex fixed-income instruments.

Instability of market relationships

Most methods of calculating VAR rely on estimates of the volatilities and correlations of market changes in order to aggregate diverse risky positions. The problem is that these correlations are highly unstable and tend to migrate towards one in times of market crises.

Instrument-specific risks

Beyond the theoretical limitation of VAR, it is important to recognise that the methodology is of no value in many hedge fund strategies. For instance, it is not possible to describe event-driven strategies such as distressed securities investing or risk arbitrage strategies with VAR methodology.

PRACTICAL ISSUES RELATED TO RISK QUANTIFICATION

Forced to recognise the practical and theoretical limits and difficulties of risk quantification, the family office hedge fund allocator must rely on prudence, prevention and judgement. The following are some of the lessons we have learned through both good and bad experiences.

Some operational risks – service providers and structure

The offshore hedge fund investor should realise that there is no proper structure in place to ensure the protection of his interests. Detailed review of the prospectus, the articles of associations, the fund structure and the service providers must be conducted. However, while this review will reduce operational risks, it will not eliminate them.

Offshore hedge fund service providers

Hedge fund investors rely on the quality and responsibility of administrators and auditors to ensure control of assets, independent NAV calculation and accuracy of financial statements. Unfortunately, all too often the basic structure is not in place in the offshore industry. We believe that today, there is a significant market opportunity for serious service providers ready to implement and enforce adequate structure in terms of administration and audit.

Administrators, who should have the role of global custodian, do not always have control of assets. As directors of their funds, any hedge fund managers have the signatory power necessary to move assets and open accounts where and when they want. In addition, it is still common for administrators to leave mark-to-market responsibilities in the hands of hedge fund managers instead of using truly independent pricing sources.

Moreover, auditors currently seem to be willing to limit their responsibilities and liabilities to the point that audited financial statements are less and less a guarantee of financial fairness. The following are extracts from a letter of engagement from one of the top five worldwide audit firms.

> "The Liability of [the audit firm name] to the company in connection with this engagement shall be limited in total to the fees paid to [the audit firm name]"

> "As you are aware, there are inherent limitations in the audit process, including, for example, selective testing and the possibility that collusion or forgery may preclude the detection of material errors, fraud, and illegal acts. Accordingly, a material misstatement may remain undetected."

Hedge fund legal documents

The fund prospectus, articles of association and the subscription agreement are the fundamental documents that structure the rights and obligations of the investor and the fund. The additional contracts to be reviewed are the investment management and advisory contract and the administration and custody contracts. As illustrated by the following extracts that have been written by a prominent US legal firm, the content of these documents should be carefully reviewed to ensure that the balance of the parties' interests are present.

"The memorandum and Articles of Association of the Company may be amended either by a resolution of members or by a resolution of Directors".

"The Fund will indemnify the Investment Manager or Any of its Partners, officers and employees with respect to any cost or expense arising from [. . .] losses due [. . .] to the negligence, dishonesty or bad faith of any employee, broker or other agent of the Investment Manager."

"The organisational and initial offering costs of the Company are expected to amount to approximately US$200,000. Such costs will be paid by the Company out of the proceeds of the initial offering of shares."

Track record quantitative analysis
The existence of a successful investment track record is often a prerequisite to any hedge fund investment. However, the predictive power of past performance and its quantitative analysis is usually extremely limited, mainly for the following reasons:

❏ the number of data point is often too small to be statistically significant;
❏ the investment strategy is usually adapted and changed over time;
❏ the financial market conditions change and are cyclical; and
❏ short volatility risks have a low probability of occurrence.

Accordingly, the use of track record quantitative analysis should be limited to an *ex post* exercise where the aim is not to predict the future but rather to question the past.

Moreover, the track record should be subject to a qualitative analysis in order to define who is ultimately responsible for it, and in what organisational context and market condition it has been produced.

The analysis of the performance engine
The study of the investment strategy and the understanding of the factors that influence its success are central to investment selection. The search for returns implies the acceptance of some market and credit risks; these need to be identified and assessed through the study of the investment strategy.

Internal factors
The investment strategy deployed is influenced by factors such as asset types, asset size, funding cost, funding availability, information flow,

portfolio concentration and diversification, leverage, and exposure to market, volatility, and event risk, etc. These factors need to be identified and their impact on the performance assessed in order to understand the risks that have generated and influenced the performance. In this respect, the risk typology, which has been graphed above, should be used as the basis for this risk analysis.

The key factor, however, is the human one. There is no hedge fund without managers. At the end of the process the investment decision is a judgment and a vote of confidence on the ethics, skills and competitive advantages of a manager. In addition, the hedge fund investor has to recognise that it is unrealistic to expect to control 100% of the hedge fund portfolio activity. The best transparency level usually available takes the form of monthly or quarterly portfolio snapshots. Accordingly, the element of ethics and "trust" vis-à-vis the hedge fund manager is paramount.

External factors

External factors are related to market conditions and provide food to the investment strategy. These factors include market direction and level, sector rotation, volatility level, IPO activity level, market flows, demand and offer, credit spread fluctuation, M&A activity, default level, etc.

It is the review and understanding of the internal and external factors that will enable the hedge fund allocator to assess whether performance has been generated because of risk, skill or luck, and to determine the extent to which past performance has a chance to be repeated in the future. Coherence of the investment strategy, stability and repeatability of the process and sensitivity to external factors should be evaluated together for a judgment to be issued.

PORTFOLIO LEVEL RISK MANAGEMENT

The selection of an independent collection of adequate hedge funds and hedge fund managers is a necessary but incomplete condition of success. The key is to extend the process into the set-up of a coherent and balanced portfolio. Our portfolio level risk management is based on the following guidelines: bottom-up approach, seasoning process, concentration and diversification rules.

A bottom-up portfolio construction approach

Hedge fund investing boils down to selecting skill, competitive advantage and risk management. Accordingly, it is crucial to place the emphasis on the selection of good managers rather than adequate strategies. Of course, our experience has taught us to avoid or maintain reduced allocation to strategies which dangerously combine leverage and illiquidity, strategies that rely on misleading and inadequate accounting standards, and strategies that tend to be short-event risk and/or volatility. But once these strategies are put aside, a bottom-up approach is critical because it helps us to avoid the temptation of filling in the pre-defined strategy allocation box with an average or poor quality manager. The corollary to this bottom-up approach is the acceptance of a running portfolio heavily allocated to US markets and US managers, overweighted in equity vis-à-vis fixed-income instruments and underweighted emerging markets.

Seasoning process

To build adequate portfolios of hedge fund investments, hedge fund allocators have to recognise and take into account the following in their asset allocation behaviour.

❑ The hedge fund mortality rate is high, especially in the early years of a fund.
❑ Hedge fund managers need to be given time to prove their competitive advantages.
❑ Asset allocators' understanding of strategies and managers increases if these are followed across a full market cycle.
❑ Early stage hedge fund investors run higher risks because of the additional business risks related to the start-up phase.
❑ Whatever the skill and experience of an asset allocator, he/she will continue to make mistakes.

We recognise these facts and have tried to take them into account in our portfolio construction guidelines. Accordingly, the portfolios we manage are structured into three different categories: farm team, intermediate and senior. The allocation will fall into one of these categories according to our subjective comfort level and knowledge of a manager and a strategy. At the farm team level, we find a large number of small allocations, while at the senior level, we have a limited number of large allocations. It will take, on average, at least four years for a manager to migrate from the farm team, through the intermediate category, to the senior level. The farm team should be limited to 15% of the portfolio, the intermediate section should be around 40% and the senior category should hold the remaining balance of the allocation.

Concentration and diversification rules

The maximum allocation to one single hedge fund should be defined according to the category the fund belongs to, the relative size of the hedge fund portfolio vis-à-vis the total wealth of the investor or family, and the risk tolerance/investment objective. The typical maximum allocation we use is 2%, 4% and 8% for the farm team, intermediate and senior category, respectively.

A more difficult question to answer as a hedge fund allocator is the adequate level of diversification (ie, how many hedge funds should be included in a portfolio?). The balance between diversification of risks and dilution of return is a subtle one. Typically, for a family who have a substantial allocation of hedge funds (above 40% of liquid assets), a total of 45 funds is often adequate. Of these, about 15 to 20 are usually in the farm team category.

The purpose is to go beyond the diversification of financial risks usually achieved with about 20 funds, and to take into account operational risks. These risks are extremely difficult to assess, and have disaster losses attached to them, although all have a low probability of occurrence. Accordingly, the maximum allocation to a single hedge fund is given by the answer to one simple question: "How much are we ready to lose should our maximum allocation suffer a 100% blow-up?"

BIBLIOGRAPHY

Alexander, C., 1999, *Risk Management and Analysis: Measuring and Modelling Financial Risk*, Volume I (New York: John Wiley & Sons).

Bekier, M., 1996, *Marketing of Hedge Funds: A Key Strategic variable in Defining Possible Roles of an Emerging Investment Force* (Berne: Peter Lang AG).

Bookstaber, R., et al, 1999, *Risk Management: Principles and Practices* (Association for Investment Management and Research Publications).

Chen, D., et al, 1999, *Frontiers in Credit Risk Analysis* (Association for Investment Management and Research Publications).

Cottier, P., 1997, *Hedge Funds and Managed Futures* (Berne: Verlag Paul Haupt).

Gastineau, G. L., and M. P. Kristzman, 1996, *Dictionary of Financial Risk Management* (Frank J. Fabozzi Associates).

Lake, R. A., (ed), 1996, *Evaluating and Implementing Hedge Fund Strategies*, Second Edition (Euromoney Publications Plc).

Molak, V., 1996, *Fundamentals of Risk Analysis and Risk Management* (Lewis Publishers).

Trone, D. B., W. R. Allbright and P.R. Taylor, 1996, *The Management of Investment Decisions* (Irwin Professional Publishing).

Global Equity and Market Derivative Market Risk, 1998, (Morgan Stanley Dean Witter).

Operational Risk and Financial Institutions, 1998, (London: Risk Books).

4

Fund of Funds: Risk Management Issues for Endowments and Foundations

William P. Miller II

Commonfund

There are many faces of risk. In the expanding investment universe, risks continually increase, and change is constant. Not long ago, endowment investing concentrated on just two asset classes: stocks and bonds. And when we talked about stocks, we essentially meant publicly traded shares in large US companies. The risks, everyone assumed, were generally quite clear. In the 1980s, endowment managers began to think seriously about other, less traditional asset classes. Because the market behaviour of these other investments differed so markedly from that of traditional stocks and bonds, their inclusion in a portfolio could actually reduce overall market risk, even while adding to the potential for gain.

But at the same time, these other investments added new specific risks to the endowment manager's worry list. Add international equity to your portfolio, and you are adding currency risk, sovereign risk and more. Add venture capital funds to the mix, and you are adding liquidity risks, custody risks and valuation risks. The list goes on.

At Commonfund, we have long been sensitive to this tendency. As the largest investment manager for educational endowments in the US, we've played more than an incidental role in expanding the variety of assets used by endowment investors.

Hedge funds are just one example. We have created vehicles for investing in a number of alternative strategies, including private capital, venture capital, real estate, and oil and gas. Since the late 1980s, over 100 of our client schools have added such "other" investments to their asset allocations.

The essential discipline

We have established a strong risk management programme coupled with an independent risk management discipline in our organisation, the establishment of the latter element being a pioneering endeavour at the time. As part of this discipline, we may advise our clients on implementing risk management in their own organisations.

When we began building our risk management activities, we had no manual of instructions for guidance. The most comparable seems to have been the quality management movement that swept through the business scene in the 1980s.

Notwithstanding that resemblance, we realised we had to create our own concept of risk management and then build it from the ground up. Now, looking forward, we hope that others can learn from our experience and thus avoid having to re-invent risk management for themselves.

So, on the next few pages, I will provide an overview of our risk management system at Commonfund, starting with a summary of our conceptual framework.

Risk beyond price

In the investment world, the interest in risk seems to ebb and flow with the swing of sentiment from fear to greed and back again. But whatever the temper of the times, investors are unlikely to deny that risk is always lurking out there, somewhere.

At heart, investors tend to think of risk as the possibility of a decline in the market prices or net asset value of their investments, and this is certainly the easiest definition for a complex condition. To give us a better handle on the chance of decline, professional investors have defined risk in terms of the volatility we can track in an investment's performance record. We then get further help from the science of statistics, which gives us a convenient marker for the range of volatility as related to the stock's net price change in the standard deviation.

Statistical analysis also gives us a benchmark for a security's volatility in relation to the overall stock market in its beta.

For bonds, we have statistical indicators of the amount by which the price of an individual security or fund is likely to rise or fall as the result of changes in interest rates in its duration, and the second derivative of convexity.

These terms, and the viewpoint they reflect, certainly work for both endowment and foundation management. But in this case, they tell us only part of the story.

The extraordinarily long time horizon we have in these investing venues tends to soften the significance of volatility in the short term. In the extended time frame (or non-frame), we have to set clear investing objectives that assure us we will be supporting our institution's objectives all along the way. An occasional dip below the targeted rate of growth will seem less critical once the objectives are met or exceeded in the longer term. When your horizon reaches to perpetuity, you have as long a term as you can imagine.

To be sure, a retreat in portfolio value can undermine an endowment's ability to contribute funds to a school's operating budget. Schools typically target around 5% of portfolio value for annual spending. A shortfall could deprive the current generation of students of its fair share. But endowment managers have employed a number of ways to mitigate this admittedly important risk, using asset allocation and other diversification strategies to support their spending policies.

In the case of hedge funds, the usual concerns about volatility are less significant. Hedge funds in many cases involve large, high-risk bets, predicated on the wisdom and experience of a fund manager with demonstrated expertise in specific investment techniques. A hedge fund's correlation with the movement of the major securities markets is in many cases slight.

In making an investment in a hedge fund, the endowment or foundation limits its risk by limiting the size of the position it takes in any one fund, while taking positions in more than one hedge fund. The hedge fund vehicles that Commonfund offers, for instance, enable those client-schools to take appropriately diversified positions in a dozen or so funds at one time.

Risks at every step

For the foundation or endowment fiduciary, and for Commonfund as one of their major resources, the challenge of risk reaches well beyond price volatility, market fluctuations or asset allocation. It extends into every corner of the investment process.

We define risk as the possibility of any failure that could impede achievement of the institution's objectives, when looking deep into the future. Our goal is always to understand the risks that our funds are taking, so that we can mitigate and control them where possible.

In this respect, risk management emulates the quality management philosophy that dominated many successful manufacturing and service businesses in the last two decades. Neither quality nor risk management can succeed as a discrete function, and neither can effectively operate on a retrospective basis. Both require a total commitment of the organisation, affecting everything it does.

In other words, risk management must work in every part of the investment management process, at every step of the investment continuum; it must be present internally and externally, in operations, in the valuation and safekeeping of assets, in legal and compliance, in guarding against fraud, in the system's data management and communications technology, and so on.

Take nothing for granted

Risk management requires a sceptical outlook at every stage of the continuum. Everyone involved must ask tough questions as a matter of habit – for instance, "how much is the portfolio worth today?"

In the past, when the portfolio might consist entirely of publicly-traded US securities, the answer was available at the end of any day, and it could comfortably be taken for granted. Now, however, it's become more complicated.

First, some of the assets may trade not on an open-auction market but dealer-to-dealer, and this could raise questions about whose pricing you've been given and whether it is the bid or ask. Some securities could be thinly traded or relatively illiquid, raising questions about the reliability or stability of the price recorded.

Second, some of the assets are likely to be traded on foreign markets; values could be changing even while you sleep. Those valuations would also, of course, be subject to foreign exchange rates and, moreover, the investment manager's currency hedging technique.

In view of the inherent complications, what is the reliability of your portfolio valuation these days? Is there a margin of variation you should know about?

Another nagging question might be, "where are our assets being held, and are they secure?" If your own custodial bank is not holding the securities, are you better protected against fraud? Will you know if the securities are placed on loan? Can you trust the valuation you are given?

The investment process is full of specific issues such as these that could, although they have no direct relation to price volatility, undermine achievement of the institution's objectives in the event of a failure. Your risk management discipline must encompass all of them and take nothing for granted.

Managing expectations

The challenge of risk management is somewhat more daunting than might have been implied by the foregoing definition and examples. In an effective risk management programme, your scepticism must dig even deeper than the institution's objectives.

The trustees will have stated the objectives in writing, clearly and "objectively". But the risk management programme must also cope with a myriad of expectations, whether stated or assumed, of all those involved.

All of the terms and conditions of the investment process, as communicated to the investors, create expectations. If we describe an investment offering as having certain objectives, and assert that the fund will be managed under certain restrictions, that presentation sets certain minimum expectations in the minds of our investors. My own expectations, and those of everyone on our staff, must emulate the collective expectations of our investors, the endowments and the foundations we serve.

Keys to effective risk management

For an effective risk management programme, we believe we must achieve the following three key attributes:

Anticipation

The system should seek to identify risks early, well before they gain any weight. To push the point further, I hold that the system should strive to raise awareness of any situation that could become risky. Surprise is a mortal enemy of risk management.

Transparency

The system should try to elicit all information relevant to the riskiness of every activity in the investment process. It should attempt to eliminate guesswork. Furthermore, the system must attempt to alert us when any risk has risen above a defined level. It works as an early warning system.

Control

Having detected risks that have reached suspicious or unacceptable levels, the firm is then able to develop programmes to address them. This could result in further investigation, negotiation, communication, or changes in practices or policies.

How do we achieve these aims? That is what our risk management programme is all about.

Our risk management process defines areas of potential risk for each activity in the investment process. From this array of potential risks, we can anticipate where risks might materialise and, consequently allocate resources to designing and implementing processes that allow us to measure our exposure to these various risks. This is an ongoing process aimed at providing the organisation with the transparency necessary to control those risks.

Commonfund's risk management structure includes both core and independent elements. The core element includes the functional areas of Commonfund, while the independent element incorporates the risk management group's direct reporting to the board of trustees. Our core-plus-independent structure gives risk management the independence it needs to function effectively, together with the interaction it needs to identify new risks as they emerge and subsequently keep them visible and under control.

This independent structure has been successful for us because of the quality of our people and the culture within which they work. Effective risk management requires willing participation of all hands and the visible commitment of leaders. Otherwise, you really need a very different approach to risk management.

Bits and pieces

I want to focus now on the process of risk management, which parallels the process of investment management.

In risk management, we must act as detectives. To achieve transparency and anticipation, the risk manager sifts through the bits and pieces of the investment process to uncover risks before they turn into failures, or disaster.

You cannot make sense of all those pieces without a map of some kind. The following table outlines our map at Commonfund. We have sorted the investment process into a continuum of 12 activities: asset allocation, benchmark determination, manager selection, etc. Another analysis might give you a somewhat different breakdown, but our 12 will suffice for this discussion.

Asset allocation (strategic/tactical)	Benchmark determination	Manager selection
Manager engagement	Portfolio construction and management	Manager monitoring
Performance reporting	Custody	Accounting
Valuation	Operations	Business/event

What can go wrong?

These 12 activities really summarise the focus we at Commonfund have for our clients. And each of these activities entails risks. So we have to look critically at each one and ask, "What can go wrong?"

Thinking this way, we can prioritise the areas of potential risk that we should be concerned with. You can see our expanded map in Table 1, with a varied number of potential risk areas linked to each activity. This matrix forms a kind of radar system for our risk management practice. Here we start the search that we later return to. Since, as fund managers, we engage in all of these activities more or less continually, we have to be managing the risks continually. It is an iterative process. With this matrix as a guide, we can make sure we review each of these checkpoints at appropriate frequencies.

The variety of risks

We apply this process to every fund we offer, though the questions we ask will vary according to the type of investment being examined. Focusing on a hedge fund offering, we would review its asset allocation in the top of the

Table 1 Investment Risk Matrix

Investment risks

Investment activity	Potential areas of risk		
Asset allocation (strategic/tactical)	Selection of asset classes/proxies; Return/correlation projections; Sufficient diversification; Liquidity	Market shocks; Market structures; Economic assumptions; Tax	Underlying models; Long term versus short term; Costs when changing policy; Cash flows; Liability projection
Benchmark determination	Selection – weight bias updates/changes	Costs	Rebalancing
Manager selection	Style – past, present, future; Misfit to benchmark; People; Compliance	Guidelines; Trading instruments; Philosophy; Controls	Concentration; Performance; Process; Separation of functions (Trading/back office)
Manager monitoring	Guidelines/controls systems	Models	Data
Performance reporting	Calculation; Independence	Presentation; Sub-custodian	
Custody		Separation of duties	Capital
Accounting	Methodology	Process; Seasonality	
Valuation	Modelling risk; Size of position		Pricing source
Operations	Business interruption; Record-keeping; Insurance	Staffing; External relationships; Systems	Internal controls; Technology; Legal/regulatory
Business/event	Currency convertibility; Credit rating shifts; Market disruptions	Reputation; Taxation	Legal/regulatory; Disaster

list by asking, "How much of the fund consists of opportunistic strategies, and how much consists of defensive strategies? What are the risk characteristics of this mix? And what would be the risks if we changed the mix?"

Then, moving to the next point, benchmark determination, we would ask, "What benchmark should we be using in evaluating this mix of strategies?"

The array of risk potentials we have defined may change from time to time. New areas of risk may emerge and certain areas may become more important than previously thought. Using our experience, we may decide to split certain areas into smaller parts, thereby achieving a tighter focus in our review process.

But we have to resist becoming too conscientious in identifying areas of risk. The array can become so extensive that it overwhelms our ability to cope. In selecting risk areas to include in our matrix, we weigh the level of probability that a failure will occur against the possible consequences of such failure.

Focusing your attention

As the independent risk management officer, I have to prioritise certain review activities that will be conducted by the independent group, or risk becoming a master of superficiality. You can't do it all, all the time, and expect to do it all well. For each investment activity, relying on input from staff and my own assessment, could determine the frequency at which the review activity would occur. Key factors in establishing such a review programme are the associated risks as well as the level and frequency of review by the "core" risk management group described earlier.

Of course, there are check-lists available to take you through a review of the hedge fund managers you're considering. But after you've done your review, completed your due diligence, and asked all those questions, what then? You still have to prioritise, asking, "Which are the areas of greatest vulnerability?"

I would point to three of the investment activities in our matrix for a closer look: manager monitoring, custody and valuation. You may not think of these as the most exciting parts of the investing experience, but this is where our most important detective work takes place.

Manager monitoring requires frequent oversight; our schedule calls for monthly iteration. In Table 1, we have defined four primary areas of potential risk: guidelines, models, data and systems.

Revisiting your guidelines

Notice that the guideline risk first appears in Table 1 in connection with manager selection. It is at that point that we have to compose the guidelines, because they will have a bearing on our selection. We use the guidelines to tell the management firm in what it can invest and the criteria it should use in making investments for us.

One additional consideration for investors is that investment guidelines for commingled funds or partnerships in general are established by that investment manager. Should you choose to invest in a commingled or partnership product, you should review those investment guidelines and assess the level of consistency with your institutions' preferred guidelines.

When we get to manager monitoring, the guideline risk appears for the second time; we again must examine this risk because the framework by which we originally composed those guidelines may, in practice, have allowed the manager to do things we did not intend. In a changing environment, the manager may have misinterpreted certain guidelines, or may have strayed opportunistically. Any deviation, for whatever reason, must be corrected as soon as possible.

The modelling challenge

Along similar lines, we have to review the modelling of risk. We use modelling to monitor the performance of managers whose investments are not entirely transparent.

Hedge funds pose a particular challenge in this respect since many managers may not want to tell investors what the fund is invested in – or at least, not immediately. This is particularly true if making the position public would be detrimental to the performance of the hedge fund. What's more, in their pursuit of adding value, the hedge fund manager could change strategies abruptly without informing the investors.

Separately, a hedge fund may provide monthly performance data, but, since some of the investments may be illiquid and not readily priced, the performance data may be estimated.

So, you may have no alternative but to use modelling to monitor hedge fund managers. You can base your model on an analysis of the sectors you understand the manager to be investing in. For instance, you might say the fund is 50% invested in high tech, 30% in health care, and 20% in consumer oriented investments, and you might create a model based on that structure. Or you might base the model on the manager's prior performance, perhaps over the last three years, identifying an index that the fund has closely tracked.

The risk here is that the behaviour of the model may not actually track the underlying assets. Therefore, you may periodically review the model to make sure it is the right model with the right data and that it is current and being executed correctly.

Getting the facts

You will have noted by now that data are identified as the third area of risk associated with manager monitoring. The risks, obviously, may include a shortage of data or the possibility that the data provided are stale or incorrect.

You have several possible defenses against the data risk: you could send in your internal auditor or ask for external audits; you may ask for process reviews to make sure the data are acquired from independent sources; or you could do a reasonableness check.

For instance, if the manager tells you the fund is heavily invested in UK Gilts, you would keep an eye on the UK currency and bond market. If you find the ups and downs of that market reflected in the ups and downs of the portfolio, you can assume, at least tentatively, that the data make sense.

Systems

The fourth area of risk in manager monitoring is identified as the systems risk, referring to the systems of people and technology by which we obtain the data to monitor our managers. The risk here is that the system as designed may not be capable of catching all the data it was intended to catch. If you do not have all the data you need, you will not have a clear picture of your managers' performance. You have to understand how your system works to be sure it is working correctly.

Custodial independence

Custody is one of the more critical areas for risk management because of the dire consequences a failure can bring about. At certain points in the processing of investments, the possibility of fraud intrudes. You could wake up one day to discover you do not actually own assets you thought you owned, or that certain assets were not worth what you thought they were.

Independence means keeping assets separated from the investment manager. When it is your custodian bank that holds and records the securities, implements transactions and reports directly to you, the possibility of fraud is decreased, though of course it still exists.

For instance, the securities delivered to the custodian bank might turn out to be forgeries; which has happened. The bank might subcontract custodial responsibilities to a bank in an emerging market, where fraud may occur. If the securities delivered to a subcustodial bank turn out to be worthless, who will indemnify you? Will their insurance policies be adequate?

Once the manager or someone other than a custodian bank has custody of your assets, the potential for loss – eg, through fraud – generally increases. You still own those assets, or at least you think you do. But what if the manager has loaned those securities out? Can you accept the valuation you are then given?

With many hedge funds, you are less likely to have custody at your custodian bank, and, therefore less likely to have ownership or valuations in which you can otherwise have the same level of comfort. If you choose to participate in hedge funds, you may have to play by the hedge fund manager's rules. As part of the price of participation, you accept this type of risk.

What defence do we have? To give us some level of comfort, we have at times had our own internal audit group review the processes in use at a hedge fund. We also consider the amount of insurance carried by the managers we select.

We also have well-known allocation and diversification techniques to help manage the risks of hedge funds. Our hedge fund offerings consist of a number of different funds, diversified among a wide range of strategies. Diversification of funds and strategies generally moderates the overall level of portfolio risk by controlling the exposure to the risks associated with any one particular fund or strategy.

Valuation ambiguities

Investors are inclined to assume that their monthly or quarterly valuations give them a reasonable estimate of the current worth of their holdings, the amount they would presumably realise through liquidation. But over every valuation hangs the risk that liquidation would, in fact, bring an amount different to that estimated.

This can be a significant issue if it is material; the expectations of investors and the assessment of managers' performance rest on these periodic valuations.

Consider a few of the ambiguities. The valuation is commonly based on a day's closing price. But the number of shares traded in one day of a traded security will normally represent only a small fraction of the total number of shares outstanding. Valuation at that price implies the assumption that other shareowners would have been willing to sell at the same price. But you have no indication that they actually would.

The valuation usually does not account for the spread between bid and ask on that last trade of the day. Had you executed a trade late that day, you might well have found that your price actually varied from the reported closing price.

And, of course, we are talking about the closing price on a specific stock exchange, if the shares are listed there. But who can say for sure whether the manager would have actually made the trade on that exchange?

Valuation entails a multiplicity of risks. In our investment risk matrix (see Table 1), we identify five risk areas: modelling, process, pricing source, size of position and seasonality.

We face the modelling risk, again, in the case of funds holding assets that are not traded publicly. Having no independent pricing source for those assets, you have to rely on modelling, on comparables, or on a combination. It becomes a matter of judgment, which is a risk in itself.

Your valuation is carried out in accordance with your established process, which may call for valuations every month, quarter, or even year. The timing makes a difference in the effect the valuations will have on further investment decisions.

For privately negotiated assets, your process may indicate use of comparables for your valuations, but with a buffer to account for the differing characteristics from the comparables. In that case, you face risks in your selection of the comparables and the amount you've selected for the buffer.

You have another potential risk in the pricing source that has been chosen. Is the source truly appropriate? Is the valuation timely, or stale? Is the pricing accurate? In the tens of thousands of transactions processed, what are the chances that a mistake will creep into just one digit of a reported price, or that one letter or number is wrong in the securities unique identifier (such as the SEDOL or CUSIP)?

In some cases, the valuation you get may be based on the initial cost rather than current selling prices, in which case the indication of volatility you would get for those holdings could appear unrealistically low.

The size of a fund's position in a holding poses a risk when the position is larger than the market can absorb without causing price distortions. If the entire position is placed on sale at once, the price could plummet. In selling out a large position, the manager must decide whether to accept a price lower than current valuation, or sell the stock off piece by piece over time.

The seasonality risk comes up later in the calendar year, in December. At the end of the year, when valuations are commonly made, you may face an unusually tranquil market. Many of the brokers have a good sense of what their bonuses are likely to be and may be reluctant to take new "risk" positions until the new year begins. So who is following the stock you are valuing? Who would be willing to commit capital? How valid are the valuations you get at that time?

How the keys work

Having discussed the risks related to these three critical activities, I think we can now better appreciate the three keys to effective risk management defined earlier in the chapter. The three keys work together: anticipation, transparency, and control.

Through the steps described above, we try to anticipate what can go wrong. That is exactly what those "areas of potential risk" are for. We want to know before anything ever happens that valuations, for instance, can go awry in any of the areas we previously touched on: in modelling, in the valuation process, in the pricing sources we use, etc.

We seek to achieve transparency through our screening process. How do we monitor all the potential risk areas surrounding our valuation activities in our modelling, our process, our pricing sources, and our position size relative to average daily volume? We strive to put sensors in place for the early detection of risk; these will collect the information for us even when we are not focusing on those activities, and alert us if a risk should develop.

For instance, you might craft a guideline for a manager which limits the percentage of the portfolio invested in any one stock. Should the manager's holdings in that stock begin to approach the limit, you are well served if you have systems in place that will alert you, allowing you to communicate with that manager and register your concern.

Comprehensive review

When we focus on one asset class in particular (in this case, hedge funds) we may seek to conduct a comprehensive review of potential risk areas, using our investment risk matrix as a general guide. We would organise a comprehensive review as an interdisciplinary undertaking. All the functional groups take part (investments, operations, legal and client services), including the independent risk management group that could take the lead in co-ordinating the effort. Our structure facilitates any sector taking the lead in addressing a risk issue.

Specifically, here are 26 topics one can address in a hedge fund review.

❏ *Master manager documents*. This involves a review of each manager document on file.

❏ *Other manager documents and files*. This involves a review of the relevant document files held throughout the organisation relating to the specific activity.

❏ *Manager review*. This involves reviewing a manager's performance, process, people and fees in conjunction with their responses to our questionnaires. Our questionnaire is organised by four main subjects: (1) general organisational information and updates, (2) investments, (3) operations, and (4) oversight.

❏ *Manager agreements*. This involves a review of the written agreement with the manager that defines the terms and conditions of the relationship.

❏ *Manager guidelines*. This involves a review of guidelines for each manager against established criteria, checking whether they continue to be current.

❏ *Fund rules*. As part of this review, each rule that applies to the entire hedge fund and its definition is revisited. You need to consider the appropriateness of each rule, whether new rules or fund descriptions should be added, or whether existing rules or descriptions should be changed or deleted.

❏ *Portfolio holdings and analytics*. The holdings of each manager are examined for risk characteristics and changes in those characteristics. The strategies of the manager are compared with the strategies originally approved.

❏ *Custody*. This involves a review of the custody arrangements for securities managed by each manager.

❏ *Valuation*. This involves reviewing the various pricing sources, and methodologies and analytics used to price the portfolios.

❏ *Partnership versus separate account*. This involves reviewing investment manager's form of organisation and its structure.

❏ *Manager monitoring capabilities*. This involves reviewing the methods and the frequencies (daily, monthly and quarterly) used in monitoring manager and fund compliance with ones rules and guidelines.

❏ *Investment monitoring filters*. This involves reviewing the use of investment monitor software and other approaches to monitoring fund/manager compliance with our rules.

❏ *Monthly checklists*. This involves a review of monthly verification of "fund within guidelines checklists" to reflect new or modified rules and interpretations.

❏ *Analytic systems*. This involves reviewing current and (possibly) other analytic systems to evaluate and monitor manager activity.

❏ *Managers' internal control testing*. This involves reviewing managers to determine the extent of their internal controls as related to activities they perform for us.

❏ *SAS 70 reports*. Here, one considers the availability and appropriateness of SAS 70 reports for major service providers, considering at the same time, more frequent audits or other testing procedures.

❏ *Performance*. This involves a review of each manager's performance calculations and methodology as well as benchmarks.

❏ *Fees*. This involves a review of each manager's fee structure, including management and incentive fees.

❏ *Reconciliation of manager to custodian*. This would involve a review of monthly reconciliation procedures used by managers, and the ways in which these are reviewed and approved by fund administrators.

❏ *Proxy voting*. This involves a review of proxy voting policies and activities.

❏ *Soft dollar activities*. This involves a review of the extent and use of soft dollar activities by a manager.

❏ *Intra/inter staff communications and reporting*. This involves a review of existing and proposed communications, and reporting procedures both within the organisation and between one's managers and custodians.

❏ *Descriptive documents*. This involves a review of descriptive documents (eg, in Commonfund's case, the Information For Members booklet), presentations, and other documents used to describe one's hedge fund offerings to clients.

❏ *Insurance*. This would involve a review of the types and amounts of insurance carried by each manager, and the ways in which these policies interface with one's own policies.

❏ *Reporting and disclosure.* This would involve a review of marketing communications and presentations made to clients about hedge fund offerings for adequate disclosures.

❏ *Current investors.* This would involve a review of clients invested in hedge fund programmes: their investment strategies and asset allocations; their level of investment sophistication; etc.

Structured for change

Now for the caveat! Even as we set up the foregoing 26-point list, it may be out of date. After all, we work in a continually changing environment. It can change. I have to assume that, as I sit here composing this chapter, new risks are arising somewhere.

How then can we rely on this list going forward? The answer is that we can't expect to pull this list out of the files a few years from now, or next year, and assume that it will still work to perfection. I am certain that most (or possibly all) of the potential risk areas that I have cited will stand the test of time. But there is no such thing as a standard, permanent risk list.

How, then, can we make sure we will be able to identify new risk potentials before they become generally visible?

Clearly, we therefore need an organisational structure that gives us the best risk management and oversight platform on an ongoing basis. In Figure 1, you can see the organisational structure we have at Commonfund.

As you can see, core risk management rests largely with the investment management group, linked formally to the independent risk management group via the internal Risk Management Committee. Other members of that Committee, the heads of Operations, Legal and Member Services, also carry core risk management responsibilities. The Independent Risk Oversight Officer serves as an integral part of this structure. The Independent Risk Oversight Officer reports directly to the Board of Directors as well as to our President. This structure is not dependent on any one individual for its success, although each plays a critical role. This structure was established by the board, with the assistance of outside consultants and management input, to best meet the needs of Commonfund's clients on an ongoing basis.

You can also see from Figure 1 that internal audit and compliance are linked directly to the risk oversight responsibility, giving us additional arms and legs to pursue effective risk management.

Questioning of the committee

As with most organisation charts, this structure looks nicely balanced; in real life, it teems with interactivity, as indicated by the arrows. You can see that we maintain an interactive relationship with Commonfund's senior

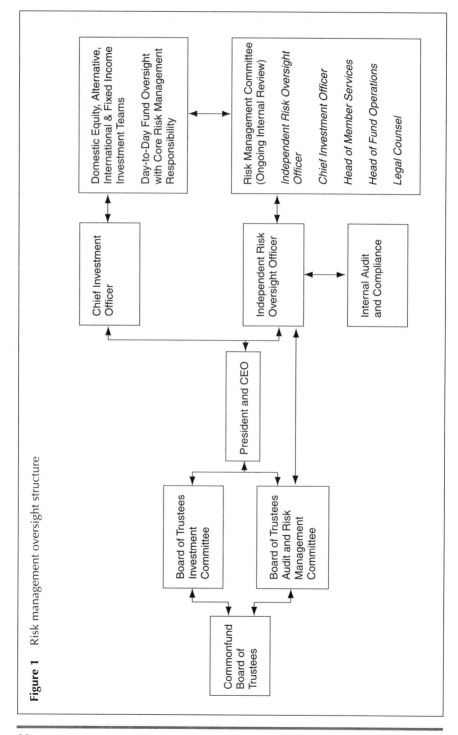

Figure 1 Risk management oversight structure

management. Each of us play a leadership role in the Risk Management Committee, which meets monthly or more frequently.

The Independent Risk Oversight Officer generally sets the agenda for these meetings and usually has relevant materials ready for the members. But the meetings do not depend on the Independent Risk Oversight Officer. We have enough momentum to allow any one of the other members to lead a meeting. We try to keep the meetings free flowing and we usually cover a broad range of issues. At our meetings, we draw our attention to current risks confronting the organisation and attempt to identify risks lurking over the horizon.

We do this, essentially, by asking questions. "Now, what about this? What about that? Have you thought about this? Have you checked that? We can lay all those checkpoints out on the table and get an update. Which have been addressed? Which are still open? Which do we have to revisit? What are our current priorities?"

These discussions let everyone tune into the risk potentials, including those risks just coming into view, and this gives us the understanding we need to report to our board on the current state of our risk management.

Why it works

This structure accomplishes a few important things. First, is that it gives risk management a conduit into every line worker in our organisation. Second, it gives risk management the visible authority of the firm's top leaders. Third, it gives the independent risk management group, the independence and leverage needed to work effectively. And, fourth, it gives us the flexibility and openness to quickly identify and address new risks.

It has worked well for us so far, but that has a lot to do with the kind of organisation we are.

I can't say that our structure would work in another type of culture. There is a lot of potential for conflict in risk management. A risk manager can make life unhappy for a lot of key people. In certain situations, it can backfire.

Stepping into this position, a new risk manager must achieve a delicate balancing act. Those who give the new manager an assignment may be expecting a quick solution. They may want to fix blame for past problems and clean house once and for all. That could work in certain situations, but, then again, it may not. It could lead to a lot of evasion, to denial, or hiding of risks.

For someone without broad experience in the investment world, and without specific experience in risk management, the assignment could be daunting.

You can see, then, that risk management in itself entails a structural risk. Each organisation must think through this issue for itself, and that's not easy. What kind of structure is right for your organisation, and what kind of risk manager is right for the job?

Everyone's responsible

Risk management ultimately has to become ingrained in the organisation's culture. Without question, every professional assumes responsibility for risk management.

If I could enter the mind of a Commonfund professional, I would hope to witness a thought process that goes something like this, "I am responsible for knowing what could go wrong in my area of activity and I have to make sure that none of those things happen. I am responsible for assuring that the investment managers in my area stay within their guidelines and that their portfolios are properly priced. In the final analysis, I am responsible for anything that goes wrong with those managers".

Achieving this state of mind starts with recruiting and hiring; a decision factor in any new recruitment must be the individual's risk sensitivity. We then develop the employee's risk orientation through ongoing internal training and our procedures manual.

Finally, this mindset is reinforced through our compensation policy. Our performance reviews include a section assessing the individual's risk management activities; they cover the full range of activities as listed above, in our discussion of process.

For the independent risk management officer, the indoctrination process must be a work in continual progress. You listen to your colleagues with all three ears, the inner one as well as the other two, and consider what needs to be done to maintain the necessary state of alert: memos, brochures, posters, training programmes, rallies; whichever will work in your organisation's culture. And don't wait till the barn burns down. At the same time, care must be taken not to cry wolf.

Know or "No"

In telling you how we at Commonfund manage hedge-fund risk, I felt it necessary to treat the issue in context and describe our overall approach to risk management. I would like to conclude by saying something about my own attitude toward hedge fund risk based on my past experiences.

I have a general bias against investments, such as those formatted as partnerships, that do not afford sufficient transparency to allow assessment of individual manager risks as well as the risks in the context of the overall portfolio. Investing in a partnership may entail the added risk of not knowing the assets in the portfolio. Alternatively, they also generally have a benefit of loss containment to the full value of the partnership. This works well for hedge funds particularly if they involve leverage.

When you have limited information about what is held in a partnership, your due diligence and monitoring can be expanded to acquire greater comfort with that investment. But then, the fund can change very fast. Within hours, some hedge funds can switch their entire strategy in pursuit of a new opportunity. In such cases, without transparency, you may have nothing to go on except your belief in the manager – plus, in Commonfund's case, its diversification across managers, added reviews and an ongoing open dialogue with that manager.

Earlier in this chapter, I stated transparency to be one of the keys to risk management. Many funds do not pass this test comfortably. In many cases, you really don't know what you have at a particular point in time. And, when you don't have enough information, there's nothing that says you have to make the investment. When you don't know, you can establish the structure, people and processes to mitigate that risk. While we believe the risks are acceptable for the return potential in our programme, they may not be for everyone. Consequently, if you do not know enough, you can just say no.

5

Fund of Funds: Risk: Defining it, Measuring it and Managing it

Robert A. Jaeger*

Evaluation Associates Capital Markets

The investment business has spawned a thriving sub-business devoted to the measurement of risk. This sub-business features a variety of wonderfully sophisticated approaches to the measurement of price volatility. However, the measurement of volatility does not improve our understanding of risk, since the essence of risk is not volatility, but uncertainty. Indeed, highly precise measures of volatility can get in the way of intelligent risk management by suggesting a level of accuracy and control that does not exist.

DEFINING RISK

Whatever risk is, it is not the annualised standard deviation of the daily (weekly or monthly) returns. Nor is it value-at-risk (VAR), measured at the 95% (99% or 99.9%) confidence level. Nor is it semi-variance, shortfall probability, or any other simple quantitative measure. These various measures may shed light on risk, and may help us to estimate risk, but they do not define the nature of risk.

People worry about risk in a wide variety of non-financial situations where the various measures mentioned above would not apply. For instance, when people worry about whom to marry, what college to attend, or whether to accept a certain job, they weigh reward against risk, benefit against cost, and upside against downside, but they do so without the elaborate quantitative machinery available to every investment professional. For indeed, the quantitative machinery is not essential to risk assessment, and may even hinder intelligent risk assessment.

* The author would like to thank Joseph McGowan, Thomas Schneeweis, George Martin, Barrett Moore and Richard Bookstaber for helpful input. The views presented here have been shaped by many years of conversation with William J. Crerend.

The key element in risk analysis, both in the financial and other arenas, is a form of scenario analysis in which the risk-related questions boil down to these: What are the possible bad outcomes? How likely are they? How bad are they? In some situations it may be possible to attach numerical values to the probabilities and the "degree of badness"; in other situations that will be impossible. For example, if Jane is trying to decide whether to marry John, it would be absurd to assign definite probabilities and "disutility units" to all the different ways in which a marriage can go wrong. Even someone worried about the risks of air travel would have a hard time calculating the probability of dying as opposed to the probability of losing a limb. And he would have an equally hard time quantifying the difference in undesirability of those outcomes, despite the fact that the flight insurance policy might pay 10 times more for death than for the loss of a limb. In many situations, the most that we can do is to *order* the scenarios, without being able to measure them. We can say that this outcome is more likely than that one, or this outcome is more undesirable than that one, without being able to attach definite values to the probabilities or the level of undesirability.

Financial professionals tend to think that investment risk is more easily quantifiable than marriage risk, career risk and air travel risk, but this is an illusion. Investors have access to an endless stream of numbers, and ways of crunching those numbers, but that does not mean that the numbers measure risk as we ordinarily understand it. We all know the story about the man looking for his keys at night under the lamppost. The joke is that he is looking under the lamppost not because the keys are there, but because the light is better there. The situation is similar with risk, the numbers can shed a tremendous amount of light, but the keys may be somewhere else.

If we had to offer a simple definition of risk it would be something like "expected pain", which would combine a rough measure of the likelihood of various unfavourable outcomes with a rough measure of how unfavourable those outcomes are. This simple definition at least captures the fact that risk judgments depend on two elements: the likelihood of various painful outcomes, and the level of pain associated with those outcomes. Think of the difference between AM radio and FM radio. AM radio works by modulating the amplitude of the signal, FM radio works by modulating the frequency of the signal. Risk combines frequency with amplitude. But this definition is, of course, an idealised over-simplification, as in most real-life situations we have no real hope of measuring either the probabilities or the level of pain. Investment situations give us the opportunity to measure standard deviations, value-at-risk, and all sorts of other numbers, but that is not the same as measuring risk.

MEASURING RISK

Since standard deviation is the most common proxy for risk (even VAR measures are driven ultimately by standard deviation), the easiest way to approach the problem of risk measurement is to catalogue the various inadequacies of standard deviation as a risk measure.

Volatility versus uncertainty

Standard deviation can be either a measure of uncertainty or a measure of volatility. Suppose, for example, that we are running a portfolio optimiser using a set of inputs that includes the assumption that US stocks will have a return of 12% and a standard deviation of 15%. The 15% figure can be interpreted as an estimate of the volatility of stocks over the forecast period, or it can be interpreted as a measure of how much uncertainty attaches to the return estimate. In the first case, we are estimating total return over the full investment horizon, and are then making an *additional* estimate regarding the character of the return over smaller time periods. In the second case, we are estimating total return over the full investment horizon, and then indicating how much confidence (or lack of confidence) we have in that estimate. In the first case, we are making two forecasts, while in the second, we are making a forecast and then adding a disclaimer regarding that forecast.

To drive home the contrast between volatility and uncertainty, consider the difference between a 10-year zero coupon bond and a venture capital partnership requiring a 10-year lock-up of capital. The bond investor can be certain of the return (ie, the nominal, pre-inflation return) on his investment, but he also knows that the investment will be highly volatile when marked-to-market on a regular basis. The venture capital investment has no price volatility, because it is non-marketable, but the investment still offers substantial uncertainty, hence risk.

A volatile investment is likely to be an uncertain investment, except for special cases (like the zero coupon bond), where a volatile investment might produce a certain return if held to the end of a definite period. And even in those cases, volatility will create uncertainty for any investor whose holding period is itself uncertain. On the other hand, uncertainty need not involve volatility, as the venture capital example illustrates. So the concept of uncertainty has much broader investment application than the concept of volatility. Indeed, "risk as uncertainty" covers career risk, air travel risk, and all sorts of other situations, whereas "risk as volatility" applies only to the marketable portion of the investment arena.

The distinction between volatility and uncertainty is central to the idea that long-term investors have a competitive advantage over short-term investors. Most investors have greater confidence in their long-term return estimates than in their short-term return estimates. For example, many people are confident that US stocks will outperform US bonds over the next

10 years, but have no idea whether stocks will beat bonds over the next two months. For these investors, adopting a long-term investment horizon does not reduce volatility, but it does increase their confidence in their expectations. This reduces the level of uncertainty, thus enhancing their ability to tolerate volatility. The art, of course, is to make sure that confidence does not become over-confidence, which is the major source of investment disasters.

Volatility and path-dependence

Even when we focus our attention specifically on volatility rather than uncertainty, standard deviation is a very imperfect measure. When investors talk about "volatile markets", they sometimes mean volatility of price, and sometimes they mean volatility of return. These two concepts are totally distinct, and both have nothing at all to do with the order of prices or returns, as the calculation of standard deviation pays no attention to order. To see these points, consider the three sequences of prices and returns in Figure 1. In each of the three cases, the total return over the full time period is 2%. Chart A shows what looks like a very volatile, or choppy, market, in which prices move up and down in a narrow band, ending up 2%. In Chart B, the prices are the same as in Chart A, but the order of the prices is changed, hence the returns change. The standard deviation of prices is the same between A and B, but the standard deviation of returns is dramatically reduced. In Chart C, we take the returns from Chart A but change the order, so all the positive returns come together and then all the negative returns. The prices are very different from Chart A, with much higher standard deviation than in Chart A, but the returns, and hence their standard deviation, are the same in both Charts A and C.

A clearly looks more volatile than B, and this difference is reflected in the

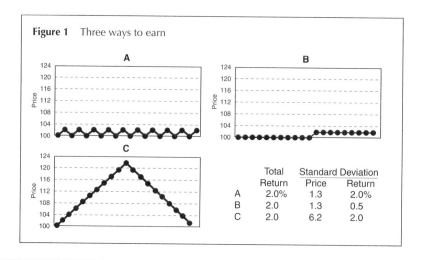

Figure 1   Three ways to earn

	Total Return	Standard Deviation Price	Standard Deviation Return
A	2.0%	1.3	2.0%
B	2.0	1.3	0.5
C	2.0	6.2	2.0

difference in standard deviation of returns. The difference between A and C is more complicated. The standard deviation of returns is the same in both cases, but the returns in A are much more jagged than in C, so the returns may look more volatile. The prices in C have a higher standard deviation than the prices in A, but which series of prices looks more volatile? The prices in C move in a much wider band, but the prices in A are more jagged. Markets that look, or feel, volatile often feel that way because of a distinct order of prices or returns: an order that involves choppy movements with frequent reversals. This kind of "order-dependent volatility" is not captured by the technical definition of standard deviation, since standard deviation is not sensitive to order.

This point has direct application to hedge fund investing, since many hedge fund managers employ trading strategies with outcomes, succesful or otherwise, relating not to the volatility of markets but to the path that markets follow. Consider, for example, the difference between convertible hedging (and other forms of "delta-hedging") and systematic trend following. The delta hedger might do unusually well in a market of big price moves and sudden reversals, while suffering in a listless market with few trading opportunities. But the systematic trend-follower would be whipsawed in an environment of sharp reversals, as the new trend would trigger a buy signal just as prices were about to turn down, and a sell signal just as prices were about to turn up.

Many of the expressions that investors use to describe "difficult" markets, such as "choppy", "trendless", "whipsaw", etc, are implicitly order-sensitive or path-dependent. It is therefore impossible to analyse in terms of standard deviation, which is path-independent. At Evaluation Associates Capital Markets, we have experimented with various tools to measure choppiness and related notions (eg, the number of times that the daily price crosses the n day moving average), but we are not yet satisfied with any single tool. And we know that, no matter which tool might seem the most appropriate, we will not be able to predict the transitions from choppiness to trendiness and back.

Standard deviation and downside risk

Many people object to standard deviation as a risk measure because standard deviation gives equal weight to deviations above and below the mean, whereas investors are likely to be more worried about "downside deviation" than "upside deviation". According to this view, the most relevant returns are returns below the mean, below zero, or below some other "target" or "benchmark" return. This has led to a proliferation of measures of "downside risk": semi-variance, shortfall probability, the Sortino ratio, etc. Ignoring the specific advantages and disadvantages of each individual candidate to represent "the true nature of risk", we would offer the following two general observations.

Frequency versus amplitude

The idea of risk as "expected pain" combines two elements: the likelihood of pain and the level of pain. The measures described above focus on one or the other of these elements, but not both. Semi-variance (and its descendant, the Sortino ratio) focuses on the size of the negative surprises, but ignores the probability of those surprises. Shortfall probability focuses on the likelihood of falling below a target return, but ignores the potential size of the shortfall. If we were forced to embrace a single quantitative measure of risk, we would offer the concept of "expected return below the target", defined as the sum of the probability-weighted, below-target returns. This measure is essentially the area under the probability curve that lies to the left of the target return level. (Note that this definition is broad enough to cover both normal and non-normal distributions.)

To illustrate this idea, suppose that the annual returns of US stocks are normally distributed with a mean of 12% and a standard deviation of 15%. Assume further that our target return is zero, so the favourable outcomes all feature a positive return while the unfavourable outcomes all feature a negative return. We can easily calculate that the probability of falling below the target is 21.2%. But this probability figure covers a region that includes small losses, large losses and very large losses. For example, there is an 8.3% probability of achieving a return between zero and –5%, and a 1.0% probability of achieving a return between –20% and –25%. What we need is the *mean* below-target return, where that mean, multiplied by the *probability* of achieving the below-target return, will be the expected below-target return. If we consider a standardised normal distribution, with a mean of 0, a standard deviation of 1, and a target return whose standardised value is z, then the expected below-target return is

$$\frac{-1}{\sqrt{2\pi}\, e^{z^2/2}}$$

and the *mean* below-target return is the above amount divided by the *probability* of achieving a below-target return. Returning to the example of US stocks, and making the appropriate adjustments for the mean of 12% and standard deviation of 15%, we find now that the expected below-target return is –1.8%, reflecting a 21.2% probability of achieving a mean negative return of –8.5%. The expected above-target return is 13.8%, reflecting a 78.8% probability of achieving a mean positive return of 17.5%. The expected below-target return of –1.8%, added to the expected above-target return of 13.8%, gives the expected total return of 12.0%.

Asymmetrical samples of symmetrical distributions

Measures of downside risk are most appealing in situations where there is reason to believe that the underlying distribution of returns is asymmetrical. But the evidence for such asymmetry can be very murky, except for very specific situations where the underlying investment process involves long positions in options. An investor who is long options is willing to accept the high probability of a small loss in exchange for the small probability of a large gain. The potential gains are much greater than the potential losses, but the likelihood of gain is much smaller than the likelihood of loss. Here there is genuine asymmetry, and a readily understandable source of asymmetry. But if you are dealing with a string of market returns, or manager returns, that are attractively skewed, you should be very cautious about inferring that the underlying return distribution is skewed in the same way. The more likely scenario is that you are dealing with a skewed sample from a symmetrical population. Skewed performance records have a nasty tendency to turn symmetrical very soon after you invest real money with the manager. In such cases, downside risk measures would have underestimated the potential risk, while plain old standard deviation would have been a better indicator. Except for the specific case of long options strategies, it is prudent to believe in investment gravity: whatever went up a lot could have gone down a lot, and may well go down a lot in the future.

Predicting risk

Past performance does not guarantee anything regarding future performance, and past risk does not guarantee anything regarding future risk. This is true even when the historical record is long enough to satisfy normal criteria of statistical significance. The problem is that, just as a performance record is getting long enough to have statistical significance, it may no longer have investment significance. This is because the people and the organisation may have changed in important ways over the years, and the strong historical record may be a prominent driver of those changes. Top-performing hedge fund managers hardly ever retire at the top of their game: the risk is that they will fade away, or blow up.

Fading away is just another example of the universal phenomenon of reversion to the mean. A manager who has compiled an excellent historical record gradually turns into just another manager, with higher risk than before, and lower return. Maybe he has lost his competitive edge, his hunger for success; maybe his historical record was just a fluke, not really a symptom of genuine investment skill. In any case, what looked like an exceptional investment opportunity turns into a disappointment: not a disaster, but a disappointment.

The blow-up syndrome takes us from the category of disappointment into the category of disaster. The pattern here goes roughly as follows: a manager puts together a superb performance record, which increases the size of assets under management and dramatically boosts the manager's confidence in his own investment prowess. At some point, confidence becomes complacency, complacency becomes hubris, hubris creates errors, and the errors breed disaster. The unwinding of Long Term Capital

Management, as well as the recent overhaul of the Soros organisation, are examples of this phenomenon. In each case, genuinely exceptional investors pushed the envelope until the envelope pushed back. The irony here is that long records of strong performance, which are the records that investors love to see, are precisely the records that should create the most anxiety. Andy Grove, the Chairman of Intel, is famous for emphasising that only the paranoid survive. Skilled money managers need to be paranoid about factors that may jeopardise the sustainability of their success. And prudent investors need to be paranoid about factors that may turn a golden record into lead.

MANAGING RISK

Given all these problems about measuring risk and forecasting risk, it might appear that risk management is an impossible task. How can you manage something that you cannot even measure? We would take the contrary position: a proper appreciation of the difficulties of measuring risk actually improves one's ability to manage risk. Those who overestimate their ability to measure risk, who have too much confidence in the sophistication of their quantitative tools, are precisely the ones most likely to get into trouble.

In constructing a multi-manager hedge fund portfolio, it is essential to have a clear view of the risk profile of the individual managers, and a clear view of the way in which those risk profiles interact within the context of a portfolio. We are talking not about a set of numbers for each manager and a correlation matrix tying those numbers together, but about a practical working understanding of risk. A Lamborghini may be preferable to a Chevrolet on a closed-circuit race course, but the Chevrolet is probably the better bet for city driving.

Manager risk factors

The risk factors that we identify at the manager level are organised as follows.

❑ *Portfolio factors: non-market related.*
  – Leverage.
  – Concentration.
  – Illiquidity.
  – Trading behaviour: cut losses versus average down.

❑ *Portfolio factors: market-related.*
  – Directional factors: long bias, short bias, neutral, opportunistic.
  – Technical factors: volatility, choppiness, etc.
  – Spread-related factors:
    – Equity: big/small, growth/value, etc.
    – Fixed income: maturity spreads, credit spreads, etc.

Organisational factors:
– Length of record
– Assets under management
  – Rate of growth
  – Nature of client base
– Ownership/compensation structure
– Risk monitoring/control systems

The thinking behind this schema is very straightforward. We want to distinguish between risk factors that will show up within the portfolio, and factors more related to people and organisations. Among the portfolio-related factors, the first group comprises those factors that can be understood by looking at the manager's portfolio and seeing how it changes through time. Many of these factors lie within the control of the manager. The market-related portfolio factors are those that can be understood only by looking more carefully at the ways in which the manager's returns are affected (either positively or negatively) by the behaviour of market-related factors.

Within the first group of factors, the first three items require no special comment, yet the fourth factor goes to the heart of the risk control problem. Some managers are deeply averse to losses: if a position moves against them, their tendency is to exit the position first and ask questions later. Other managers are more contrarian, or value-oriented: if a position moves against them, the position is now even more attractively priced, hence the manager may be tempted to add to the position on weakness. Managers in the first category tend to have a shorter investment horizon than managers in the second category. At the extremes, both approaches are self-defeating. The excessively loss-averse manager becomes so impatient that he cannot withstand any adverse movements, the result being enormous trading costs and no profits. The excessively value-driven manager becomes so convinced that he is right and the market wrong, that his hands remain frozen to the wheel as his portfolio crashes into the wall. In the real world, away from the extremes, the issue is to locate the manager, at least roughly, on the spectrum between "cut your losses quickly" and "buy low, buy lower."

Within the group of market-related risk factors, the directional factors are mostly self-explanatory. It is comparatively easy to assign managers to the long bias, short bias, and market-neutral categories. The opportunistic category is more complicated. This category is reserved for those managers who have the mental flexibility to vary their net portfolio exposure from net long to net short and back. However, in the real world, managers often turn out to be less flexible than they originally appeared. Throughout the course of the powerful US equity bull market that began in 1982, many managers who appeared to be opportunistic wound up fighting the tape with portfolios that were chronically net short. For these managers, "short biased" turned out to be the more appropriate category.

The technical factors are especially important for those managers who are either market neutral or opportunistic. Even if a manager does not have an enduring directional bias, his returns may be affected (either positively or negatively) by such factors as volatility, choppiness, etc. As we discussed earlier, a convertible hedger might thrive in an environment of sharp reversals, whereas a systematic trend-follower would struggle in such an environment.

The spread-related factors are particularly crucial for those managers who profess to be market neutral. For example, an equity-oriented manager might be neutral to the broad market but still have a tendency to be long value and short growth, or long small capitalisation names and short large capitalisation names. The portfolio would thus contain major style bets even in the absence of any market directional bets. This can be seen in the fixed income world as well. For example, hedge fund managers sometimes construct "hedged" positions in which the long side emphasises high yield corporate bonds, or emerging market debt, while the interest rate risk of the long side is "hedged" with short positions in US Treasury bonds (or futures, or other derivatives). But these so-called hedges are really just spread trades in which the manager is betting that the non-Treasury leg of the trade will outperform the Treasury leg. The trade will fail if the yield spread widens, and will fail dramatically in the special case of the long side of the portfolio falling for sector-specific reasons, while the short side rallies on a flight to quality. That was exactly the case in Autumn 1998, when emerging markets debt fell in response to the Russia/LTCM crisis, while US Treasuries rallied sharply in a stampede for safety.

The organisational factors speak for themselves. One needs to be cautious about managers whose assets have grown very fast, whose client base includes significant amounts of "hot money", etc. Ownership and compensation need to be structured in a way that incentives for good people to stay, while the manager needs to have systems in place that demonstrate his own concern for risk monitoring and management.

Prevention versus cure

Preventing disease is usually much cheaper, and more effective, than curing disease. The same is true in risk management: staying out of trouble is much more effective than getting out of trouble. The keys to avoiding a crisis are diversification, prudent levels of leverage and liquidity, and a continuing respect for one's own fallibility. The keys to managing a crisis are more limited and less satisfactory: either do nothing, or reduce positions sharply. Doing nothing is often the right thing to do, and will certainly appeal to the longer-term, value-oriented manager, but sometimes the temptation to do something can be overpowering. Reducing positions seems very prudent (the manager is, after all, "protecting the value of his portfolio"), but the implementation costs are enormous, since the manager is selling long positions that may be in free-fall and covering short positions that are spiralling upwards. For managers with a very large asset base, or a preference for less liquid situations, risk control in the sense of "crisis management" is simply not a realistic alternative. The only viable form of risk control is to stay out of trouble in the first place.

PRUDENCE

Risk is complicated, as is risk management, so we are chronically suspicious of the idea that risk can be boiled down to a single number. A proper appreciation of the complexities of risk is an essential part of being a prudent investor. Prudence, like risk, cannot be boiled down to a single number. For the last word on prudence, we turn to the US government, whose nautical charts are indispensable for those who need to find their way about on the water. Every US chart bears this warning, "The prudent mariner will not rely solely on any single aid to navigation, particularly on floating aids". Investing is just like navigating, except that there are only floating aids.

6

The Critical Path to Effective Hedge Fund Risk Management: Control, Transparency and Risk and Performance Measurement

Virginia Reynolds Parker

Parker Global Strategies LLC

Risk management is both an art and a science. An inquisitive investor contemplating this statement may wonder exactly what is meant by *art*. The art of risk management is the *experience* that the practitioner develops over time. This chapter shares the perspective of risk management from the position of a trading manager for multi-manager hedge fund strategies. The role of a trading manager is similar to that of a manager of managers. The trading manager customises multi-manager hedge fund strategies for clients, carefully addressing the investor's rate of return objective, risk tolerance, time horizon, liquidity needs, legal and regulatory issues, and any unique circumstances. The trading manager's role is active and continuous, to ensure that the portfolio continues responding to the objectives of the investor.

With the institutionalisation of the hedge fund industry since the late 1990s has come the debate over the appropriate approach to risk management. Views range from managing risk through extremely broad diversification, so that one or two blow-ups will have minimal effect on a portfolio's overall performance, to a fully transparent, risk controlled structure with continual independent oversight. This chapter focuses on the significant merits of the controlled, transparent approach to managing the risk in a multi-manager hedge fund portfolio.

History offers numerous examples of investment disasters. Many, many billions of dollars have been lost over the years because of inadequate, independent oversight. There are recent examples in the hedge fund arena like Long Term Capital Management's demise during the summer of 1998, and more recently, Manhattan Capital, Phoenix Research and Trading, Maricopa and Blue Water. But one need not be invested in hedge funds to be exposed to potential, devastating losses. Some of the best examples of extraordinary losses have included publicly registered mutual funds, brokerage firms, investment banks, corporations, and municipalities. The source of losses may include fraud and cover-ups, mis-priced securities, flawed accounting practices and mismatched hedges, to name a few.

In July 1993, the Group of Thirty published "Derivative Practices and Principles for Dealers and End Users". Among the report's objectives was to help establish "best practices" in addressing the risks inherent in dealing and/or investing in derivative instruments. Publication of the report followed several well-publicised losses in derivative instruments. The report's recommended "best practices" are applicable for all types of instruments. The standards suggested in this report provide a critical path to effective hedge fund risk management for trading managers. The major tenets of these practices and principals include:

❏ determining the scope of activities and policies at the highest level of management;
❏ valuing derivative positions at the market;
❏ performing stress tests and forecasting cash and funding needs;
❏ establishing an independent, middle office reporting directly to senior management; and
❏ installing systems capable of measuring, managing, and reporting risks in a timely and accurate manner.

CONTROL

Effective risk management must begin with the establishment of control. It is nearly impossible to manage risk in a fund of funds if the manager does not have any control beyond the ability to redeem at some point in the future – 30 days, 90 days, 180 days or 365 days after a notification period that may be equally as long. And what good is portfolio transparency, if one cannot redeem until sometime in the future when it may be too late? In the Spring of 1998, there were several examples of very skilled fund of funds' managers deciding that they wanted to redeem from certain hedge funds where the fund of funds managers were concerned about style drift. The managers put in their redemption notification. By the time the redemption date arrived, several months later, most of the hedge funds assets were gone. Portfolios had sustained unrecoverable losses in the Russian bond market. The style drifters were US high yield managers who decided to try their golden touch with Russian GKOs. The managers knew little about sovereign risk, Russian politics, and Russian counterparties.

Ideally, the trading manager should strive to have the hedge fund manager run a managed account, if the allocation is of sufficient size warranting the structure. Assuming that the running of a managed account is feasible, then the trading manager is in a position to select the counterparties to the transaction, including the prime broker, custodian, administrator, auditor, other counterparties, and cash manager (where applicable). The trading manager then negotiates the terms and conditions of each of the agreements, including the hedge fund manager agreement. In the hedge fund manager agreement, the trading manager may outline the trading policies for the account. This way, the trading manager and the hedge fund manager have a document to which each may refer, which stipulates the agreement between both parties.

An investor in hedge funds, like an investor in traditional asset classes, is exposed to many sources of potential risk. Risks include market, credit, counterparty, operational, model, legal, and sovereign risk, to name a few. The more risks that the trading manager is in a position to monitor and to attempt to mitigate the better off the investor. By being a party to the many and varied relationships in a hedge fund investment, the trading manager is in a better position to protect the investor's interest. If one reads the offering memorandum of the typical US based hedge fund manager, one notes that the document is quite one-sided in favour of the hedge fund manager. The litigious nature of the US is unfortunate for investors in hedge funds, because attorneys advise their hedge fund manager clients to include minimal restrictions. This is good for the hedge fund manager; but this is not so good for protecting the interests of investors.

Trading managers are not always able to have a separately managed account. Perhaps the manager is unwilling; perhaps the allocation is too small; perhaps the operational burden of the strategy makes a separate account unfeasible. Nonetheless, the trading manager or other type of investor should perform extremely rigorous due diligence. This due diligence should include a review of *each* agreement to which the hedge fund or the hedge fund manager is a party. The trading manager or investor should request the opportunity to review each of the agreements listed above and *each* investor side letter that is outstanding. One must look for the exposures to risk contained in these documents.

With the institutionalisation of hedge funds, and the fiduciary role that many allocators to hedge funds must assume, there may be a development of managed account structures for hedge fund investments. Although we do see such structures today, the managed account tends to be the exception as opposed to the rule. Managed account structures have become available for large investors in mutual funds who preferred to have separate managed accounts. The hedge fund industry and regulators may make such structures easier to manage *en masse* in the years ahead. In fact, there is a need in the hedge fund industry for investment structures to keep pace with demand from sophisticated investment fiduciaries. When one considers the extraordinary risks inherent in investing in a hedge fund that provides no transparency and no control to investors, one must truly question the prudence of fiduciaries electing such a path for assets in their care.

TRANSPARENCY

To imagine that significant investors would not require meaningful transparency of their hedge fund investments is difficult. Consider the behaviour of banks, broker dealers, insurance companies, corporations, endowments, foundations, and pensions where there is internal investment activity. How many employees of such organisations are allowed to cover their investment activities hidden beneath an opaque cloak, because knowledge of their positions could be detrimental? If internal investors are not allowed to pursue unmonitored investment activities, why should external managers be allowed to pursue unmonitored, and in many instances, unregulated investment activities? Traditional investment managers are accustomed to providing transparency to their clients. Why should institutions and significant private investors not require transparency in strategies that by their very nature have the ability to be riskier than traditional investments? Hedge funds may:

❏ employ leverage;
❏ short securities;
❏ purchase illiquid and complex derivative instruments;
❏ suspend redemptions;
❏ provide pay-in-kind securities in lieu of cash redemptions; and
❏ have a mismatch between portfolio liquidity and redemption policy.

There is a reason that the investment and trading activities of banks, broker dealers, and insurance companies are regulated – without regulation and oversight, a few banks, broker dealers, and insurance companies have engendered a financial debacle. Even under regulation and scrutiny there have been well-publicised failures over the past decade like Kidder Peabody and Barings. Who would have imagined such staid, venerable institutions would virtually disappear?

Requiring transparency is *not* a call for the regulation of hedge funds. In fact, transparency for significant investors is a tool that will assist in the development accepted, sound practices for the hedge fund industry. Transparency provides the very foundation of effective risk management. Without the information that transparency delivers, one is unable to perform risk management, risk measurement, and performance measurement. Prime brokers, as the counterparty to hedge funds that clear trades, provide financing for leverage, and lend securities, require transparency. After a prime broker, the party with the greatest financial exposure to a hedge fund is the investors. The investors may lose their entire investment in a hedge fund; where the prime broker may lose more than the hedge funds assets, should the fund fail. Prime brokers require continuous transparency; investors should require full transparency. Investors do not necessarily need daily transparency to effectively manage and measure risk and performance, but investors should have at minimum weekly transparency. Transparency should not be a one-day snap shot for the week; the information should include all adjustments to the portfolio since the last snap shot.

RISK MEASUREMENT

Transparency requires quantitative tools for undertaking the measurement of market risk in a portfolio. Fortunately for trading managers and investors, the quantitative tools of risk management are readily available and computer systems become more powerful and less expensive with each passing year. Prime brokers have become an excellent source of risk measurement analytics for investors. Risk measurement tools must be objective. The trading manager's purpose in measuring portfolio risk in hedge fund strategies is to formalise the monitoring role and behave proactively in the event of actual or pending problems in the portfolio.

Some of the more popular risk measurement tools include value-at-risk (VAR), correlation analysis, downside deviation, key drivers, stress testing, leverage and sector analysis, and scenario analysis. Some of the quantitative tools of risk measurement, like VAR and correlation analysis, apply statistical analysis to the distribution of historical returns or implied volatility for forecasting potential market moves. There are several important issues with these measurement techniques.

❏ Much of the analysis assumes normal distribution of the data, although market returns tend to be lognormal, (skewed to the right).
❏ Much of the analysis depends upon historical returns. Historical returns show what did happen, not what could have happened. Historical returns represent *discrete* time rather than *continuous* time.
❏ Many derivative instruments are not actively traded, so we must mark-to-model rather than to market.
❏ Liquidity must be factored into our pricing and our models must demonstrate integrity.

Despite the shortcomings of our current risk measurement techniques, the tools are nonetheless extremely helpful. VAR studies the body of risk; stress testing studies the tails. Specifically, VAR calculates the risk band of expected volatility, the expected maximum move – up *or* down – for a position, market, or portfolio over a given time horizon and within a given confidence interval. The significance of VAR is its ability to characterise risk across a broad spectrum of instruments according to a single variable – expected volatility.

The selection of time horizon and confidence interval depends upon the objective of the analysis. Hedge fund managers often have a very short-term perspective, whereas investors have a much longer perspective.

Users of VAR require a confidence interval, or percentile cut-off, small enough to expect regular violations of risk bands. One may test the integrity of the VAR model by comparing *expected* deviations to *actual* deviations. For example, the risk band of a three standard deviation model, expecting one out of 100 observations to deviate, is too wide to be useful on a regular basis. Most market participants apply a confidence interval ranging from 90% (1.65 standard deviations) to 95% (2 standard deviations). The 90% confidence interval implies that data should fall outside the risk band in 10% of the observations; the 95% confidence interval suggests data should fall outside the risk band in 5% of the observations.

Given the dataset including volatilities and a covariance matrix, the calculation of VAR is quite simple. For example, consider a balanced US$10 million US portfolio with 60% allocated to the S&P 500 and 40% allocated to US Treasury bonds:

Position	260 Day σ	One Day σ	95% Confidence Interval (2σ)	Position VAR
US$6 million S&P	9.96%	0.62%	2*.62%	US$74,400
4 million US Bonds	4.36	0.27	2*.27	21,600
				US$96,000

One takes the annual volatility of each position, here 9.96% for the S&P 500 and 4.36% for US Treasury bonds, measured over 260 equally weighted, daily observations. Next we divide the annual volatility by the square root of the number of observations, or 260, for a daily volatility. For a 95% confidence interval, or 2 standard deviations, we multiply the daily volatility by 2. We then multiply the resulting percentage by the position size to determine VAR. The additive VAR for both positions is US$96,000. The next step is to apply the correlation coefficient (0.62) to arrive at the net correlated VAR of US$89,000.

$$\sigma^2 p = \omega_1^2 \sigma_1^2 + \omega_2^2 \sigma_2^2 + 2\omega_1 \omega_2 COV_{1,2}$$

$$\sigma^2 p = (.6)^2 (.62)^2 + (.4)^2 (.27)^2 + 2 (.6)(.4)(.62)(.27)(.62)$$

$$\sigma = .447 \quad 2\sigma = .89$$

$$\text{US\$10 million} * .89\% = \text{US\$89,000}$$

where
p	=	portfolio
ω_1	=	weight of the first asset
σ_1	=	volatility of the first asset
ω_2	=	weight of the second asset
σ_2	=	volatility of the second asset
$COV_{1,2}$	=	covariance of assets 1 and 2 .

One may extend the analysis of VAR to include contribution to risk, incremental risk, and risk attribution. *Contribution to risk* in a portfolio considers what percent of total VAR each asset provides. An asset with a negative correlation to the portfolio will have a negative contribution to risk. For example, a portfolio hedge brings down the total risk of the portfolio in proportion to the hedge's weighted, correlated offset. A trading manager, considering the addition of another manager to the portfolio, may consider contribution to risk at the hedge fund manager level. A hedge fund manager with a negative contribution to risk will diversify the portfolio of managers, according to the statistical analysis.

Incremental risk

This measures a portfolio's VAR with the asset and then without. An asset with a low correlation to the portfolio will have a low incremental risk. An asset with a negative correlation will have a negative incremental risk, meaning that the asset diversifies the portfolio. Without the asset, the portfolio's overall volatility risk increases. Analysing incremental risk is particularly powerful when considering the addition of a new asset to the portfolio or adjustments in allocation. Again, the trading manager may apply the analysis of incremental risk at the hedge fund manager level as well.

Finally, risk attribution applies VAR analysis to the sources of risk in a portfolio. For example in a global fixed income portfolio risk attribution would identify spread risk, yield curve risk, and currency risk among others.

VAR and its extensions, including contribution to risk, incremental risk and risk attribution, are valuable not only for risk management purposes but also for fine-tuning asset allocation decisions. The trading manager may then determine whether the sources and concentrations of risk are acceptable given future expectations of return and volatility. The trading manager may also consider the correlation among markets and whether the portfolio's expression of market expectations through asset selection and allocation are the most efficient.

Correlation risk is an often-tracked measure of portfolio risk. Correlation is an input to the calculation of covariance, which, of course, drives VAR. But correlation is also used as a stand-alone measure to determine the expected similarity in performance between two assets, or even two managers. In measuring correlation, one must be careful to consider the number observations and the efficacy in the pricing of the assets, or the p/l of the managers. Adding to the complexity of the analysis is the fluid nature of correlations. Correlation measurement is important to consider, but the weaknesses of correlation measurement must be understood. Like most statistical measures, correlation relies on historical returns. The fewer the observations, the less reliable the estimate. But even with thousands of data points to compare performance between two assets, correlations may suddenly reverse going from negative to positive, from positive to negative, or from perfect correlation to no correlation whatsoever. By the time correlation statistics have enough data points to pickup a reliable trend, a new trend may be underway.

Downside deviation measures the negative performance of an asset or a manager. A frequent criticism of standard deviation as a measure of risk for examining the riskiness of an asset, especially when that asset is a hedge fund manager's performance, is that the manager is unfairly penalised for upside deviation. Many hedge fund managers have an upside deviation that is higher than the downside deviation. While downside deviation is interesting to consider, the prudent allocator to hedge funds is well advised to pay careful attention to a high standard deviation of performance in a manager. Often that upside deviation turns to downside deviation all too quickly. Some hedge fund managers are skilled at reducing position sizes when market volatility heats up. Others are refugees from the long-only side whose alpha, in downwardly volatile markets, has yet to be developed.

A trading manager is advised to know the key portfolio drivers at both the individual hedge fund level and for the aggregate portfolio. If the trading manager has a mandate to perform hedge overlays, the trading manager may offset a portion of key portfolio drivers during volatile market times. Occasionally, a portfolio's key driver may not be present in the portfolio. For example, a long short US equity strategy with a long bias may have US interest rates as a key portfolio driver. In an environment of rising rates, the portfolio may be vulnerable to a rate rise, especially if the portfolio is in long economically sensitive sectors. One must try to understand both the internal and external influences and risks for the hedge fund portfolio.

Stress testing is a quantitative tool useful for trying to predict the size of portfolio loses given certain changes in the markets. One may stress the portfolio through:

❑ assuming a portfolio move of 5+ standard deviations;
❑ setting portfolio correlations to zero or to one;
❑ moving key portfolio drivers by several standard deviations; or
❑ increasing the VAR time horizon out to address illiquidity in the market.

The above list is an example of several stress tests that may be applied. The potential list is endless. Crisis in the markets has been occasional, versus constant, over the past decade. Stress testing is helpful for estimating funding needs or the potential size of losses when the market enters crisis. A trading manager cannot effectively manage a portfolio as if the markets are always in crisis; otherwise little risk would be taken. But the trading manager must consider what might happen during a crisis, there is certainly some balance between the ability of a portfolio to withstand risk taking during normal markets versus during crisis markets. Often when a crisis arrives, it is too late to adjust commitments.

Leverage and sector analysis

This analysis is another important risk measure for long/short equity portfolios, because equity portfolios, like corporate bond portfolios, have specific risks as opposed to simply systematic risks. VAR analysis must be complemented by leverage and sector analysis. There are many other types of analyses, but at a minimum these two should be considered. Leverage analysis looks at gross and net exposure at the aggregate portfolio level. The trading manager should take this to the next step to consider gross and net leverage by sector. These reports help pinpoint where the hedge fund manager, or the aggregate portfolio, is taking its bets. Large gross exposure may be less risky than *neutral* net exposure. Likewise small gross exposure may be more risky than large net exposure. Sector analysis becomes extremely important, because the seemingly small risk portfolio may have a *huge long* or *huge short* bet on exactly the wrong sector. Without drilling down to the sector level, the trading manager may miss the real market risk in the portfolio. Adding an interesting challenge to sector analysis over the past three years has been the evolution of the sectors. For example, some old utilities transformed into an important component of the TMT group. This development was great for the conservative utility (telephone) investors who owned these darlings of the new economy, until the old economy again met the new, and investors realised sectors of the 21st century are as unstable as correlations. Value becomes growth becomes value.

Finally, there is the risk measurement of *scenario analysis*. Applied for years by traditional asset allocators, macro hedge fund managers, and the banks and dealers with proprietary trading positions, this too can be a helpful risk tool. Scenario analysis helps trading managers establish a framework applying "what if" scenarios to guesstimate the effect of market moves, policy changes, election outcomes and the like, on a portfolio of positions or managers. The scenarios are meant to outline a range of outcomes and the resulting market effect. Then the user may assess the probability of each of the scenarios, and determine the best allocations given the range of possible outcomes.

PERFORMANCE MEASUREMENT

Investors invest in hedge funds to target positive returns. Some investors are aggressive; others may be quite conservative. Hedge fund strategies have a very wide range of performance and risk. In the final analysis, successful hedge fund investing is determined by performance measurement. The concept appears simple, but, beneath the surface, performance measurement is perhaps the most challenging analysis of hedge fund investing.

Why? To appropriately measure performance, one must drill down again and again.

Performance, or an estimated or declared NAV, may have been accurate for a moment in time. Or perhaps, never anywhere near accurate. After all, performance, or profit and loss, is not truly known until performance is realised. Until the time positions are actually liquidated, performance is an estimate. Sometimes this estimate may be close to accurate. Other times performance, and thus NAV calculation, is a number in progress. Many administrators do not consider the size of the hedge fund and the difficulty of liquidating large positions. Even exchange-traded instruments may have marks that are relevant for only a portion of a position, because of its size relative to market volume.

Part of the importance of portfolio transparency is the need for accurate performance measurement. How can one properly judge the quality of performance without transparency supporting the process that generated the performance? Frequently, with the hedge funds that experience blowups, the difficulties are evident months before investors become aware. Consider Long Term Capital Management. The fund realised it needed more capital as early as February 1998, although the eruption came in August.

In evaluating the quality of performance, one must look for the red flags. Were there one or more very concentrated positions? Who marked the less liquid positions? Were the marks aggressive? Did the fund avoid markdowns in certain positions? One must consider performance on a risk-adjusted basis. A manager who takes twice the risk of another manager to generate the same performance has inferior performance. Risk adjusted performance may be easy to measure applying a Sharpe ratio or return divided by VAR. But what if the performance is an estimate at best, because a significant portion of the portfolio is composed of less liquid securities? If one analyses the Sharpe ratio of the various HFR indices, one discovers that among the very highest are Reg D hedge funds. Experienced investors understand that part of the reason these returns appear so consistent is that the positions are so illiquid. Rare would be the investor who could actually redeem on a monthly basis at the NAVs that the administrators strike for Reg D funds. Many arbitrage strategies enjoy attractive risk-adjusted performance. What investors sometimes miss is that these strategies are burdened with event risk. Often the event happens suddenly, so those managers have little opportunity to reduce portfolio positions. Some arbitrage managers mark portfolio positions to maturity as opposed to market. Such an accounting practice makes for a very smooth return stream and an unrealistic measurement of true performance. During explosive market turmoil, many arbitrage funds sustain such large losses that managers decide to liquidate their funds.

The possibility of liquidation of hedge funds is an important reason one must track hedge fund performance, especially at the universe level, with caution. Survivorship bias is a major weakness of the many hedge fund databases available on the market. Unfortunately, many of the vendors elect to drop all previous performance for hedge funds that are no longer operating.

The trading manager must dissect the inputs to performance to judge the quality of a hedge fund manager's earnings for investors. By adhering to a portfolio structure that provides control, transparency, and risk measurement, the trading manager has a much stronger information set for evaluating performance. Performance should receive haircuts for portfolio complexity, illiquidity, large size, and concentrated positions. These variables are missed by the traditional risk-adjusted measures like Sharpe ratios and VAR. This is not to suggest that complex, less liquid strategies are not suitable investments, but to suggest that adjustments should be made to address some of the less obvious risks inherent in these strategies.

CONCLUSION

Risk management is most effective when the trading manager has control over the many facets of the programme, along with transparency. Transparency provides the path along which accurate risk and performance measurement may be generated. Without the critical information that transparency provides, the trading manager must perform ongoing risk analysis at the manager and portfolio level and performance evaluation in a vacuum. With an open, controlled and transparent process, the trading manager may independently confirm portfolio information. The trading manager is in a position to be proactive and take steps to remedy situations in a timely fashion. Risk management does not create positive performance, nor does it prevent losses. But the discipline of independent, skilled risk management oversight provides a sophisticated approach to hedge fund investing that works to serve the best interest of investors over time.

Part II

Perspectives from the Counterparties

7

From a Dealer's Perspective

Irenee duP. May, Jr

JP Morgan

Like most things there is a degree of art and science to managing hedge fund risks from a creditor's perspective. While it is convenient to group and categorise funds, it is important to recognise that each fund is different. Each has its position regards the markets and the opportunities. Each has its own risk tolerance and management teams. And each has its own strengths and weaknesses based on items as disparate as technology, service providers and personal lives. Therefore, every client needs to be assessed individually in a way that enables the creditor to decide whether to do business, and if so, how much, of what type, and under what circumstances.

Whether consciously or not, every decision to do business implies an answer to these four questions. Any one of the four could dominate to the point of making others irrelevant. Nonetheless, each has been answered by the time a trading relationship is established.

To do or not to do?

The answer to the question of whether to do business depends on two factors. One is character and the other is profitability. If the assessment is negative on either of these two components, there is no reason to move forward.

Though an entire chapter could be written on character, its actual assessment can be consolidated into two simple questions: "Do I feel comfortable doing business with the manager?", and, "Do I believe that the fund will make every effort to meet its obligation?" If the answers are affirmative, proceed. If not, defer. This is so critical, because character is both your first and last line of defence. Without character, the creditor is exposed to unquantifiable risk.

While the question of profitability seems simple, it is intriguing how often the analysis is overlooked on the way to establishing a relationship.

Often the fact that a trade "can get done" seems to be sufficient. However, recognising the full cost of doing business includes calculating not only the marginal expenses of additional research and sales coverage, but also the cost of capital that supports the credit.

The long journey to capacity

Assuming that the basic factors of character and profitability are met satisfactorily, answers to the questions of how much credit, of what type, and under what circumstances, need to be established.

In search of these answers, a creditor needs to develop a credit view based on a fundamental analysis of the fund and the management company. When establishing credit capacity, a number of considerations come into play. In addition to the risks a fund is taking, other issues include the creditor's broader appetite for risk, and its ability to track, quantify and monitor the exposures. Once the investigation is complete, the creditor must develop covenants and negotiate documents to protect itself against the risks identified through the analysis.

The final factor influencing the capacity of a bank is the degree of confidence the creditor has in their ability to fully and accurately capture, understand and control the risk outlined above. This is true not only for those embedded in the fund, but also for those residing in the creditor's firm.

FUNDAMENTAL ANALYSIS
Capital

To effectively analyse the risks in a fund, the creditor must consider the amount of capital under management and the likelihood that it will be there to meet credit obligations. It also needs to assess the risks that the capital bears, given the strategy employed and the infrastructure in place to support the business and manage the risks.

Size

The first and foremost consideration is size. While in some respects size should have no independent value in and of itself without some appreciation for the risk inherent in the fund, a slight "bigger is better" bias exists. There is some justification for this as large amounts of capital tend to attract and retain resources and tools that broadly contribute to greater financial stability. These resources can take the form of personnel, systems or credit arrangement, with a number of counterparts, all of which can assist in time of difficulty, in making the fund a better credit.

Redemption rights

While size is a leading indicator of credit worthiness it is by no means a guarantee. Shareholder redemption rights may in fact be more important, as even the threat of withdrawals can cause tremendous strain and ulti-mately cause a fund to fail. The key here is to compare the time horizon of the strategy versus the redemption rights of the investors. These consider-ations are no different from those used to manage assets and liabilities in any financial institution. Typically, managers should avoid a significant mismatch between their strategy and redemptions. The classic example of this problem is the emerging markets manager who allows monthly liq-uidity with 10-day notice in a fund that holds large positions in Russian and Latin American equity. While he may have been hedged adequately for large market movements, any quickly departing capital concerned with market volatility may leave him with no time to allow for his long and short positions to rebalance in the market, or even to liquidate in an orderly fashion.

Redemption rules may, on the surface, appear straightforward, with monthly or quarterly rights, but the details make a significant difference. Notice periods and the time a manager has until cash payments are made play an important role in extending terms of investment. Quarterly liquid-ity with 10-day notice and payment required the following day is significantly different from 45-day notice with 30 days to pay. While in both cases the investor has quarterly redemptions, in the second instance the creditor sees a manager with significantly greater opportunities to liqui-date positions to a size more compatible with the expected remaining capital. Finally, some funds have a clause enabling a manager to suspend redemption rights for extended periods of time, if, in his judgment, with-drawals would impair valuations of the remaining shareholders. This can be particularly reassuring to a creditor in times of market crisis or illiquid periods. Often the manager is a significant remaining shareholder, so the suspension comes at a time when the manager and creditor have overlap-ping interest.

Investors

Also important to the risk of a fund is the make-up of the investors. The ideal situation is a large number of diverse and sophisticated investors whose investment in the fund is only a small portion of their net worth, and whose view of that investment is long term. Additional comfort arises when a significant portion of the fund's management team's net worth is invested in the fund. This model is appealing because typically it creates a stable equity base that remains largely invested over a longer period of time, with investors and managers having significant and similar interests.

Though it is often difficult to get a manager to reveal specifically who the fund's investors are, most managers readily provide sufficient insight to allow for general determination on the above criteria. With this perspective gained, it is also important to check redemption activity, ie, to compare the redemption history and performance. Did investors leave quickly after a poor performance period or did they tend to remain? Gain a sense of the make-up of those redemptions. Did the departing capital represent a diverse group of investors or a few? Was it representative of full redemption by those investors, or just an incremental decrease in their allocation? Also, look at other times when performance might have been good, but redemptions increased. This could be a sign of changes in the organisation that were apparent to insiders but less so to others. Also, it can be interesting to note withdrawals following good performance, particularly resulting from a difficult market period. This can be an indication of a concentration of fund-of-fund investors as they are forced to rebalance allocations to their managers, or to meet their own redemptions. An example of this occurred at the end of 1998, when a number of profitable managers lost as much as 15% of their capital because fund-of-fund investors, who constituted 30% of their investor base, were having as much as half of their money redeemed by their investors.

Another circumstance that bears consideration is a manager who has one significant investor whose departure, for whatever reason, could put a significant strain on the position liquidity or the economic viability of the manager. The departure of this investor could cause the collapse of the fund either directly or indirectly by influencing others to leave as well.

Market risk

After considering the size and nature of the capital, the next area of focus for fundamental analysis is the risk, both intentional and unintentional, that the capital bears. These risks arise from a variety of sources including investment strategy (and the tools used in its management), organisational structure, operational activity, liquidity management, along with as reputational and counterparty risks.

Investment strategy

The most obvious risk of a fund is that associated with trading positions. It is important to assess the strategies employed by a manager to properly understand what he is attempting to accomplish. A good starting point is how a manager has positioned himself with his investors. What are the fund's expected returns and volatility? What asset classes and geographic focus does it have? And in what kinds of markets does the strategy work best? These answers should offer up an overview of a manager's basic goals.

While most managers can fit into a single strategy type, in practice they typically incorporate a number of different market approaches to generate revenue. Managers allocate capital across these strategies, given market condition and their assessment of the best opportunities. For example, a relative-value equity manager may have capital employed in convertible bond strategies, merger arbitrage or long-short equity positions, depending on what he thinks will provide the best returns. On the other hand, an emerging markets manager could take risk in equities, interest rates and foreign exchange of a particular country, depending on his views.

When analysing these investment strategies, a manager's experience is another consideration. Ideally, an alignment of a manager's background and the strategies employed should provide the creditor with the greatest comfort.

Trade ideas

Once a perspective of the manager's general approaches to the market is formed, it is useful to obtain a more detailed understanding of the themes or specific trade ideas they employ. These trade ideas or themes represent his current expectations for market movement, whether it is volatility of the broad market or some more idiosyncratic risk between companies, or securities. Themes are analogous to hypotheses and the manager, through position-taking, tests these hypotheses.

It is useful for the creditor to know the source of these ideas and the process a manager goes through when deciding upon a trade. A disciplined process that sorts, analyses and selects trade ideas is preferred over a more casual approach. A manager with the resources to develop their own ideas, or who has a process to check ideas that the "street" provides, is in a better position to leverage good ideas and avoid being herded into the poorer ones. A strategy that has specific entry points, with targets for return and reasons for exit, provides comfort as a creditor can establish a metric to gauge performance and behaviour once going forward. An understanding of what represents a full position or maximum allocation, and how a manager gets there, are also useful for assessing an enterprise. Some strategies are designed to build up the position as it performs well, while others build up as the trade performs badly. Knowledge of a manager's tendency can help in predicting when a fund might be in trouble upon a dramatic market turn.

A creditor also cares about the dynamic around the decision-making process and the question of who is ultimately responsible for the risk. Once a position is adopted, how often is it checked or reviewed? In one extreme, there is concern about having only one person in charge without checks or controls. In the other extreme, the concern is having too many responsible participants, none of whom will exercise the necessary leadership to make the appropriate move at the right time.

Concentration

Another component of risk assessment is understanding a portfolio's concentration, the themes in place and their structure. The goal is to prevent one specific event or a combination of events from significantly affecting the value of the entire portfolio.

Depending on the type of strategy employed, the manager might have as few as five themes or more than 50. The number in place and the nature of capital allocations are critical to gaining an overview. However, for true insight, a creditor needs to be aware of and understand the actual positions on the books and the types of market movement that create profit and loss.

Often, in the manager's mind, each theme captures an independent market development. But in practice, the positions are sometimes also vulnerable to other, more systemic, market forces. The fact that a manager has 200 trades may not necessarily mean his portfolio is diversified. When analysing concentration risk, one needs to recognise that while on the surface themes may appear independent, they may all be susceptible to one or more potential market developments. As a simple example, a manager who has a US swap convergence trade, a long European equity portfolio and a long dollar/yen position is at risk. While these all look significantly different, a change in the confidence of the US financial system would negatively affect all of them. Swap spreads would widen, the dollar would devalue, and a general lowering of overall risk appetite by investors would drive down the stock market. Therefore, assessing the risks that the capital bears requires getting into the specific trades.

To manage concentration concerns, many managers have diversification rules in place that state limits on the size of positions allowed. Such limits can include a cap on the amount of exposure to a given credit or name, both in equity and bonds. They can limit allocations to market sectors, geographic regions or countries, as well as instrument types. The creditor needs to assess these guidelines for their appropriateness given the strategy, and also needs to conclude whether the manager has in fact lived within them.

Leverage

After recognising the types of market exposure the manager is exploiting, it is important to assess the leverage they are employing. Leverage in and of itself is not an indication of risk. Often, leverage is a risk mitigator. For example, owning a 10-year note and selling a note with a nine-year maturity in similar amounts lowers the risk of the owner's portfolio, despite increasing the leverage. Therefore, it is very important to look at leverage in the context of the portfolio.

In many instances, however, leverage is used as an accelerator of the market risks that reside in the themes established by the manager. Ultimately, the creditor cares about the rate of change in the fund capital deriving from any change in the basic risk expressed by the positions held. So, while one is often tempted to ask how much leverage is used, the more important insight is gained by getting the manager to express the risk in terms of changes in capital arising from any change in the market.

Once the creditor knows what types of market movement will create P/L, and the magnitude of that P/L due to leverage, they are in a strong position to understand the inherent risks in the investment strategy. As a check, the banker uses this perspective to compare the fund's performance with ongoing market movements. Also, depending on the length of history, a comparison of the fund's past performance during significant market events allows the investigator to see if the fund's volatility resembles their expectations.

Instruments
The next step in understanding the risks in the portfolio is knowing the way in which various positions are constructed. Choice of instruments used is critical, as it provides additional perspective on the types of risks embedded in the portfolio. The use of futures for hedging in a convertible bond portfolio for example, is considerably different to the use of an interest rate swap or credit default derivative. However, in all three cases, it is correct to say that the portfolio is "hedged". The use of options also creates different risk characteristics, which may not be initially recognised when a manager expresses his views on the market and his position within it. There are also differences in the underlying liquidity of positions, depending on the instruments utilised, which create distinctly different risk characteristics. Finally, and significantly, the instruments used also establish the kind of infrastructure necessary to properly support the portfolio.

Investment horizon
Knowledge of the investment horizon is a useful check on a number of issues raised earlier. As already mentioned, comparing the investment horizon to withdrawal rights is a very simple way of seeing whether there is a basic balance between the assets and the capital. Second, understanding the investment horizon provides a potentially confirming perspective on the level of volatility the manager may actually be willing to take. A manager with a short investment horizon should not be taking significant losses in any positions, and should use relatively liquid markets with narrow bid-ask spreads. In general, they cannot afford it otherwise. Finally, knowing the investment horizon and the trade volumes also contributes to an understanding of the infrastructural requirements necessary for for proper support and manage the organisation.

Market risk management
Closely associated with the investment strategy is the approach used to manage the market risks of a fund. To gain perspective, the creditor needs to understand the tools that the manager uses to track and guide trade management decisions. Answers to the questions of who sees the risk reports and the nature of the influence they bear in the actual risk management process also contribute to a clearer picture of the risk management infrastructure.

Tools

Not every strategy requires the same level of sophisticated risk management tools. The more complex the strategy, the more developed the risk management tools need to be. A cash-based, long-short US equity portfolio requires far less than a relative value mortgage backed security (MBS) strategy with significant prepayment risk. Often, querying the capital a manager is willing to risk on a particular trade, or the rules in place to manage a poor performing position, helps to outline the basics of a fund's risk management system.

However, in every instance, the creditor looks for evidence of approaches and tools that appropriately address the needs. In its simplest form, a risk management tool should capture all the risk positions and provide some metric for risk assessment, whether it be a market instrument equivalent, like the S+P 500 index, or a value-at-risk (VAR) estimation. By highlighting positions both good and bad, the tool should also reveal poorly performing positions that are ripe for action, consistent with the strategy employed. For downside management, stop-loss triggers are the easiest tools, but some managers argue that they are more dangerous than useful. In the end, there needs to be recognition that the manager can be wrong and, for the benefit of the fund, appropriate rules for anticipated behaviour put in place to address this. Also, the point at which remedial action takes place should relate to the capital of the fund and not some esoteric view of the market. Additionally, some overall measure of the portfolio decline resulting from poor performance, separate from any one bad performing position, should exist, indicating the point at which the manager will exit the market prior to jeopardising the ongoing viability of the fund.

If a manager uses a risk-based model, then considerations around the assumptions used to manage the risk are important. A strategy that has large illiquid positions should not use one-day market volatility and one standard deviation moves as guidance, because there would not accurately reflect the risk borne in the portfolio. Also, some methodology that recognises the existence of correlation is important. To address this last point some managers assume that all trades are fully correlated – but there can be danger here too. While it can appear disciplining, it is human nature to become insensitive and overlook signals that do not consistently apply to our world. Therefore, over time, a manager could easily ignore these signals, rendering them useless at the time they are most accurate.

Whatever tools are used, one that should ideally be included is a tool for stress-testing using actual market events. While stress-testing using higher sigma moves can be useful, it still tends to assume a modelled relationship between factors. By using a variety of actual distressed market conditions when stress testing, the results reflect circumstances where traditional and expected relationships break down, providing a better basis on which to judge what risk the portfolio bears.

Price discovery
Price discovery is another important component. While there is always concern about managers marking their own portfolios, in some instances, it is reasonable to do so on certain types of positions. However, it is important to have checks and balances in place. These can be achieved by third party marks provided by more than one broker/dealer, and certainly by other dealers to the one who sold the position. Manager marks can also be confirmed by some form of regular portfolio turnover. If somewhat random and diverse, these regular trades establish real prices reflecting the point at which the market clears the risk carried in the portfolio.

Liquidity
Another major issue surrounding risk management is liquidity.

In recent years, it appears that this portfolio risk is the most likely to cause a problem in a fund. Liquidity risk comes in two closely related forms: one associated with the cash available to meet margin calls, and the other with unwinding positions. To take a lot of risk in one area requires the manager to limit risk in the other. To do otherwise eliminates the fund's flexibility in times of crisis.

While most managers have some concept of how easy it is to get out of their market positions, it is important to bring a disciplined approach to this as well. The slippage that results in a manager's inability to get out of positions can make most traditional risk management tools ineffective predictors of risk, as they assume free and abundant liquidity within the confines of expected volatility.

An example of this problem is a manager who has a simple basis trade in the portfolio involving the cheapest delivery of a 10-year note against the future. In normal times, the future and the bond move in the opposite direction and the margin requirements match up. However, in very volatile times, given limit moves on the futures exchange, the future may not be able to adjust as far as the cash markets. If this were to occur, the value tied up in such a future would be unavailable to meet the margin on the bond for several days. By then, if not properly anticipated, a fund could be out of business. Therefore, a creditor looks for a liquidity management approach to assess the potential requirements during difficult market conditions and identifies where a limited source of liquidity might be found. This analysis should be tied into the stress test model as well, thus ensuring a consistent and full approach to risk management.

Other counterparties
Associated with considerations around liquidity are the fund's other counterparties and any arrangements that are in place. These arrangements incorporate secured lending lines, committed debt facilities or prime

brokerage relationships. One of the lessons learned from the financial crisis of 1998 was that one of the factors most critical to a fund's survival – or at least to an orderly dissolution – there is identification of its counterparties. Far more important than the risk positions in those volatile markets was the manager's ability to find liquidity. When a major provider of financing abruptly pulled support from a fund in 1998, it had significant repercussions on the fund's ability to receive and deliver securities, make payments, meet margin calls, and ultimately protect its NAV. There were funds that claimed to have sufficient capital to bear the risk and cash to meet its obligations, but that were nonetheless forced out of the market.

Operational risk

Another source of risk in a fund is operational risk. This includes trade capture, confirmation, settlements and reconciliation. While they are often considered less important, these risks can unexpectedly bring down a firm as quickly as any other type of risk.

For example, if the fundamental operating systems and structures are not in place to capture all the positions, systems such as risk and liquidity management tools are not dependable. As mentioned earlier, when reviewing the back office, the creditor keeps in mind the trading profile of the fund. Daily turnover, the number of assets classes and instrument types, as well as counterparties, all contribute to the level of risk in the fund and demand sufficient infrastructure to manage the activity. A creditor looks for robustness in the operations and resources to support the business. This includes personnel sufficient in number and skill-sets, as well as processes and systems. Often, managers in start-up phases de-emphasise these areas, but it is to their own peril. A lost trade or insufficiently controlled environment exposes them to unintentional mistakes as well as to malicious intent. The existence of formal back-office policies and adequately senior individuals responsible for these functions' performance combine to reflect an operational quality that gives the creditor comfort. Indications of operational strength come in the form of consistently met margin calls, speedy and accurate trade confirmations, and a limited number of failed trades along with quick dispute resolution.

Another factor affecting operational risks is organisational change. Significant growth or decline in the capital under management can raise concerns. Changes in strategies or the addition of new portfolio managers can also have an adverse effect, and need to be watched closely. The departure of significant people, whether on the trading or operations side, is an additional event that requires tracking.

Other considerations when investigating operational risks are the non-market service providers. Administrators, lawyers and auditors can either lend creditability to, or create concern about, an organisation. Creditors look for a reputable firm with experience. Like the manager, a crisis is a terrible time for the counterparty to realise that a fund's service providers have under-performed.

ESTABLISHING CAPACITY

Once the due diligence is complete and the risk borne by the capital is assessed, the creditor's task is to establish the capacity it has for the fund, answering the questions of extent, type and conditions. The five drivers effecting the capacity are transparency, legal documentation, monitoring, overall credit risk appetite and revenue.

Transparency

The degree of transparency a fund provides to a creditor is particularly important as it directly affects the creditor's confidence in his assessment of the risk embedded in the fund's market position. High transparency eliminates a significant portion of the uncertainty the creditor must protect against, thus enabling the fuller allocation of capacity against the known risks, such as capital size, redemption rights and portfolio risk. While the rules of transparency are often codified in the documentation, a greater exchange of information can also occur in practice, contributing to a creditor's comfort and willingness to accept increased exposure.

Documentation

A second driver of capacity and a tool for risk management is the legal documentation. The documents are important because they outline the creditor's recourse to guide the relationship during the normal course of business and to manage in times of difficulty. The terms outline the manager's obligations to meet certain requirements and the consequences if he does not. Regular reporting of NAVs and risk information, timely audit reports and additional information upon request are typically listed as terms of an agreement. Documents often also provide the creditor with the rules surrounding the use of collateral. Risk to market exposure is a constant with all managers, so terms incorporating margin arrangements for various types of instruments and maturities, as well as changes in mark-to-market values, are a regular feature. In addition to terms on market risk, the documents address other issues, based on the due diligences assessment described earlier. The other risks that may have been recognised in the fund include key man risk, changes in strategy, defaults, or significant changes in relationships with other counterparties.

Depending on the credit view of these exposures, along with the risk in the market portfolio, and the size of the capital, thresholds will be set for the exchange of collateral, these reflect the creditor's appetite for the fund. Usually, there are provisions for up-front margins or initial collateral to mitigate risks associated with the timing difference (between the time when positions are put on and the time when additional collateral can arrive to meet changes in mark-to-market values). Collateral can also be used to address additional concerns. Useful in this respect are collateral triggers, which increase the amount of initial margin required if certain conditions develop, such as a significant drop in NAV. Collateral triggers protect a creditor who provides aggressive amounts of exposure to a manager, based on a previous level of capital. Consequently, if a serious deterioration of that capital occurs, or a dramatic shift in the risk profile of the fund clearly develops, the creditor has some way of mitigating his risk.

Domicile

Another point of risk that falls under legal issues is where a fund is domiciled. While in many cases, jurisdictions such as the United States and the United Kingdom are used in disputes with offshore funds, this is not always the case. Creditors need to be aware of the differences that exist in bankruptcy laws in the countries where funds are set up. Rules on who has control over the assets and liabilities, netting rules, reciprocity, and the length of time for resolution vary, and can have a very significant effect on the recoverable value of a creditor's exposure after the collapse of a fund.

Measure and monitor

A counterparty's ability to measure and monitor its risk is critical for the effective management of hedge fund exposure. Similar to the requirements of a fund manager and his market risks, a counterparty needs to have the systems and processes in place that allow for proper capture, analysis, and reporting of exposures. The better and more sophisticated the approach, the higher the degree of confidence in the information and the greater the capacity for exposure.

Aggregation

Fundamental to the successful management of exposure and the maximisation of the value of the business with funds is the ability to aggregate positions across the firm, so they can be tracked and managed on a portfolio basis. If a creditor cannot do this, they are constantly in a position of trying to estimate the exposures' potential impact. The lower the degree of confidence in the reporting, the greater the margin of error they have to create when allocating exposure to a particular manager, as well as to the industry as a whole.

The biggest hurdle to successful aggregation is technology. Being able to interface the various trade capture and reporting systems, so that all positions including cash, swaps, futures and exotic options are included, is key. However, given the different system legacies that exist in most organisations and the co-ordination required to create a robust calculating engine, this is not easily done.

One of the issues that complicates the aggregation process is how to treat a creditor's inter-entity exposures – ie, those between associated companies within the creditor's overall organisation. The difficulty arises, for example, when a fund has exposures to the creditor's futures clearing merchant, security dealer, and separately capitalised swap entity. While the exposures are separate and distinct, an unassociated risk control process that does not net may overstate the real impact of a fund's collapse to the creditor, and thereby limit the amount of capacity a counterpart might have for a fund.

Reporting

Another issue at the crossroads of technology and monitoring is the speed and accuracy of the information available. In most instances for on-going monitoring, the goal is a regularly available, reasonably accurate estimate of the whole exposure. This is more useful than a very accurate estimate of a portion of the exposure, which is available only periodically.

Once the technology is in place to effectively monitor the exposure, the creditor needs to analyse the data in a number of different ways. The first level of analysis is that associated with an individual fund. Here, the fund's positions and expected current market exposure are captured and reviewed. This information can usefully be compared with the credit lines, the fund's capital and liquidity. The second order of risk comes from the exposures in aggregate of all funds using leverage strategies. Consolidating and analysing this data enables the creditor to recognise the risks associated with the positions as a whole. It provides insight into risk concentration, as well as the benefits of correlation. So while a creditor may be concerned about a particular manager, on a portfolio basis – if that fund went out of business – the creditor's losses would not necessarily cause a significant deterioration of the portfolio. To effectively analyse the risk in an overall portfolio, the data needs to be malleable enough to report across a number of categories. Ideally, the categories will include specific names or credits, industry or sector risks, as well as concentrations in geographic regions, or even types of strategies.

The third order of risk, which is often overlooked, views the consolidated exposure of the creditor's own market positions along with those positions generating credit risk exposure from the portfolio of hedge fund clients. This analysis reflects the best estimate of the impact of market movement to the creditor's capital, if all the funds were to go out of business.

When viewing all orders of risk, it is also important to be able to stress-test the exposures. While it is appropriate to analyse exposures on an "as expected" basis, it is important not to rely on that alone. Markets do not always act as expected. Often, it is these unexpected moves that cause credit events with managers, producing knock-on effects on other funds, the creditor's trade positions and ultimately the capital of the creditor itself.

Ongoing due diligence

One final observation about monitoring is that it is imperative to conduct ongoing due diligence with clients at some level. How much effort is made is a function of the degree of impact a problem with that fund will have on business. While you might be more likely to experience a loss with a small account, the size of that exposure may be so insignificant that the resulting expected loss is not worth much follow-up. However, with bigger exposures, the creditor needs to be on top of the manager. This effort is to ensure that the creditor's assessment of the underlying risk remains up to date and accurate. Changes in apparent concentration or expected volatility reflect potential shifts in business and therefore warrant additional investigation. As mentioned earlier, changes in the organisation or declines in operational performance raise warning signals.

Creditor risk appetite

The fourth driver of credit capacity is the creditor's own appetite for hedge fund risk. In assessing this, a counterparty needs to consider some of the issues also used in analysing a manager. The creditor needs to consider the various risks that the capital of the firm bears, plus how much of that risk it wants associated or correlated with a hedge fund portfolio. They need to ensure that the portfolio has sufficient diversification, and that overall limits are consistent with the capital base, so that no single or series of events can put the firm at risk. Also, issues surrounding internal monitoring and control affect the capacity of the creditor as mentioned above.

Revenue

Finally, revenue is a driver of credit appetite. A creditor is running a business with the goal of an attractive return on investment. That investment includes running expenses, as well as the cost of capital required to support the market-making and the credit risk. To the extent that adequate returns can be made on incremental expenses and credit exposure without a greater incremental increase in risk, the capacity for the fund or the portfolio should increase.

CONCLUSION

The process of risk management is not static and linear, but constitutes a constantly changing balance between factors. Depending on the information available, the confidence in that information, and compensation for the risk, a creditor tries to find the right portfolio of capacity for his firm. There are many well-developed models used to manage risk. However, none fully capture the changes that occur in the markets or the industry. Therefore, the task of the creditor is to understand the types of market movement that create profit and loss, and to recognise the assumptions that are embedded in his own risk management model. The ultimate challenge for the creditor is to remain flexible enough to allow for the constant dynamic, incorporating the newest tools without losing sight of the basic truths of risk management. This requires a degree of art amidst the science.

8

A Structurer and Enhancer

Susan Webb

CDC Capital Markets

Over the last year and a half, CDC North America has become increasingly active as a portfolio enhancer in structures involving both total return funds and structured credit portfolios (CDOs). Our role has been as simple as intermediating a total return swap and as complex as modifying the duration of a CDO structure through portfolio restructuring. Typically, we are providing a protection option on the performance of an underlying structure or fund. Regardless of the final structure we use, the methodology we employ is analytical, comprehensive and rational.

The cornerstone of CDC's approach is an attempt to understand the liquidity of the underlying fund or trust investments that we are protecting. A complete understanding of this risk, as it relates both to the fund and the structure we are implementing, is analysed through a variety of methods. First, the structure and strategies of the fund are explored. Secondly, a careful examination of the underlying assets and their respective liquidities is undertaken. Finally, we compare and contrast both aspects relative to the level and control of CDC's proposed involvement.

The rationale for this framework is supported by the methodologies we use in structuring around the funds we agree to immunise. The risk of the structure hinges primarily on a fund performing within agreed parameters with mutually agreed constraints. When established barriers are breached, signals are set off and a variety of triggers are hit. The fund or trust must then take specific actions to return the fund to compliance within the agreed structure. If the situation is not speedily addressed, the underlying risk must be liquidated. We attempt to correctly access the speed with which this can be done, the price slippage that might occur, and the market risk CDC will bear (if it is a proxy hedge) in the event of a termination.

CAREFUL EXAMINATION OF THE UNDERLYING FUND

This review aims to obtain a clear understanding of the fund strategy and the characteristics unique to the fund. These include, but are not limited to, the degree of leverage employed in the context of the underlying assets, the lock out features of the particular fund, and the pricing and valuation mechanisms employed by the fund. We also carefully examine the risk management techniques used and the fund's financing sources, which includes the origin and commitment level of the investors. Each of these differentiating features will be explored below.

Fund Manager review

We begin our examination of each fund with a manager review. This requires a complete understanding of the fund manager's backgrounds and particular market expertise. We focus on the manager's previous trading experiences and general market reputations. In a team approach, it is equally important to examine the group dynamics. We must feel comfortable with the allocation of roles and the co-ordination of investment strategy implementation.

A clear explanation of the fund's particular investment strategy and philosophy is a prerequisite for continuing the fund review. It is important that this is articulated in how a fund invests and allocates its investments, and also in how they deal with the management of their positions on an ongoing basis. The investment implementation should be coupled with a clear methodology for taking profits and cutting losses. We look for a clear allocation of trading authority from both directions. If this is not being readily addressed, then the ability to satisfy our risk management concerns will be found lacking.

The firm's internal risk management processes are equally important. Well-run funds have regular meetings to discuss positions and to monitor adherence to their own established guidelines for portfolio position management. If these policies are in place, we try to confirm that they are actually implemented. To accomplish this, we read newsletters and examine a fund's performance over a number of previous periods (looking at sector and position allocations). We attempt to determine if there are any inconsistencies in stated and implemented policies. None of these methods are perfect, but when taken cumulatively, we obtain a clearer picture of the fund's internal management both from a risk management and internal investment discipline perspective. This research is invaluable later on when we try to implement limits and constraints that will control manager style drift.

A final factor is the manager's uniqueness. We are particularly concerned if there is primarily one individual implementing the investment strategy. In this case, the necessity of an independent risk management group with clear-cut authorities is essential. Additionally, we try to assess if they are the only qualified individual to implement the monitoring of positions. Will they be able to train others to support them and duplicate their efforts, or will this be a solo performance? If it is, then the emotional state of the fund manager is always a concern, and the investment discipline and risk management procedures become even more important.

Liquidity and leverage

The amount of capital that a fund may possess can be significantly different from the notional amount of assets under management. Funds may obtain leverage through a variety of means, such as repo transactions, lines of credit from banks, futures, options and other exchange-traded instruments, as well as over-the-counter derivatives. All of these instruments enable a fund to control a larger amount of underlying assets in return for posting a smaller amount of collateral. The collateral or "haircut" a fund must post is determined by an exchange, or is assessed by each institution entering various lending arrangements with the funds. Normally, this haircut is actively maintained and the positions are marked-to-market daily; additional collateral can be called as the market moves against the fund. In examining leverage in the context of the fund, we are trying to determine whether the degree of leverage employed by the fund is appropriate given the fund's investment strategies and the underlying assets. We also attempt to assess the overall leverage employed by the fund and determine whether we can monitor this on an ongoing basis.

In determining whether the leverage is appropriate, we try to predict the vulnerability of a fund to significant market movements. To correctly assess this, we must understand the volatility of the underlying assets over a variety of scenarios, the correlation across various assets, and the ability of a fund to correctly address the market movements. The amount of readily available cash and the various financing arrangements of the fund are part of this analysis.

Well-managed funds will maintain a variety of relationships with several banks and financial institutions. Additionally, they will attempt to match the financing of their assets against the probable holding period of the investment and try to maintain some draw on a "liquidity" facility in the case of an unexpected cash need.

Assessing the liquidity of the underlying assets and estimating if adequate financing exists requires an understanding of the valuation of each asset. The source of valuations is a key variable in determining this. Is the fund relying on third party valuations, and are these real mark-to-markets? If a real liquidation event were to occur, what type of bid/offer spreads would we expect, and how deep would the market be in terms of trade size and volume? To do this, we perform our own spot checks on various positions using third-party pricing as well as our own internally developed models.

A final but frequently overlooked variable in accessing a fund's financial flexibility is its investors and any constraints that they may be under. With this in mind, we examine the lock-out features of each fund. Does it vary by investor? Some investors may have monthly liquidity whereas others may have a year or more. The term of the lock-out should be largely determined by the probable holding period of the bulk of the underlying positions. Equally important is the notice period that investors must give before withdrawing assets. A long notice period can lengthen a lock-out from monthly to quarterly, which clearly works in favour of the fund. As an enhancer, a long lock-out period limits our ability to liquidate if the fund violates its parameters, and we may ask for an exception, as it relates to the structures we protect.

The type of investor is also crucial. If the investors are a stable group, sophisticated and aware of the fund's strategy and possible volatility, this will enable a fund to implement its strategies with additional security. As a structurer it gives us added certainty that in times of negative performance, this will not be exacerbated by the withdrawal of equity. Investors that have a reputation for departing a fund at the first sign of performance troubles add an additional layer of concern. This can be mitigated by the fund retaining more liquid assets than it normally would and by the enhancer maintaining a cushion against such withdrawals in the form of a tighter exit trigger.

We also look to the level of personal financial involvement the fund managers have. This is a good indicator of their level of commitment, and tends to prevent irrational handling of investments should an unforeseen market event occur.

Creation of the structure

Once we have completed our initial fund analysis we begin to refine the structure we hope to use. Just as each fund has a unique approach to managing money, we provide each fund with a tailor-made solution for protecting their performance for investors.

The basic structure requires that the fund provide CDC with performance data on the underlying funds. These data are requested daily, weekly or monthly, depending on the liquidity and volatility of the underlying assets. Equally important is the level of other external monitoring and information gathering we might be undertaking. In a large number of the structures for which we provide performance options, we will work closely with a third party. This is typically a fund-of-fund or other fully equipped monitoring entity that will provide us with accurate fund data and constant fund monitoring.

We rely on these firms to receive the prime brokerage reports and segregate the data into the risk buckets we may require. This may include detailed breakdowns of positions, percentage of portfolio in each asset class, country risk sector allocations, and currency buckets. We can then perform our own volatility and risk assessments on these numbers, or we may rely on the firm to do basic volatility tests. Any exceptional gain or loss we will examine in greater detail. Fund NAV changes due to increased purchases, and redemption will also be monitored very closely.

Where the variations in positions or the underlying may warrant it we will perform a value-at-risk (VAR) for the appropriate time horizon. In other cases, we perform stress scenarios based on historical or projected future market and liquidity events. Losses from both cases are used to judge the riskiness of CDC's liability and alert us to the need to more closely examine the funds and assets involved. Deals may have several limits imposed on the fund and these limits will be observed closely. Projected risk scenarios are communicated to a fund manager before a limit is reached.

We also actively monitor general world conditions. These include world equity performance and volatility, G7 country swap yield levels and spreads, currency volatility, the shape of yield curves, interest rate volatility, credit spreads, MBS and ABS and agency markets. These are all monitored daily to help identify potential problems at some funds.

In the context of the above, we work to establish signals and triggers that will satisfy our risk management needs and our desire to retain the correct cushion should there be a need to liquidate. We must balance these desires against the fund managers' need for flexibility in managing their assets and following their investment strategies.

The creation of the structure, analysis of the underlying assets and the final conclusion is as much an art as it is a science. As we have discussed, CDC draws upon a number of factors before arriving at its final decisions. But ultimately, it relies on the internal experience level and knowledge base of the personnel involved in the deal process.

CDC possesses many levels of highly qualified and staff who have experience in dealing with a variety of structures and underlying. The company is an active participant in the mortgage market with experience in IOs, POs, and whole loans both commercial and residential. It can also confidently analyse the risk of a variety of corporate credits, both investment grade and some non-investment grade. The group has actively managed equities as well as commodities. Experience with a wide variety of underlying as well as their various derivatives is crucial when analysing the liquidation risk we work hard to monetise.

Secondly, CDC has analysed and dealt with a variety of structures, CBOs, CLOs, CMBS, and a variety of asset-backed securities deals. CDC has also worked on deals that are a synthetic variety of all the above, and the combination adds to our understanding of both risk and structuring.

Finally, we have internal legal staff who are adept at understanding and evaluating the risks inherent in the context of this broad array of underlyings and structures. They work actively with us to implement a structure that will address the concerns of all involved parties: investor, fund manager and CDC as the enhancer.

To complete your understanding of how CDC views risk when analysing total return funds as a structure and enhancer, we also include two sample term sheets. Hopefully, these inclusions will clearly illustrate the means by which we have attempted to structure the risk of enhancing fund performance.

CAISSE DES DÉPÔTS
———— GROUP ————
CDC FINANCIAL PRODUCTS, INC.

DEAL SUMMARY

RE: ABC Fund Linked Note   DRAFT ONLY

In continuing our discussions with ABC Asset Management, we agreed to specify in more detail the portfolio guidelines and reporting requirements that we would require. Some of these were listed in our draft termsheet, others are new. I propose this list as the starting point of our more detailed negotiations with ABC and ask you for comments and omissions.

- Average Days to Liquidate (precise definition to be determined) less than 30. No single position over 45 days to liquidate.
- Historical volatility less than 30% annualised.
- Prospective volatility less than 30% annualised.
- No stock with less than 100 days of trading price data.
- Volatility weighted allocation to any market sector less than 25%, no two sectors combined over 40%. Regardless of volatility, no sector over 40%, or two sectors combined over 60%.
- Leverage less than 3.0.
- No position added to if allocation is over 5% of the portfolio.
- No position to exceed 5% of the market capitalization of a firm.
- Volatility weighted allocation to any country not to exceed limits to be determined (e.g., US 100%, JPY 20%, etc.).
- No short option positions. No equity index options.
- No long option position longer than 6m to maturity, no exotic (eg, asian, basket, quanto) options.
- No outright currency positions (possible exceptions for equities with dominant roles in foreign countries).
- No convertible bonds or other embedded options.
- Reporting requirements:
- Daily: NAV, sector allocations, aggregate days to liquidate.
- Weekly (or on request): Daily data plus position data.

9 West 57th Street, 36th Fl., New York, New York 10019 Telephone: 212.891.1990

CDC FINANCIAL PRODUCTS INC.

DRAFT

Indicative Term Sheet: European Fund Principal Protection

Fund:	Multi-Manager European Fund TBD
PPO Provider:	CDC Financial Products, Inc.
Notional:	USD 100MM maximum
Offering Price:	USD 1000 per share
Settlement:	TBD
Coupon:	none
Subordination:	none
Rating:	Expected AAA from Moody's, NAIC-1 from SVO of NAIC.
Maturity:	5yrs
Portfolio Manager:	ABC Strategies LLC
Trading Advisors:	At settlement, a) Alpha, b) Beta, c) Theta, d) Rho, e) Pi. Advisors to be added over time at mutual agreement between the portfolio manager and the PPO provider.
Trading Asset Allocation:	Max [100% of NAV, 5*(NAV-S(t))], where S(t) = price of a theoretical 2% bond priced from the USD Libor curve at an assumed funding cost of Libor –20bp.
	Trading assets to be reduced from this figure if realised 60 day volatility exceeds the target level of 9% by more than 2%.
Asset Allocation Guidelines:	To include the following:

a) Minimum of 5 trading advisors
b) No more than 5% of assets used for options premiums
c) No short uncovered options
d) No more than 30% of assets used for margin and/or options premiums
e) No more than 10% of assets in any single position
f) No more than 25% of assets allocated to any manager

FAX (212) 891-6112 9 WEST 57TH STREET, 36TH FLOOR, NEW YORK, NY 10019   TEL. (212) 891-6275

CAISSE DES DÉPÔTS
———— GROUP ————

CDC FINANCIAL PRODUCTS INC.

	g) Daily Value at Risk limit for each manager h) Daily Value at Risk limits by country and sector
Defeasance Trigger:	If NAV per share is less than 2% above that of S(t), as defined above.
Fund Fees:	As specified in the offering memorandum
Offering Expenses:	None
PPO Provider Fees:	100bp per annum, payable quarterly, 2yr lockup
Reporting Requirements:	Daily NAV, pricing, and risk reports to be agreed upon
PPO Payment:	PPO provider pays the difference, if and only if positive, between (A) the product of (i) the offering price times (ii) the outstanding number of shares and (B) the NAV of the Fund at maturity.
Form of Documentation:	Total return swap, credit default swap or other as mutually agreed upon
Calculation Agent:	CDC Financial Products, Inc.

Offering as of 31/10/00 at 5:03 PM
Note: All offerings are subject to market conditions.

FAX (212) 891-6112 9 WEST 57TH STREET, 36TH FLOOR, NEW YORK, NY 10019   TEL. (212) 891-6275

CAISSE DES DÉPÔTS
GROUP

9

From the Practitioner's Perspective as a Prime Broker

Graham Rowlands*

Lehman Brothers

Prime brokers are service providers to the hedge fund industry. Most major investment banks offer prime brokerage as a core product area. A wide variety of services are available to the hedge fund industry, ranging from the structuring, executing, financing and settlement of transactions through to custody, accounting, fund start-up (including capital introduction) and the various aspects of risk management. Although many of the above are related, the focus of this chapter will be the risk management issues that arise from the perspective of the prime broker in this business. Emphasis will primarily be placed on the credit, market and legal risk issues of the participants. Credit risk relates to the potential for loss resulting from adverse changes in creditworthiness of entities whose securities are held, or with whom there is a trading relationship as counterpart. Market risk is focused on the potential for trading losses flowing from changes in market factors such as price, volatility, correlation, market depth/liquidity and the ability to fund. Legal risk centres on the conditions under which liquidation of the hedge fund's positions is available to the prime broker, and the appropriate processes for effecting such liquidation.

Hedge funds are privately organised, pooled investment structures typically unavailable to the general public and administered by professional investment managers. These structures are not homogeneous: size, mandate and objectives can vary enormously. Funds range in size from those controlling market participation measured in billions of dollars to those of less than one million. Mandates for these funds include, but are not limited to, the following strategies:

* The author wishes to acknowledge the assistance of his colleagues within the prime broker business and Corporate Risk Management group at Lehman Brothers, notably Peter D. Seed, James K. Cunningham III and Roger E. Canton, in the preparation of this work.

❑ global macro;
❑ fund of funds;
❑ arbitrage;
  ❑ statistical arbitrage;
  ❑ index arbitrage (ie, bond/bond index versus futures/futures equivalent, equity index/futures/futures equivalent);
  ❑ risk/merger/event arbitrage;
  ❑ convertible arbitrage;
  ❑ warrant arbitrage
❑ long only and/or short only;
❑ major market (ie, G10);
❑ emerging market;
❑ distressed debt/equity;
❑ country or region;
❑ sector; and
❑ risk factor (ie, volatility, correlation, term structure).

ORGANISATION

For an investment bank, risk management issues are typically addressed at both corporate and business product levels. A central feature of the corporate risk function is the management of risks at the aggregate level of activity between the investment bank and the hedge fund community that is the bank's client base. This function determines and monitors the scope of activity undertaken by hedge fund clients with the various businesses within the investment bank. Corporate level risk management is also involved in setting policy regards the nature and magnitude of the risks that the bank as a whole has an appetite for and is prepared to assume. Although these determinations can seem very high level, it is worth emphasising that the granularity of the analysis undertaken at the corporate and product levels may be similar; there are circumstances where it is appropriate that the focus reaches right down to the individual transaction level. The differentiation between corporate and product functions can be viewed as a difference of emphasis on related priorities. Prime broker businesses use their own risk management function to concentrate on the measurement, reporting and mitigation of risks specific to their activity. This concentration addresses internal control issues and so requires a control infrastructure specific to this purpose. The control infrastructure, in turn, can provide the foundation for a prime broker risk-monitoring/risk advisory service to the hedge fund client. A large element of this role concerns measurement and production of reports to match the client's needs and perspective; daily interaction with the client in the context of a proactive advisory role is also ensured.

RISK OVERVIEW

The risk associated with this business may appear unusual amidst the more vanilla activity that investment banks undertake, as it comprises a true hybrid of credit and market exposures in circumstances where there is a strong relationship between the two. The issue of the market risk of the portfolio of hedge fund transactions becomes most significant where the hedge fund defaults on the agreement between the parties. In these circumstances, the market risk characteristics of the portfolio, prevailing market conditions and the extent of any indebtedness determine the credit exposure to the defaulting fund. This dynamic therefore drives the choices of risk management technique. The estimation of risk focuses on infrequent events, such as the estimation of likelihood of fund default, or the combination of adverse market conditions and a number of client defaults overlaid by a model of orderly liquidation.

A technique often adopted by investment banks to mitigate credit risk exposure is to maintain a number of hedge fund relationships that yield a blend of trading strategies in a variety of products and markets. This introduces an element of dispersion into the market and credit risks assumed by the prime broker. It is very unlikely that all the funds a prime broker finances should experience extreme adverse movements in their positions and become unable to satisfy their margin requirements at the same time. Therefore, the effect of individual fund default is diluted. Naturally, this effect applies equally to the hedge fund, in the sense that its credit exposure to the prime broker can be mitigated through the adoption of multiple prime broker relationships.

Market risks are determined from an analysis of historical and prevailing market conditions and the asset mix in the portfolio. For portfolios of primarily linear assets, such as equities or government/high grade bonds, the dominant risk factors are liquidity, volatility and correlation. Where the portfolio contains concentrations within countries, sectors or issuers, the effect of these concentrations must be comprehended by any analysis. If the portfolio contains non-linear assets (such as convertibles, listed derivatives or perhaps structured transactions) with higher level or perhaps more subtle risk factors, the result is that the analysis increases in sophistication to account for the contribution of these risks. Examples of the risks that could be included are listed below.

❏ *Delta*. The long or short market exposure based on the appropriate netting methodology.
❏ *Gamma*. The rate of change of delta exposure with respect to change in underlying asset price.
❏ *Vega (Kappa)*. The rate of change in asset price with respect to an incremental change in volatility of underlying assets.

❑ *Nu*. The rate of change in vega with respect to underlying price movement.

❑ *Epsilon*. The rate of change of vega with respect to change in implied volatility.

❑ *Theta*. The rate of change in asset prices with respect to time.

❑ *Rho*. Rho risk can be considered as the combination of the risk summarised below under the rho heading.

❑ *Rate Rho*. The rate of change of asset price with respect to change in interest rate.

❑ *Dividend Rho*. The rate of change of asset price with respect to change in dividend actual or dividend yield.

❑ *Chi*. The rate of change of asset price with respect to change in currency exchange rate.

❑ *Omicron*. The rate of change in asset price with respect to change in credit spread.

❑ *Price Spread*. The effect of changing the spread between bid and offer prices.

❑ *Cross Gamma*. The effect of change in embedded correlation on asset price.

❑ *Correlation*. The effect of offsetting behaviour in groups of more than one asset.

❑ *Currency*. The effect of foreign-exchange rate movement on the value of an asset with respect to the base currency.

❑ *Recall*. The risk that an asset that is being borrowed or lent will be recalled by the lender or returned by the borrower.

❑ *Liquidity*. The effect of freely traded volumes on holding period.

The trading strategies currently undertaken by hedge funds characteristically exhibit different concentration weightings and mixes of the risk factors identified above. Techniques used to combine or separate risk factors (or risk aggregation/disaggregation techniques) are employed to develop understanding of the magnitude of potential loss resulting from each risk factor within either the context of a prime broker/hedge fund relationship or the inventory financed by the prime broker as a whole. The choice of methodology used is crucially important and has a direct bearing on the effectiveness of any such analyses. An appropriate choice can empower the prime broker to develop extremely cost-effective risk-mitigation strategies when circumstances dictate that they are necessary – eg, in adverse market conditions or when a hedge fund is experiencing funding liquidity problems. The prime broker can also gain an enhanced appreciation of appropriate margin rates and adjust accordingly, thus aiding the hedge fund's objective of maximising its yield on capital.

MARKET RISKS AND METRICS

Prime brokers frequently use the following techniques to assist them in their understanding of the market risks that are assumed in their relationship with hedge funds:

❏ value-at-risk (VAR);
❏ stress/scenario analysis;
❏ market liquidity; and
❏ funding liquidity.

The first three techniques are used to develop understanding of the behaviour of the inventory and to assess the size of the risk, whereas funding liquidity analysis delivers the prime broker's perspective on risk appetite.

The concept of VAR has become a widely applied and accepted measure within the industry. VAR aims to quantify expected losses with a probability measure over a defined period of time. The characteristics of this measure and the many techniques used to derive it are also well understood. Three approaches (and variations upon them) are most widely used:

❏ estimated variance/covariance;
❏ historical walk/simulation; and
❏ Monte Carlo simulation.

VAR estimates are often calibrated by backtesting with historical observations to confirm their predictive power. It is worth considering two aspects of the VAR estimate within the context of prime brokerage: the confidence level and the holding period (or time horizon). Both of these scalars have to reflect the nature of the relationship between the prime broker and the hedge fund. The holding period should be adjusted to reflect two considerations: the time that will elapse before a liquidation process can commence and the time that the liquidation process will take to complete. The confidence level should reflect estimates of the prevailing market conditions when a default/liquidation cycle occurs.

Many prime brokers recognise that VAR techniques should be augmented by other techniques, such as a stress/scenario analysis. These approaches are useful for portfolios with significant non-linear risk contributions, or those where critical risk factors exhibit characteristics in market conditions that prevail on an infrequent basis and are inadequately captured by inputs or assumptions in the VAR estimate. Stress tests are used to determine the consequence of user-defined perturbations on observed market characteristics such as correlation, volatility surfaces and credit spreads. Scenario tests aim to estimate potential losses associated with previously observed market events – eg, the 1998 credit crisis – by applying the changes observed in these situations to the portfolio under consideration.

Market liquidity measures redesigned to predict or model the availability of sufficient depth for the disposal or recovery of assets in that market in an orderly manner, such that any adverse effect on the price of those assets is insignificant. These techniques can range from simple impact analyses on an asset-by-asset basis, usually by reference to historical observations of market volume, to more complex approaches that seek to develop risk- or variance-reducing strategies for liquidation. The question is whether to liquidate as quickly as possible or to liquidate with the objective of minimising risk. For a portfolio of assets, the approach of liquidating as quickly as possible may lead to increased risks, for the characteristics of the portfolio that remains after highly liquid positions have been removed can have a less desirable risk profile than the original portfolio. Market liquidity analysis can be helpful in adjusting the holding period assumptions used in VAR estimates; or, it may result in modifications to asset valuations.

Funding liquidity analyses goes to the ability to finance asset positions and meet collateral calls (margin requirements) and other payment obligations to investors, credit providers and market counterparts. This issue is central to the relationship between the prime broker and the hedge fund, as each is concerned with prudent management of the assets that are leveraged by the relationship, and each endeavours to avoid a funding liquidity crisis. The steps that characterise such crises broadly conform to the following pattern.

1. The hedge fund experiences a loss or the withdrawal of a significant investor, or the prime broker decides to increase collateral requirements.
2. To meet collateral obligations or obligation to return funds to the investor, the hedge fund must liquidate positions to free up the necessary resources.
3. The market conditions prevailing at the time of the liquidation mean that there is insufficient liquidity within the market leading to a significant adverse price movement.
4. The significant price movement forces the fund into further forced liquidation in adverse market conditions.
5. The cycle accelerates until the amount of collateral raised through liquidation is insufficient to meet the fund's obligations.

Except in situations where a hedge fund is using the services of a single prime broker, the primary measure from the prime broker's perspective (ie, of resources available to the fund) is collateral placed to meet margin requirements, plus any excess in the fund's account(s). This collateral is generally described as the 'equity' of the fund and it will typically comprise cash or highly liquid G10 government securities. Equity may be augmented by unsecured credit lines available from third parties. This information can be supplemented by profit-and-loss tracking, particularly in circumstances where the prime broker is providing accounting services to the hedge fund. Therefore, the prime broker is able to detect – at least for the portion of the inventory that it is providing financing – trading losses that can be considered in the context of the fund's equity.

The following ratios of risk to equity provide a measure for controlling the level of margin requirement requested by the prime broker:

❏ value-at-risk/equity;
❏ stress risk/equity;
❏ scenario risk/equity; and
❏ market liquidation risk/equity.

In some markets, notably outside the US, the use of these ratios, or similar metrics, to determine margin requirements is increasing. Within the US, the regulatory environment associated with prime brokerage describes a rule-based approach to determining margin requirement.

CREDIT RISKS AND METRICS

The management and control of credit risks in the relationship between prime brokers and hedge funds represents one of the most challenging areas for the corporate credit function of investment banks. The hedge fund community is experiencing a potent combination of rapid growth and innovation. For these reasons, an independent credit control fulfils an important role. This role relates primarily to protecting the investment bank from the loss potential of hedge fund default situations. Secondarily, it prevents hedge funds from funding liquidity crises. The following aspects of the role ensure its effectiveness.

❏ Independence ensures that credit officers are removed from the commercial pressures associated with the business relationship between prime broker and hedge fund.
❏ Open relationships are maintained with hedge fund clients.
❏ Close working relationships exist with other control functions within the investment banks, such as legal, compliance, market risk control, operations and margin management.
❏ Close working relationships exist with the prime brokerage business.
❏ The role harbours the ability to assimilate quantitative and qualitative measures as inputs to decision-making (many of the metrics described within the previous section are used by corporate credit control).

In extreme market conditions, this control function is one of the main conduits for communication both within the investment bank and between the investment bank and hedge fund.

Corporate credit is involved at the inception of any relationship between prime broker and hedge fund. This phase of the relationship involves infor-mation-gathering and the assimilation of consequent data to those decision processes concerned with enabling and defining a financing relationship. The list below indicates some of the issues that are covered.

❏ Documentation:
  ❏ partnership agreement;
  ❏ offering memorandum/prospectus;
  ❏ investment advisory agreement;
  ❏ audited financial statements;
  ❏ quarterly interim financial reports (if available); and
  ❏ monthly performance summaries of returns and net asset values (NAV).
❏ General:
  ❏ contact person for documentation, financials, etc;
  ❏ use of sub-advisors (if any) and criteria for selection;
  ❏ maximum level of manageable assets;
  ❏ fee structure (management and incentive) – ie, whether a high-water mark is used;
  ❏ number of employees, breakdown of trading versus administrative;
  ❏ whether the fund is staffed to trade on a 24-hour basis;
  ❏ number of significant trading counterparties, top five relationships;
  ❏ counterparty selection criteria (credit rating, services offered, etc);
  ❏ any past or present criminal, civil or administrative proceedings;
  ❏ firm registrations (if any); and
  ❏ administrators.
❏ Counterparty corporate structure:
  ❏ domicile;
  ❏ investor base (ie, "accredited investors" only), major shareholders;
  ❏ capital structure;
  ❏ subscription and redemption policies (initial lock-up period); and
  ❏ legal form of the fund.
❏ Background of principals:
  ❏ depth of investing/trading experience;
  ❏ track record of managing funds;
  ❏ percent of personal net worth invested in fund or percent of fund capital;
  ❏ other business involvement (officerships, directorships, other partner-ships);
  ❏ principal registrations; and
  ❏ professional references (where appropriate).
❏ Trading strategies:
  ❏ permitted investments;
  ❏ example portfolios;

❏ targeted returns;
❏ portfolio diversification (average number of positions, correlation);
❏ number of major strategies, sub-strategies;
❏ markets traded;
❏ portfolio turnover;
❏ liquidity management (bank lines of credit, redemptions);
❏ use of leverage (limitations);
❏ discretionary versus systematic trading (if systematic, describe methodologies); and
❏ use of derivatives (hedging versus speculation), products used, and whether or not they hedge existing exposure or contribute to overall long or short positions.
❏ Management controls:
  ❏ investment decision-making process;
  ❏ individual decision authority levels and controls for sales and trading functions;
  ❏ research and analytical approach;
  ❏ stop-loss mechanisms (maximum daily loss);
  ❏ maximum percentage of capital in given strategy, market; and
  ❏ portfolio stress testing (impact of shifts in yield curve, decline in S&P, etc).
❏ Systems and reporting:
  ❏ risk management systems;
  ❏ depth and frequency of management reporting;
  ❏ back office infrastructure; and
  ❏ number and extent of other prime broker relationships.
❏ Performance:
  ❏ maximum drawdown; and
  ❏ against which benchmarks (if any) the fund's returns are measured.

When the business relationship is under way with a hedge fund, the corporate credit group establishes a monitoring, advisory and control relationship with the prime broker. The extent of acceptable credit exposure, whatever the source, is defined and the mechanisms for controlling this exposure are agreed (eg, the level of margin rates and risk concentration criteria). This role is enhanced by corporate credit's independent relationship with the hedge fund. Such a relationship typically includes follow-up reviews which may address changes in circumstance (eg, new funds or strategies), difficulties in timely resolution of margin payments, and trends identified in audited and unaudited reporting.

LEGAL RISKS

The main risk that the prime broker seeks to control through legal means is the closing-out process. This is the process whereby prime brokers seek to liquidate the positions of a customer that is insolvent, or has failed to meet a margin call, or is otherwise seriously in default of its obligations to the prime broker.

On such a liquidation, the prime broker must be certain that the subsequent obligations to and from the customer can be netted off against each other. The broker must rely on expert legal advice regarding the enforceability of netting when setting up and running its operations; this is particularly so when netting on insolvency. However, they must also be certain that it has the right to liquidate when it is desirable to do so. Equally, where the prime broker takes other forms of security, such as letters of credit, guarantees or charges over assets, it must satisfy itself that the security is both valid and effective, and that it can be relied upon in the circumstances of a liquidation.

One significant feature of prime-brokerage documentation is that it provides the prime broker with a wide discretion in setting margin rates and determining whether circumstances warrant a liquidation. That discretion should never be compromised either by them, acting in a way that is inconsistent with its rights under the documentation, or by negotiating away its discretion. An increasingly common exception to this arises where, for reasons of stable financial management and certainty, the hedge fund requires the prime broker to fix margin rates for a set time and requires notice before such rates can be changed. In agreeing to such a provision, the prime broker must exercise great care in setting conditions that must be met for the margin rate to remain fixed. Such conditions will include limits on concentrations in securities of a particular issuer, sector or country.

Documentation should also preserve the prime broker's unfettered discretion to mark-to-market the hedge fund's positions and to determine the existence and size of equity deficits (and, therefore, of margin calls), both on a trade and settlement date basis. It is essential to the proper operation and risk management of the hedge fund's account that there be no scope for disputes in relation to margin calls. Margin calls, once made, must be met by the hedge fund urgently, generally within one business day. This point seems obvious, but often in the negotiation of documentation, hedge funds will ask that this mark-to-market process is conducted by the prime broker in a "reasonable" fashion. At first blush, this would seem to be fair. However, because the courts are the arbiter of what is reasonable, such a requirement would open the margin call process to dispute and therefore delay. Delay in the meeting of margin calls is an unacceptable threat to the integrity of the risk management system.

Because the ultimate risk management tool at the disposal of the prime broker is the liquidation of the hedge fund's positions, prime brokerage documentation tends to emphasise the rights of the prime broker in such circumstances. Clearly, the prudent setting of margin rates and the monitoring and adjustment of those rates are important pre-conditions to successful liquidation. Equally important, however, is the requirement that the hedge fund should not have any ability to control the manner or timing of a liquidation (other than its failure to meet a margin call). The pricing and closing out of all positions must be effected by the prime broker through reference to independent and verifiable sources, and not, under any circumstances, by the hedge fund.

The development and increasing sophistication of financial products and services offered to hedge funds by prime brokers inevitably bring risk management function into closer contact with legal counsel. A recent example was the introduction of cross product netting, in which the prime broker nets its exposures to the hedge fund across a number of financial products, enabling the hedge fund to gain enhanced leverage by taking into account its equity across the product range. New services and products such as this place increased demands upon the risk manager and their counsel, and highlight the fact that risk management and legal professionals can each benefit by closer cooperation and a deeper appreciation of their respective disciplines.

FUTURE DEVELOPMENTS AND INNOVATIONS

Within many investment banks, prime brokerage has previously been the domain of the back office, where, in the absence of significant competition and with limited pressure on margins simple rule-based control processes used to be adequate. Recent years have shown that this situation has changed radically as more investment banks become interested in offering a prime brokerage product to the market. Technological innovation, such as the increasing use of the Internet as a forum for seamless interaction between hedge funds and prime brokers, is a driving force. In order to compete as a full range service provider, the investment bank must offer research and global product execution. This naturally leads to a demand for financing services through this new medium. Prime brokers are also growing from providers of leveraged finance to providers of a much wider range of services. The services on offer, as discussed here, most notably include risk management analyses. We should also anticipate, through the Internet, a more open asset borrowing and lending market, and the growth of markets that make the investment performance of hedge funds more visible and participation in these funds easier.

The hedge fund community is becoming larger, is attracting more capital, and hence is more influential within the markets. Institutional investors are seeking greater involvement in alternative investment vehicles as regulators around the world become comfortable with providing a domicile for hedge funds and prime brokers alike. There is also pressure for a standardisation of risk measures from fund-of-fund investors, where the issue of assembling risk-reporting from multiple prime brokers can inhibit asset allocation decisions.

The climate of innovation will lead prime brokers towards cutting edge risk management techniques for identifying the mechanisms through which risk factor concentrations are both measured and used for internal control purposes, and delivered to clients for their own use. This could be the basis for proposing and pricing hedging strategies that can be shared between service provider and client and which make the best use of capital.

Hedge funds are also looking for mechanisms to protect themselves from the effects of default by seeking principal protection guarantees from their prime brokers and margin rate protection during significant market events.

10

Operational Risk

Marcelo Cruz and Jonathan Davies[1]

UBS Warburg

Operational risk (OR) has earned considerable attention in the last four or five years in the wake of huge losses that took place at investment banks such as Barings and Daiwa. Yet, the fact is there is still no agreed industry definition of OR and if there is no agreed definition, how do banks identify it? To some institutions it is the risks not covered by market or credit risks. To the Basle Committee on Banking Supervision it is "the potential for unexpected losses to arise from inadequate systems, operational problems, breaches in internal controls, fraud or unforeseen catastrophes". It is also the losses that follow from acts undertaken (or neglected) in carrying out business activities. Thus, when a transaction is priced solely in terms of market and credit risks an important risk is missing from the product pricing. This can produce devastating financial consequences for a bank, an asset manager or a hedge fund.

From a banking perspective, OR measurement enables proper performance measures, including risk capital, to incorporate all risks. It is best determined by analysing an institution's historic internal loss information. This analysis will highlight risky business activities and assist management towards reducing this diverse category of risks.

The development of a quantitative model for measuring OR begins with modelling a database of operational loss cases. Each event should identify the loss amounts, the business activity responsible for the event and the risk indicators to prevent and prevent the event from occurring. Establishing and managing such a database is key to understanding the control environment in which an organisation operates. Investment banking losses result more often from processing a high volume of transactions, and will show up as interest payments to counterparts, fees and fines paid to exchanges. In contrast, retail banks will typically be more exposed to

[1] The views expressed in this article are those of the authors and do not necessarily reflect UBS Warburg or UBS AG views.

fraud, legal and liability problems and small claims arising from processing errors. The database will facilitate analysis for each business unit and for each potential loss-making activity.

Hedge funds and asset managers who employ sound operational risk management practices might demonstrate to investors that operations, in particular transaction processing and compliance activities, are being closely watched. Such practices protect an organisation and lower costs by reducing the number of operational errors. Some asset managers already publicise this to attract customers. It might only be a matter of time until the presentation of good operational risk standards become the standard.

OPERATIONAL RISK IN HEDGE FUNDS

The most publicised OR-related event in the fund management industry took place in 1996 in London. An asset manager at Morgan Grenfell Asset Management (MGAM) exceeded his limit in small cap shares and lost a considerable amount of money. This attracted considerable negative publicity and a severe fine from UK regulators. Though less regulated, hedge funds still suffer most of the same problems of traditional asset managers and some of those of investment banks. In general, traditional asset managers have a lower position turnover than hedge funds. Since hedge funds try to arbitrage the market they have a volume of transactions akin to those of an investment bank. Therefore, the potential for errors in transaction processing is greater and the resulting losses could affect the profitability of a transaction.

To better illustrate the hidden costs in operational risk consider the following example. Suppose a hedge fund FX trader bought US$100 million at £1.50 sterling and sold almost immediately at 1.5005. This resulted in a gain of US$50,000 profit for the transaction. When the transaction went to the back-office some of the trade details were incorrect and the hedge fund leg in one of the transactions was not settled. The transaction settled correctly three days later. Given that market practice allows the counterparty to fairly charge interest claims for these three days at 10% per annum (cost of funds plus penalty charges), the cost of the operational error was approximately US$82,000.00. What was a good transaction for the front desk actually resulted in a loss for the hedge fund of US$32,000.00! This situation happens with remarkable frequency and is often not apparent.

A robust operational risk measurement/management system will ultimately identify these types of errors by each individual trade and trader and will reveal both the frequency and severity of loss. The same procedure is applied to the other types of operational risk such as compliance, legal, liability, etc. Having a clear understanding of where, when and how they happen is the first step towards reducing these errors.

The regulators of the financial industry have woken up to these additional risks, both as a result of analysing the causes behind some of the major events but also as a consequence of changing the rules governing capital against market and credit risk. Needless to say there is currently a great deal of discussion between the financial institutions and the authorities on this subject.

STAGE OF REGULATORY DISCUSSIONS BETWEEN BANKS AND THE BASLE COMMITTEE

The Basle Committee, an organisation composed by the central bankers and regulators of the most developed countries, is currently redrafting the 1988 "Accord" that specifies the capital requirements of an individual financial institution and for the system as a whole. For the first time operational risk will be included in the framework. It is expected that the Accord will be reissued by the end of 2001.

During the last five years, the financial industry has evolved to finally acknowledge operational risk to be a meaningful risk category that could ultimately threaten the safety and stability of individual financial institutions. These risks need to be supported by an appropriate level of economic and regulatory capital. However, in order to be effective and to avoid some of the shortcomings that have hindered other regulatory capital frameworks, financial institutions believe that the regulatory capital rules governing operational risk must adhere to certain principles, such as the two below.

1. Regulatory capital requirements should be limited to those activities or risks that pose a meaningful threat to individual institutions or constitute a systemic "safety and soundness" risk for the financial industry. Therefore, categories such as business, strategic, reputation and certain other risks should be exempt from regulatory capital requirements altogether. While these risks and other risks do exist and require economic capital, there is no meaningful evidence that such risks pose any idiosyncratic or systemic threat to depositors in financial institutions.
2. The identification of a series of evolutionary stages for operational risk capital assessment recognises that financial institutions are at different stages with regard to operational risk management. It is necessary to ensure that all financial institutions will be able to meet regulatory requirements, and still provide an incentive for all financial institutions to manage operational risks more proactively.

Proposed stages of an evolutionary process

There are four stages currently being considered by various regulatory and industry bodies. The financial industry believes they could meet both regulatory requirements and financial institutions' needs.

Stage 1: Basic indicator approach

This is the most simplistic approach to the "measurement" of operational risk. Capital is calculated by applying a set of factors ("risk rates") to general "risk indicators", such as revenue or total assets. The selection of both risk rates and risk indicators are determined by regulators. We can represent this in the following formula:

Required capital = (Risk indicator 1 × Risk rate 1)
                 + (Risk indicator 2 × Risk rate 2)

Example:

Required capital = Assets*α + Revenue*β

Stage 2: Standard approach

This is an elaboration of the basic indicator approach, with the key differences being that the standard approach distinguishes between different business lines, with risk indicators selected to reflect the underlying driver of activity in each business line. Key features of this approach are listed below.

❏ A financial institution is divided into a limited number of standardised business lines.
❏ Capital charge is based on a percentage (risk rate) of a risk indicator for each business line.
❏ Risk indicators are selected to reflect, as far as possible, the volume of the central activity in each business line. For example, total turnover might be selected as an indicator for investment banking.
❏ Regulators determine appropriate risk indicators and risk rates in consultation with the industry.
❏ Individual capital charges for each line of business are summed to arrive at a charge for each financial institution.
❏ The total charge could be subject to an additional capital charge to reflect "other", less quantifiable risks, at the discretion of the regulators. This charge might be applied to "outlier" financial institutions only. This includes those firms perceived to have extraordinarily exceptional or poor control environments.

We can represent this approach in the following formula:

Required capital = $\sum_{i=1}^{n}$ [Risk indicator [i] × Risk rate [i]]

Stage 3: Internal risk-based approach

The key distinguishing feature of the internal risk-based approach is that financial institutions can determine the risk rates applied to each risk indicator based on their own internal loss data. The freedom of banks to determine their own risk rates is subject to the regulators approval, based partly on the availability of historical data to validate the rates chosen.

Regulators may impose an additional capital charge if the reality deviates significantly from the risk rates applied.

This internal risk-based approach is further classified into the following two categories according to the way the business lines and risk indicators are determined.

1. *Basic*: business lines and risk indicators are both determined by regulators. Banks are only able to set the "risk rate".
2. *Advanced*: business lines and risk indicators are both determined by each financial institution, in addition to the "risk rate".

The key features of the internal risk-based approaches are compared with those of the standard approach below.

❏ Financial institutions are divided into a more granular number of business lines than under the standardised approach.
❏ Each business line may have multiple risk indicators, each of which will be associated with its own risk rate. The base capital charge for each business line is the sum of these products.
❏ The total capital charge for the financial institution is the sum of the charges for each line of business.
❏ Capital charges for each line of business may be adjusted to reflect the perceived quality of the control environment, as in the standard approach.
❏ As with the standard approach, the total charge could be subject to an additional capital charge to reflect "other", less quantifiable risks, at the discretion of the regulators
❏ The individual capital charges for each line of business are summed up. We can represent this approach in the following formula:

$$\text{Risk capital} = \sum_{i=1}^{n} \sum_{j=1}^{m} (\text{Risk indicator } [i, j] \times \text{Risk rate } [i, j])$$

Where: n = Number of business lines, and
m = Number of risk types

At the fourth stage, financial institutions will be able to establish an operational value-at-risk (VAR) based on their own internal database and modelling.

MODELLING CRITERIA

To establish a defendable VAR for OR, a methodology is required that combines statistical/actuarial methods with loss data to estimate the distributions of severity and frequency. When combined with econometric techniques the results can be linked to measures of the environment. This can form the basis for scenario analysis.

Our broad requirements are that the results of the model must be easily understood, requiring no expert statistical interpretation which means, for example, that it must be computationally efficient and require no elaborate simulation studies. If we could mimic the VAR measures widely used in market and credit risk computations, so much the better. A financial institution might want to sort its losses into "expected loss" to be absorbed by net profit, "unexpected loss" to be covered by risk reserves and "stress loss" requiring core capital or hedging. The "expected loss" per transaction can easily be added to the premium charged. Therefore, if a business unit handles 5,000 transactions in a typical week, with weekly "expected losses" estimated at US$82,000 – US$16.40 per transaction would cover them. It is the rare but extreme stress losses with which the institution must be most concerned. Extreme value methods can be used to model these losses.

EXTREME VALUE METHODOLOGY

The normal distribution that forms the basis of much of statistical inference in risk management does not accommodate a loss distribution showing a thicker upper tail. The lognormal distribution has historically performed this role in econometrics theory and the Weibull distribution for reliability modelling. Because of the paucity of extreme observations we cannot hope to model with any precision the entire upper tail distribution (the excess distribution) despite its importance for understanding aggregate loss. Therefore, we restrict ourselves to estimating only extreme quantiles, e.g. 95-99%. This corresponds to market risk VAR that uses a 99% confidence interval to set a maximum limit on potential losses.

A typical operational losses database will present a distribution that is not Gaussian. In general, an operational risk database is composed of a few very large events and several smaller ones. Nevertheless, for some businesses, a transaction processing back office in an investment bank for example, due to the huge number of transactions processed daily, a quasi-normal distribution of losses could appear. For risk management purposes, we are interested in knowing the behaviour of the tail of this curve (or the maximum losses). The question to be answered by the risk manager is: "How much economic capital should I allocate to a particular business to protect against an eventual operational catastrophe?". The answer comes from analysing the distribution of losses which arise from extreme value distributions.

The application of extreme value theory (EVT), as the theory that supports this type of distribution is known is still at an embryonic stage in risk management. Some recent work with application to engineering, meteorological and insurance problems can be seen in Embrechts *et al* (1997). Suppose that X can denote the operational losses on the database provided by a bank. Let $X_1, X_2, ..., X_n$ be the monetary losses observed in a certain period. Extremes are defined as maxima and minima of the n ordered random variables $X_1, X_2, ..., X_n$. Let $X_{1,n}, ..., X_{n,n}$ be the order statistics of this series, with $X_{1,n}$ denoting the highest value (the maximum) observed during the period; $X_{2,n}$, the second largest, and so on. To find a non-degenerate limiting distribution, the maximum random variable $Y = X_{1,n}$ is standardised by location, scale and shape parameters, chosen to give a proper distribution of standardised extremes. We therefore focus on the asymptotic behaviour of the extremes.

Three important extreme value distributions are those defined by Frechet, Gumbel and Weibull (see Cruz *et al*, 1998). A convenient representation of these is given in the GEV (generalised extreme value) distribution. This three parameter distribution, $F_{\xi,\mu,\psi}$, arises as the limit distribution of normalised maxima of iid (independent, identically distributed) random variables. It can be represented (in the three-parameter form) as follows:

For the random variable $Y = X_{1,n}$, we let

$$Z = (Y - \mu)/\psi \text{ and } z = (y - \mu)/\psi$$

where μ and ψ are location and scale parameters respectively, then

$$P(Y \leq y) = F_{\xi,\mu,\psi}(y) = F_{\xi,0,1}(z) = \exp\{ - (1 + \xi z)^{-1/\xi} \}, 1 + \xi z \geq 0$$

where ξ is the shape parameter. Letting $\xi \rightarrow 0$ which gives the Gumbel distribution; $\xi > 0$ the Frechet distribution, and $\xi < 0$ the Weibull distribution.

We might have chosen to work with any heavy-tailed model, but selected the GEV distribution, which encompasses the distributions (Weibull, Frechet and Gumbel) which arise as limit distributions for the largest observation in a sample. The estimation procedure takes the largest loss observed in each of the preceding 12 months, and obtains the parameters of the GEV best fitted by these 12 values. Estimation procedures are described in Embrechts *et al*, (1997). The results can be updated daily, weekly or monthly on a rolling 12-month basis. The estimated 100p% quantile is called the maximum amount at risk at confidence level p (MaRp). In view of the heavy-tail characteristics, a very high quantile such as 99% can give very high figures, suggesting an economic capital allocation beyond that which would be deemed appropriate, so the 95% quantile might prove more suitable. The table below shows values similar to those that were obtained from a typical fraud database of a clearing bank handling millions of transactions per day, with about twenty frauds in excess of £100,000 sterling attempted each year, and only one massive fraud over a period of five years.

The single extreme case is seen to distort the shape of the fitted distribution. However, insurance premiums are similarly dependent on the previous year's claims history. Simulations (see Embrechts *et al*, 1997) demonstrate the problems of estimation for heavy-tailed distributions even when the exact model is known and there are plenty of data. Tests of fit for any particular heavy-tailed distribution would lack power to detect a lack of fit, as was seen in Cruz *et al* (1998).

Table 1 Maximum amount at risk (£million sterling) at year-end using 95% and 99% quantiles, with the estimated annual net premium (£million sterling) for stress loss.

Year	1992	1993	1994	1995	1996
Loss frequency	586	454	485	658	798
Stress loss frequency	21	17	17	19	21
MAR 95%	2.9	5.9	14.0	1.1	5.1
99%	12.9	29.2	122.9	3.3	28.1
Net premium at					
95%	0.10	0.22	0.49	0.03	0.13
99%	0.46	1.09	4.31	0.10	0.74

HEDGING OPERATIONAL RISK

The development of better hedging possibilities for OR is one of the most important consequences in the recent advancement of quantitative techniques in this area. In the near future, it will be possible to hedge any category of operational risk. Until now, hedging has been limited to simple insurance with limited cover offered. With the development of new products such as OR securitisation or OR derivatives these risks can be more effectively protected whilst offering new and exciting products to the capital markets. These products would offer enhanced yields with a pay-out subject to risks that are uncorrelated with other market instruments, (see Cruz 1999). As such, they could be attractive investments to hedge funds.

CONCLUSION

The development of OR measurement techniques will bring the financial industry to a new level of control by reducing costs and risk in processing transactions, and by making the hedging alternatives cheaper and more diverse.

BIBLIOGRAPHY

Cruz, M., 1999, "Taking Risk to Market", *Risk*, Operational Risk Supplement, November.

Cruz, M., R. Coleman and G. Salkin, 1998, "Modelling and Measuring Operational Risk", *Journal of Risk* 1(1), pp. 63-72; reprinted in *Extremes and Integrated Risk Management*, 2000, (London: Risk Books).

Embrechts, P., (ed), 2000, *Extremes and Integrated Risk Management* (London: Risk Books).

Embrechts, P., C. Kluppelberg and T. Mikosch, 1997, "Modelling Extremal Events for Insurance and Finance", in *Applications of Mathematics* 33 (Berlin: Springer-Verlag).

Part III

Perspectives from the
Hedge Fund Managers

11

Risk Management for the Asset Management Firm

D. Sykes Wilford, Erik Norland and José M. Quintana

CDC Investment Management Corp

Financial theory tells us that earning high returns and controlling risk are part of the same process. Yet although sophisticated investors have long known the value of high risk-adjusted returns, it took recent problems at Long Term Capital Management, Tiger, Quantum and other trading operations to refocus the asset management industry on risk management. Gone are the days when asset management firms differentiated themselves largely on the basis of how much return they could earn. These days, the focus has shifted to risk-adjusted returns. Of course, as cynics say, the financial industry only learns after losing large amounts of money. But while the asset management industry has relearned the importance of the words "risk management", what will really differentiate firms are their respective methods of interpreting and applying risk management.

For example, Wall Street first adopted duration as a standard tool in the early 1980s, after the Federal Reserve Board's October massacres of 1979 and 1980, which sent interest rates to record highs in short order and led to large losses on bank balance sheets. The convexity lesson was learned after a well-known trader at a large brokerage house figured his duration correctly in a trade dividing securities into interest-only strips and principal-only strips, yet neglected convexity – an oversight which cost the firm more than US$200 million. Consequently, convexity became the watchword of the mid-1980s. Further crises led to the development of options-theoretic approaches to risk management, until a new word appeared in the late 1980s: correlation. It seemed that each crisis led to a new mantra, and that each new mantra was labelled "risk management". It also appeared that each new tool had been around for a long time: duration since the 1930s, correlation and VAR analysis from the 1950s (in financial terms), options theory and convexity from the 1960s and 1970s (Wilford, 1995).

Even the exact definition of risk management is nebulous, the term being frequently used in different firms to mean different things. Many, if not most, institutions now employ very sophisticated models to evaluate the risks of their portfolios. In fact, many even have a department called "risk management." Ironically, while the term "risk management" implies action, the departments that use VAR models and scenario tests to provide very important services to the firm actually do very little by way of *managing risk*. Rather, they *measure risk*. "Risk management" departments tend to be divorced from the decision-makers who actually allocate risk, their role being more akin to an accounting department which independently verifies the traders' P&L estimates; risk management departments provide upper management with an honest, unbiased account of risk levels. However, relying upon such departments to manage risk can be injurious to portfolios because measurement is, quite simply, not the same thing as management.

As in previous crises, the most recent round of manager explosions and implosions will give rise to "new" risk measures – measures that were very likely considered in financial literature years ago. Managing risk is more than just measuring the degree of risk inherent in portfolios that have

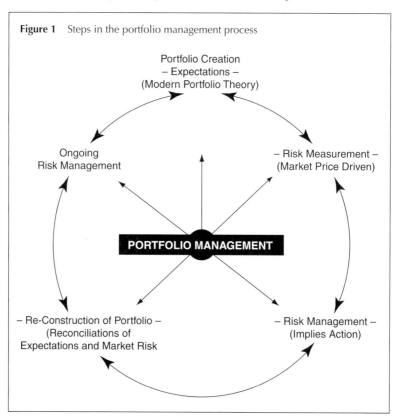

Figure 1 Steps in the portfolio management process

Portfolio Creation
– Expectations –
(Modern Portfolio Theory)

Ongoing
Risk Management

– Risk Measurement –
(Market Price Driven)

PORTFOLIO MANAGEMENT

– Re-Construction of Portfolio –
(Reconciliations of
Expectations and Market Risk

– Risk Management –
(Implies Action)

already been put into place: it entails using certain risk measures to allocate risk optimally among different assets, while using other types of risk measures to monitor exposures and make refinements. There is, unfortunately, no one single risk allocation process that can be applied to all types of investment strategies.

By now, nearly all asset managers and sophisticated investors are familiar with the basic tool of allocating risk and modern portfolio theory. And yet, while they are keenly aware of the potential benefits of modern portfolio theory and diversification, the theory is surprisingly difficult to apply correctly. The goal of this chapter is to provide a guide for asset managers and firms who manage the risks of their investments both in the initial portfolio construction process and on a continual basis for existing portfolios.

STAGE 1: PORTFOLIO CREATION – A SEQUENTIAL PROCESS
Perhaps the first question that those responsible for the asset management firms should ask their portfolio managers is, "Where do you expect to generate return and in what areas must you take risk in order to generate it?" Portfolio managers should, of course, be allowed and encouraged to take risk in their respective areas of expertise, while being strongly discouraged from taking risks outside those areas. For example, a manager of a mortgage backed security (MBS) portfolio may be excellent at choosing which securities to purchase and which ones to avoid, but will probably be unable to forecast interest rate levels, the risk from prepayments, or changes in the shape of the yield curve. The asset management firm should restrict the ability of the MBS portfolio manager to take risks in the areas that are not part of their expertise or which, more generally, may be beyond the control of any portfolio manager.

Much the same can be said of domestic equity managers. There are a variety of reasons why most equity managers chronically underperform on benchmarks. One key reason is that they charge fees, but most of the other reasons boil down to managers taking risk in areas outside their skill set, attempting to time markets and holding too much cash and big industry bets, as well as over investing in small companies (Putnam, 1997, 1998).

Once an asset management firm has determined the investment universe of a manager, bearing the manager's strengths and weaknesses in mind, it is time to develop a process for making allocation decisions. When creating a portfolio, one decides how to allocate risk. Allocating risk requires a more specific set of tools than when merely measuring it for informational purposes. Risk measures used for allocating risk ought to be forward-looking estimates of return, forecasting accuracy and the correlation of forecasting errors. If one is merely measuring risk, then it is perfectly acceptable to use historical, retrospective information. This is not the case when attempting to allocate risk. Historical VAR indicates only how volatile markets have been in the past; it does not provide managers with an accurate indication of their forecasting accuracy. This is a subtle, but crucial, difference (see Smithson, Smith and Wilford, 1995, for a simple discussion of this principle). Table 1 summarises these differences.

When Harry Markowitz developed modern portfolio theory, he was very specific about the inputs needed to construct efficient portfolios (see Markowitz, 1987). These are:

❏ expected returns;
❏ forecast accuracy, as measured by the standard deviation of the forecasting errors; and
❏ correlation among the forecasting errors.

These inputs are very different from those related to historical VAR. Markowitz recommended measuring the difference between expectations and outcomes rather than historical averages and outcomes, using standard deviation as the measure of volatility (see Figure 2). For example, imagine that one has been able to forecast the return of a volatile asset with perfect accuracy. One's insight into that asset's return is flawless. From the perspective of Modern Portfolio Theory (MPT), says that investors ought to be concerned with maximising risk-adjusted returns and that they can create such a risk-return optimal portfolio with three mathematical inputs: expected return, forecasting error and the correlation of forecasting errors. One should be willing to take a large position in a market where one's views have been very accurate. However, using a historical measure of risk, it would appear that, because the asset had been volatile historically, such a portfolio position would be very risky. By the same token, we could also view the opposite example: imagine a model that made extreme forecasts for a low volatility asset. In this case, a historical measure would tell us to go ahead and take a large position because, historically, there has been little risk. In reality, our understanding of the behaviour of this asset has not been accurate, meaning we probably should take a more modest position.

Table 1 Different definitions, different tools

	Risk Measurement	Risk Management
Definitions	The act of determing how a portfolio will react to movements in the prices of the securities that it holds.	The act of allocating risk among different assets in the investment universe, based upon the strength of one's insights.
Tools	Historical value-at-risk (VAR) Monte Carlo Scenery Analysis	Estimates of expected return Forecast accuracy (variance of forecast errors) Correlation of forecasting errors

Markowitz is very insistent that the process of portfolio construction should include the process for generating expected returns. As such, creating the expected returns, error estimates and error correlation estimates are all part of the same process and should be conducted simultaneously (Quintana, Putnam and Wilford, 1998a). Quantifying these three inputs is no easy task and usually requires a quantitative model. The expected return part of the process is not especially difficult: most investors have some idea of expected returns before they invest. The risk component, however, presents a significant challenge. Human beings are notoriously poor at calculating probabilities and tend to be too confident in their forecasts (Buede and Watson, 1987).

Correlation also poses a problem. A manager with only two or three assets in their portfolio can usually keep track of correlation quite well. However – and this is unfortunate for people who do not like using computers – the number of correlations one must keep in mind grows quadratically with the number of assets in the portfolio. With three assets, there will be three correlations. With 30 assets, there will be 420. On the

---

Figure 2   The recommendations of Harry Markowitz

What Harry Markowitz did say:

Expected return of an asset, i is: $\mu_i = E(r_i)$

Variance of an asset i is: $V(r_i) = \sigma_{ii} = E(r_i - \mu_i)^2$

Covariance of assets i and j is: $\sigma_{ij} = E[(r_i - \mu_i)(r_j - \mu_j)]$

Note that Markowitz explicitly relates volatility and covariance to expectations of returns. From this point of view, they are part of a seamless whole and so for the purpose of portfolio construction t not be calculated simultaneously.

What Harry Markowitz did not say:

Variance of an asset i is:

Covariance of assets i and j is: $\sigma_{ij} = E[(r_i - \bar{r}_i)(r_j - \bar{r}_j)]$

Where $\bar{r}$ is the average historical return of an asset i or j.

Note that Markowitz never defines variance and covariance in terms of differences between outcomes and historical averages, although he does not explicitly say that this is incorrect. And yet this is how many people in the financial industry apply (or, in our opinion, misapply) his theory with regard to constructing portfolios.

Source: Markowitz, 1987.

---

other hand, computers do an excellent job of dealing with probability, assuming that they have been properly programmed to do so. Consequently, the critical importance of proper programming cannot be overstated (Norland and Wilford, 2000).

Given that modern portfolio theory is inherently quantitative and requires proper inputs based in a sophisticated model, it follows that managers employing it blend their judgement and expertise with the discipline of a quantitative model when allocating risk. Although judgement with quantitative discipline can be put to use in the portfolio creation process in many different ways, the following logical steps are incorporated within such a process.

1. The development of an initial quantitatively driven portfolio.
2. A managerial review of the quantitative portfolio with special attention to risk and opportunities outside the models' range of information and interpretative ability.
3. The revision of the quantitative portfolio to reflect additional risks and opportunities.
4. The re-optimisation of the portfolio, given revisions to the risk estimates or the expected returns.

When developing the initial quantitative portfolio, it is important to keep in mind what Arnold Zellner terms the "KISS principle" (Zellner, 2000). Zellner's version of the KISS principal differs from the "Keep It Simple Stupid" acronym with which most of us are familiar, as he points out that simple and stupid are sometimes one and the same. Instead, Zellner's version of KISS reads, "Keep It Sophisticatedly Simple." Models that are sophisticated and simple can work well in financial markets; models that are simple and stupid nearly always fail.[1]

This kind of MPT-driven process has the potential to work well for managers who trade in liquid markets, where time series' of historical data on securities are easily available. Managers who deal in less liquid markets such as corporate bonds, mortgages or emerging markets may find it more difficult to apply the theory correctly. Nevertheless, these managers will still want to achieve high expected returns per unit of risk. This will require them to develop metrics of risk that are more specific to the types of securities in which they are dealing. But the goal of optimally allocating risk remains the same.

Once the manager decides upon a final portfolio, it is time to measure the risk of the portfolio from different perspectives.

STAGE 2: RISK MEASUREMENT

With the portfolio creation process completed, the manager must focus on managing the risk of the existing portfolios. First, the manager must begin by asking what the risks are, both obvious and hidden, and what sorts of information are necessary to evaluate them. A variety of questions can be asked.

❏ What is the expected volatility of the portfolio?
❏ What is the expected contribution of each position to portfolio risk?
❏ How will the portfolio perform if prices in a particular asset class change?
❏ How much will overall risk increase if the risk of an individual position doubles or triples?
❏ Will the volatility of the portfolio increase or decrease in the event of a crisis in which correlations within an asset class or between asset classes change significantly from their average?
❏ Could the portfolio withstand a liquidity crisis in which correlation within an asset class approaches 1 and changes rapidly between asset classes, as in August, 1998?
❏ Will the portfolio return be sharply negative if there is a collapse in a particular asset class, such as equities in October, 1987, or bonds in early 1994?

The three most commonly used tools associated with the measuring and managing of existing risks are historical VAR, scenario analysis and Monte Carlo simulations. Each has specialised uses, advantages and limitations.

VAR

Based upon a variance-covariance measure of risk similar to the one adopted by modern portfolio theory, VAR is the most widely used tool, being especially appropriate for liquid assets with time series of historical prices. VAR often involves calculating volatility over the last 100 trading days but could, in principal, be used with other intervals, such as weeks or months, and focus on longer time periods. VAR excels at shock-testing portfolios and with easy manipulation shows how portfolios might behave if correlations change or volatility rises.

Before discussing the potential benefits of shock-testing portfolios, it is important to note that VAR does have limitations. First, it does not function well in illiquid markets in which time series of prices may not be reliable, eg, mortgage markets. Second, it will tend to underestimate risk significantly prior to a crisis and over-estimate risk after a crisis. Third, using VAR calculations based on daily information may be misleading for assets that trade in different time zones. When markets are not open simultaneously, correlation estimates tend to break down and average risk may be improperly estimated.

For hedge fund managers, one of the more useful exercises is to "shock" the portfolio by assuming the worst from normal markets. For instance, observe what happens to the calculated VAR, assuming that all the volatilities within an asset class double. How does the portfolio behave? How much does the calculated VAR increase? It is also useful to allow correlation with an asset class to go towards unity. When this assumption is reflected by the variance-covariance matrix, does the risk of the total portfolio increase or decrease? In a well-constructed long-short portfolio, risk can actually fall under these circumstances. Among long-only portfolios, however, risk often soars under these assumptions.

Events like these seem to occur much more frequently than the normal distribution, upon which VAR analysis is based, would predict. For some managers, it may be useful to test the opposite assumption, that correlations can approach -1 between risky assets on the one hand, and assets that have traditionally been safe havens during flights to quality on the other. This assumption could be useful for managers who take positions in both equities and government debt, because during a crisis, bond markets often rally sharply as equity prices tumble. With the benefit of hindsight, such an analysis might have been useful for fixed income portfolio managers in 1998, when many of them were long lower-quality debt and short government debt, which tend to move in opposite directions when equity markets lose confidence. Shocks of this type allow managers to identify weaknesses in the construction of the portfolio, while providing the information necessary to take appropriate action in the case of a crisis (Putnam and Wilford, 1998).

Scenario analysis
Scenario analysis enables managers to test the returns of their portfolios in various hypothetical market events. These are especially useful for managers for whom VAR is difficult to use or inappropriate. Scenario tests supply answers to questions such as, "How would my bond portfolio perform if the events of 1994 were to be repeated?" or "What would my long-mortgage, short-treasury portfolio do in a re-run of August, 1998?" The chief limitation of scenario testing is the manager's imagination. But sadly, managers, like models, rarely anticipate crises; if they were to, crises would not occur because they would have been factored into expectations in advance.

Monte Carlo simulations
Monte Carlo simulations can be used for any kind of asset, but are especially useful in estimating the risk of options strategies and other strategies where historical time series are difficult to come by and payouts are complex non-linear functions. Here, too, the strategy's usefulness is dependent upon the manager's assumptions.

Having applied the appropriate measures of risk to an existing portfolio, shock-testing or scenario testing can help to expose additional weaknesses. The manager needs to assign a probability to such outcomes. If it seems that such outcomes are extremely unlikely, the manager may decide not to adjust the portfolio. However, if such a crisis situation begins to emerge, the manager may then be able to devise an action plan to cope with it.

STAGE 3: RISK MANAGEMENT – AN ONGOING PROCESS

To convert the above information into decisions, the asset manager must evaluate these scenarios and their implications, and estimate what type of risk is most likely to occur at which time. Having identified risk, the manager must then place a value on it and decide what instruments to use to reduce the risk.

If a portfolio has been constructed with the aid of quantitative tools, it is often helpful to view changes in the portfolio in the context of the original set of assumptions used. Here, it is important to remember which portfolio positions are intended to generate returns and which are intended to reduce risk as hedges. For obvious reasons, it is important when reducing high-expected return positions to pay close attention to the possibility that offsetting hedges may also need to be reduced.

Action requires separating theoretical exercises. Even the most well-constructed risk management systems in the world will not protect a portfolio. That is the manager's job. Risk management implies action. The manager has identified a real or potential crisis, has a good handle upon what generates the risk, can evaluate the types of events necessary to create these outcomes, and possesses information about the sources of expected returns in the original portfolio.

Armed with these data, the manager then needs to start making decisions. Is the average risk too high? Are these scenarios where portfolio losses would be too great? Would sudden changes in volatility lead to unacceptable levels of portfolio risk? With this information, the manager can decide what, if anything, to change.

STAGE 4: RE-CONSTRUCTION OF THE PORTFOLIO –
RECONCILIATIONS OF EXPECTATIONS AND MARKET RISK

At this juncture, the portfolio manager has the information needed to make decisions. He knows the risks under varying circumstances; he recognises the places where average historical measures of volatility and correlation differ from measurements of his own forecast errors; and he has good information about where he expects to make and lose money in the existing portfolio. These data can lead to several types of action.

❏ No action need be taken. Let the portfolio stand because in crisis situations the portfolio behaves well. For the manager of long-short portfolios who has used effective optimisation as outlined above, this will often be the case. The manager can still sleep at night without making any adjustments.

❏ No action need be taken but a watchful eye must be kept for a certain set of events. The risk measurement process will, if executed correctly, define areas where the potential for highly volatile swings will occur. In this case, the manager is made aware of and should focus on the events that presage these possibilities, knowing what prior events are unacceptable. Is it an announcement? What date could it occur? Is it an emerging market crisis? And so on. Often this is the most important part of the whole process. With the risk analysis having identified key events, this portfolio will likely be acceptable as long as a careful outlook is maintained for these critical factors.

❏ Often the portfolio can be adjusted so that the expected return does not change significantly – marginal analysis capability is critical in this adjustment. As a result, the most offensive positions, which would be damaging during a crisis, are mitigated. This may be accomplished directly by changing those positions under the watchful eye of the quantitative process, or indirectly, by adding or changing other positions that have an offsetting effect during a crisis but which don't significantly alter the portfolio's performance, if the month or week or quarter proceeds as expected.

❏ The risk of the portfolio can be massively changed. Perhaps, after the analysis, the risk-reward ratios simply do not justify taking those risks. In this case, large portfolio operations may be needed, including moving to the benchmark or cash until alternatives have been identified.

Most managers usually confront a mix of the above scenarios. In making adjustments to portfolios, two factors are critical:

1. the quantitative systems for understanding the implications of changes need to be in hand and utilised; and,
2. the manager must have a profound understanding of the relationship of his quantitative system to the developments in the market that are of concern.

One of the above without the other is very dangerous and can lead to unintended consequences for the manager – he may attempt to decrease one set of risks, but unknowingly create others.

STAGE 5: CONTINUING RISK MANAGEMENT

Even after the portfolio is up and running, the risk management process does not end, especially in situations where the portfolio has been identified as being particularly susceptible to shocks. The following question must always be in the manager's mind: "Is X occurring and must I do Y to reduce the odds of a very costly scenario developing?" Marginal risk analysis is very useful in this situation, as it enables the manager to identify trades that could be implemented to mitigate deleterious effects should an unfavourable scenario arise. Performing marginal risk analysis also allows the manager to measure the cost of these trades in expected return or expected risk should the events fail to occur. Again, having tools available to accomplish this analysis is critical. Additionally, marginal risk analysis enables the manager to keep track of both positions intended as hedges and positions expected to generate return. If one decides to reduce risk in positions that are designed to increase return, such an analysis might also reveal the need to rein in some of the hedges as well (Putnam, Quintana and Wilford, 2000).

In a sense, the portfolio management process is about ongoing risk management from the time the portfolio is created until it is reset again. Therefore, it is important for the management team to keep abreast of news items that could impact the portfolio. Often, new events arise quickly and there may not be time to re-run portfolio construction models or conduct sophisticated risk analyses. Still, action may be necessary. Marginal risk analysis, as mentioned above, can help the manager make changes quickly, in a way that does not compromise the integrity of the portfolio.

CONCLUSION

Undoubtedly, there will be more crises in the future, leading to the implementation of risk management techniques currently unused by most practitioners. That does not mean, however, that those risk management instruments do not yet exist. Diligent managers can keep one step ahead by maintaining an active research effort and refining risk models, thereby tailoring them more closely to the reality of markets.

Transparency is also likely to become more important for clients. Investors may receive some degree of comfort from knowing that their managers employ state-of-the-art risk management systems. Nonetheless, they might derive even more comfort if the manager provides fast access to portfolio allocations and risk estimates. With the Internet, a number of systems are coming on-line that will allow investors to do just that. Such systems may also reduce the need for manual provision of such information, for investors will be able to simply access it over the Internet.

---

1   Sometimes, when practitioners apply modern portfolio theory incorrectly, their optimisers yield bizarre looking portfolios with extreme allocations, known as corner solutions. These managers typically then apply various constraints to limit position sizes. The need to apply such restrictions is indicative of problems with the inputs for the optimiser, not with the concept of applying mean-variance optimisation itself. Such restrictions do not usually reduce risk. In fact, they sometimes have the perverse effect of increasing risk, because managers have to take more aggressive positions in other areas. Thus, portfolio constraints nearly always have the effect of reducing risk-adjusted returns (see Putnam, 1997 or

Quintana and Wilford, 1998. For a more in-depth discussion of the potential benefits and drawbacks of using quantitative systems to construct portfolio and to measure risk, please see Norland and Wilford, 2000).

We also believe that quantitative models are likely to better apply to financial markets if they are adaptive as well as integrated. Adaptive models have the advantage of assuming that volatility as well as factor sensitivities change through time. We believe they can help to reduce the problem with fat tails (Quintana and Norland, 1998).

BIBLIOGRAPHY

Buede, D.M., and S.R. Watson, 1987, *Decision Synthesis* (Cambridge University Press).

Markowitz, H.M., 1987, *Mean-Variance Analysis in Portfolio Choice and Capital Markets* (Oxford: Blackwell).

Norland, E., and D.S. Wilford, 2000, "All Tooled Up", *Hedge Funds Risk and Reward*, Spring, pp. 19–25.

Putnam, B., 1997, 1998, "Why active managers underperform the benchmark", *Global Investor*, December/January 1998), pp. 62–4.

Putnam, B., 1998, "The Flaws in the US Asset Allocation Model", *Global Investor*, March, p. 42.

Putnam, B., and D.S. Wilford, 1998, "When Correlations Converge Towards One", *Global Investor*, July, pp. 46–8.

Putnam, B., J.M. Quintana, and D.S. Wilford, 2000, "Understanding Risk is Key to Long-Term Return Management" *Risk Budgeting: A Cutting-Edge Guide to Enhancing Fund Management* (New York: Institutional Investor Inc).

Quintana, J., B.H. Putnam, and D.S. Wilford, 1998a, "Mutual and Pension Fund Management: Beating the Markets Using a Global Bayesian Investment Policy", Proceedings of the section on Bayeslan Statistical Science, American Statistical Association.

Quintana, J.M. and E. Norland, 1998b, "Dynamic Estimation to Control Portfolio Risk", *Global Investor*, February, pp. 43–5.

Smithson, C.W., C.W. Smith, and D.S. Wilford, 1995, *Managing Financial Risk: A Guide to Derivative Products, Financial Engineering and Value Maximization* (New York: McGraw Hill).

Wilford, D.S., 1995, "Risk Management Adapts – Yet Again", *Global Investor*, June.

Wilford, D.S., 1997, "Techniques for Today's Global Asset Allocation", *Investing Worldwide VIII*.

Wilford, D.S., 1999, "Risk Management, Risk Measures and Asset Management: Not Three Sides of the Same Coin", *Global Investor*, June.

Wilford, D.S. and J.M. Quintana, 1998, "The Unfettered Manager is the Successful Manager", *Global Investor*, October.

Zellner, A., 2000, "Keep It Sophisticatedly Simple", forthcoming in H. Kuezenkampf, with M. McLeer and A. Zellner, *Simplicity in Economic Modeling*, Cambridge University Press.

12

Sound Practices for Hedge Funds

Tanya Styblo Beder

Caxton Corporation

During the 1990s, hedge funds were blamed for significant losses by well-known dealers and investors in particular funds. As academics, practitioners and regulators studied these newer losses, such as Long Term Capital Management (LTCM), and reflected on older losses, such as Granite, risk management for hedge funds landed in the spotlight. A useful by-product of this spotlight has been an increased focus on greater education, information and market transparency at the highest level of public and private organisations. In this chapter, I examine some of the key aspects of risk management for large hedge funds, as detailed in the February 2000 report, "Sound Practices for Hedge Fund Managers", in which Caxton Corporation was an active participant. I also examine the key ingredients of a successful risk function.

It is vital to acknowledge here that not all hedge funds pose the same risks: some are inherently riskier than others. The level of risk also depends upon the risk appetite, risk control discipline and common sense of the hedge fund management. Nevertheless, there are common elements of risk management that define the current practice for hedge funds. Two important premises underpin my discussion.

1. Risk unto itself is not bad. What must be avoided are risks that are taken without proper compensation, risks that are left unmanaged, or risks that are too large relative to the capital (this includes activities that are too leveraged for capital at hand).
2. Not taking risk may be bad. For example, insufficient exposure to an asset class may be equally or more risky than not using that asset class at all. Similarly, not investing in hedge funds may be equally or more risky than the use of hedge funds for many investors. This is because hedge funds are often uncorrelated to other returns and risks in the market place.

COMMON ELEMENTS OF RISK MANAGEMENT FOR HEDGE FUNDS

Following the LTCM crisis in late 1998, the President's Working Group on Financial Markets[1] published its report, entitled "Hedge Funds, Leverage and the Lessons of Long-Term Capital Management", in April 1999. This report recommended that "a group of hedge funds should draft and publish a set of sound practices for their risk management and internal controls [including] how individual hedge funds could assess their performance against the sound practices for investors and counterparties".

The hedge fund group that came together and produced this report included Caxton Corporation, Kingdon Capital Management, LLC, Moore Capital Management Inc, Soros Fund Management LLC, and Tudor Investment Corporation. "Sound Practices for Hedge Fund Managers" was consequently, published in February 2000 and recommended that the following risk functions be performed.[2]

1. Consistent with its agreement with the hedge fund's governing authority and disclosure made to investors, senior management of the hedge fund manager should determine the appropriate overall level of risk for a particular fund.
2. This overall level of risk should then be allocated (among portfolio managers, strategies, asset classes, etc).
3. Once the risk allocation is determined, portfolio managers should choose the specific risks (consistent with the policies established by senior management) to be assumed, and enter into transactions in order to gain exposure to those risks.
4. The risk actually assumed by a Fund must then be analysed and monitored by an independent risk analysis function, or "risk monitoring function". The resulting risk information must be disseminated to senior management and, as appropriate, portfolio managers.
5. Senior management must ensure that risk levels are acceptable and consistent with established risk policies and parameters.

These summary remarks are further explained in the report in the form of 34 specific risk recommendations that include examples and a discussion of how application varies across types of funds.

The document defines a hedge fund as "a pooled investment vehicle that is privately organized, administered by a professional investment management firm ... and not widely available to the public". As such, a wide variety of investment vehicles are included in this definition – small and large (in assets or staff), operating in one market or many, following a single, simple strategy or a combination of complex strategies, operating on-shore or off-shore under varying organisational structures, etc. Given this breadth of definition, application of the risk recommendations can and should vary according to the type of investment fund to which they are applied.

To illustrate the importance of this concept, Figure 1 considers two funds that are following different strategies in different markets.

The implementation of such sound practices is substantially different for these two funds. Suppose Fund 1 controls US$200 million in combined long/short positions, is fully invested and turns its entire portfolio each week, and has 40 to 200 positions at any point in time and a maximum of 10,400 positions over the course of one year (52 x 200). To perform position, risk and return analysis on its portfolio at the instrument level, Fund 1 maintains a database of all US large cap equities plus their positions. For such instruments, data at the instrument level are widely available from single vendors. The historical period for the database must be long enough to perform the specified computations, including back testing and stress testing. Fund 1 is fortunate in that the scale of this database is quite manageable with common data platforms. Note that information on other market sectors (eg, correlation data) will need to be collected as well, depending upon the sophistication of Fund 1's analyses.

In order to perform peer group comparisons, selecting a benchmark (or constructing a custom benchmark) for Fund 1 is relatively straightforward. For example, if Fund 1 is broadly diversified, the first step should be to select S&P indices as an index. Second, if Fund 1 specialises in certain sectors, then a benchmark could be created through a weighted combination of specialty equity indices. Finally, because Fund 1 has a small number of positions in a single market sector at any point in time, computations became very manageable.

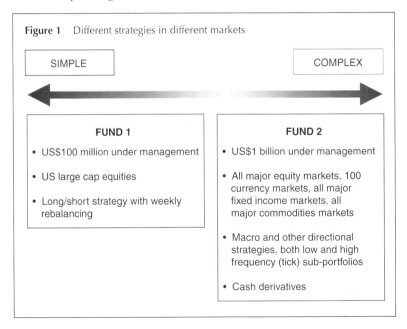

Figure 1   Different strategies in different markets

SIMPLE

COMPLEX

FUND 1

- US$100 million under management

- US large cap equities

- Long/short strategy with weekly rebalancing

FUND 2

- US$1 billion under management

- All major equity markets, 100 currency markets, all major fixed income markets, all major commodities markets

- Macro and other directional strategies, both low and high frequency (tick) sub-portfolios

- Cash derivatives

Fund 2 presents a much larger challenge. If Fund 2 controls US$2 billion in long and short positions, trades plain vanilla derivatives (eg, futures, options and swaps) and runs high frequency sub-portfolios (eg, a foreign exchange portfolio or long/short equity portfolio to capitalise on intra-day moves), it may have tens of thousands of positions at any point in time. This adds up to millions of positions over the course of a year, compared to the maximum of 10,400 positions for Fund 1 (Fund 2 has many more positions in a day than Fund 1 does in a year.)

Due to its macro activities, Fund 2 may be invested in different market sectors at different points in time. This is quite a contrast to Fund 1, which only trades in one market – US large cap equities – at all points in time. To perform position, risk and return analysis, Fund 2 must maintain data on the thousands of instruments that it may trade at any point in time; Fund 2 would maintain Fund 1's data universe of US large cap equities merely as a subset of its total data.

While high/low/close data are sufficient for Fund 1, they may not be sufficient for Fund 2, depending on the scope and scale of its intra-day trading. If tick data are required, these must often be drawn from multiple vendors in contrast to Fund 1's ability to obtain its data from a single source. This drastically increases the size, complexity and administration needs of the database, thereby raising Fund 2's need for more complex data platforms and more sophisticated personnel. To be timely, computations will require greater technology infrastructure than is the case for Fund 1. Finally, large data sets beyond position and pricing information will be required, including correlations, volatilities and other items.

Advances in technology – and technology's impact on trading styles – will also have an impact on the type of risk management required. Higher frequency trading styles and more complex strategies will continue to evolve. These create larger operational dependencies and are by their nature more difficult to monitor without a substantial risk management infrastructure.

KEY INGREDIENTS FOR A SUCCESSFUL RISK FUNCTION

Once an investment fund establishes its sound practice requirements, it must turn to the issue of implementation of the risk function. A risk function that performs such a role is often only a few years old within the investment manager community. Another issue is that no two firms tend to have identical risk functions as each varies in its strategy, return targets, investment horizon, risk appetite, systems and other items. The following two factors often impede the success of a risk function.

1. *Limited resources*

A lack of funds, staff, systems or time have deterred many. In general, large hedge funds, mutual funds and other investment managers have been quicker to implement a risk function than pension funds or other plan sponsors. However, market events such as the Russian crisis and the unexpected correlation moves of 1998, the dramatic fall in the Nasdaq and the technology sector in early 2000, plus the volatility of the energy sector during the past few months, continue to increase budgets and the pace of implementation.

2. *Perceived lack of value*

This may be summarised by remarks such as "we already do this all day long as part of our normal investment process", or, "what could this possibly add to our investment process?"

Put simply, there are two forms of risk functions – those that work and those that do not. Many of those that do not work are often viewed as a "big brother" nuisance to the investment process. Others that do not work are perceived (rightly or wrongly) as producing information that is not helpful to the investment process. In some cases, the risk manager may be relegated to filling out reports that no one reads, or may be perceived as being at the firm for appearances sake alone. In others, the risk manager is perceived as an individual who wishes to kill risk at the expense of too much return, thereby destroying individual performance. Yet in other cases, the risk manager is perceived as an impediment to new investment ideas or markets, delaying and disrupting progress. Whether such views are perception or reality, they may cause the risk function to fail.

In virtually all cases, successful risk functions are collaborative and have the buy-in of portfolio managers, senior management, traders and other key players (eg, the board, auditors, operations, etc). But do note that collaboration and buy-in do not automatically jeopardise the independence of the role.

To summarise, the key ingredients for successful risk functions include the following.

❏ *A mission understood by all*

Risk managers, portfolio managers, senior management and other key players should agree on the roles and responsibilities of the risk function.

❏ *Perceived value added*

The risk function should add value. It should help to identify, measure, monitor and select the risks that matter, and offer a considered opinion on risk and return from a strategic perspective. Reporting and information should be deemed useful for the front, middle and back offices (note that these often vary by area as well as by recipient).

❏ *A collaborative process*

The risk function should be viewed as a resource and should collaborate frequently with the front, middle and back offices. It should also be seen to be sensitive to the needs and concerns of all three areas and to acknowledge the expertise of others. For example, if things aren't working, productive dialogue and resolution to issues should be possible.

❑ *Education*
The risk function should facilitate the use of current and innovative products and risk tools through education at the front, middle and back office levels for quantitative and qualitative techniques. Further, the risk function should translate quantitative techniques into English (or the appropriate language) and assist in the interpretation of risk measures on absolute and relative bases.

❑ *Knowledge and perspective*
Risk managers should be knowledgeable about the investment process and the need to provide competitive returns. Further, they should understand how the investment process (and therefore the risk function) varies from the activities of banks and dealers. They should be proficient with benchmarks (including custom benchmarks where appropriate) and understand their role as it relates to risk and return.

❑ *A well-defined process*
All aspects of the risk function – from data collection to exception reporting and escalation procedures – should be well-defined. The process should be methodical, consistent and fair. For example, this risk is if the same risk should be viewed the same way across instruments or portfolios and an established process is used to approve "new" activities.

❑ *Healthy scepticism for the numbers*
Risk managers should be well-versed technically yet do not place too much faith in the numbers. They should understand what the numbers do and what the numbers do not do, as well as the limitations of the quantitative and qualitative measures. Risk managers should be able to implement appropriate stress testing, back testing, simulation and risk-adjusted performance measures, and they should understand what cannot be measured. Finally, they should believe that the maths is necessary but it is not in itself sufficient to manage risk.

❑ *Aligned responsibility and authority*
The risk function should have sufficient authority to act in its areas of responsibility. Reporting and organisational structure should be clearly defined and understood by all, including all delegated responsibilities and authorities.

❑ *Sufficient resources*
The risk function should have sufficient staff, systems, data, and budget to succeed. Risk managers are sensitive to and do not deny the realities

of peer pressure for results and reduced staff/budgets in other front, middle or back office areas. Further, they should be able to offer perspective regarding the trade-offs between the desire for overnight results versus "perfection" for the long run.

❏ *Independence*
Oversight of compliance with risk policies should be independent of line investment activity, or, if separation is not possible due to limited staff, should implement alternative checks, balances and controls. However, risk managers should not have so much independence that they check on themselves.

CONCLUSION

"Sound Practices for Hedge Fund Managers" is an excellent starting point for a fund seeking to perform a self-evaluation of its risk management practices. Investors or counterparties to a particular hedge fund should be encouraged to discuss risk management as a part of their normal dialogue with that fund. Current market practice is that hedge funds offer differing degrees of information regarding their activities, and, while disclosure varies, this is consistent with many other types of firms. The question, "what is the right level of disclosure by hedge funds?" is of interest to hedge funds and investors in hedge funds alike. This topic has been taken up by an industry group known as the Investor Risk Committee (IRC). The IRC operates as one of the working committees of the International Association of Financial Engineers and its goal is to provide the consensus of a substantial group of hedge fund managers and institutional investors regarding the question, "what is the right level of disclosure by hedge funds?" The IRCs work is in progress at the time of writing, but is due to be published in October 2000 on the International Association of Financial Engineers' website (www.iafe.org).

1   Comprised of the Secretary of the US Department of the Treasury and the respective chairs of the Board of Governors of the Federal Reserve System, the Securities and Exchange Commission and the Commodity Futures Trading Commission.
2   This report is reprinted as the first part of the appendix in the present volume.

BIBLIOGRAPHY

Sound Practices for Hedge Fund Managers. Url:http://www.hfmsound, practices.com [February 2000].

Hedge Funds, Leverage, and the Lessons of Long-term Capital Management. Url:http://www.cftc.gov/tm/hedgefundreport.htm [April 1999].

13

Risk Management for Hedge Fund Strategies

Mike Boren

Sawtooth Investment Management LLC

Global fixed-income involves relative value investing many of the same risks experienced by other fixed-income investment strategies, including exposure to interest rate fluctuations, credit default, foreign currency rate fluctuations and unpredicted correlation among unrelated securities. Analysis and management techniques for these risks are well developed and understood by most professional investment managers. This book offers many insights into such strategies.

Relative value investment strategies differ from other investment methodologies in that they involve significant amounts of leverage. Leverage on a large scale introduces certain unique risks for which even the experienced professional investor may not be prepared.

In fixed-income markets, relative value trading can be leveraged to a very high degree. For example, an investor might simultaneously purchase a US Treasury note with two years and one month to maturity, commit to pay fixed on an interest rate swap with two years to maturity, and finally purchase some out of the money options on US Treasury two-year note futures contracts. Using the repo/reverse markets, the investor might push final settlement of the transaction six months into the future. This strategy involves three or four separate transactions (four trade confirmation tickets). A creditworthy investor with good dealing relationships might be able to transact US$100 million notional value of this strategy (long US$100 million versus short US$100 million) while putting up collateral of less than US$500,000.

Some investors may find it difficult to select the appropriate size for this type of transaction. One common approach is to calculate the dollar amount of risk per notional unit of the specified transaction, determine the dollar amount of risk that is appropriate for any single position in a given investment portfolio, then divide the second number by the first to arrive at the number of notional units that should be transacted. This requires several judgment calls on the part of the investor. For example, how is risk calculated? What types of risk are considered? What is the appropriate amount of risk per position in a portfolio? How does this position fit into the rest of the portfolio? What is the appropriate amount of risk for this position? The answers to these questions shape the portfolio and result in varying investment returns for different investors.

For example, you may be managing a five hundred million dollar portfolio. How much of this two-year notes versus swaps trade should you execute? The answer is that you should begin with a thorough risk analysis. Most investors will analyse each factor that could influence the outcome of the strategy to see what effect changes in that factor will have on the strategy's value. One such factor is the shape of the yield curve. If the two five year segment of the yield curve changes by two standard deviations, how much should that change the value of the strategy on a US$1 million position? If six-month Libor increases by 20 basis points, what effect does that have on a US$1 million position?

Having analysed all the factors, you may decide to manage to a specific dollar risk target. You may decide that you are willing to risk 1% of your portfolio, or US$5 million, on the trade. Let's assume that your risk analysis indicates that a two standard deviation adverse move in the position would result in a loss of US$500 per million dollars of notional value. Let's also assume that your analysis indicates an expected gain of US$500 per million dollars of notional value, after assessing probability of each possible outcome. For a fixed-income relative value investor, this looks like a good trade. Now you need only figure out the appropriate size. US$5 million risk limit divided by US$500 potential loss per million is 10,000; multiplied by one million dollars – your desired notional size of this strategy would be US$10 billion! That may sound like a large trade, but your prime broker would require only US$50 million of collateral from you to carry this position.

Let's now assume that your investment goal is to earn net returns of 15–20% per year, while limiting risk to 15% of assets. That means you would be willing to suffer a loss of 15% once in a while, as long as your average annual returns, including the losing periods, averaged more than 15%. If the risk-free rate that you can earn on your collateral is 5%, you need to make 10–15% from your investment strategies. The two-year notes versus swaps trade mentioned above has an expected profit of 1% of your portfolio's net asset value over a six-month horizon. If three of every four such trades is a winner, you probably need around 20 of these trades a year to reach your target profitability. With a time horizon of six months, you might have around 10 of these trades in the portfolio at any given moment. Obviously, we are making all kinds of assumptions here, but they seem reasonable enough and we have to make some assumptions in any analysis.

Here is where fixed-income, relative value investing gets tricky. If you construct a portfolio of ten relative value strategies with large enough positions to earn 1% on the total portfolio over a period of six months or less, most of your capital will be committed to collateral with your prime broker and other counterparties. In the example we have been using, 10 strategies with similar risk characteristics would require 500 million dollars in collateral; your entire investment portfolio. While that may be extreme, it is not uncommon for fixed-income, relative value investors to commit a large majority of their capital to collateral on trading strategies.

When markets are calm and rational, there is no problem with this strategy. Most of the trades will be profitable. Those that are not will be manageable, and you will enjoy relatively steady returns. In these conditions, it often seems the only problem with leverage is that you can't get enough of it.

The hidden flaws are not revealed until the system is stressed. Consider the tenuous nature of your position. With only US$500 million, you are controlling positions that have a notional value of US$200 billion (US$100 billion long; US$100 billion short). In most cases, you have achieved your leverage by borrowing from your counterparties. These are not your friends. They are involved in two businesses: first, they trade for their own proprietary accounts, and second, they broker transactions. While they would like to see you stay in business so they can continue to broker your trades, their trading desks would like to make money by trading with you. Their proprietary trading desks engage in relative value, fixed-income strategies on a regular basis. Although your banker has a vested interest in your ability to repay your loans, in this case he also has an interest in making money by trading with you. What happens when a few of your positions lose a little money and your counterparty asks you to post more collateral? You may not have enough money to cover the margin calls without liquidating some of your positions. Sometimes, you may not have time to liquidate your positions in an orderly manner, and may end up paying a substantial bid/ask spread to get out of some positions in time to have enough cash to post collateral on other positions. There have been incidents in the past where investment banks forced relative value investors to liquidate positions on a holiday in order to meet margin calls. Of course, the only traders who were available to make markets on those positions were the traders who worked for the investment banks that posted these calls. As would be expected, their bids were less than competitive, and this was very costly to the investors.

Now consider what might happen to market valuations when you start liquidating positions. Consider the two-year notes versus swaps trade. If you hold a US$10 billion position in a two-year note, your position may represent 90% of the total size of the issue. Granted, it is a leveraged transaction. This means you have committed the note as collateral on a repo transaction, so it is not actually in your possession. When you start to look for bids, however, it does not matter whether or not you have financed the position. You are trying to find a lot of buyers. It is very similar to a US Treasury auction, except you don't enjoy the same deal pipeline as the Treasury. You may find that you move the market significantly while trying to liquidate the position. Consequently, that will in turn result in greater losses for you, probably forcing you to liquidate other positions to help cover these losses. You will have even greater difficulty liquidating your other positions, as investment banks and other large institutional investors start to get wind of your predicament.

You are now captive to your extreme leverage. A single margin call on one of your positions might easily destroy your entire investment portfolio, simply because you will be forced to liquidate positions under adverse market conditions. If your positions are large enough, a forced liquidation of one position could create adverse market conditions for the remainder of your portfolio. Suddenly, you realise that not only is it possible to get enough leverage, but you have far more than you can handle.

These are the unique risks of leveraged investments. They cannot be hedged by executing more transactions. However, it is possible to avoid these risks through careful protection of liquidity. There are certain steps you can take to insulate your portfolio from these risks. We will now discuss these.

First, set portfolio and individual trade liquidity limits. This will prepare you for margin calls and make it far less likely that you will suffer a liquidity crisis. For example, rather than leveraging a strategy to the point where it is expected to earn a specific dollar target, set a leverage target that leaves plenty of liquidity in volatile markets. For a fixed-income, relative value investor, it may be wise to keep as much as 50% of capital in liquid investments, available to meet margin calls on short notice. Depending on the investment strategy, you may need to restrict the amount of collateral that can be employed by any individual position.

Next, consider market depth before setting trade size. You should never accumulate positions that will be difficult or impossible to liquidate over the course of a few days. It is usually unwise to take a position that represents more than 10% of the float on any security, and, for more esoteric derivatives transactions, the limit should be set even lower. You do not want to saturate the market when you need to get out of a position.

Maintain a high degree of confidentiality regarding your investment strategy and the positions in your portfolio. When you have large positions, do your best to conceal them from other investors, brokers, news media, etc. It is not uncommon for salesmen who cover your account at investment banks to try to find out what you are doing. They may ask questions such as, "Why are you buying that bond? What are you trading against it? Is this part of an arbitrage strategy?" When asked why they need such information, they typically reply that it will help them find better trading opportunities, obtain better prices from their traders, or obtain better credit terms on your behalf. Do not succumb to these requests. If your positions or investment strategies are revealed, other investors may try to mimic your investment strategies. This will reduce your ability to find similar trades in the future and may jeopardise your ability to unwind existing positions profitably. Require your prime broker and all other counterparties not to divulge information about your positions. Never give details of your investment strategies to any counterparty or competitor.

Finally, negotiate agreements with each counterparty that protect you from volatile market conditions. Depending on your relationship with each counterparty, you may be able to eliminate the risk of an adverse liquidation. Some of the terms you should seek include cross-market netting of positions, two-way posting of collateral with reasonable thresholds, and a restriction on forced liquidation of positions. Cross-market netting reduces the frequency and magnitude of margin calls, and reduces exposure to any single counterparty. Two-way posting of collateral reduces counterparty exposure to a specific threshold number and ensures that profits from open positions held with one counterparty can be diverted to cover losses on positions held with other counterparties. Restrictions on forced liquidations might include limiting margin calls to business days, giving the customer a full business day to satisfy a margin call, requiring mid-market valuation based on quotes from three independent dealers for any forced liquidation, etc. Many investment banks offer terms such as these to most creditworthy investors, thereby greatly reducing the risk of a liquidity crisis.

To be successful in relative value fixed income trading, the investor must employ leverage. To successfully employ leverage through an entire market cycle, the investor must pay attention to liquidity and must take measures to protect the portfolio from liquidity risk. Some investors may find it difficult to set liquidity-based restrictions on the investment portfolio. Although such restrictions may reduce profitability when markets are stable but survival is usually a better goal than a few extra percentage points of profitability.

14

Risk Management for Hedge Fund Strategies: US Equity Market Neutral

Jane Tisdale*

State Street Global Advisors

US equity market neutral strategies are viewed to be among the most straightforward and easily understandable types of hedge fund. Such strategies are designed to take advantage of the spread between returns of attractive stocks (on the long side) and unattractive stocks (on the short side). A manager's ability to capture this spread is a function of stock selection skill as well as other lesser-known or understood considerations. This chapter will discuss several of the issues investors need to explore and understand before venturing into the market neutral arena.

Investors are increasingly turning to hedge funds in an effort to maintain satisfactory returns while reducing portfolio volatility. Typically, edge funds are highly uncorrelated with traditional asset classes, and therefore provide good diversification benefits along with the potential for very strong investment returns. Long-short market neutral US equity strategies are among the more popular hedge funds for achieving this goal. These strategies use stock selection to capture excess returns while targeting a beta exposure of zero. By investing both long and short, the manager can neutralise market exposure while doubling the potential for excess return. Investors find varied uses for long-short market neutral strategies within their portfolios: an attractive alternative to fixed income; an equity alternative when coupled with equity futures; or an inclusion in their alternative investment category, if they have one. According to HFR, long-short market neutral strategies have grown in assets by nearly US$22 billion during the 1990s, at a time when hedge fund assets grew dramatically[1].

Broadly, there are some misconceptions around this strategy. One is the

* The author wishes to thank those who contributed and reviewed this chapter, including John Serhant, David Hanna, Susan Reigel and Michael Arone of SSgA and HFR and Goldman Scahs for their comments and industry information.

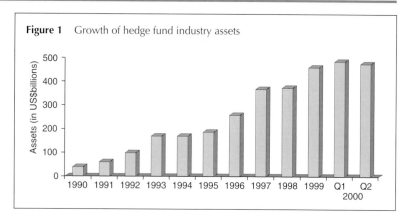

Figure 1   Growth of hedge fund industry assets

opinion that long-short market neutral strategies somehow provide a free lunch due to the double alpha, or return, of the strategy. What is often forgotten is the double omega, or active risk, associated with the strategy. This means that while a skilled manager may have double the positive value-added, an unskilled manager may have double the negative value-added. Another is the view that long-short market neutral works in all market conditions, when in fact market conditions play a significant role in the ability of the process to succeed. For example, extreme market volatility over the last several years has resulted in significant return "punishment" for managers whose selection skill waned – the stocks that underperformed having done so in double figures. Long-short market neutral strategies, however, will work regardless of market direction, unless conditions are unfavourable to the management approach. A third misconception is that market neutral means the same thing to everyone and that strategies are easily comparable. The reality is that managers and investors alike must understand the exposures (stock, style, industry, etc) of each strategy, because techniques differ.

When evaluating market neutral strategies, these misconceptions and other potential risks need to be understood and explored rigorously. Generally, the risks fall into four categories: investment process, implementation, personnel and firm.

ISSUES ASSOCIATED WITH THE INVESTMENT PROCESS
The manager's judgement
The greatest risk for a long-short market neutral strategy is that the source of return will vanish. Ultimately, the success of most long-short market neutral strategies comes down to stock selection. Therefore, if the stock ranking process is invalidated, the manager's edge is lost. Over the years, managers have experienced periods when their process was "out of favour" during times when market conditions or structure were changed. Sometimes, these changes reversed and the approach returned to favour,

yet sometimes they did not. For example, in 1999, when expensive stocks just kept running up in price, strategies that relied solely or largely on valuation to rank stocks were raked through the coals as returns of their highest ranked (low price-to-earnings) stocks trailed those at the bottom of the ranking. As the end of 2000 approaches, this phenomenon appears to have subsided, and managers who consider company valuations are performing well.

Changes in market structure

Changes to market structure can also be an impediment to manager success. For example, the emergence of new industries needs to be taken into account because as they grow, remaining neutral towards them becomes an issue. Consider the rise of the Internet industry. Companies now classified as "Internets" were previously in market segments as diverse as financial services, media and computer hardware. Because they looked expensive compared to their then industry counterparts, many long-short market neutral funds held them short. In aggregate, this left the strategy short the Internet industry at precisely the wrong time. Bringing them together into the same industry allowed for the comparison of like companies. The same experience is occurring with genomics companies – these were classified in the drug industry, but are now behaving differently to the more traditional drug companies, and should therefore be reclassified as their own industry.

Business categorisation

The phenomenon goes beyond the identification of new industries, it is also important to understand a company's business so as to ensure the appropriate industry classification. Corning exemplifies this matter, as it began in the late 19th century as Corning Flint Glass, a consumer products company. Consumer products remained an appropriate category for this company until, in 1971, it developed the optical fibre that enables voice, video and data to be sent via lasers. This was a fundamental shift in the company's business that was not immediately reflected in its industry classification. The bottom line is that businesses and industries emerge and change, and investment managers must be aware of these changes in order to be successful.

Incomplete information and valuation

As we look to the future, there are many areas that could influence a manager's ability to add value. One example involves the relationship between investment bankers and brokerage houses – will polluted information flow into the market from brokers who are swayed by business conducted on the other side of the Chinese wall? Another example is the ongoing concern about the quality of earnings and cashflow information – does this really reflect the value of the company, or does it mislead as a result of pension accounting and options? To illustrate, consider employee stock options – they enabled high-flying technology companies to attract stellar employees while avoiding extravagant salaries. What is not so well-known is that while option plans are not reflected on the income statement, their cost is reflected on corporate tax returns. This leads to a bonanza when stock prices are rising and employees are cashing in their options. Recently, a Wall Street Journal article referred to a study by Bear Stearns[2], which found that options-based tax benefits contributed upwards of 20% to the operating cash flow of Qualcomm, Dell Computer, and Cisco Systems among others. In addition, according to Bernstein[3], options in the technology sector have added 7–10% to earnings growth; for the market as a whole, option accounting has boosted annual earnings growth rates by over 3% since 1996. What happens on the flip side? When stock prices decline, the favourable tax impact recedes as employees hold on to their options making the cash flow and earnings look even worse than they otherwise would.

In conclusion, managers must be aware of the various influences on their approach, from accounting manipulations to changes in industry structure, and aim to manage them through steps including incorporating dynamic approaches to stock selection, portfolio construction and industry classifications. The key to success is staying ahead of the curve, so investors must take care to identify the manager who can accomplish this.

A final, though often overlooked, area of investment process risk goes beyond individual managers. Investors should identify how their long-short managers generate their excess returns and learn whether all use the similar techniques. If they do, diversification of process risk is called for within their alternatives category.

IMPLEMENTATION

Correctly selecting stocks is only half the job when it comes to managing long-short market neutral strategies. Implementation holds additional challenges for the manager and additional considerations for the investor. First, there are the issues of liquidity, capacity and borrowability. Second, there are those related to interaction with prime brokers and traders.

Implementation risks

Capacity, liquidity and borrowability risks are other areas that investors should evaluate when considering long-short market neutral managers. A major factor in long-short market neutral strategies is lack of capacity on the short side. As with small cap strategies, capacity constraints arise as a result of the stock universe and fund size. In addition, liquidity may affect the portfolio manager's ability to implement the strategy if the fund is so large that it cannot short positions in the necessary size, or if it needs to short positions that are not in good supply (generally in the small cap range).

Along with liquidity, it may be difficult to borrow certain securities, especially names that are not typically found in large institutional funds. The bulk of institutional equity assets, which form the lion's share of security lending assets, are invested in large cap companies. By identifying an appropriate investable universe, investment managers can avoid many of the issues of capacity, liquidity and borrowability within their long-short market neutral strategies.

Broker selection

Selection of the prime broker is an important decision because the prime broker plays an integral role in the daily management of the long-short market neutral process. Criteria for selecting a prime broker include their internal and external access to stock on loan, industry experience and resources. First, access to loaned stocks is critical to the effective implementation of the long-short strategy – if a manager cannot short a desired security, there is a lost opportunity. Prime brokers should use electronic locates and other techniques to improve implementation. Second, expertise in the operational and management issues associated with long-short strategies is also crucial. Experienced prime brokers are often able to help managers avoid potential execution pitfalls. Third, information management is a significant part of what the prime broker does, a strong support structure is therefore required. A good prime broker can trouble-shoot potential problems and act quickly when problems arise. They are also efficient and timely when it comes to reporting – advanced technology (including, though not limited to, internet reporting and trading analytics) is an essential component of this. A final consideration is security in this age of freely flowing information; it is important that client data are protected with the prime broker. Many prime brokers provide individual security identifications to each member of the portfolio management team to ensure tight security.

Personnel

Personnel risk includes the risk that a manager is not qualified, or is qualified but ready to leave the firm. Experience and competence are difficult to discern because they are often masked by the aura of age, education and industry exposure. Although these provide an investor with a level of comfort, they may not tell the whole story. In today's dynamic environment, it may be more important to consider a person's ability to remain on the leading edge rather than the fact that they *used to be* on the leading edge.

Incentives and personnel loyalty

Once comfortable with a manager, you need to make sure that person is motivated to stay at the firm. A manager will move on if compensation is not competitive, if the surroundings and corporate culture are not satisfying or if the future is uncertain – for either firm or manager. Investors can usually gain a sense for these issues by asking specific questions about the compensation structure and the amount of time spent on the road; it is always useful to visit the manager's site during the due-diligence process to gain an impression of other issues. Keep in mind that there may be two sides to an issue, particularly compensation. Often, it is believed that if managers invest in their own long-short market neutral portfolio, they will work harder to provide excess returns. There may be some positive motivation in such circumstances, but there may also be negative, since a manager is more willing to take chances in order to recognise superior returns. If the compensation structure is fair and the manager is motivated in other ways the manager's objectives should be in line with those of the participants regardless of personal participation.

FIRM
The commitment of the firm

Investors should also look at the investment management firm, because the firm's commitment to the strategy and the surrounding structure are critical to its success. Commitment shows in the form of resources to insure leading edge technology, competitive compensation, and resources for investment research. In today's high-tech market environment speed and access to information is vital, as without the necessary data, technology and hardware investment opportunities may be lost. Along with manager compensation, this is another way that a firm shows its support for the strategy.

A firm's internal support structure

A solid firm structure is important in supporting the activities of the portfolio management team. Many areas, including sales/marketing support, keep managers focused on day-to-day management. Support is offered through asset gathering; operational support to insure readily available portfolio cash and trading data; and, compliance support to ensure careful monitoring and fulfilment of guidelines.

Structure can also be considered from the perspective of firm size. This attribute provides benefits that are less visible. Larger firms are typically more heavily regulated and therefore may exhibit less business risk. Additionally, larger firms have significant bargaining power when it comes to trading and technology. The brokerage community tends to value prime brokerage and trading relationships with prime brokers because of the volume of trading generated; prime brokers are more responsive and also provide more competitive pricing.

CONCLUSION

Long-short market neutral strategies offer many benefits compared to traditional management approaches, including diversification relative to traditional asset classes, attractive absolute return and low volatility. To realise these benefits, investors must carefully evaluate their manager choices, keeping in mind a variety of considerations, including the long-term viability of their investment process, their ability to implement the approach, manager qualification and motivation, and the management firm's strength and commitment to the strategy.

1   HFR Copyright 2000. All rights reserved. www.hfr.com
2   McGough, Robert, 2000, "Stock Options Pad Cash Flow of Soaring Technology Issues", *Wall Street Journal*, (July 17th), pp. C2–C4.
3   August 2000, "Bernstein Disciplined-Strategies Monitor" by Bernstein Research

15

Long/Short Japanese Equities

Alex Balfour and Alastair MacGregor

Balfour Capital Limited

George Bernard Shaw once remarked that England and America were two countries divided by a common language. Interestingly enough, one could almost say the same about attitude to risk, with both nations each adopting an opposite pole of the risk spectrum. In the United States, risk is a highly systematic mathematical issue, which tends to be measured purely quantitatively, and is therefore rather inflexible and does not take into account exceptional circumstances. The British attitude is rather more qualitative but risks being rather woolly and vague, on the basis that risk management is not an exact science. At Balfour Capital, we believe that the ultimate form of risk management is both quantitative and qualitative, in that it should have strict statistical parameters, but should also take into account potential scenarios that cannot be measured by history alone. After all, risk assessment is only a historical approximation of the future. Risk for us is paramount: as a long/short manager we view our brief to be to maximise return for risk. In this chapter, we do not cover all the different areas of risk because many will have been covered elsewhere. Instead, we have sought to present those risk factors which are quintessential to Japan, based on what we perceive to be roles inherent to the Japanese market. Inevitably, much has been coloured by our personal experience of running money in Japan over a number of years.

We have split this chapter into two parts. The first focuses on what we consider to be the principal risks of investing in Japanese equities, as well as what we think is particularly idiosyncratic about this market. In the second, we discuss the tools we use to assess risk both on a quantitative and a qualitative basis. Given that we view risk control as more of an art than a science, this explanation is critical to our thesis.

THE PRINCIPAL RISKS OF INVESTING IN JAPAN
Liquidity

Liquidity is one of the prime risk areas in Japan, particularly since the bear market began in 1990. The reason for this is that volumes have been extremely low, making it very difficult to cut "bad" positions. Indeed, in February 1999, liquidity in the Japanese market was so bad, that on a day of exceptional trading for Dell Computer, there was more volume in that US stock than in the entire Tokyo Stock Exchange for that week. This might be an unsurprising story if one were talking about an emerging market. Nevertheless, Japan is the second largest stock market in the world after the United States, and this effectively makes managing money in any quantity somewhat difficult. Even with little over US$100 million, we have found that we have to considerably restrict our investment list to meet our objective of being able to liquidate all positions within one to two days at most. The "portfolio liquidity ratio" is at best an approximation of how easy it would be to liquidate the portfolio, as it is based on the six-month average liquidity. As discussed below, volumes in certain stocks can suddenly dry out and the individual liquidity figures for any given number of stocks can change dramatically. This was particularly true during the euphoria of the technology boom and the inevitable bust that followed. An important, contributory factor was the participation of individual investors, as well as the relative novelty of many of these stocks. Individuals as a whole tend to be far more emotional than institutional investors, and this is particularly the case in Japan. On 13 March, 2000, we found that our value-at-risk (VAR) assessment was completely innaccurate because the market as a whole did not act in accordance with history. The

Figure 1   Topix Communications Index down 11.3% on 13 March 2000

Source: Bloomberg

extreme participation of individual investors, who had not only been major buyers for many months, but were also buying on margin, led to precipitous declines. These became far more important than they should have been due to high levels of gearing. As a result, most of the technology favourites were down between 10–12% on that day, as opposed to being down a more normal 3–5%.

Many of the stocks that individuals panicked out of were new technology stocks, which meant that they effectively had no trading history at all. Whereas the individual VAR calculations suggested potential drops of 5–6%, because stocks such as Hikari Tsushin had even in recent times been more volatile than the likes of Sony, nobody could have been prepared for a fall of 15% or more in one day, given the trading history. Of course, this is something that the fund manager who focuses on qualitative risk would indeed understand. At Balfour Capital, while marginally over-geared at this particular point in time, the exposure to potentially illiquid stocks was immediately decreased in the ensuing short-term correction. This proved to be the correct move, given the sustained dry-up in liquidity and sustained falls that followed.

Macroeconomics

Macroeconomic factors are always an important risk measure and can generally be viewed in a quantitative context, although occasionally there might be a qualitative overlay, particularly with foreign exchange. The importance of the exchange rate to a Japanese fund manger is rather perverse. In normal circumstances, one would assume that a strong yen would be bad for electrical stocks which tend to be foreigners' favourites. This was certainly true until the mid-1990s. Since then, however, the relationship has been almost exactly the opposite. The qualitative explanation for this has been that foreigners have become the swing investors in Japan, and therefore their behaviour tends to be the driving force. Foreign asset allocators tend to view the yen-dollar exchange rate as one of the most important reasons for allocating to Japan, given that most of them do not hedge back into dollars. It therefore follows that the prospect of a strong yen will tend to encourage them to increase their allocations to Japan. Fund managers will then be faced with a requirement to buy their current list, which will include the foreign favourites, most notably the electrical exporters. As a result, a strange feature has occurred: on some occasions when the yen has risen, the price of Sony has also gone up.

There are other critical macroeconomic factors. We tend to look at overall GDP growth, interest rates, inflation and the price of oil. The latter has become increasingly less important in Japan, witness the recent lack of impact crude prices have had on the economy at large. To assess macrorisk, we have tended to use Schroder Salomon Smith Barney's Risk Attribution Model (RAM), which, as well as analysing the variance and co-variance of stocks in a portfolio, also examines each stock and the total portfolio in relation to seven macroeconomic factors. This has been a very useful tool in giving an impartial statistical health-check of the overall portfolio.

Ownership

Ownership is an increasingly important element that needs analysing. There are three main categories of investors who make a major difference to stock prices and to the performance of portfolios in the Japanese market. Previously, we referred to foreign investors, who in the late 1990s, became the swing investors, largely because domestic institutions were either on the side-lines or were sellers of equities. Foreigners can make a huge impact upon the performance of individual stocks, particularly when there is a ceiling on foreign ownership – eg, with broadcasters, foreigners cannot own more than 20% of the common stock. Where foreigners have an important participation in a stock, there tends to be a rather higher degree of risk. This is partly because foreigners tend to be rather more fickle and will quite happily pull out of a stock altogether because it has reached a certain valuation. Nevertheless, the major factor is that foreign portfolio managers who invest in Japan are completely at the mercy of asset alloca-tors who manage a whole international portfolio. A decision to reduce a portfolio's exposure to Japan can have a dramatic impact upon foreign favourites such as Sony and Honda. We saw a large measure of this in the second and third quarters of 2000.

The next most volatile investor category is individuals. This is particu-larly true in Japan because there still remains a "casino" class of investor, despite the long bear market – the stubborn bulls of the "bubble economy" of the late 1980s. These investors know relatively little about professional valuation techniques and growth assessments, and rely instead on the tip-sters – or, indeed, hearsay. This makes them a volatile group, and one which is prone to being swayed by the domestic stock-broking firms. They have a more than proportional impact on the market because many of them buy or sell on margin, thereby adding a considerable degree of gearing. We referred to 13 March 2000 above – a remarkable day for Japanese markets in recent history. The significance of that day was the degree and wide-spread nature of the fall in the market. This was a classic case of individuals driving the market – panic selling whatever the price. Institutions, or indeed dealers, would have traded far more cautiously. If they had wanted to sell, they would have done so up to a limit. At some stage, and in the absence of complete panic, prices would have simply been too oversold, and these participants would have pulled their offers. Instead, individuals who were beginning to have hefty margin calls instructed their brokers to sell at whatever price.

Cross-shareholdings, or the process of business associates owning each others' shares to cement their relationship, have been significant in post-war Japan. The process of unwinding these holdings has been accelerating recently, but this is likely to plateau sometime in the next few years. The cross-holdings used to represent more than half the Japanese market, but thanks to recent changes, now only make up about a quarter.

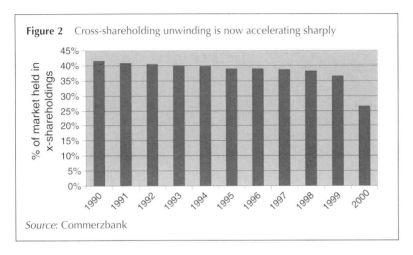

Figure 2 Cross-shareholding unwinding is now accelerating sharply

Source: Commerzbank

During the past few years, as the tight relationships between the banks and industrial conglomerates known as *keiretsu* have broken down, both parties have been selling each others' stock, thereby increasing the effective free-float. This has been tantamount to increasingly supply. The impact has been as negative as if the companies had issued stock, except that this process has been a steady trickle rather than an avalanche. Still, at the stock level, it has been essential to check that a stock is not likely to underperform because every time it goes up another cross-shareholder comes out of the woodwork. A recent example of this is Shin-Etsu Chemical, a manufacturer of silicon wafers for semi-conductors and of PVC, that, for the first time in many years, has enjoyed the boom of both businesses at the same time. The company keeps on revising up and yet, at the time of writing, the share price languishes at the same level of ¥5,000. Cross-shareholders do not tend to sell low, but they can certainly prevent a stock from rising.

Balance of risk to earnings

With reference to stock-specific risk, the most important aspect is the balance of risks to earnings. This is something that we at Balfour Capital stress, particularly in our fundamental analysis. Of all the developed markets, Japan has historically been the most correlated to earnings growth. Value investing in Japan has generally not been successful. As such, assessing future earnings is without doubt the most important criterion in making long-term investment decisions. Getting these forecasts right is

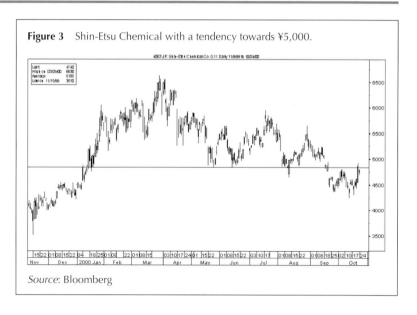

Figure 3 Shin-Etsu Chemical with a tendency towards ¥5,000.

Source: Bloomberg

where the risk analysis comes in. To some degree, this is a qualitative process. The Japan fund manager will have a good idea of what many analysts are forecasting, not only from database services such as IBES, but also from a select list of analysts that he trusts. Nevertheless, most analysts tend to project uni-directionally – ie, they tend to follow the current trend – and they tend to have too much faith in Japanese management. This is a critical issue, because Japanese management teams tend either to be super bullish or ultra conservative. There are relatively few in between. In addition to this, despite widespread exaggeration from foreign observers, Japanese management are at times economical with the truth, although marked differences in performance have to be reported according to the rules of the Financial Supervisory Agency (FSA). However, there are inevitably shocks that nobody expects. Analysing what those shocks could be is difficult, but nonetheless possible. We have engaged in the rather clichéd notion of SWOT analysis – Strengths, Weaknesses, Opportunities and Threats. Although clearly "Streetese", this methodology is effective because it looks at the balance of risks. Understanding the opportunities and threats of a business allows one to identify the balance of risks to earnings.

On the negative side of balancing risk, the best example of 2000 is clearly Hikari Tsushin. Although Balfour Capital was not amongst the enlightened few who got out at the absolute peak of ¥240,000, we nonetheless were not amongst the heavy pack of aggressive managers who continued to hold on in the hope that the stock would one day recover.

Indeed, the main "threat" to Hikari's earnings was that something would happen to its bread-and-butter business or retailing of mobile

Figure 4   The rise and fall of Hikari Tsushin.

Note the series of "limit-down" days in March and April when buyers were
virtually non-existent for 16 market days in a row
Source: Bloomberg

phones. When it became apparent that Hikari had actually guaranteed
payments to its agents regardless of whether a sale had taken place, and
was subsequently accused of forging parental signatures allowing minors
to purchase a phone, it became clear that the franchise was at risk.
Although the SWOT analysis did not reveal this particular eventuality, it
was clear that the operators who chose to sell their phones through Hikari
could either choose another firm, or might even start selling their phones
themselves.

On the positive side, understanding the "opportunities" of Fast Retailing
allowed the Japan manager to commit to the stock with far more confidence. In this instance, the critical piece of the jigsaw was to understand the
disenchantment of the Japanese consumer, who has been dying to discover
a new formula that represents value for money. Any non-American understands this perfectly when travelling to the US: high quality, well-designed
clothes available at very low prices. The Japanese have spent years buying
either designer clothes at sky-high prices, or buying frumpy, cheap imports
from Asia. Many fund managers were sceptical of Fast Retailing, not only
because GAP has been expanding in Japan already, but also because they
could not accept that the company would be able to reach out to young
consumers. Fast Retailing baffled them by having a management structure
that had the flexibility to swiftly understand changing consumer tastes,
and to produce what the consumer wanted cheaply, thanks to state-of-the-
art factories in China. It is a tribute to the management that the company
has been able to produce increases in same store sales in excess of 100%

year-on-year, while the department stores continue to see their figures decline by over 5%.

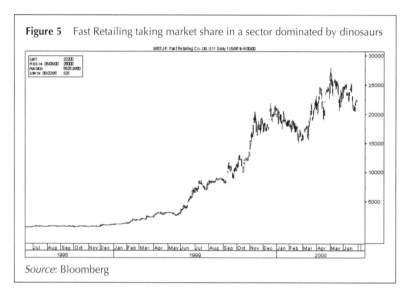

Figure 5   Fast Retailing taking market share in a sector dominated by dinosaurs

Source: Bloomberg

In terms of portfolio specific risk, the most striking aspect is the correlation of all stocks with each other. Clearly, if all the stocks in a portfolio move in tandem, the fact that the entire portfolio has a beta of one is irrelevant. The portfolio can end up underperforming the market substantially, because few stocks buck the trend to get an average performance equivalent to that of the market. For a long/short fund, the situation can be even more precarious because of the risk of what is known as "double negative alpha". Broadly speaking, this is the nightmare scenario in which the shorts go up and the longs go down. Anyone who thinks that a long/short portfolio is necessarily less risky than a long only portfolio clearly does not understand risk. We have therefore placed great emphasis on the correlation of stocks within a given portfolio. The RAM calculates the co-variance of each pair of stocks and factors this into the overall calculation of the variance of a portfolio.

Rotation

From a more qualitative perspective comes the risk of "rotation". This is an aspect that is particularly powerful in Japan, but which also exists in other markets. A market with a great deal of sector rotation, or indeed one with no direction at all, can be a far riskier market than might at first appear. These markets tend to exist when there is little in terms of fundamentals or technicals to drive the market. Instead, safe havens are found, or rather spurious investment themes abound, usually meaning that areas where there are good prospects for earnings, or where valuations are sound, are rendered weak due to consequent selling. These periods can extend for quite some time, leading to potential underperformance. The only real way of protecting against this is to use less capital.

THE BEST TOOLS TO ASSESS RISK IN JAPAN

We have made numerous mention of various risk tools that we use and we have discussed the different levels at which we assess risk. In order to tie this together, we feel it important to go through the process in sequential order, describing the methods used at each stage.

The initial risk management takes place at stock level, because we aim to screen out those stocks carrying too high a risk, in order to narrow down our universe. It would be a waste of our time to carry out rigorous fundamental and technical analysis on a particular stock, only to find out that it carries an unacceptable level of risk from a liquidity stand-point. This narrowing down is undertaken through a normal screening process, focusing primarily on liquidity. Our filters are two-fold: market capitalisation and average six-monthly trading volume. We aim to be able to liquidate substantially all our positions in one day; this screening immediately reduces our universe from a potential of over 3,300 stocks to roughly 500 stocks. We then do a manual screening to check for those that have an unacceptable level of cross-shareholders ie, low free-float.

Once our narrowed-down universe has been established, we then carry out our fundamental and technical research, which is very much a risk assessment process. The expression "balance of risk to earnings" mentioned above is critical at this stage of the fundamental analysis. We need to assess as accurately as possible what the risks are for earnings either to overshoot or to undershoot. We need to be aware of what expectations actually are, and of the likelihood of their being met. This will be based on the record of management predictions as well as the composition of the profit and loss account. The gearing of profits to sales is generally the key question.

At a technical level, charts do not necessarily tell us where a share price is going. Instead, it gives various scenarios, and often provides probabilities for the various scenarios. For example, if a stock has been in a continuous upward movement with a strong base line, the balance of probability is that this growth will continue. Anyone attempting to short that stock either has great insight, or is simply quite reckless. Conversely, once a strong upward trend line has been broken, it is a warning signal. If the stock continues to fall,the point is, of course, obvious. If, however, the stock recovers to its trend line and continues the same ascent many observers would argue that it is back on course. We would argue, however, that the probability of the stock breaking down has multiplied.

The exact converse is true of shorts. If ever we see a stock's chart

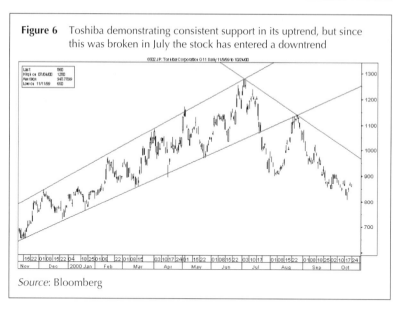

Figure 6   Toshiba demonstrating consistent support in its uptrend, but since this was broken in July the stock has entered a downtrend

Source: Bloomberg

breaking up through a downtrend, we will immediately reconsider our position. Clearly, there are occasional overrides during very "choppy markets", when exceptions are made. This was the case in Autumn 1998, but the choppiness we saw exactly a year later was probably a warning as to what would happen to "tech" stocks after the new Millennium.

At portfolio level, we use the RAM primarily to look at absolute risk. This is critical, because our mission is to deliver superior absolute returns. The model has a two-pronged approach: it examines variance as well as macroeconomic risk. It is useful because it looks at seven years' worth of data. We find this an ideal timescale, because anything much longer than this takes into account the bubble years, whereas anything much shorter puts too much emphasis upon the boom in technology. The other advantage of this model is that it can look at the combined risks of long and short positions in combination, rather than subtracting one from the other. This is thanks to the co-variance of stock pairs described above. In addition to this, RAM gives us an impartial assessment of how vulnerable our portfolio is to macroeconomic factors. For example, it is probable that most good portfolio managers will have considered how their portfolio is likely to behave if the yen strengthens, but how many people look regularly at the effect of rising oil prices? The same is true for both long and short-term interest rates.

In assessing market risk, we also look at Beta. This is notoriously unreliable, particularly in Japan. But like any other risk model, it gives one an impartial photograph of what the portfolio looks like. We particularly like to use Beta in the context of the net position of the portfolio. A fund may on the surface appear to be market neutral at a particular instant, but, having adjusted for Beta, one might find that it is actually net short. This does not mean that we regard our true exposure to be only the Beta-adjusted version. But we do take it into account. Given that we determine our gross exposure and consequent gearing according to confidence level (a very qualitative process), understanding the gearing of the long and short books on their own merits is critical. For example, let us assume that we are market neutral, with a long book of 60% of capital and a short book of 60% of capital. We will then be 120% geared. Our risk, in theory, should be relatively contained, although the level of gearing would suggest a high degree of confidence in our current stock selection. Assuming that the Beta of the long book is 0.7, and the Beta of the short book is 1.7, the picture changes dramatically! Essentially, the risk assessment process needs to focus very much on the short book. The risk of the long book pales into insignificance.

Fundamentally, we view risk measurement and risk control as an art, not as a science. Like most arts, however, one uses tools that are to some degree mechanical to assist in this process. The concert pianist uses an instrument which, however lovingly assembled, has essentially been made by machines. The same is true of a sculptor who uses a series of chisels that have been made in a factory. So it is with risk. Those who rely entirely on a risk model, especially for "optimisation" purposes (the model suggests how to tweak the portfolio to achieve a given level of risk) should be indexers. This is one of the great mistakes that some of the large "money-collecting" fund management firms have made. They are trying to establish a niche away from indexing, while offering largely quantitative analysis and risk tools. On a recent trip, I was reminded how dangerous scientists can be in our industry. I was introduced to a Swiss professor of Physics who was very friendly and asked lots of questions. When he found out that I had read modern history at Oxford before going into fund management, he was aghast. How on earth could I have entered the industry without a qualification in one of the sciences or in economics? I replied that I thought this not to be essential and then gave him my views on risk models, citing the then recent example of John Meriwether's Long Term Capital Management. He retorted somewhat like Hercule Poirot: "Ah... but you see the model was wrong!".

We believe passionately that this attitude is wrong. This game is all about maximising return for risk at every single stage of the process (at whatever level has been agreed between manager and client). Managers must use every single tool at their disposal, both quantitative and qualitative, to achieve this aim. The tools together are the ultimate pair.

16

The "Risk" in Risk Arbitrage

John Paulson

Paulson & Co, Inc

One of the great practitioners in risk arbitrage, seasoned by over 40 years of investing, once said to me, *"risk arbitrage is not about making money, it's about not losing money"*. In effect, the true skill in risk arbitrage is about avoiding losses. And to avoid losses, one must understand, evaluate and manage risk.

Risk arbitrage[1], or merger arbitrage, entails capturing the spread between the price an acquirer has agreed to pay for a target and the price the target trades at after the deal is announced. In a cash deal, the arbitrageur would merely buy the target at a discount to the cash offer price and exchange the target stock for cash at its completion. In a stock deal, the arbitrageur would buy the target and, in order to lock in the spread, short the acquirer in an amount equal to the number of shares the arbitrageur is due to receive in exchange for the target's shares. The spread is the discount the target trades at to the merger consideration and can be expressed in either absolute, percentage or annualised terms.

Since spreads are typically small in relation to the premium paid in a deal, the downside one takes to earn the spread can be significant. The graph in Figure 1 illustrates the magnitude of the risk/return trade off in a typical transaction.

In this example, Chirex Inc, a US-based pharmaceutical service provider, agreed, in a cash tender offer, to be acquired on July 24, 2000 by Rhodia SA, a French specialty chemical manufacturer, for US$31.25. Chirex stock jumped 10½ points on the day of the announcement, from 20¼ to 30¾. The spread, at US$0.50, provides a gross return of 1.6% and an annualised return of approximately 17%, assuming a 35-day close. However, many factors can affect the rate of return. If the deal incurs delays and takes three months to close, the annualised return will fall from 17% to 6%. If the price is subsequently cut to below US$30.75, the deal will turn from a profit to a loss. Or, in a worst case scenario, the deal might break altogether and the

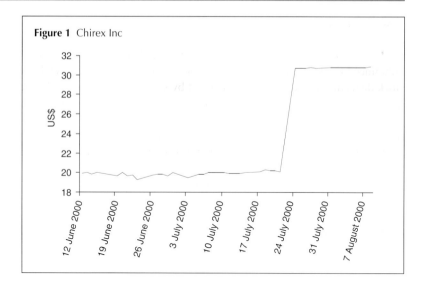

Figure 1 Chirex Inc

stock will fall to its pre-announcement levels or lower. *The "risk" in risk arbitrage is therefore anything that affects the deal's completion, the timing of completion, or the amount of consideration received at completion.* The magnitude of the risk can be substantial. In the Chirex example, the potential loss, as measured by the premium, would be US$10.50, or 21 times the potential gain.

What should be apparent from this example is that risk arbitrage is not for the average investor. The potential downside is substantial in relation to the small upside.

Using the economics of the previous example, if one were right 95% of the time in similar situations, one would only break even. The average investor may not be able to accurately assess the myriad of risks in a transaction and would be likely to lose money in this strategy. Paradoxically, the reward for the experienced manager would be stable, non-correlated returns with less volatility than the market, but able to provide comparable returns over the long term.

To manage the "risk" in risk arbitrage, one must first identify the specific risks, and then manage risk in a way that produces the desired returns. We divide risk into two general categories:

- *macro risks*, which pertain to general economic forces such as market volatility, interest rates, exchange rates and commodity prices; and
- *micro risks*, which pertain to the specific transaction such as earnings, financing and regulatory issues.

MACRO RISKS
Market
In merger arbitrage, one can generally hedge market risk by investing in announced transactions. In cash deals, the consideration is fixed, while in stock deals the consideration can be fixed by shorting the acquirer's stock in an amount equal to the merger ratio. By locking in the spread, the expected returns are earned regardless of the direction of the market, as long as the deal closes. Sometimes, the ability to lock in a spread in stock deals can be more difficult because the ratio is not fixed and is subject to a pricing period, or a collar structure, in which the amount of stock issued will vary. However, by matching the short sales to the terms of the collar or the pricing period, the consideration can generally be locked in.

While small market movements may have minimal effect on transactions, a sharp movement, either up or down, may increase the risk of deal completion. A rapidly falling market, for example, may cause merger financing to dry up, or may cause buyers to re-evaluate the merits and/or the price of an acquisition. In September 1998, the high yield market almost shut down completely and banks used market-out covenants to rescind financing commitments, causing many leveraged buyouts to break. Similarly, financial buyers may try to negotiate a lower price if they think they can buy the company cheaper. Generally, in a rapidly falling market, cash spreads may widen due to the increased macro uncertainty while spreads in stock deals may contract or stabilise due to the "cushioning effect" of the gains realised on the short side.

A rapidly rising market can create problems in arbitrage as well. For example, the Internet fever of 1999 caused rapid run-ups in the stock price of many buyers, causing the target's stock price to rise to levels where huge loses would be incurred if the deal were to break. The rapid increase in the potential downside caused spreads in certain deals to widen. In January, 1999, the At Home acquisition of Excite was announced. At Home ran from US$50 on the day of announcement to over US$94. This caused Excite to rise from the mid-US$60s before the deal was announced to over US$170, creating potential downside of over US$100 per share. The spread responded accordingly and widened from US$8 when the deal was announced to US$30. Numerous other examples exist including, most recently, JDS Uniphase's acquisition of E-Tek Dynamics and JDS Uniphase's proposed acquisition of SDL Inc.

Interest Rates
A rise in interest rates negatively affects certain deals and is a red flag in arbitrage. Higher interest rates will make financing more difficult, affecting the ability of borrowers to incur debt, and increasing the cost of debt. Higher interest rates will also negatively affect earnings for certain industries, such as banks, insurance and automobile companies. Difficult

financing conditions, combined with negative earnings surprises, may cause buyers to terminate deals and cause the stocks of targets to collapse.

Other economic factors

Commodity prices, exchange rates and other economic factors may negatively affect the profitability of particular industries, which in turn could increase the probability of deal termination. To avoid losses, arbitrageurs must be aware of these trends and the impact they may have on targets.

MICRO RISKS

There are many risks pertaining to particular transactions that may give rise to a deal breaking. After 20 years in the merger or risk arbitrage business, I still uncover new risks because markets are always evolving. However, I have attempted to highlight some of the important risks that may affect a deal's outcome.

Earnings

One of the most common reasons for a deal to break is due to an unexpected decline in the target's performance. Buyers typically value an acquisition based on a multiple of earnings and the projected growth in earnings. If, between the announcement of a deal and its closure, the target fails to meet the buyer's earnings expectations, the buyer may attempt to negotiate a lower price or terminate the transaction. The result can be devastating. The example in Figure 2, while one of many, illustrates the risk of an earnings disappointment. In this case, the Warnaco Group cancelled its purchase of Authentic Fitness Corporation (AFC) and stated, "After it

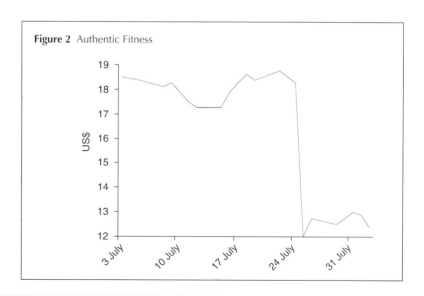

Figure 2 Authentic Fitness

became clear that AFC will report a loss for its fourth quarter and report earnings below street estimates for its fiscal year, the board unanimously concluded to terminate the merger agreement".

Financing

In cash transactions, the ability to finance the purchase of the target may, in certain circumstances, pose a substantial risk to deal completion. While all buyers believe they can raise the money at the time of announcement, a rise in interest rates, an earnings decline in either the target or the acquirer, or a decline in the stock market may all cause financing difficulties. In a recent deal, PSC shares plunged after Welch Allyn called off the merger as it "was unable to obtain sufficient financings" (see Figure 3).

Legal

A thorough understanding of legal issues is imperative to evaluate the risks in a transaction. Such issues include the specifics regarding tender offers, exchange offers, cash mergers, stock mergers, spin-offs, state takeover statutes, corporate by-laws and articles of incorporation. One must also be familiar with litigation risk as the buyer, or the seller, may be involved in litigation which could affect the deal's completion. Consider the US$145 billion judgment against Philip Morris in Florida State Court, announced after Philip Morris agreed to buy Nabisco, or the US$800 million patent infringement suit filed against Seagate in the midst of its proposed merger with Veritas. An understanding of a broad spectrum of legal areas is paramount in assessing the risk of a transaction.

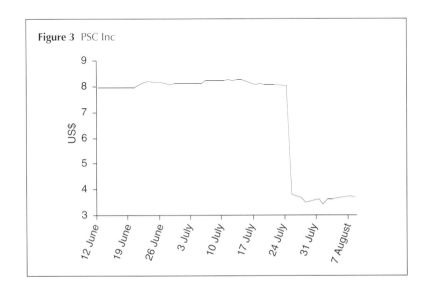

Figure 3 PSC Inc

Premium

The premium the acquirer pays for the target can be used as a starting point in estimating the downside risk if the deal fails. Generally, the greater the premium, the greater the downside risk. Premiums of 75%, 100% or even 150% are not uncommon in risk arbitrage. In such situations, the arbitrageur must carefully weigh the risk/return trade-off and avoid those situations where the return is not adequate for the risks assumed.

Merger Agreement

Not all merger agreements are created equal and, in fact, vary widely in the parties' degree of commitment to completing the transaction. The weakest form of a merger agreement is an agreement-in-principle or a letter-of-intent, both of which virtually allow either party to walk from the transaction at will. Even definitive agreements can vary widely as to the circumstances under which the buyer can walk from a transaction. Merger agreements must be examined closely to investigate any due diligence conditions, any performance tests, material adverse change clauses, drop-dead dates, walk-away provisions, and regulatory outs. Clearly, the tighter the merger agreement, the greater the certainty of deal completion.

Taxes

A dollar in cash is not always a dollar in cash. The after tax proceeds to the investor can vary widely, depending on the tax structure of the transaction and the tax status of the shareholders. This is especially true as more and more transactions are cross-border deals involving multiple tax codes and investors of different nationalities.

For example, the receipt of cash in a merger may sometimes be taxed as a dividend and not as a capital gain. While this may have limited impact on a US fund, it could be disastrous for an offshore fund which, although it incurs no tax on capital gains, is subject to a 30% withholding tax on dividends. Consider the situation where the arbitrageur buys Company A for US$19.50 and sells it to Company B for US$20.00, earning a US$0.50 spread. If the transaction is taxable as a dividend, 30% of the US$20 (ie, US$6.00) will be withheld by the depository and paid to the IRS. Instead of a US$0.50 gain, this example will provide a US$5.50 loss for the offshore investor.

Consideration

While most deals involve either all cash or all stock, there are a near infinite number of possible permutations. Merger consideration could include:

- a mixture of cash and stock in fixed proportions;
- cash and stock in fixed amounts subject to proration;
- cash and stock in unlimited proportions;
- fixed dollar amount of stock subject to a collar;

- fixed dollar amount of stock subject to a pricing period;
- fixed ratio of stock with a dollar cap;
- stock and a spin-off;
- stock, a spin-off and debt; and
- stock, a spin-off, debt and cash.

The risk the form of consideration poses to the arbitrageur is in the ability to lock in the value of the consideration at the time of closing to ensure a positive spread. This may not always be possible if the consideration does not trade, is illiquid, is contingent, is based on a random pricing period or is subject to an unknown proration. The following quotation from the press release regarding the acquisition of Trimark by AMVESCAP highlights how complex the form of consideration can be:

> AMVESCAP will offer Trimark shareholders a mix of consideration valued at approximately CDN$27.00 per share. Total consideration will include a fixed amount of cash of approximately CDN$760 million and, at current prices, approximately CDN$1.97 billion in shares or other AMVESCAP linked securities, all subject to proration. Trimark shareholders may elect either AMVESCAP Ordinary Shares or shares of an AMVESCAP Canadian subsidiary which are exchangeable into ordinary Shares ("Exchangeable Shares"). If the trading price of the underlying AMVESCAP Ordinary Shares increases or decreases by up to 12.5% from the current level, the number of shares to be issued will be adjusted accordingly. The final value of the consideration to be offered will be based upon the weighted average of the Canadian dollar equivalent of the trading prices of AMVESCAP Ordinary Shares on the London Stock Exchange for a period of five consecutive trading days ending the day that is three business days prior to the closing. Additionally, Trimark shareholders may elect to receive consideration in the form of up to CDN$1.3 billion in principal amount of equity subordinated debentures ("ESDs") subject to a minimum ESD issuance of CDN$100 million. The ESDs are a form of convertible debenture security with a 6.0% coupon, three year term and a strike price at the AMVESCAP Ordinary Share price calculated as of the issue date and an appreciation cap of 20% above the strike price.

Acquirer

One must examine the acquirer as well as the target in a merger transaction. In a cash transaction, for example, one must ensure that the acquirer has the ability to raise the cash to complete the transaction. Also, one needs to know the reputation of the acquirer, as some acquirers are known for being tough negotiators and may try to negotiate the price downward given any opportunity. In stock deals, a recurring risk is that the acquirer itself may become a takeover target. This is one of the biggest risks in risk arbitrage. Since the arbitrageur is long the target and short the acquirer, a bid for the acquirer could cause the acquirer to rise and the target to fall, resulting in losses in both the long and the short side. This happened in the proposed acquisition of Ocular Science by Wesley Jensen. Only two days after the two companies signed a definitive merger agreement, Bausch & Lomb bid for Wesley Jensen, causing the deal with Ocular to break, Ocular's stock price to fall and Wesley Jensen's stock price to soar, leading to large losses for some arbitrageurs.

Fraud

Unfortunately, fraud is a risk that may be difficult to uncover until it is too late. While infrequent, many examples exist, including the creation of Cendant through the merger of HFS with CUC International, the proposed sales of North Face and Sunbeam, and, in the biggest fiasco of all, Bre-X. In the cases of CUC, Northface and Sunbeam, management used irregular accounting practices to overstate earnings. When the frauds were uncovered, the stocks collapsed. Bre-X was the most bizarre story of all. Advised by JP Morgan, Bre-X was billed as the largest, lowest cost and most profitable gold prospect in the world, with a value estimated by mining analysts of US$11 billion. Bre-X became the target of a fierce bidding war between Barrick Gold, Freeport McMoran and Placer Dome, with bids exceeding US$5 billion. In the end, Freeport prevailed, only to find out that the mine was a complete fraud, supposedly masterminded by an employee who then, supposedly, committed suicide. Ultimately, the stock price of Bre-X declined from a high of US$27 to zero.

Regulatory

"In the risky realm of arbitraging mergers and acquisitions, government scrutiny can be perilous and costly", states Marcelo Price of Dow Jones (From Dow Jones News Service). Very true. Regulatory concerns frequently cause spreads to widen, leads to delays in closing and ultimately cause deals to unravel. The most common form of government scrutiny would be antitrust. In the United States, either the Justice Department or the Federal Trade Commission reviews mergers to ascertain their competitive implications. In Europe, each individual country has its own regulatory authority investigating mergers, eg, the Federal Cartel Office in Germany and the Monopolies and Mergers Commission in the United Kingdom. In addition, the European Commission investigates mergers for their impact on the European Union. Many deals have broken due to antitrust enforcement, including such landmark cases as Staples/Office Depot and Lockheed Martin/Northrop Grumman.

However, anti-trust authorities are not the arbitrageurs' only regulatory concern. Many industries have their own specialty government watchdogs. In the United States, these include the Federal Communications Commission for communication deals; the Committee on Foreign Investment for national security concerns; the Federal Reserve for bank deals; State Insurance Commissions for insurance deals; and State Public Utility Commissions for utility, cable and telephone deals. Some deals cause a virtual regulatory quagmire. Our firm's analysis of the merger of Entergy and FPL Group ended promptly after we read the following paragraph from the press release:

> The merger requires the approval of shareholders of both companies, the Securities and Exchange Commission, the Federal Energy Regulatory Commission, the Nuclear Regulatory Commission, and the Federal Communications Commission; the expiration or termination of the waiting period under the Hart-Scott-Rodino Antitrust Improvements Act; and the completion of regulatory procedures in Arkansas, Florida, Louisiana, Mississippi, Texas and the city of New Orleans. The companies' objective is to complete the transaction within 15 months.

Timing

Not only must the arbitrageur predict the outcome of a transaction, but he must also estimate the time to completion. If a deal takes significantly longer to complete than anticipated, the rate of return will decline to uneconomic levels. Intense regulatory review will frequently prolong the time to closing. Dow Chemicals' acquisition of Union Carbide, announced on August 4, 1999, had still not received antitrust clearance as of its first anniversary. If one had put the transaction on the day of the announcement, the annualised return-to-date would be less than 5.0%. Other regulatory reviews have taken longer. Consider the following Bloomberg news story: "The Federal Energy Regulatory Commission rejected Wisconsin Energy and Northern States Power plan to merge and told the companies to come back in three months with a new plan. The two companies first proposed their merger two years ago".

Due Diligence

Announced mergers with due diligence conditions always raise a red flag and create uncertainty as to when, and if, the deal will be completed. Some due diligence clauses are open-ended while others have a specific time, or event, to their completion. One must always research whether there are any due diligence conditions, and be wary of any deals with such clauses. The following news stories are not unusual. "Banyan Corporation announces that it has signed a Letter of Intent to merge with Echo Marketing Corporation. Additional details will be made available as soon as both companies conclude their due diligence". Four months later, "Banyan Corporation announces that after extensive due diligence it has withdrawn from its merger with Echo Marketing Corporation". Or, "EDS today announced it has withdrawn its proposal to acquire Policy Management Systems after completing due diligence".

Other

There are many other risks that may need to be considered including, environmental liabilities, customer concentration, shareholder vote requirements, and management issues. Each of these risks has affected a deal's outcome in previous situations. The important point for the arbitrageur is to know which potential risks are relevant to which particular situations.

Risk management

Once the arbitrageur understands the "risks" in risk arbitrage he can then begin constructing a portfolio of deals that balances risks and limits downside exposure. Unfortunately, every deal has risk, so one cannot avoid risk entirely. Instead, one must prudently manage risk to produce a desired return with minimal drawdowns and low market correlation.

To manage portfolio risk, we first examine the potential downside in a transaction. We eliminate, up front, the riskier arbitrage transactions, which over time have proven a poor or even negative expected value. Instead, we look for deals whose characteristics imply a high probability of closing (see Table 1).

By avoiding low quality deals and focusing on high quality deals, we reduce both the micro and macro risks of our portfolio. For example, by eliminating from our portfolio deals subject to financing or deals with poor performing targets, we remove deals that have a lower probability of closing in a stable market as well as a higher probability of breaking in a deteriorating macro economic environment. On the other hand, by focusing on the strategic combinations of solidly performing targets by large acquirers, we increase the probability that deals in the portfolio will close in all market environments.

To further reduce the risk of our portfolio we:

- constantly monitor events which could alter the risk profile of a transaction, and, when necessary, adjust positions;
- diversify the portfolio across industries to avoid the influence of any industry specific risks;
- diversify the portfolio amongst deals to limit the impact any unforeseen event could have on a portfolio position;
- diversify the portfolio across cash and stock deals to mitigate the effect of rising or falling markets;
- size individual positions according to their potential downside and the probability of that downside;
- hedge stock deals according to their full merger ratios and use "put" protection, when necessary, to limit downside loss; and
- focus on deals with structures that perform better in declining markets.

Table 1 Screening criteria

Avoid
- Agreements in principle
- Deals subject to financing
- Deals subject to due diligence
- Targets with poor earnings trends
- Targets with negative earnings
- Deals in cyclical industries
- Deals in highly regulated industries

Focus
- Definitive agreements
- Strategic rationale
- Large acquirer
- No financing condition
- No due diligence condition
- Solidly performing target
- Reasonable valuation
- Limited regulatory risk

CONCLUSION

The same wise gentlemen who told me "risk arbitrage is not about making money, its about not losing money" also told me, *"if you watch the downside, the upside will take care of itself"*. To manage the downside, one must first have a thorough understanding of the "risk" in risk arbitrage. Using that understanding, one must then construct a portfolio that eliminates poor quality transactions and focuses on high quality deals. To further manage risk within the portfolio, one must constantly monitor one's positions for any changes, hedge all positions, limit position size, and broadly diversify across deals and industries. By implementing these criteria, the manager will be able to deliver the benefits of this strategy: non-correlated, low volatility returns.

1   In addition to mergers, risk arbitrage may also include situations such as spin-offs, recapitalisations, partial tender offers and other forms of restructurings. "Event arbitrage" situations have higher risk/return profiles, as the value of the ultimate consideration is less certain. For the purposes of this chapter, we will limit our discussions to merger arbitrage, the segment of risk arbitrage pertaining to announced corporate mergers and acquisitions.

17

Convertible Arbitrage

Michael A. Boyd, Jr and John Michael Pagli, Jr

Forest Investment Management LLC and Forest Global Convertible Fund Ltd

Convertible arbitrage is a well-established alternative investment strategy in terms of its broad acceptance and history. In the realm of alternative investments, it is known as a *relative value, risk-controlled* strategy. In its most basic form, convertible arbitrage is an investment technique that entails the purchase of a convertible security and the partial short sale of the related equity security.

Our interest in, and the usefulness of, convertible arbitrage is predicated upon two basic precepts that are largely borne out in reality. First, the unique, hybrid composition of convertible securities provides for an asymmetrical relationship between upside return potential and downside risk. The ability to hedge the convertible security's price movements with a correlated underlying equity security enhances risk/return modification. The second precept is that the return streams from convertible arbitrage tend to have lower inherent volatility, as measured by standard deviation. This reflects the relative steadiness of periodic returns and lower and shorter periods of drawdown with sharper and quicker snapbacks.

Awareness and use of the strategy has grown significantly over the last decade, and is expected to continue to grow. Underpinning this is the significant growth of the global convertible securities market over the past decade; ongoing development and adaptation of enhanced hedging techniques and risk management tools; and investors' need to balance investment portfolios in an increasingly volatile environment.

This book is about risk management. Before we address the specific approaches to risk management on the bases of security selection and portfolio construction, we will provide some background on convertible securities and convertible arbitrage theory and practice and discuss the inherent risks. This is intended to be a distillation of our long experience as a leading pure-play convertible arbitrage firm. Appropriate risk-adjusted returns will be the by-product of judicious application of risk management and the experience of the portfolio management team.

A BRIEF OVERVIEW OF CONVERTIBLE SECURITIES THEORY

A convertible security is a corporate security that is usually issued with a corporate bond yield. This is issued in exchange for a conversion feature that allows the holder to convert the security into a fixed number of shares of the company's underlying common stock at any time prior to maturity or redemption of the instrument. Typically, the convertible security is call protected for a number of years after which the issuer may induce conversion or call the security for cash. As termed in this discussion, convertible securities typically mean bonds convertible into common stock, although other hybrid instruments such as preferred stock, warrants, PERCS (Preferred Equity Redemption Cumulative Shares) and LYONS (Liquid Yield Option Notes) may also be used.

As the holder of a convertible security may convert it into a predetermined number of shares of the issuer's common stock, there is often a high degree of correlation between the convertible security's value and that of the related equity security. Therefore, as the common stock price appreciates or depreciates, the convertible security's valuation follows. However, the degree to which a change in value of an underlying security is reflected in the value of the convertible security depends on the convertible security's premium over conversion value. Understanding the relationship between convertible security and stock prices is very important in convertible investing since, generally, the higher the premium, the lower the correlation between convertible securities and common stock movements.

The premium over conversion value is defined as the amount paid for a convertible security in excess of the value receivable upon conversion into the underlying security. For example, if a bond trading at par (US$1,000) converted into 100 shares of an US$8.00 stock, the conversion value (also known as parity value) would be US$800. The premium level, therefore, would be the difference between the US$1,000 par value and the US$800 conversion value, a total of US$200 in premium. Since premium is typically expressed in percentage terms over conversion value, this security would have a 25% premium (US$200 ÷ US$800).

There are various factors that affect a convertible security's premium. Generally, the higher the yield of the convertible security, the higher the premium given that the convertible security acts more like a fixed income instrument as it trades closer to its investment value (ie, theoretically, that level where the issuer could issue non-convertible debt). Therefore, investors pay more for the convertible security's yield component rather than its equity component. Conversely, as the common stock appreciates, making the convertible security ultimately trade higher above par value, the premium falls since there is a likelihood that the issuer will call the convertible security and force conversion. The degree of narrowing of premium at these levels is often heavily dependent on the amount of call protection left in the security and the volatility of the underlying equity.

While this premium relationship generally holds true over time and across a broad base of convertible securities as they trade between investment value and potential call point, there are many independent factors which also alter an individual convertible security's premium relationship on a daily trading basis. For example, for various reasons, there is rarely in practice a dollar-for-dollar correspondence between the price and movement of a given convertible security and that of its underlying security. A convertible security, as a hybrid instrument having elements of both debt and equity, responds to different market forces than that of a pure equity instrument such as common stock. For example, the market price of a convertible security will tend to move inversely to changes in interest rates in recognition of its debt-like characteristics, whereas a common stock's sensitivity to interest rate fluctuations might be more closely related to the perceived macroeconomic causes and effects of such fluctuations. Liquidity, or size of issue and frequency of trades, and the issuer's credit rating generally have a greater impact on the relative valuation of a convertible security than on a common stock. Earnings announcements, credit rating changes, market sentiment and supply and demand for a particular security all contribute to a unique personality for each convertible issue.

In theory, hedging positions in convertible securities employs the short sale of the underlying equity security or related instruments that create an offset to the long position. The principal risk in the purchase price paid for the convertible security is offset by the proceeds realised from the short sale of the underlying security. Therefore, due to the inverse correlation, the price fluctuation in either position is theoretically offset by a contra price fluctuation in the related position. The gain which would be realised from an increase in the resale of a long convertible security position would be offset against the loss which would be realised from an increase in the repurchase of the short underlying security position. The theoretical net result of all the movements should be a neutral or profitable US$ outcome.

There is no single, fixed formula dictating the movement of an underlying security as a function of its corresponding convertible security, but rather a range of factors having varying levels of predictive value. To assist in evaluating these various factors, we have constructed a computer based "target system", which maintains a database of relevant information particular to each convertible issue, and various analytical models, which reflect our subjective values and weights over various time periods with respect to such information as relative volatility, cashflows, upside forced call price, investment value, related premium levels and credit spreads.

When the Target System is overlaid with these proprietary analytical models a total return profile for each convertible security is established. Thus, while a statistical foundation is employed by our managers in trading these securities, we believe that its three-tiered, hedge oriented approach magnifies a portfolio's potential returns by recognising and taking advantage of the unique fundamental and statistical aspects of each security on an individual basis.

In our view, an overall portfolio combining the use of a convertible total return profile with an in-depth knowledge of the underlying equity and credit risk, can be used to create hedges that outperform on a risk-adjusted basis a direct investment in the underlying equity. This approach reduces the need for market timing, allows for statistically superior performance and enhances capital preservation over time.

RISKS AND RISK MANAGEMENT
Structure and globalisation of the convertible securities market

The events of 1998 highlighted, if not precipitated, the maturity and integration of the convertible market as all sectors of the global capital markets seemed to converge. Among the critical features characterising modern capital markets are the globalisation and securitisation of many asset types. This has led to the integration of essentially all capital markets. In the late 1980s and 1990s, many asset classes were being securitised, and these new securities were being issued globally, supplanting much of the capital provided directly by the banking system. These securities include high yield bonds, emerging markets bonds, asset-backed securities, mortgage-backed securities, securitised loans, collaterised bond, loan and debt obligations, and tradeable private placements of debt and equity. The development and growth of securitised instruments in the cash market has been complemented by the development and growth of the derivatives market to capitalise on trading opportunities and manage risk within and between all markets globally, including the convertible securities market. This has led, in turn, to greater volatility in liquidity, credit spreads and prices.

Within the convertible securities market, there have been a number of significant developments over the last decade. These include the growth of the convertible securities markets in developed economies such as western Europe and Japan; the plethora of new issuance in 1999 and 2000 by investment grade issuers; the emergence of hedge funds as the new dominant participants in the convertible market and a historic widening of credit spreads off the Treasury yield curve. The combination of these factors has led to the emergence of a new market landscape for convertible securities hedging in terms of opportunity and risk. This new landscape has necessitated, in our view, a tactical shift in security selection, hedging and portfolio construction.

In western Europe, the growth of the convertible securities market in recent years has been driven by the combination of the need for higher returns by pension funds, banks and insurance companies, and the need by corporate issuers to finance growth and acquisitions efficiently as well as to monetise cross-shareholdings in as tax-efficient manner as may be necessary. Much of the western European convertible securities market is investment grade. While the yields tend to be low, and the static returns, in turn, tend to be low, the convertibles tend to have a determinate, and reliable, bond floor. Additionally, new issues have tended to be priced advantageously for investors with respect to implied versus historical volatility, thus providing the opportunity to capture trading profits, or *gamma*. Given these features, western European issues have become an increasingly important component of many convertible portfolios. The size of the market now approximates that of the US at US$180 billion. The Japanese convertible market, which only a few years ago was the largest at roughly US$400 billion, has contracted significantly. However, there are selected trading opportunities that do arise. We would expect the Japanese market to expand again when there is a need for efficient growth financing and as new issues are attractively priced and structured.

The US convertible securities market, in contrast to those of western Europe and Japan, is still largely sub-investment grade. The market during its renaissance in the 1960s, and through much of the following decades, was a localised, niche market for growth financings for sub-investment grade companies. Many of the early issues were by airlines and conglomerates, and later by industrial and technology companies. Whereas much of the return profile for western European and Japanese issues is characterised by higher trading profits and lower yields, US issues tend to have higher yields, reflecting lower credit quality, with cash and carry characteristics.

In the latter stages of the recent bull market, particularly in 1999 and the first quarter of 2000, there was heavy new issuance by US companies in the new economy sector, much of which had been of sub-investment grade quality. More recently, as the bull market faded, a bear market developed and the extension of credit has been constricted. Consequently, default rates have escalated, credit spreads have widened significantly and bond floors have become much less determinate and reliable. Since the second quarter of 2000, up to the time of writing there have been a number of new issues from investment grade and larger capitalisation companies, with favourable make-whole and change of control terms for investors. These issues tend to be structured and perform in a similar manner to western European issues.

With the expansion of the global convertible securities market and the development and increased use of asset swaps and credit default swaps, particularly since 1998, the larger, more sophisticated convertible hedge managers, Forest among them, have emerged as the dominant market participants. They are well positioned to commit meaningful amounts of capital to new issues of their choice and to hedge *rho*, or interest rate, risk and the risk of credit spread widening. As the size of the US market has broken the US$100 billion threshold, many issues have become swappable either through asset swaps or credit default swaps. The marked bifurcation between lower sub-investment grade issues and larger cap, investment grade issues has become more marked.

Liquidity

Liquidity is a key driver of financial market performance and risk. Many alternative investment strategies are particularly vulnerable to the vagaries of capital flows, some more so than others. In this regard, convertible arbitrage is no exception. There are a number of factors that determine, or otherwise influence, liquidity. Among these are government and central bank policies; credit extension by prime brokers; market-making by broker-dealers; market participation by cross-over buyers; the swap market; participation by hedge fund managers; and market bifurcation and segmentation.

Liquidity is as much a catalyst for, as it is the object of, events and government central bank policies. Interest rate movements by the Federal Reserve precipitate fluctuations in liquidity. As we learned from the implosion of Long Term Capital Management in the summer of 1998, the confluence of events and factors driving liquidity were intertwined and inextricable. Through decisive intervention by the Federal Reserve, liquidity was restored to the global financial markets to avert further damage to the financial system and the economy.

The events of 1998 and central bank policy since then have had significant impacts on the global financial markets. After injecting liquidity in the financial system in the latter half of 1998, the Federal Reserve embarked on a restrictive monetary policy. Extension of credit by lenders, prime brokers among them, has been rationed; market-making by broker-dealers and participation by cross-over buyers has shifted away from riskier assets and toward higher quality instruments. Many hedge fund managers, Forest among them, have adopted a more defensive posture and credit spreads in the cash markets and swap markets have widened significantly. There has been, and there remains, a clear flight-to-quality which has resulted in a more pronounced bifurcation and segmentation in the capital markets with respect to credit quality, market capitalisation and industrial sectors. The synchronicity, or linkage, between issuers's access to capital and liquidity of investments has never been so direct.

Within the convertible securities market, the flight to quality is very marked. Prime brokers apply heavier margin haircuts on lower quality companies. Market-making activity by broker-dealers in lower quality issues has been greatly curtailed, while in higher quality issues, it has grown substantially as the number and size of such issues has been increasing. Cross-over buyers from the high yield and balanced fund sectors have increased their participation in the convertible market in search of higher and safer total returns that may be available in the higher investment grade segment. And of course, the larger, more sophisticated convertible hedge fund managers themselves, as noted above, have increased their participation. Convertible hedge fund managers are generally well positioned to manage the risks and capture the trading opportunities associated with fluctuations in liquidity, interest rates and volatility by virtue of their trading methodologies, expanded array of risk management tools, and skills in delta trading. Additionally they may serve as a source of elastic demand given their ability to use leverage opportunistically to expand and contract their portfolios.

Interest rate risk

As fixed income securities, convertible securities and convertible arbitrage portfolios are subject to interest rate, or *rho*, risk. The shape of the yield curve, the price at which the convertible security is trading and the remaining maturity of the issue are key determinants of the impact of interest rate movements on a convertible. As interest rates increase, the bond component and, in turn, the bond floor are likely to decrease in value, while the embedded option component, as a key determinant of the convertible premium, is likely to contract.

Fluctuations in interest rates can also result in fluctuations in credit spreads. In the short-term, an increase in interest rates to the extent that it reflects a strong, growing economy and access to capital is not constricted, is positive for credit spreads. However, sustained high interest rates or a series of interest rate increases, in combination with constriction of capital access, can result in widening of credit spreads as the economic environment slows. As a result, a convertible security's bond floor is prone to accelerated erosion the lower the issuer's credit quality and market capitalisation.

Along the convertible price curve, certain risks are more important than others. To obtain the maximum benefit from the risk management process, the most appropriate risk management techniques must be applied where the risk is greatest. In our experience convertibles trading between 70% and par are generally most subject to rho risk, and will therefore be most responsive to interest rate risk management. The gamma, or trading profits, that are capturable on the downside result from the widening of the spread between the long convertible and the short stock positions as the stock price moves down more than the convertible. Above par, they are more equity sensitive, and the emphasis on delta hedging increases. Below 70% of par, credit risk is most dominant.

The use of asset swaps or the sale of treasuries or futures matched to the weighted average duration of the block of interest rate sensitive convertibles in the portfolio can be used effectively as well as other techniques. The option adjusted spread and credit spectrum must be taken into account. However, during periods of coincident credit spread widening and a flight to quality, such as was experienced during the milieu of 1998, the long convertible exposure and short treasury exposure will compound loss. In such a scenario, the use of asset swaps or credit default risk management instruments may be more appropriate. Other complementary forms of interest rate risk management include shortening the duration and maturity structure of the portfolio and rotating away from interest rate sensitive issues and sectors.

Volatility: a key ingredient to exploit

Fluctuations in liquidity, capital markets conditions, and the fundamentals of the economy, industries and companies are the bases for volatility. With the integration of the global capital markets, increased cross-over buyer participation, the growth of the swap market, the implementation of full disclosure requirements, and the instantaneous impacts on credit spreads and securities prices, volatility has never been greater. For investors who invest on a long only basis, volatility is generally a major negative factor, all the more so if the direction of the markets has a downward bias. However, for true hedge fund managers that employ long-short strategies, particularly market neutral strategies, volatility is a critical ingredient to exploit regardless of the direction of the markets. Of course the quality of volatility is critical. Muted or erratic volatility is far less capturable than that which has a semblance of regularity, optimally like a sine wave, and sufficient amplitude.

The objective of a market neutral convertible arbitrage strategy is to capture and profit from the volatility, or upward and downward price fluctuations of the long convertible position and short equity position, along with the static return. Capturing volatility does not happen by itself nor is it assured. The delta hedge ratio must be properly determined and set. As the prices of the convertible and the stock may fluctuate frequently, and as the relationship of price changes, or the *delta*, may fluctuate, the delta hedge ratio must be re-determined and re-set on an ongoing basis.

Trading profits result from the build-up of gamma of the convertible moving asymmetrically with the common stock. As the stock moves down in price, and as the convertible moves down towards its bond floor, positive gamma results from the effective creation of the equivalent of a *put option* on the basis of time value. The *time value* of the put option increases because bond value is built up as the security approaches maturity. As the stock moves up in price, and as the convertible moves up, positive gamma results from the effective creation of the equivalent of a *call option* through a *long volatility position*, where the excess long position of the convertible over the short stock position should exceed the decline in premium. In a market neutral context, the delta hedge must be set and re-set such that the positive gamma can be captured in the same magnitude, albeit on different paths, on the bases of upside and downside price movements to resemble a *straddle*.

Convertible premium cycle: supply, demand and the business cycle

Just as global financial markets overall and individual asset classes are subject to cycles, so are investment strategies. In our experience, and by empirical observation that bears out that experience, there has been a rolling three- to four-year cycle for convertible premiums in the United States. Troughs in convertible premiums were hit in 1962, 1966, 1970, 1973–74, 1978 to some degree, 1982, 1987, 1990, 1994 and 1998. Although the European convertible market is still somewhat nascent, given its size, structure and momentum of growth, we envision it converging with that of the US and fluctuating much in tandem. While the common denominator for all of the cycles is the business cycle itself, each business cycle has its own complexion, arising for different reasons and ending for different reasons. Each cycle, at least up to 1998, has been precipitated by, if not exacerbated by, some marked event. In 1998, the structure and complexion of the convertible securities market in the US changed and caught many participants unaware.

The impacts on the convertible market manifest themselves in the forms of pronounced premium spread contraction and expansion. The contraction can be precipitated, and exacerbated, by widening credit spreads and erosion of bond floor. The peaks and troughs of the cycle are amplified by the homogeneity of the investor base, which consists largely of hedge funds, proprietary trading desks, mutual funds, banks and insurance companies. This may result in a marked imbalance between supply and demand.

Awareness of the existence and process of the convertible premium cycle permits an experienced convertible arbitrageur to make appropriate adjustments to minimise the impact of premium contraction. The key variables to control are leverage, credit quality, hedge ratios, exposures to issuers that are particularly vulnerable to tight liquidity or capital markets conditions, and interest rate exposure. The portfolio manager must anticipate problems and be resolved and agile enough to manage through the cycle.

Security specific risks

Like any security, there are risks on the downside, but in the case of convertible securities, there are also risks on the upside – and all along the convertible price curve.

Downside risks: bankruptcy, default, credit spread widening and interest rate sensitivity

As fixed income, or credit based, securities, convertibles are subject to all of the downside risks associated with non-convertible fixed income securities, namely bankruptcy, default, credit spread widening and interest rate sensitivity. Depending upon which market and the market environment in which one is invested, the degrees of these risks vary.

The credit risk management process is multi-faceted. The first aspect of the process is traditional credit risk analysis, where the key elements determining a borrower's ability to repay are analysed. Under the acronym of CAMEL, these are Capital, Assets, Management, Earnings and Liquidity. Credit analysts should be well trained and experienced through the credit cycles and across industries. The securitisation of many types of financial assets and the integration of global capital markets provides instantaneous and continuous information feedbacks. In the context of credit risk, credit spreads and credit spreads fluctuations reflect the market's expectations on future defaults. Sophisticated models drawing on both fundamental and credit and equity market variables are now being employed to determine credit quality on a real time basis in line with market expectations. Apart from company-specific fundamentals, a key determinant is the market capitalisation of a company. Generally, the lower the company's market capitalisation, the more susceptible it is to credit spread widening and, in turn, reduced access to the capital markets under adverse market conditions. Once the credit risk profile of a given issuer, convertible security and industry group is ascertained by the analysts, the analysis should be reviewed with the portfolio managers to determine the optimal means in which to invest.

The next element of the credit risk management process is the determination of the equity hedge. Generally, the lower an issue's credit quality, the greater the price volatility of the convertible and underlying equity securities.

A critical element of the credit risk management process, as well as portfolio construction, is diversification across credit quality, industrial sectors, geographic sectors, types of convertible securities, duration and type of trade. The manager must continuously assess the relative contribution of each position to the whole portfolio on the bases of return, risk and correlation.

To reduce credit risk exposure further, the market for credit derivatives, although still somewhat nascent, provides a variety of products and strategies. Much of this has been encouraged by the risks and benefits of crossover buyers participating in and alongside of the high yield and convertible securities markets. They take the form of asset swaps, credit default swaps, index-based or basket-based credit default hedges, and credit spread hedges. Such instruments can be used efficiently and effectively to reduce exposure and to alter the risk-return profile of a given position or a portfolio as a whole.

Upside risks: early redemption
On the upside, money can be lost through early redemption. Convertible securities are typically issued to enable the issuer to pay a lower coupon as a debt-type instrument with the added benefits of future, less dilutive

equity issuance, by virtue of the conversion premium at which the securities are issued. Upon conversion, the investor receives stock and the issuer reclassifies the convertible security as equity and no longer has an obligation to repay or redeem the principle.

Typically, but not necessarily, a convertible will be called when its price exceeds 15% to 20% of the call price after the call date. When the convertible is called, the investor exchanges his convertible for stock and loses the premium that he paid in purchasing the convertible. In the case of convertible bonds, he might lose the accrued interest as well, which may be as much as six months worth of accrual.

The rationale for investing a portion of the portfolio in convertible securities that are or may soon be callable is predicated upon their relative inefficiency, and in turn cheapness. Much convertible investment, as distinct from trading, is done by outright buyers.

To manage early redemption risk, a manager can: avoid investing in callable securities altogether; limit exposure; and contact issuers whose securities are callable, or that are suspected of being called, to determine what the issuers' intentions are. Increasingly, issuers are incorporating various types of "make-whole" provisions to minimise, if not eliminate, the risk of loss due to calls. The risk of early redemption is better measured than managed in that the benefits of investing in callable securities can meaningfully exceed the losses of early redemption.

Other risks

Along the pricing curve, there remain a handful of other investment risks. These include corporate event risk, short squeeze, increases in the short common stock dividend, and spin-offs.

In the case of corporate event risk, generally in the form of a cash merger, the manager may have paid more for the convertible securities of the target company than the value based on the merger, thus resulting in a loss. Simultaneously, there may be upward price movement of the target company's stock that has been sold short by the manager, also resulting in a loss.

To manage this risk exposure, a careful reading and understanding of the indenture is required. It is the indenture that specifies the terms and conditions under which investors will be treated in change of control situations. Research is also critical in the assessment of the likelihood of takeover, to the extent that it is possible. As takeovers tend to be a surprise, the risk management platform may not capture that risk in a timely manner. For some convertible arbitrageurs who are sufficiently skilled, such a trade may be converted into a risk arbitrage trade. Fortunately, the negative effect of corporate event risk has abated somewhat amidst strong takeover activity with the inclusion of change of control features in new convertible issues.

The risk of *short squeeze* can materialise in connection with takeover activity or a price decline below US$5.00 per share. Given a convertible arbitrageur's short position in a stock, and an unexpected and strong upward price movement of that stock, a short squeeze could develop whereby there is insufficient stock to deliver. The convertible can be converted into stock to cover the short. This will, at the very least, minimise loss. To avoid or otherwise manage the risk of a short squeeze, the manager must proactively assess the technical signals and the borrowability of the stock.

Another salient risk in convertible arbitrage is the risk of an increase in the short dividend on the underlying common stock. As the dividend rises, the standstill return is reduced, the stock price would predictably increase, and the convertible itself might even decline a bit as its relative attractiveness on a yield basis would diminish. Such a risk is generally predictable on the bases of a company's rising cash balances, weak or lacklustre stock price and no meaningful plans for growth.

The risk associated with a spin-off, where a division of a company is being spun off to common stock, is that the indenture may not provide for an adjustment to the conversion ratio of the convertible security to keep the investor whole after the transaction. Again, careful analysis of the indenture is required in advance of making an investment.

Putting it all together: total portfolio risk management
The risks inherent in convertible arbitrage are not readily apparent from the generally low volatility of the strategy's return stream, as measured by the standard deviation. The risk is in all the moving pieces not being managed individually and all together. Indeed, the return stream and resultant low standard deviation are by-products of appropriate risk management at both the individual security selection/position setup and portfolio levels.

Our portfolio management process is iterative, must adhere to strict disciplines and be subjected to continuous stress testing as critical variables change and the interrelationships between and among those variables change. The process begins with a top-down macro-geopolitical and economic analysis as the basis for allocation to the US, European and Japanese convertible markets. It then drills down to broad economic sectors, industrial sectors, which compose each economic sector, and then to the company level.

Traditional credit risk analysis and a host of new credit quality determination models, as discussed above, are used in tandem with statistical analyses and fair value analyses to assess the relative attractiveness of a given position and its contribution to the risk and return profile of the portfolio on a pro forma basis and on an ongoing basis. To that end, a well constructed convertible arbitrage portfolio designed to achieve a risk/return profile within a definable range will give consideration to a multi-faceted portfolio risk analysis. Our teams of portfolio managers and research analysts focus on, issue size exposure, industry exposure; stock borrow availability, position exposure as a percentage of portfolio capital, position exposure as a percentage of capital by balance sheet characteristics, credit quality and market capitalisations perhaps an overall credit grade limitation depending on market conditions and type of convertibles. Portfolios are regularly stress-tested for sensitivities to rho risk, vega risk, credit spread widening and credit default.

Risk Metrics: measures by which to benchmark risk and performance

Each strategy has its own risk/reward configuration. Within each strategy, the risk/reward configuration may differ to varying degrees depending upon each manager's approach. As a discrete hedge fund strategy, convertible arbitrage tends, ignoring some outliers, to produce annualised returns within a range of high single digits to high teens, with volatility, as measured by the standard deviation in the low single digits to low teens. The differences among convertible arbitrage managers are: geographic allocations, leverage, degree of market neutrality or biasing, portfolio credit quality and rho and vega risks, industry exposures, the tactical use of asset swaps and credit default swaps, the overall portfolio management process, and size and capacity.

Our market neutral portfolios are opportunistically diversified across geographic regions and industrial sectors subject to strict parameters and are managed with moderate leverage. The complexion of the portfolios' credit quality and related rho and vega risks are a function of our views on the landscape of risk and opportunity. In an environment such as that of the period following the latter half of 1998 to the beginning of 2000, a more defensive posture was appropriate in our portfolio management process. Whereas in the bull market years of 1995 through much of the first half of 1998 a more aggressive posture was appropriate.

With that as a foundation for where our portfolios fit into risk/return space, our target returns are in the mid teens range, with a standard deviation in the lower single digit range on a rolling three- to four-year cycle. Tying risk and return together, the resultant Sharpe ratio, which is the quotient of an investment's annualised return over the risk-free rate, typically the three-month US Treasury bill, and the standard deviation of the investment's returns, is in the range of 1.6 to 1.8. The Sortino ratio, which is the ratio of an investment's annualised return over the risk-free rate over the standard deviation of an investment's negative returns, exceeds 1.9. Integral to risk and return, we believe our approach to convertible arbitrage adds value to a diversified portfolio by virtue of high positive alpha, or excess return over the risk-free rate, very low beta, as a measure of market sensitivity, of –0.01 to +0.02, and non-correlation to stocks and bonds in all market environments.

CONCLUSION: A PRESCRIPTION FOR INVESTING PRUDENTLY

To obtain the most from any given investment strategy and in turn a total portfolio strategy, investors and their managers need to find a common understanding with respect to investment objectives and risk tolerances. It is a matter of beginning with the ending in mind, of matching investment objectives to be achieved within a defined, or definable, time horizon, with investors' risk tolerances. This is a process of matching assets with liabilities.

Regular, open dialogue between a manager and his investors and discipline in the investment process by the manager and the investing process by investors must buttress the relationship. Lack of dialogue and discipline can undermine an investor achieving his objectives. There is a delicate balance between investors' temptation to time the market and second guess their managers and managers' ability to maintain investors' confidence as they remain invested through the cycle. As part and parcel to managing risk, that balance must be determined and managed.

18

Mortgage Strategies

Eric Keiter

MKP Capital Management, LLC

Valuation and risk management methodologies used in mortgage-backed securities (MBS) investing have advanced considerably during the past 15 years. Sophisticated models and more powerful computers can analyse securities with greater accuracy than ever before. And yet, the MBS market continues to evolve, as the securitisation of new types of collateral, innovations in security structures, and changes in prepayment and default behaviour create opportunities through which savvy investors can profit.

The goal of this chapter is to educate both investors and market practitioners about risk management in MBS strategies, and to leave readers with a better sense of what this process actually entails. Managing risk in mortgage hedge fund strategies (or any libor-based mortgage strategy) is too multifaceted a topic to comprehensively cover in one chapter, but an attempt will be made to focus on the subjects of most importance to the mortgage hedge fund manager. Some basic background information on the mortgage market will be reviewed, followed by a detailed discussion of risk management.

Risk management in MBS strategies can essentially be distilled to the understanding of portfolio exposures to changes in interest rates, credit spreads, prepayments and volatility. While quantifying these risk exposures can seem more complex than in other hedge fund strategies, in practice, an MBS manager employs readily available tools to simplify the analytic process.

Mortgage arbitrage centres on the identification of those mortgage-backed and asset-backed securities that offer excess compensation for assuming their embedded optionality and/or credit risk. In mortgage-backed and asset-backed securities, the return advantage over Treasuries is primarily compensation for cashflow uncertainty, credit and liquidity. Cashflow uncertainty (ie, the uncertain timing of principal and interest payments to the bondholder) is a result of the prepayment options held by the underlying borrowers, and is what makes MBS unique within the fixed income universe. With proper hedging, returns are generated over time through a combination of cashflow yield and price convergence. Price convergence may result from market repricing, a credit rating upgrade, or a re-securitisation of portfolio holdings.

THE MORTGAGE MARKET

The outstanding mortgage debt in the United States for residential and commercial borrowers exceeds US$5 trillion. Much of this debt has been securitised, making the MBS market the largest fixed income market in the world. A tremendous variety of securities, in terms of structure, credit rating and liquidity, exist within it. (While this chapter focuses exclusively on US MBS, a growing market exists in international MBS as well.)

Residential MBS are created by pooling a relatively homogeneous group of underlying homeowner mortgages. These securities can consist of 30-year, 15-year, or adjustable-rate mortgage (ARM) loans. The majority of residential mortgages are guaranteed by one of three Government-sponsored agencies: Fannie Mae, Freddie Mac and Ginnie Mae. Fannie Mae and Freddie Mac are private entities carrying the implied sponsorship of the US Government, while Ginnie Mae is a Government agency, backed by the full faith and credit of the US Treasury. The resultant "agency" mortgage pass-through security (ie, principal and interest are passed through to the investor) has a credit rating considered to be AAA. The mortgage pass-through securities market is extraordinarily large and liquid; the mortgage market benchmark indices are chiefly comprised of these securities.

The remaining residential mortgage loans that do not conform to Government-sponsored agency guidelines are issued by private entities with no ties to the government. Included in this group are investment banks, commercial banks and mortgage banks. Without the implied government guarantee, the capital markets have developed various forms of credit enhancement, including the tranching of credit through subordination and third party bond insurers. Through the process of subordination, investment banks create securities from these loans. These represent the full range of credit classifications, from AAA-rated down to below-investment grade. Non-residential mortgages, including commercial mortgages, home equity loans, manufactured housing loans, and credit card and auto loan receivables have their securities created in a similar fashion.

As a result of investor need for certain mortgage security cashflow characteristics, the collateralised mortgage obligation (CMO) market developed. Over the years, myriad structures have evolved with different maturities, payment profiles, embedded leverage and liquidity. For example, a 30-year mortgage pass-through can be divided or restructured into short, intermediate and long maturity securities. These securities better fit the needs of banks, insurance companies and pension funds, respectively.

Other structured securities involve insulating certain mortgages from pre-payments, leaving others with more cashflow variability. Additionally, not unlike Treasury strips, interest-only (IO) and principal-only (PO) strips have been created to tailor prepayment sensitivity. Moreover, securities with different coupon payment schedules have been created, such as those with floating rate and inverse floating rate coupons. Each class of securities offers different reward/risk characteristics.

UTILISATION OF MODELS
Option-adjusted spread
The uniqueness of mortgage-backed securities within the fixed income uni-verse comes from the embedded prepayment option. At any time, the borrower, usually without penalty, may pay back more principal than required by the amortisation schedule. The option is usually exercised in the form of a refinancing into a lower rate loan, essentially making a mort-gage-backed security a "callable bond". As a result of this option, the timing of the stream of principal and interest cashflows is uncertain, affecting different mortgage-backed securities in different ways. Accurately understanding and valuing this prepayment option through quantitative methods is the cornerstone of a successful MBS investment and risk man-agement effort.

One of the primary investment tools employed in managing a portfolio of MBS is an option-adjusted spread (OAS) model. OAS is the yield spread a security is expected to earn, on average, over its life, taking into account embedded optionality. This model, comprised of an option-pricing model and a prepayment model, is able to price all bonds with embedded options and interest rate derivatives in a consistent manner. To analyse a particular security, an arbitrage-free Monte Carlo process simulates hundreds of random interest rate paths, and the prepayment model projects an expected prepayment vector for each interest-rate path, given the underly-ing mortgage coupon rate and other loan parameters. Employing this prepayment vector, the cashflows of a particular MBS are generated along each path. The present value of these cashflows is then calculated by dis-counting with the interest rates along that path, plus an added yield spread. The OAS of a security is the sole value for this yield spread that causes the average of the present value for all paths to be equal to the actual market price. OAS calculations attempt to make MBS (and all bonds with embedded options) comparable to other fixed income securities. (The OAS of a non-callable bond is roughly equal to its spread to the curve.) Once an OAS calculation is carried out, all risk measurements can then be calculated as well.

As stated above, the OAS is the anticipated spread, but never the actual spread, which can only be determined with the benefit of hindsight. Therefore, it is important to ascertain the distribution of possible outcomes in order to determine the quality of the OAS number. This can be accomplished in two ways: by examining the distribution of calculated prices for all interest-rate paths, and by measuring the sensitivity of a security's OAS to changes in model inputs. If the price distribution is unusually skewed or dispersed, and/or the security's OAS exhibits unusual volatility by changing a particular input (prepayment levels, interest rates, etc), the security's potential value is unlikely to be easily extracted through hedging. In these cases, a security's investment value should be questioned, even if an attractive OAS arises from the model calculations. In practice, the market usually builds an uncertainty premium into more volatile securities. The goal in MBS hedge fund management is to construct a portfolio that offers attractive investment returns in the majority of market environments.

As a topical aside, early in 2000, the issue of whether to use a Treasury-based or libor-based (interest rate swap curve) model came to the forefront. As the Treasury budget surplus and debt reduction news emerged, the Treasury curve inverted, significantly diverging from the still positively sloped swap curve. When valuing the embedded prepayment option in a security, if a disproportionate number of paths project forward rates lower than they actually are, the value of the option will be overstated, and errors will be introduced to all subsequent risk measurement calculations. Since mortgage securities, although of high credit, are not Treasuries, the swap curve is more appropriate when calculating forward rates and option values. Once the swap curve is used to calculate option values, an OAS can still be calculated over the Treasury or libor curve.

Prepayments

The prepayment model is truly the engine that drives fundamental MBS analysis. A prepayment model projects prepayments for the underlying mortgage loans backing any security over their entire life for any interest rate scenario. There are two key components of prepayment behaviour that need to be modelled when analysing residential mortgages:

❏ Housing turnover, or baseline, non-economic prepayments. These result from normal homeowner mobility, death and divorce, partial prepayments and equity "take-out" refinancing.
❏ Refinancing, or economic prepayments. These result when the prepayment option is exercised to lower the mortgage loan rate.

A sophisticated prepayment model is able to analyse different loan cohorts based on issue year (age), interest rate and term, size, origination programme, and economic demographics, such as geographical and credit considerations (loan-to-value, home price appreciation, etc). The model should attempt to reflect actual homeowner behaviour and, as far as possible, be forward-looking, rather than just a regression fit of historical prepayment data. Most importantly, the model should be tested for accuracy and revised at regular intervals, as inevitable changes occur in overall economic conditions, loan programmes and regulations, and refinancing efficiency, capacity and transaction costs.

Although not as advanced as residential mortgage models, prepayment models have also been developed for other types of mortgage loans, including home equity and manufactured housing loans. Commercial mortgage loan prepayment models are still in their infancy, but these securities typically offer excellent call protection because of their contractual no-prepay lockout provisions and/or significant prepayment penalties.

The prepayment option embedded in MBS can never be perfectly modelled, for in many ways it is akin to modelling human behaviour. Changing economic fundamentals, from home price appreciation to employment levels to stock market value, can alter prepayment levels in both directions. In addition, the advent of technology has already made it less time consuming and less costly to process applications, while the Internet can provide the homeowner with much more timely information, allowing more informed decisions to be made. Finally, the impact of new mortgage products (recently hybrid ARMs) can offer the homeowner more refinancing options, and change the demographics of the mortgage loans underlying different mortgage products.

Although the market does not conform to any single prepayment model, the models employed by different dealers and investors have advanced to the point where they are relatively consistent. Some market participants have suggested using a market-implied prepayment model for valuation and risk measurement calculations. This model is constructed by setting the various prepayment model parameters to levels that make the OAS of all prepayment-sensitive securities (interest-only and principal-only strips) identical. In this way, the market is revealing its estimation of the correct model and pricing of prepayment risk. While some risk information can be gleaned from such a model, this author believes that the market is too inefficient and inaccurate to make extensive use of such a model in the overall investment process.

RISK PARAMETERS

When managing a libor-based, mortgage-backed securities portfolio, the main approach to understanding risk is to calculate risk parameters for each security in the portfolio, and then aggregate them to quantify overall portfolio risk. With the exception of credit risk, all risk parameters are calculated using the OAS model, as the effect of the embedded optionality must be taken into account. Once risk parameters are calculated for securities, they are aggregated to determine the risk in the overall portfolio. Risk parameters are calculated based on current market conditions, and need to be recalculated every day as the market environment changes.

Interest rate exposure
Duration

Like all fixed income arbitrage strategies, the most important risk parameter is option-adjusted or effective duration, defined as the percentage change in price for a given move in interest rates. For a market neutral strategy, the market-weighted sum of the duration of all securities (long/short assets and hedges) should add to zero. In theory, the portfolio is then insulated against changes in interest rates. The effective duration for individual securities is calculated from model prices obtained by shifting the yield curve up and down in a parallel fashion, while holding OAS and other model parameters (volatility, mortgage rate spread) constant.

Of course, the yield curve does not always shift in a parallel shape. For MBS investing, understanding yield curve exposure takes on added importance for two reasons. First, MBS do not have bullet maturities, but instead pay back their principal over many years. Second, the shape of the yield curve, and hence the forward curve, will directly impact the value of the embedded options, and thus the overall value of the security. Key rate or partial yield curve durations are calculated from model prices obtained by shifting specific points on the yield curve, while holding the other yield curve points, OAS, and other model parameters constant. A set of key rate durations can be calculated for the entire yield curve and by hedging appropriately, market neutrality can extend across the yield curve.

As stated above, the calculation of effective duration involves holding OAS constant. However, for various reasons, it is not uncommon for certain mortgages to trade at different OASs based on their proximity to par. For example, due to prepayment uncertainty, a discount mortgage passthrough may trade at a slightly tighter OAS than a premium mortgage passthrough. Factoring in this small adjustment can be important in understanding true market price sensitivity to interest rates, and is referred to as an "OAS-curve" effective duration. Also, MBS managers can readily observe a security's market price change as interest rates move, which is commonly referred to as an "empirical" duration.

Convexity

While duration is the most important risk parameter, option-adjusted or effective convexity is also essential in managing interest rate risk. As stated above, the duration of a security can predict the price change in the event of interest rate movement. However, due to cashflow discounting effects and embedded optionality, the price will drift away from this linear approximation as interest rates shift. Convexity provides a way to measure this error by quantifying the drift of a security's duration as rates move. Most MBS exhibit some negative convexity because the prepayment option is likely to be exercised in low rate environments. (Deeply discounted MBS like principal-only strips, MBS with excellent call protection like commercial MBS and many mortgage credit subordinates have positive convexity.) Thus, MBS durations contract in a rally as principal is prepaid early, but extend in a market decline as it becomes uneconomical to prepay the mortgage. The convexity value of a security is calculated as a by-product of the duration calculation. For moderate to large moves in interest rates, hedging the portfolio convexity can be crucial to risk management in MBS strategies.

Interestingly, like duration, the convexity number for a particular security is not constant. For example, a mortgage passthrough can be positively convex when it is trading at a deep discount to par, since the prepayment option is so far out of the money that local moves in interest rates do not change the mortgage's cashflow, meaning it behaves like a non-callable bond. As interest rates drop, the security will turn negatively convex as its price moves up and through par, reaching its maximum negative convexity when its price trades at a small premium to par, where the mortgage is most likely to be refinanced. However, once the mortgage pass-through trades at a large premium to par, the negative convexity actually declines, because fast prepayment speeds will exist locally, with the option being so far in the money. This changing convexity behaviour stems from the shape of the prepayment function, which has a floor (due to baseline housing turnover prepayments) and a ceiling (as refinancing prepayments top out after a certain point, due to mortgage banker capacity constraints and borrower prepayment "burnout").

In hedging convexity, the manager will usually employ some type of options strategy to "buy back" convexity in the portfolio. Two important points must be kept in mind when hedging out this risk parameter: first, since negative convexity is derived from the mortgage rate, which is driven by the intermediate-to-long end of the curve, most of the negative convexity resides in the five-to-ten year key rate durations; and second, the manager must be cognisant of the changing convexity mentioned above, and optimally set up the options strategy to account for this.

Prepayment exposure

While the absolute level of prepayments can have a substantial impact on the overall MBS market, this prepayment exposure risk relates to the *differential* between model expectations and actual prepayment rates. Prepayment duration is defined as the percentage price change for a given change in model prepayment projections. With this number, the manager can quantify the portfolio risk exposure to prepayments coming in faster or slower than model projections. The prepayment duration is calculated from model prices obtained by speeding up and slowing down the overall prepayment model, while holding the yield curve, OAS, and other model parameters (ie, volatility, mortgage rate spread) constant. As the value of almost all MBS is to some degree directly impacted by prepayments, understanding this risk is vital to overall portfolio risk management.

Beyond calculating the market value sensitivity to changes in prepayment projections, it is also extremely important to understand their impact on effective duration. If the prepayment option becomes more efficient, this will lead to a decrease in duration, as the higher prepayments seen in a rally will limit a security's potential price appreciation above par. In many cases, an MBS may exhibit a very low prepayment duration, but will still be susceptible to prepayment model errors, arising from the potential impact of hedging to miscalculated duration.

While the prepayment duration is a useful number, it is only the first step. Often, there is hidden prepayment risk in a portfolio whose aggregate prepayment duration is equal to zero. For example, different loan programs and types (eg, Ginnie Mae, Fannie Mae/Freddie Mac, non-conforming residential mortgages, commercial mortgages, etc) will give rise to different prepayment exposures. Another hidden prepayment risk stems from having exposure to different mortgage loan rates or coupons, this being equivalent to having exposure along different parts of the prepayment function. Some securities might be more exposed to housing turnover prepayments, while others may be more susceptible to changes in the shape or strength of the refinancing function. A more sophisticated set of prepayment duration risk numbers can be run that quantify the sensitivity to both parts of the prepayment function.

A more subtle form of prepayment risk is seen in securities with actual cashflow structures depending on the path along which prepayments occur. This behaviour is typical in CMOs that have been structured to be more or less susceptible to prepayments than the underlying mortgage collateral. Unlike a mortgage pass-through (which has an average life roughly the same whether prepayments come in fast then slow, or vice versa), these CMOs can often have a different average life depending on which prepayment path is taken. While the OAS model will value this correctly, the character of these securities can change significantly over time.

The importance of understanding the effect of prepayment model error can be seen from the prepayment waves of the past decade. In 1993, when prepayment modelling was in its infancy, generational lows in mortgage rates caused prepayment speeds to exceed most street models by almost 100%! In early 1998, a combination of similarly low mortgage rates, a strong housing market, and the advent of the Internet caused prepayment model errors of 10% to 20%. While the error was not nearly as large as in 1993, the impact was still evident in changing security valuations. Prepayment risk is often mispriced in the market, including times when the market overestimates future prepayments. This was the case in 1995, when a weaker housing market and the after-effects of the 1993 prepayment wave led to prepayments that were much lower than expected, despite low interest rates. As interest rates move, market prices usually behave in an anticipatory fashion, eventually readjusting to more correct pricing levels as actual monthly prepayment data becomes available.

Spread exposure

As MBS are part of the larger universe of fixed income spread product, understanding the portfolio's spread exposure (either to libor or Treasuries) is extremely important from a risk perspective. The spread duration is defined as the percentage price change for a given change in OAS. For individual securities, the spread duration is calculated from model prices obtained by shifting the OAS up and down, while holding the yield curve and other model parameters (ie, volatility, mortgage rate spread) constant. The challenge with this risk measure is that for prepayment-sensitive MBS, moving mortgage spreads also alters prepayment projections, since the mortgage rate is moving higher or lower as well. This effect can overwhelm the economic effect of a spread change – an adjustment is made to account for this by simultaneously altering the mortgage rate spread in the model when calculating spread duration. This is called the "mortgage-spread" or "current-coupon" duration, and using this allows the MBS manager to obtain a clearer picture of the true exposure to changes in spreads. The best example of this effect is evident in an interest-only mortgage strip security (IO). This security only receives coupon payments from a mortgage. Therefore, if mortgage prepayments speed up, there will be less interest paid over the life of the security and the IO's value will decrease. If mortgage spreads widen, the ensuing reduction in prepayment rates from a higher mortgage rate actually makes the IO security more attractive, giving this mortgage security a rare negative mortgage spread duration.

Two other complications arise when quantifying and managing spread risk in an MBS portfolio: first, as in interest rate partial durations for an MBS, spread duration exposure is distributed along different parts of the yield curve and must be quantified to understand overall spread risk; second, the relative movements in various spread products must be taken into account. A typical MBS portfolio can contain a variety of 30 and 15-year mortgage pass-throughs, ARMs, CMOs, commercial MBS, agency debentures, interest rate swaps, etc. The MBS manager must be conscious of the impact of different spread movements between each of the securities (assets and hedges) contained in portfolio. Statistical studies, quantifying correlations between different spread products and the magnitude of their relative spread movement, allow the manager to model the overall spread risk in the portfolio.

Credit exposure

As investments are made in non-agency securities, credit risk is introduced into the portfolio. Non-agency securities include residential and commercial MBS that are not guaranteed by a governmental agency, as well as asset-backed securities. For the most part, triple-A credit enhancement is provided "internally" through the subordination of principal and interest cashflows. This subordinate class of securities is then subdivided into the full range of credits, including investment grade, below-investment grade and unrated. Triple-A ratings are also achieved by external guarantees from mono-line bond insurers such as MBIA, FSA and FGIC. Mortgage credit risk differs from corporate or sovereign credit risk in that the exposure is to large, well-diversified pools of borrowers rather than to single entities.

In the credit-sensitive arena, while other risk factors (especially spread risk) still apply, the introduction of the credit component adds new analysis to the risk management process. Specifically, considerations include:

❏ the credit rating;
❏ deal structure credit enhancement/support;
❏ the nature of the collateral pool;
❏ the experience and strength of the loan originator and servicer; and
❏ relevant loan performance data, including changes in property values and delinquency/default statistics.

Analytical systems must be utilised to assess the impact of both projected prepayment and default rates on the structure and credit of a particular investment.

Investing in credit-sensitive MBS requires a pre-investment loan-level collateral review and on-going surveillance of both loan characteristics and performance (delinquencies and defaults). This becomes increasingly important as one moves down the credit-rating spectrum. (At the triple-A level, credit risk is minimal, meaning other risk considerations will dominate.) At all rating levels, the loan originator/servicer (who is also typically the issuer) should be scrutinised for financial health and frequency and quality of issuance. Non-agency securities are structured by the rating agencies to be independent and unaffected by the long-term viability of the issuer. However, if the entity servicing the underlying loans experiences financial difficulty, the securities are likely to suffer some temporary price dislocation, with the valuation impact increasing at lower credit ratings.

In terms of overall sector risk management, diversification of security types, underlying properties, and issuer/servicer concentrations is one of the best ways to reduce overall risk. For example, commercial mortgages have much stronger prepayment protection than residential mortgages, but the default risk is greater. Also, the MBS manager must be aware of any developments in related credit markets, namely corporate and high yield debt, as spread movements in these sister markets can affect mortgage credit spreads.

Volatility exposure

A typical option becomes more valuable as the volatility of the underlying instrument rises, because there is a greater probability of the option becoming exercisable. In a similar manner, the level of implied-option volatilities directly impacts the value of the embedded options within MBS. Most MBS are negatively affected by increases in volatility, since the prepayment option that the bondholder is short becomes more valuable. (Many positively convex mortgages, including some mortgage derivatives containing other embedded options, can be positively affected by volatility increases.) Looking at this another way, options are needed to hedge the negative convexity; if they become more expensive, MBS will appear less enticing, as more money needs to be put to work to hedge the securities.

A security's volatility duration is defined as the percentage price change for a given shift in implied volatilities. This is calculated from model prices obtained by shifting all model volatilities up and down, while holding OAS and other model parameters (ie, yield curve, mortgage rate spread) constant. A more detailed analysis might include calculations of the price sensitivity to changes in cap and swaption volatility separately. Like spread duration, changes in implied volatilities directly affect mortgage spreads, which in turn alter prepayment projections through shifts in the mortgage rate. Therefore, in a manner similar to spread duration, a correction must be made to the volatility duration, which will give an MBS manager a clearer picture of the true exposure to changes in volatility.

As most of their optionality is derived from the longer-term prepayment option, the majority of MBS are more affected by longer maturity volatility (ie, a 5x10 swaption), rather than shorter-dated options. One of the challenges of MBS investing is that the embedded option is an amortising prepayment option, for which a market does not exist. Therefore, the MBS hedge fund manager will typically buy swaptions, Treasury options or other MBS to hedge out this exposure.

OVERALL PORTFOLIO RISK MANAGEMENT

Once the individual risk parameters of securities held in the portfolio have been quantified, they must be aggregated so that the overall risk dimensions of the portfolio can be understood. Setting acceptable limits for these portfolio risk parameters is the essence of MBS portfolio risk management. Each aggregate risk parameter can be thought of independently, although there are often minor correlations between them. For each risk factor, the average historical daily move and standard deviation of that move are calculated. Using these data, each risk parameter can be moved by any number of standard deviations, with the commensurate change in portfolio market value calculated. Thus, for any probability or confidence level, a daily VAR for each risk parameter can be estimated, and limits in relation to capital can be set to ensure that no excessive risk is taken. Monthly VAR numbers are calculated in a similar way.

Quantifying portfolio exposures to interest rate shifts and volatility is fairly straightforward, as there is a wealth of historical data available. In the case of spread risk, spread volatilities can also be calculated from historical data, including the correlations between the spread sectors themselves. Further spread risk analysis can be carried out by stressing the correlations between different spread sectors. For credit risk, delinquency and default volatilities in each credit sector can be calculated. Finally, for prepayment risk, it is harder to determine historical volatilities of model error, but reasonable estimates can be made based on the past ten years of data and market experience.

These statistical measures must be continually updated for each risk parameter as new data points become available. An MBS manager must always be aware that calculating VAR numbers based on past data can be misleading, as the data set may not be representative of possible future distributions. For instance, in late 1998, the market exhibited significantly higher volatility than would have been predicted by utilising previous data. Therefore, not only is it important to stress the portfolio in unlikely scenarios, but the integrity of the data must also be tested. Also, when calculating historical volatilities, one can use a fat-tail distribution (as opposed to a normal distribution), which gives a higher probability of outsized moves than might otherwise be expected.

Unfortunately, except for very small shifts in risk parameters, VAR numbers for different risks cannot be added to give a total VAR number for a portfolio. This is because of the changing nature of MBS in different market environments. For example, during an interest rate decline, the change in portfolio market value can be estimated, but as durations shorten because of the embedded prepayment options, the spread exposure can actually decline, reducing that risk. This offsetting effect of risk parameters is common in MBS hedge fund management. Of course, at any time, shifts in these risk parameters may become correlated in different market environments. In this instance, scenario analysis must be run, whereby several risk parameters are shifted simultaneously so that combined market value changes can be calculated. Such an analysis may reveal a scenario in which the portfolio value declines significantly. Combining the risk–parameter VAR calculations with the effects of simultaneous shifts in risk parameters in a projected total rate of return scenario analysis gives the MBS manager a fairly accurate depiction of the portfolio risk for small or large market moves.

Armed with this set of risk calculations, the MBS manager can now set VAR limits on overall portfolio risk and carry out market transactions to implement them. It is important that the MBS manager explicitly targets risk, or the chance of loss, instead of returns. Targeting a particular return often leads a manager to take excessive risk in order to achieve it. Thus, the manager determines the appropriate levels of risk for the overall portfolio, and then evaluates returns relative to the risk taken to achieve them.

Additional risks

Hedging risk

Hedging strategies are used in the investment process to reduce or eliminate risks that a manager chooses not to assume. The purpose of hedging is not to eliminate all risk, but rather to isolate those risks that are perceived to be mispriced. With this in mind, a manager utilises available instruments based on their hedging efficiency, defined as effectiveness and cost. When hedging risk in MBS strategies, non-mortgage hedges (Treasuries, futures, agency debentures, swaps, etc) have potential basis risk with respect to MBS investments. Of course, this basis risk shows up in the risk parameter calculations. Often, using other MBS securities as hedging vehicles can minimise some of this risk. Moreover, securities that can reduce less easily hedged risks are favoured in the investment decision process. Overall, it is much more efficient to hedge at the portfolio level, since some of the risk parameters of certain holdings can offset those in other parts of the portfolio.

Generally speaking, if a complex, illiquid, and/or costly hedge is required to extract excess value from a particular investment, that investment will become less attractive from a risk/reward perspective. An example of this trade occurred in 1995, when several market participants used amortising interest-rate floors to hedge inverse IOs, a mortgage derivative that looks somewhat like this hedge without factoring in the prepayment component. Not only did the market participants lose as the market rallied, but volatility rose considerably, making the hedge more costly to cover; the bid/offer in this hedge at the time was several percent. Even if the trade had been hedged more appropriately, amortising floors would still have proved a poor hedging vehicle, as the illiquid and costly nature of this hedge was prohibitively high.

Sector concentration and portfolio diversification risk

Sector concentration risk relates to an investor's portfolio that contains a significant percentage of the float in any one sector. (This applies to any hedge fund strategy in any market.) In the well-publicised MBS hedge fund difficulty of early 1994, a single hedge fund portfolio contained a high concentration of mortgage derivatives, which represented a significant percentage of the overall float in that sector. (There were other risk issues as well.) Upon liquidation, the next set of buyers were at significantly lower prices, and each wave of supply further depressed prices in that sector. Therefore, an MBS manager must be disciplined to make sure that the fund's positions do not represent a sector unto itself.

Portfolio diversification, then, is central to risk reduction. Certainly, the MBS manager can attempt to quantify the correlations in different investment opportunities. However, investment correlations tend to rise during more turbulent market environments. Since many of the investments tend to revolve around taking advantage of market inefficiencies, it becomes especially important for the manager to diversify risks as much as possible.

Financing risk

There are two risks that need to be addressed with regard to financing risk. The first is the cost of financing a leveraged position. As finance rates move, the portfolio may be adversely affected by an increase in funding costs, either through increases in short-term borrowing rates or through particular hedges having special repo rates due to a shortage in the security being borrowed.

The second risk involves lender risk, which also applies to all leveraged strategies. Whenever securities are financed, a certain amount of control is granted to the lender. Without delving into this topic too deeply, it is safe to say that the MBS hedge fund manager must ensure that financing counterparties are sufficiently strong and diversified, and that backup mechanisms are in place if a credit squeeze occurs. Cash management systems should also be employed, as significant intra-month cashflows can result from principal and interest flows, normal margin payments, flows resulting from changing margin requirements, etc.

Leverage and liquidity

Liquidity risk in the portfolio can be quantified from individual security average bid/offer spreads, and aggregated to calculate an overall portfolio bid/offer spread in market value terms. Clearly, this number should not be disproportionately high in relation to the returns that can be produced. In any investment, a manager should contemplate whether the potential return is sufficient given the liquidity of the security, and whether there are more liquid ways to create a similar risk exposure.

The leverage level of a hedge fund portfolio is probably the most commonly asked question by investors, and yet it only reveals the asset to capital ratio without giving a true picture of portfolio risk. In many instances, the quoted leverage can be surprisingly misleading, especially since it does not account for security types, inherent leverage contained within securities, liquidity, etc. This does not mean that it is unimportant, rather that when viewed against risk parameter VAR analysis, it is less meaningful. Leverage can be, however, a good measure of external financing, with the provision that the more credit is needed, the greater the possible risk.

Event risk
Event risk can be defined as an unexpected event that causes significant shifts in security valuations. Several sources of event risk pertaining to MBS strategies include:

❏ a sudden stock market decline;
❏ an unexpected portfolio liquidation by an investor;
❏ an accounting or regulatory change which can cause market participants to favour (sometimes uneconomically) some security sectors over others; and
❏ a change in the composition of widely followed market benchmark indices.

The only way to avoid the pitfalls from these types of events is to maintain a diversified and liquid portfolio.

CONCLUSION
The risk management process in MBS hedge fund strategies enables managers to measure and set limits on portfolio exposures to changes in interest rates, credit spreads, prepayments and volatility. Investment returns cannot be made without taking risks, but quantification of these risks is necessary in the overall investment process. By controlling risk through comprehensive risk management systems, the excess alpha extracted by the MBS manager will, over time, smooth out the inevitable fluctuations that occur, producing a healthy absolute-return stream with low performance volatility.

The utilisation of models in MBS investment strategies has been comprehensively covered in this chapter. Ultimately, however, models are not enough to analyse risk, as they can never truly represent reality. Just as aircraft pilots do not rely solely on their instrumentation, the MBS hedge fund manager must artfully balance model output with real market information. For example, there is no substitute for empirically observing actual fund profit-and-loss volatility. If the swings in portfolio returns are greater than the VAR estimates suggest, the portfolio may be too risky and should be re-evaluated. Subsequently, research can be carried out to determine whether any flaws might exist in the risk analysis process itself.

All of the well-publicised MBS hedge fund difficulties over the last several years can be directly linked to one or more significant mis-estimations of risk. Following these risk management principles correctly will never insure against a losing month or bad investment judgment, but it ought to insulate the fund from a significant market value decline.

An MBS hedge fund with a well-defined, disciplined investment philosophy and a meticulous approach to risk management can be a compelling investment opportunity. It can offer long-term capital appreciation with low-return volatility and low correlation to other investment vehicles, including other fixed income or equity based strategies. The MBS market is still a structurally inefficient, over-the-counter market with imperfect information flow, and this causes fundamental mispricings of certain risks to appear at various times. The myriad actively traded security types and structures dwarf that of any other market, creating far greater potential for inconsistent valuations. Furthermore, the capital markets have consistently demanded more compensation for cashflow risk compared to credit risk, and this can be exploited in the MBS credit markets. For example, the spreads afforded to commercial MBS investors for taking on credit risk typically exceed that for corporate or emerging market debt, despite the fact that mortgage credit has been proven to be of higher quality. Through the market expertise of MBS hedge fund managers and employment of a disciplined and balanced investment process, these anomalies can be taken advantage of to produce attractive investment returns.

19

Risk Management for a Distressed Securities Portfolio

Marti P. Murray

Murray Capital Management, Inc

Murray Capital invests in the debt claims of troubled companies. The investments are primarily in distressed bonds and bank debt of companies undergoing financial difficulties because of underlying operational issues or serious and material litigation matters, such as product liability disputes. The investment objective is to maximise total return by identifying securities that are undervalued due to market inefficiencies. Our goal is to identify opportunities that will increase in value over time as the troubled company pursues a restructuring, either in the context of a chapter 11[1] bankruptcy or through an out-of-court restructuring, thus restoring financial health. While maximising total return is our foremost objective, we seek to do so in a controlled, risk-averse manner. There are three areas in which we seek to control risk: managing the risk of the underlying investments, managing the risk of our portfolio overall, and managing the potential risk posed by general market dislocations where trading liquidity might become an issue.

MANAGING RISK IN INDIVIDUAL INVESTMENTS

The best way to begin the risk management process in distressed securities investing is to carefully do the homework. By this, we mean that investment decisions should be subject to a rigorous analytical process that has clearly identified the potential rewards and risks of the investment. Third party research is a useful analytical tool, but should always be supplemented with independent analysis.

Buying securities in a rush increases risk. At Murray Capital, we prefer to follow the progress of situations for a significant amount of time before committing capital. This careful approach allows problems to be uncovered so they may be properly evaluated.

Access to management is also an important risk reduction technique. We prefer to invest in situations where we can have a dialogue with management and visit with them at their offices. This allows us to get much closer to the investment and develop a better understanding of the situation than would be possible through simply looking at papers and speaking to people on the telephone. We are wary of companies that do not talk to the investment community.

Our research process on a potential investment begins by identifying the key drivers that will make an investment either a success or a failure. Once these issues have been identified, they are then analysed. The variables will be different for each investment – sometimes we may be analysing a legal claim or entitlement, sometimes we may be evaluating a company's ability to improve its cashflow or maintain its credit rating. In all cases we are evaluating the quality of management as well as their objectives.

Once we are confident that the key drivers have been properly identified and analysed, we then put together three scenarios for how we believe the investment might perform on a going-forward basis. These three scenarios are the upside, the base case and the downside. In the upside case, we are evaluating what our potential return will be if the outcome of our key variables is favourable. In the base case, we determine how our upside will be impacted if, for example, timing is delayed or valuations are lower than in our upside. In the downside scenario, we evaluate what our risk is if things do not go our way – in other words, how much money will we make or, conversely, how much money might we lose? It is the outcome in the downside scenario that actually eliminates from consideration most of the investments we look at. If we find that we could potentially lose a material amount of money in an investment, we will eliminate it from consideration regardless of the upside. We would always prefer to be in a series of investments where the upside is attractive and the potential downside is extremely limited, than in a group of investments with double the upside yet bearing significant risk of major capital loss.

AMF Bowling

AMF Bowling provides a good example of how we seek to mitigate risk in our analysis of individual investments, and how we choose the investments we think are the most appropriate fit for the firm's risk-reward profile. AMF is not only the leading bowling alley operator in the United States, but also manufactures and sells bowling alley equipment. The company was acquired in a leveraged buyout transaction in 1996. The management's objective was to pursue a "roll-up" strategy by acquiring smaller bowling centre operators, achieving operating synergies and eventually realising a higher valuation on a larger business than the multiples of cashflow paid. However, two negative developments impacted AMF: (1) the company was unable to achieve some of the operating synergies originally anticipated, and (2) the market for bowling alley products fell off precipitously during 1997–98, when the Asian economies experienced severe difficulties. Sales in Asia had been a major contributor to the company's cashflow until that point, so the decline in Asian business weakened AMF's financial condition, as it was highly leveraged from the original leveraged buyout (LBO) and the acquisitions completed.

Murray Capital first analysed a potential investment in AMF Bowling in 1998. There were a number of different debt securities in the company's capital structure available for investment, but we were primarily interested in evaluating a potential investment in the bank debt and the senior subordinated notes, which represent an unsecured debt obligation where the rights to payment come after that of the senior lenders. In evaluating the bank debt, we noted its senior position in the capital structure and the fact that it was secured by all the company's assets. The financial leverage through the bank debt was approximately 4.3 times cashflow, a level we found reasonable, as we believed that the business was worth at least that multiple, while the cashflow was not in a steep decline. We also performed a liquidation analysis on the company to determine what cash value the assets would generate in a straight liquidation. We determined that the bank debt would be covered by approximately 90% in such an event. We then performed an evaluation of the senior subordinated notes. The notes ranked below the bank debt in priority, and the leverage through these notes was approximately 6.7 times cashflow, materially higher than the multiple through the bank debt. We also noted that in the event of a liquidation, the senior subordinated notes would get a recovery of zero.

The results of our upside, base case and downside scenarios is outlined in Panel 1. We viewed the potential bank debt investment as having a relatively attractive upside of approximately 21% with a downside of +1% return. The notes indicate a better upside of approximately 30%, but with a much greater downside at –38%. Our view was that the bank debt was the better investment of the two and that it was, in fact, an appropriate investment for our portfolio. We were comfortable with the return scenarios and felt we had a reasonable chance of achieving the upside because of solid management at the company, a strong equity sponsor, and AMF's leading market position in the bowling centre business, which, although not a growth industry, was regarded as being stable. While the senior subordinated notes would do very well if we were right about AMF's prospects, the cost of being wrong was too great in our judgement, with potential exposure to a 38% loss of capital.

Consequently, we held our bank debt position for a number of months and made a small profit in it. Over time, however, we became concerned about the company's lack of progress in increasing its cashflow, and felt that the risk of a restructuring was intensifying, meaning that it was becoming less likely that we would achieve our full upside. As a result, we

PANEL 1.

AMF Bowling: Bank Debt versus Bonds

Bank Debt investment:

❑ Description: Senior Secured Bank Debt due 2002, L+225 coupon, rated B1/B

❑ Leverage through Bank Debt: 4.3x latest twelve months (LTM) EBITDA of US$130MM

❑ Liquidation analysis indicates that Bank Debt is 90% covered by hard assets

	Downside	Base case	Upside
Assumptions	Debt is purchased @ 90.75; trades to 87 (4.3x projected downside EBITDA of US$120MM – 8% lower than LTM) in 6 months; earns interest	Debt is purchased @ 90.75; trades to 96 (360 bp off vs. current spread of 570 bp off) in 12 months; earns interest and capital appreciation	Debt is purchased @ 90.75; trades to 96 in 6 months; earns interest and capital appreciation
Return (annualised)	+1.0%	+14.9%	+20.7%

Bond Investment:

❑ Description: Senior Subordinated Notes due 2006, 10.875% coupon, rated B3/CCC+

❑ Leverage through Senior Subordinated Notes: 6.7x LTM EBITDA of US$130MM

❑ Liquidation analysis indicates zero value for the Senior Subordinated Notes

	Downside	Base case	Upside
Assumptions	Bonds are purchased @ 83; trade to 46 (6.7x projected downside EBITDA of US$120MM –8% lower than LTM) in six months; earn interest	Bonds are purchased @ 83; trade to 90 (800 bp off versus current spread of 950 bp off) in 12 months; earn interest and capital appreciation	Bonds are purchaed @ 83; trade to 90 in six months; earn interest and capital appreciation
Return (annualised)	–38.0%	+20.9%	+29.5%

decided to exit the position. After we had exited, the financial performance of AMF moved sideways for a time, neither improving nor deteriorating dramatically. Nevertheless, due to the passage of time and looming debt obligations, the company announced that it would need to restructure its balance sheet. Since this announcement, the bank debt has traded to the downside price we had originally anticipated in our analysis of 1987, while the bonds traded to the downside we had anticipated. In fact, while the bank debt held up quite well in the face of an actual downside scenario, the bonds did not.

In the investing process, it is critical to have a point of view about outcomes. In the case of AMF, we believed that the company would most likely do well and that we would achieve our upside or close to it. From a risk management perspective, however, the important question for the portfolio manager is, "What happens if I'm wrong?". It is this question that we attempt to address as we perform our analysis of the downside. Many strategies and portfolio managers employ an "expected return" methodology, in which various potential outcomes are assigned probabilities and a weighted average expected return is calculated. If we had employed this methodology in the case of AMF, the results might have been as follows:

Upside probability:	60%
Base case probability:	30%
Downside probability:	−10%
Bank debt expected return:	$(20.7\% \times .6) + (14.9\% \times .3) + (1\% \times .1) = 16.99\%$
Senior subordinated notes expected return:	$(29.5\% \times .6) + (20.9\% \times .3) + (-38\% \times .1) = 20.17\%$

From this analysis, we might conclude that the senior subordinated notes are a good investment and are in fact, superior to the bank debt because the expected return is in excess of 20%, while the expected return of the bank debt is 17%. This conclusion would have been a big mistake and would have led to a loss of capital for the investing portfolio. While we at Murray Capital employ expected return methodologies in our analysis of investments, we add another simple layer of analysis: what is the expected return and is it attractive? And what does the downside scenario show (just in case we are wrong)? If the bank debt investment had indicated that we had more than an acceptable level of downside, we would have eliminated the investment from consideration, regardless of any upside or attractive expected return that might have been calculated using the technique described. The second level of analysis, in which we methodically remove investments from consideration where the downside is significant, is critical to our risk management function.

MANAGING RISK OF THE OVERALL PORTFOLIO

Once we have identified the investments that we believe are appropriate for our portfolio, we can then focus on how these investments will work together in the context of a portfolio. We require a portfolio that will provide us with an attractive return without losing our focus on the reduction of risk. All final investment decisions are made centrally by the portfolio manager and are based on the recommendations of the research analysts. This in itself is a risk reduction technique, as final accountability lies with one portfolio manager as opposed to a system of multiple sub-portfolio managers or traders whose decisions can cancel each other out. In addition, a system in which two or more individuals analyse a potential investment before it is made is always preferable. It is likely that important issues, which may have gone through in a single review, will be picked up on the second review (as the research analyst works through the investment with the portfolio manager).

When examining the overall portfolio, our concerns fall into three areas: maximising return, minimising the volatility of returns and minimising the correlation of the portfolio's performance with that of the broader debt and equity markets. Excessive industry concentrations are also to be avoided. In managing this process, we use a proprietary model developed at Murray Capital to project our performance for six month intervals. The model provides us with certain information on each position we own, such as the type of security, industry exposure, expected interest income from the position (if any), current trading price, and expected future price in six months. These data show us what type of return we might expect from the portfolio for the next six months if we are right in our investment selection. Consequently, we can evaluate whether our expected returns are being generated by a diversified group of investments or whether there are any undue concentrations in a few names that might increase our risk of under-performance should one of our investments fail to achieve the target price we have set. Because each position is also coded for industry, we can also evaluate whether we have any unintentional industry concentrations of investments in any particular industry.

In addition to the information gathered for each position as described above, the model also identifies whether the target price for each position is achievable if the stock market or bond market is unfavourable. This analysis helps us decide whether or not we think the success or failure of each investment will have any correlation to what is going on in the markets generally. With some investments, it is clear that there will be no correlation at all. For example, take an investment in which the success or failure is tied to the outcome of litigation in which the ultimate distribution is expected to be in cash. Using our model, this would be coded as a non-correlated position, because the outcome would have nothing to do with markets, but rather with an issue very specific to the given situation. Conversely, an investment in a distressed company in need of an operational turnaround, where the likely distribution will be received in newly issued equity securities, might be highly correlated to the stock market. As valuation multiples in the company's industry change in a gyrating stock market, so will the value of the distressed securities. These types of positions would therefore receive a correlated code in the model.

As a result of this analysis, we can evaluate how much of our expected return is being generated by positions that we believe will be impacted by the market. While we are willing to accept some correlation in the portfolio, it is limited. The methodology we employ allows us to determine whether we are above the limits we set, or if we have some room to add a new position that has very attractive return characteristics, but which we feel might also have some correlation.

The use of any model, including our performance projection, is an art rather than a science. At Murray Capital, we find its use beneficial because it provides a framework within which we can evaluate our portfolio and more fully understand not only its potential upside but also its exposures. The most important risk control aspect of this model is that it is reviewed every week at a meeting with the portfolio manager and the research analysts. In this meeting, we review the current trading and target prices for all the positions in the portfolio. As time passes, information changes, as do trading prices, and it is critical to constantly review where we think the upside is for our investments, and why. It is also critical, as prices change, to review again the downside for an investment, because while the downside might have been acceptable at one trading price, it may not be so at another. For instance, if the security has moved up in price, the downside might also have increased, and we need to determine whether we are still comfortable with the investment.

In the process of reviewing the projection, if an analyst is finding it difficult to arrive at a target price for one of the positions that indicates an attractive return, it is time for a serious conversation about whether the investment still makes sense for us. This may be the case for a position that has performed very well for us in the past, but where the upside from the current price is difficult to see; it may also be the case for an investment that has been a laggard and disappointment. In distressed securities investing, this sometimes occurs when the timing of a bankruptcy or out-of-court restructuring is continuously stretched out and it becomes difficult to see the light at the end of the tunnel. If we cannot see a way to make an attractive return in a particular investment it is sold. We do not allow ourselves to become sentimental.

Clinical detachment is also critical if you own a security that for unknown reasons is declining in price. My view, which is a result of almost 15 years' experience in distressed securities investing, is that where there is smoke, there is usually an inferno. If a security drops in price for unknown reasons, the best course of action is to sell immediately and re-evaluate the situation when you do not own it. It is much easier to think clearly when the mind is not trying to justify what was possibly a mistake.

MANAGING RISK OF MARKET DISLOCATIONS

Market dislocations such as that experienced during August–October, 1998 are, unfortunately, periodic occurrences that need to be managed. While maximising return is our utmost priority at Murray Capital, our objectives also include constructing and holding a portfolio that we believe will be able to weather any storm. The key issues we evaluate include the level of expected correlation of the portfolio's securities, the use of leverage (historically, we have not used any), the use of derivatives in the distressed debt portfolio, and the historical liquidity of the investments we are choosing. While there is no way to eliminate all risks of a market dislocation, careful attention to these areas will certainly help minimise their impact. It may allow the portfolio to survive relatively intact and in a fashion that allows the portfolio manager to make some smart purchases during a difficult market environment. Others may be less prepared to weather such difficult conditions.

We have already discussed the techniques we use for limiting what we view as correlated positions in the portfolio. While we will accept some correlation, it is restricted, as we would like the bulk of our expected returns to be coming from investments in which we believe the outcome will not be heavily impacted by debt and equity market gyrations. At Murray Capital, we want to own securities that will be the last positions a distressed securities portfolio manager would want to sell. We call these positions flight-to-quality investments and consider their characteristics to be as follows.

Short time to work out
The investment will conclude in six months or less. The shorter the expected time to completion, the less volatile the securities will be in the interim, because it is easier to determine the outcome for the investment. Our fundamental analysis would therefore indicate a limited downside for these securities. These positions tend to be later stage investments and therefore further along in their bankruptcy reorganisation or out-of-court restructuring process.

Easily valued back-end distribution
The distribution to be received at the investment's conclusion will typically be cash or an easily valued debt security.

Limited downside
The fundamental analysis performed indicates not only an attractive expected return but also limited downside.

Historical liquidity, issue size and trading frequency
The size of the debt issue is large enough to encourage numerous holders, frequent trading, tighter bid-ask spreads and increased interest from the

dealer community. We would look back over the trading history for securities to determine whether they have historically been more or less tradeable, and at what types of bid-ask spreads.

It has been our experience that in the distressed debt sector, flight-to-quality investments will hold their value better and recover more quickly than other potential investments which do not fit the criteria as outlined. In a severe market downturn where participants are faced with an intense liquidity squeeze, it may be that flight-to-quality investments are the only securities in the sector that are saleable, because bids may completely disappear for earlier-stage and more risky investments. It is possible to see prices drop for flight-to-quality names as severely tested managers look to liquify their portfolios. While it may appear as though the flight-to-quality investments are actually underperforming the rest of the sector during these periods, this is clearly an illusion, as these investments will generally be the only securities where a bid is readily available. The cause of the illusory underperformance is more a function of pricing issues for the riskier paper than actual valuations. Such discrepancies tend to be resolved over a period of weeks as markets either stabilise (in which case the flight-to-quality names tend to bounce back more quickly), or get worse (where portfolio managers are forced to move into the riskier parts of their portfolio and unload positions at truly fire sale prices).

Use of leverage

Clearly, the use of leverage in a distressed securities portfolio will enhance returns in the upside but it also increases risk, particularly during market dislocations. At Murray Capital, we have historically avoided the use of leverage to enhance returns as it does not fit with our risk-return profile. In distressed debt investing, there are several forms of leverage that may be employed by the portfolio manager. The first is typical margin borrowing from a broker or dealer who will lend against a portfolio of securities or distressed bank debt.

The second form of leverage are derivatives transactions known as total return swaps. In a total return swap, the portfolio manager essentially makes an investment equal to 20% of the purchase price for a given debt instrument, borrows 80% and pays interest on 100% as though the investment has been fully financed. In exchange, the portfolio manager receives the economics on 100%, even though his initial investment was only 20%. Essentially, in this example, it is a purchase of the underlying securities using 4/1 leverage. The portfolio manager does not own the underlying securities, but the portfolio receives the economics of the bonds or bank debt as though it were a regular long position. What the portfolio manager actually owns is a swap. In some cases, these swap positions can be rather difficult to manage during periods of market dislocation. A typical downside scenario might be where liquidity dries up in the securities underlying the swap and the counterparty calls for more collateral, citing a value for the underlying securities which is at odds with the portfolio manager's perception of value. Resulting pricing issues or the desire to unwind the swap may ensue. In these situations, owning a swap (as opposed to just being long the underlying securities) can turn into a disadvantage. The swap may not be readily saleable to an interested third party, whereas the underlying securities might be more saleable and more liquid. Total return swaps can be beneficial for enhancing total returns, but they must be managed and monitored with extreme caution.

It is clear that different portfolio managers in the distressed debt investing community have varying styles and approaches to maximising return and minimising risk. As a result, equally gifted managers may have very different return patterns with varying levels of return, volatility and correlation. Murray Capital takes a balanced approach in which we seek to maximise return, but in a way that clearly takes into account minimising volatility, correlation and risk in a turbulent market environment. Our techniques, while certainly not the only way to manage risk in a distressed debt portfolio, have the benefit of history. We have been through many market cycles and have been able to observe and learn how different types of securities tend to react. We therefore attempt to continuously incorporate and leverage off what we have learned from past investments in our approach to making new investments and managing the portfolio.

1   Under US bankruptcy law, a chapter 11 restructuring provides a company with court protection from its creditors while it addresses either the financial or legal issues that caused the bankruptcy.

20

Short Selling: A Unique Set of Risks

A.R. Arulpragasam and James S. Chanos

Arktos LLC

Over the last two decades of the 20th Century, the bull market in US equities has taken valuations to unprecedented levels as measured by most methodologies. As this market matures, it becomes increasingly appropriate for sophisticated investors to include short selling as an important part of their overall portfolio. In this chapter, we seek to present all of the major risks faced by short sellers and discuss ways to manage those risks to the greatest possible extent.

Investing in equity securities necessarily involves many types of risk. The initial risk is trade execution risk, which is involved with every purchase and sale. Second, there are the obvious risks of general market performance and the relative performance of an individual stock. Depending on the nature of the portfolio, there may also be significant portfolio dynamics risk, especially when the portfolio contains derivative instruments. Finally, there are the often overlooked legal, tax and regulatory risks, which no investor really wants to deal with, but which are of critical importance to all investors over the long term.

The business of short selling, or investing in a portfolio of securities sold short, is also subject to all the above risks. However, securities sold short must first be borrowed to effect proper delivery on the trade settlement date. This single extra step of borrowing the securities, and then maintaining that "borrow" until the shares sold short are bought back and returned to the borrower, creates a set of important risks that are unique to the short seller.

BORROWING SHARES TO SELL SHORT

Short selling is the reverse of owning, or "going long" securities. Short-sale transactions are opened by selling short a security and are closed out by buying back that security. The mechanics of short selling involve selling securities that one does not yet own and then borrowing shares to make delivery. Therefore, before a short sale can be reasonably contemplated, the "borrow" of the stock must be arranged. This entails several significant risks, including share availability, the stability of the borrow, negotiation of the short interest rebate, short squeezes, and the quality of the relationship with the prime broker.

The "borrowability" of a stock is ostensibly based upon its issued shares outstanding, or its capitalisation. As such, there are severe limitations on one's ability to borrow (and, therefore, to short) small cap stocks. In fact, many very large money managers are essentially unable to borrow even mid-cap stocks in the quantities required by their portfolios. In reality, the borrowability of a stock is further restricted to the outstanding float and even more so to the percentage of that float actually available to be lent out. For example, stocks held in the cash accounts of retail investors cannot be lent out, whereas stocks held in their margin accounts can be. Similarly, stocks held by institutional investors are not available for borrowing unless the prime broker already has a stock-loan arrangement in place with that customer.

Institutionally, there are two major sources of stock from which to borrow. There are actively managed portfolios, which are potentially unstable, and there are passive portfolios, which are more secure. Active managers are constantly trading their portfolios and allow their securities to be lent out primarily for economic reasons (ie, to earn part of the so-called "short rebate"). This source of shares presents certain risks to the short seller. First, the stock will be recalled when the active manager trades out of the long position (or worse yet, decides to short it himself). In this case, it is the job of the intermediary (the prime broker or trustee) to find another source of the stock to borrow. This risk is often small, as the stock may be seamlessly borrowed elsewhere. A second, more sinister risk is when the active manager decides that the short sellers are "ganging up" on his beloved stock, and consequently decides to fight back. In this case, the manager calls in his shares – despite the loss of short rebate income – to intentionally disrupt the short sellers and engineer a temporary "short squeeze". This presents a serious risk to the short seller, as it can result in a vicious short-term upward spike in the stock price, as traders simultaneously rush to cover stock that they can no longer borrow. Fortunately, prime brokers are as reluctant as short sellers to allow this to happen; engineered short squeezes cause their short-selling clients anger and hurt. All too often, the active manager engineering the squeeze fails to sell quickly enough into the price spike and also fails to profit. Additionally, other clients may be attracted to the upward momentum in the stock and purchase shares, only to suffer losses on the inevitable retracement. In any case, a short squeeze creates unwanted volatility in the stock and may also violate certain anti-manipulation clauses of the US securities law. This is a no-win situation that prime brokers wish to avoid and will do their best to mitigate. In many cases, the better brokers will intentionally over-borrow in names that they expect to become tight and that may be subject to such a short squeeze.

In addition to the occasional engineered short squeezes, short sellers are also subject to the risk of the involuntary short squeezes that occur when there is a sudden large increase in the demand for a stock. For example, when a company goes into distress and has debt outstanding, it is not uncommon to find every available share borrowed all the time. Similarly, in risk arbitrage situations where a high probability profit is evident, the arbitrageurs will do as much of the trade as possible (which is typically limited by the shares available to be borrowed on the stock sold short). In addition, it is often difficult to borrow sufficient quantities of certain thinly traded, or foreign, stocks. These involuntary squeezes create all sorts of ongoing, day-to-day buy-in pressures that are neither malicious nor engineered, but are simply situations in which too many people are trying to borrow a stock that is in relatively limited supply. Involuntary squeezes tend to happen far more frequently than engineered squeezes. Fortunately, in the case of fundamental short selling, they tend to happen near the end of the game (after the whole world realises that the stock may be going to zero!). As such, they usually result in profit reductions rather than outright losses in the position.

In both of these types of short squeeze, the degree of risk to the short seller is often dictated by the prime broker's buy-in policy. Most brokers use a "last in, first out" policy. However, other brokers either effect *pro rata* buy-ins, buy-in small clients before large clients, or buy-in retail clients before institutional clients. Clearly, it behoves the short seller to fully understand the buy-in policy of the prime broker prior to borrowing stock.

Another poorly understood aspect of stock-loan is the "short rebate". When shares of a stock are sold short, the seller is responsible to the purchaser for the payment of all dividends that become due, so long as the short sale is on the books. However, the sale of the shares also generates cash, which is known as "restricted cash". The restricted cash remains at the prime broker and earns interest at a rate that is linked to the fed funds rate or the libor rate. Under normal circumstances, in which the stock is freely available for borrow (ie, general collateral), most of that interest is credited to the short seller and is known as the "short rebate". The balance is split between the lender of the securities and the prime broker. As the supply of a stock diminishes relative to the demand, however, the stock goes on "special" and the short rebate is reduced. In this case, the interest earned on the restricted cash remains the same and, typically, the lender of the stock is paid the same rate, but the prime broker retains a larger portion of the short rebate (a reflection of the free market at work). Recently, there have been some rare cases in which stocks have actually gone to negative rebates, in which short sellers have received no short rebate and have actually had to pay additional interest to borrow the stock! The short rebate can be a significant portion of the income in a short-selling strategy, and failing to properly negotiate those rates presents another source of financial risk to the short seller.

Clearly, many of the risks associated with short selling revolve around the related activity of borrowing the shares to be sold short. The choice of prime broker and the strength of that relationship have a major impact on the short seller's ability to properly manage the borrowing risk. It is important to note that the prime broker is an intermediary who serves as agent for both the lender and the borrower of stock in every transaction. Fortunately, brokers have come to realise that the stock loan business is highly lucrative and can be a major profit centre for the firm. Accordingly, the past few years have seen a marked improvement in the systems and capabilities of the prime broker and, consequently, the level of service provided to successful short sellers.

EXECUTION RISKS

Once the availability of shares to be borrowed has been verified, the short sale can be executed. At this point, the usual execution risks apply. Short sellers are subject to possible bad fills due to poor liquidity, "fast market" conditions or clumsy order execution by the broker. Unlike long investors, however, short sellers are severely handicapped by an execution constraint called the "tick rule," more commonly known as the "uptick rule." The tick rule, adopted by the Securities and Exchange Commission (SEC) in 1938, requires short sales on US exchanges to be traded only on plus ticks or zero-plus ticks. This rule effectively prevents short sales on a stock exhibiting weak price behaviour (the point at which a short seller would ideally like to short it) and significantly increases the risk that many of the short sale ideas with the greatest profit potential never get executed at all!

There are several exceptions to the uptick rule. For instance, legitimate market makers in a security do not need an uptick to sell that security short. In turn, these exceptions have led to some questionable interpretations. If, for example, a broker dealer initiates a short sale in its proprietary account, is that truly a part of their overall market-making function, or should it be considered separate and apart? A few creative traders have managed to circumvent the uptick rule by executing their trades on non-US exchanges, such as in London, where the rule does not apply. The good news is that the SEC is quietly championing the abolishment of the uptick rule, which is now generally recognised as an anachronism. The introduction of individual stock futures is currently under serious consideration and, as there are no restrictions on selling futures short, it would not make sense to continue the uptick rule for cash trades. Nevertheless, so long as the uptick rule remains in effect, it poses a major risk to short sellers and is a severe impediment to their ability to execute trades.

Trading in over-the-counter stocks can lead to another risk unique to the short side. In certain cases where only one or two underwriters control the trading of a stock, these underwriters will sometimes refuse to execute any short sale transactions. While plenty of trading in the stock may occur, for various political reasons (eg, so as to not alienate the corporate finance client) the short sales do not get executed. This is not a major risk, but when it does occur it forces the short seller to trade anonymously, electronically or otherwise, and such trading comes at an increased cost.

Many investors believe that shorting IPOs (Initial Public Offerings) is prohibited until 30, 60 or 90 days after issuance, but that is a myth. In fact, the shorting of IPOs is allowed at any time. However, shorting IPOs is often impossible for several months, until sufficient shares have settled into institutional investment portfolios to facilitate borrowing the shares.

The aforementioned execution risks pertain to the opening (ie, shorting) side of the transaction, but buying back shares to close out a short sale can also present problems. Very few investors are aware, for example, that short sellers are prohibited from covering shorts by purchasing shares in an underwritten secondary offering, unless the short has been executed prior to the offering announcement. This restriction exists because the SEC considers that activity to be facilitating the distribution of stock, thereby rendering the short seller a 'constructive underwriter'.

It is also important to understand that short selling actually creates tradable float. When a person purchases shares from a short seller, those shares are being borrowed from someone else, meaning that two people now own them. Under normal circumstances, that does not pose any problems. For example, in the case of a dividend payment, the new holder of the stock receives the dividends and the short seller is obligated to pay the missed dividend to the lender. In the case of tender offers, proxy issues and special (return on capital) dividends, however, the lender of the stock may be entitled to receive only prorated consideration for their stock. In such cases, the lender may choose to recall the shares in order to receive full consideration. These corporate events create unexpected buy-in risks for the short seller.

PORTFOLIO DYNAMICS RISKS

The absolute movement of the overall stock market and the relative movements of individual securities within an investment portfolio can cause significant shifts in the portfolio's risk profile. These portfolio dynamics risks are generally the most essential risks to be managed over the short term.

The risk that is best understood by all investors is the risk of unlimited loss that can occur when a stock that has been shorted continues to rise indefinitely. This potential loss of all one's investment capital, and the theoretical risk of infinite loss, is the major reason that most investors will never consider short selling. Conversely, this psychological barrier creates inefficiencies and tremendous opportunities for professional investors who engage in short selling with appropriately managed risk. The risk of infinite losses can be effectively mitigated by using proper diversification, reduced position size limits, and occasional judicious stop-loss rules.

A more insidious portfolio risk, which is appreciated by very few investors, is the paradoxical effect of performance on position size, or inverse tracking error. One of the great difficulties of short selling is that the more successful your investments, the less invested you become. Let us consider a simple example. Assume an initial trading capital of US$100 that is invested 100% in a portfolio of stocks sold short – ie, the value of your short portfolio is US$100. If you are correct and the stock portfolio falls 50% in value, you earn a 50% profit. Therefore, your equity rises to US$150, but your short portfolio is now worth only US$50, meaning you are now only 33% invested. The net effect is that as the shorts begin to work, there is an ongoing struggle to keep selling more shares to maintain the desired level of investment. Worse still, the decline in these stocks means there is an increased risk that there will not be enough upticks on which to sell more shares. Furthermore, as a stock falls, the supply of shares available for borrowing tends to dry up. The short seller must vigilantly manage this dynamic risk. The converse is even worse. When a short position goes against you (ie, when it rises in value), you become increasingly overexposed to this bad investment. Rigorous adherence to maximum position size limits is a good way to mitigate this risk. Stop loss orders can also be useful, although during periods of increased volatility, they can sometimes yield disastrous results.

TAXATION RISKS

As we have seen, the risks associated with short selling are numerous and are quite different to the risks faced by long portfolio managers. However, just to ensure that absolutely no short sellers have any fun, all gains from short sales are currently taxed in the United States at the higher short-term rates – regardless of how long the short position has been held. This is yet another cost of short selling, which translates to an increased risk that the strategy will not be profitable. A future risk might be the imposition of a tax surcharge levied against short sellers, although we are not currently aware of such tax legislation being seriously considered.

Another important taxation risk associated with short selling involves the unrelated business taxable income (UBTI) issue for US pension funds and charitable remainder trusts. For many years, it was unclear as to whether or not short sales gave rise to acquisition indebtedness, and whether or not the income from short sales should be considered UBTI. Then, in 1988, a private-letter ruling was issued to allow a pension fund to participate in short selling. In 1994, the US Internal Revenue Service (IRS) issued Revenue Ruling 95–8, which clarified that tax-exempt organisations could indeed engage in short selling without triggering any UBTI. Since then, tax-exempts have started to do some short selling, although it remains a highly under-utilised portfolio strategy.

REGULATORY RISKS

The regulatory risks associated with short selling ebb and flow according to the current political climate. These risks are generally at their greatest during or following severe equity bear markets. Prior to the Great Crash of 1929, there was little support for federal regulation of the securities markets. During the Crash and the ensuing depression, public confidence in US markets plummeted. There was a growing consensus that for the economy to recover, the eroded public faith in the capital markets needed to be restored. Congress held hearings to identify problems and find solutions, and subsequently passed the Securities Act of 1933, established the Securities and Exchange Commission (SEC) in 1934, and passed the Securities Exchange Act of 1934. These laws were designed to restore investor confidence in US capital markets by providing structure and government oversight. The SEC's charter was to enforce the newly passed securities laws, to promote stability in the markets and to protect investors.

The regulatory environment for short sellers in the US has not really changed much since the Securities Acts of 1933 and 1934. In Europe and Asia, however, the environment has been a lot more hostile from time to time. Although we have not experienced bans on short selling here in the United States, both Europe and Asia have enacted bans on short selling from time to time (eg, in Hong Kong after the 1987 crash).

By and large, the SEC has been generally friendly to the short selling community. Although it has profited from falling stock prices, the short selling community has often accomplished this by exposing frauds, accounting abuses and other attempts to defraud investors through false information or misleading behaviour. As such, short sellers are actually helping the SEC to perform its oversight role.

LEGAL RISKS

Issuers of corporate stock understandably do not have much appreciation for people who sell their stock short, in anticipation of the company's value tumbling. Most such issuers, being public companies, understand that they are subject to the many and varied opinions and investment decisions that stem from public scrutiny. Some CEOs, however, take the short sellers' attacks on their company rather personally. In these cases, it is not unusual for a CEO to threaten to sue a short seller, although it is very rare indeed that such a suit is actually brought. This is often because the company has absolutely no desire to see the short seller's analysis and reasoning discussed openly in a public hearing. In the few lawsuits that have been brought, very few plaintiffs have been victorious. Although a CEO may feel that the short seller is spreading "false and malicious rumours", the fact is that the short seller is generally just expressing an opinion based upon reasonable analysis, which does not in any way constitute libel; the short seller is also protected by the First Amendment right to free speech.

A celebrated case in which a corporation did bring suit against a short seller was Sullivan & Long, Incorporated Vs. Scattered Corporation (argued November, 1994 and settled February 8, 1995). The plaintiffs alleged that Scattered's massive-scale shorting of LTV Corporation shares resulted in market manipulation and violations of securities laws. Scattered did, in fact, short 170 million shares of LTV at a time when only 122 million shares existed. In this case, despite the fact that Scattered could not possibly borrow the shares that they had shorted, the presiding Chief Judge Posner found that "since the conduct in which Scattered engaged appears to have served rather than dis-served the fundamental objectives of the securities laws, we are not inclined to strain to find a violation of a specific provision". The lawsuit was soundly rejected.

CONCLUSION

Short selling certainly shares many of the risks known to long portfolio managers. However, the short seller also faces additional risks unique to the short side. The most significant of these is the borrowing risk, which is a prerequisite to even entering a short sale transaction. This risk can be greatly reduced through the choice of an appropriate prime broker and the building of a strong relationship with that broker. A superior prime broker will be very proactive in securing stock to loan out to the short seller and will be communicative about the changing stability of the borrow. Many of the other risks faced by short sellers cannot be eliminated and must be dealt with through risk management techniques such as diversification and position limit rules.

Short selling is definitely not for the faint of heart. However, the tremendous bull market of the 1980s and 1990s has led many investors to realise that short selling will have to be a part of their overall portfolio strategy in the very near future. The dearth of investors and investment capital has yielded some enormous opportunities. It is our hope that this exposition will help investors to understand that short selling is a viable investment strategy and that the unique set of risks faced by short sellers can be effectively managed.

BIBLIOGRAPHY

The Chicago-Kent College of Law Website: http://chicagokent.kentlaw.edu/7circuit/1995/94-2015.html

The Securities & Exchange Commission Website: http://www.sec.gov/asec/wwwsec.htm

21

Risk Management for Hedge Fund Strategies – Foreign Exchange*

A. Paul Chappell

C-View Limited

A hedge fund manager undertaking strategies in foreign exchange is con-fronted with several types of risks. These are market risk, liquidity risk, regulatory risk and – usually by deferral – credit and delivery risk. In this chapter, we cover the issues related to each of these categories and high-light a number of the techniques used to address them.

MARKET RISK

The risk most apparent to any foreign exchange strategy is market risk. It arises from the possibility that market variables such as interest rates and exchange rates will move in an adverse direction, creating a requirement to have some effective limitation on the size of exposure undertaken. Market risk is compounded by the volatility of any currency pair – the speed at which the price can change – and also by the availability of market makers and the depth of the market.

Originally, the primary technique for addressing market risk was the use of nominal limits for each currency, derived from an analysis of historical volatility and, particularly, the liquidity in that currency. Liquidity in this instance covers the depth of market and the availability of price. This process incorporates the notion that certain more actively traded major cur-rencies have higher levels of liquidity and thus warrant larger exposure. Indeed, many managers today still manage their foreign exchange activity based on nominal limits and, in a number of instances, restrict their activities

---

* This chapter has been written with assistance from Kenrick Ramlochan of Bank of America Risk Management Group. The views expressed in this chapter are those of Paul Chappell and Kenrick Ramlochan and do not reflect the views of Bank of America, N.A. or any of its affiliates (the "Bank") and the Bank accepts no responsibility for, nor has it approved, any of the statements made in this chapter.

solely to the G7 currencies; this illustrates that only those currency pairs exhibit sufficient liquidity to justify reasonably large exposures.

From a hedge fund perspective, market risk can be considered in absolute and relative terms. Absolute risk is measured in total monetary terms, while relative risk is measured against a benchmark, typically agreed with the client. Any deviation from the benchmark is termed tracking error. Market risk and value-at-risk (VAR) are dealt with more comprehensively under Determination of Currency Positions, below.

LIQUIDITY RISK

Foreign exchange trades predominately for settlement at a future date. In the over-the-counter (OTC) market, it involves the nominal exchange of currencies on that future date. The forward exchange rates for each currency beyond spot are derived from the prevailing interest rate differential between any two currencies at the time the deal is struck. Sizable adverse movements in a currency, or indeed large shifts in inflation or debt levels within the countries, may cause rapid changes in interest rates that counteract those movements or reflect the effect that currency pressure is having on the prevailing interest rate structure. In instances where pressure is severe, it often manifests itself most in the cost of very short-term liquidity and thus in short-dated interest rates. This may, *in extremis*, affect a short-term position with few days to delivery; thus any transaction where there is a mismatch in maturities contains an element of liquidity risk.

This drives the need to have forward foreign exchange or gap limits to contain mismatches in maturities. These limits constrain the absolute amount of mismatched maturities and are intended to protect against a lack of availability of liquidity or balances. They are usually only applied to short or over-lent positions in a currency. Gap limits for long or over-borrowed positions are either substantially larger than for short positions or are not applied at all, depending on the currency. Thus, the technique for addressing liquidity risk incorporates the introduction of forward foreign exchange limits for each currency that allow for only limited mismatch in maturities in FX exposures right along the maturity scale.

Forward limits reflect the maximum-netted forward exposure and the maximum allowable exposure in any one calendar period as opposed to another, as well as in all calendar periods. That calendar period may be one day or one week, but is most often defined as a calendar month. Limits will also define the maximum cumulated exposures in a forward book. There may also be gap (or straddle) limits allowing only a certain time span between two legs of a forward position. The general emphasis is that the longer in tenor the exposure, the greater is the risk, of interest rate volatility before it comes to maturity with greater limitation.

As described earlier, the forward foreign exchange rate is a reflection of the differential in interest rates between two currencies. It follows that forward foreign exchange can be used to capitalise on anticipated movements in interest rates by the deliberate creation of mismatches in forward books. Able managers, when perceiving the likely pressure on a currency, will, from a trading perspective, ensure that they take in balances for future dates in order to benefit from the resultant upward effect upon interest rates. This makes gap limits important, and helps desks to avoid taking too high risks.

The undertaking of trading in futures rather than OTC instruments obviates the majority of liquidity risk issues. However, as futures exposures have specific maturity dates, futures contracts need at some stage to be either rolled over or liquidated. This in turns means that adverse pressure on a currency will cause a larger movement in the outright price than in the spot price as interest rates adjust alongside the deteriorating spot price. Futures limits need to be scaled to reflect this. Again, the technique of using foreign exchange to capitalise on movements in interest rates can be achieved by mismatching futures contract dates by buying one maturity and selling another, although this activity needs to be subject to limitation. Intelligent risk management scales limits on currency futures mismatched exposures to the amount of limitation applied to similar mismatches in the OTC market.

There has been an upswing in the desire from the corporate and investor community to hedge or undertake exposures in some less liquid currencies, irrespective of the fact that there is limited availability of liquidity in the local, usually onshore, market. This has lead to the development of the non-deliverable forward (NDF) market. NDF contracts – also called dollar-settled forwards – are synthetic forwards, which entail no exchange of currencies at maturity. Instead, settlement is made in US dollars, based on the difference between the agreed contract rate at inception and a market reference rate at maturity. NDF contracts can be used to establish a hedge or take a position in a growing number of minor currencies in the emerging markets, where conventional forward markets either do not exist or may be closed to non-residents. As offshore instruments, NDF contracts offer the advantage of eliminating convertibility risk, since no emerging market currencies are exchanged at maturity.

The NDF market is different only in that the effect on the outright price may be further accelerated by the offshore nature of the activity. Price volatility of the outright rate will be greater if it is not benefiting from the damping effect of a robust local money market to reflect the actual cost of interest expenses. Therefore, the implied NDF price of an interest rate may occasionally be far higher for managers requiring balances or liquidity to cover short positions in that currency than the actual prevailing local interest rates. Liquidity limits for NDF currencies need, therefore, to be commensurately smaller than for freely convertible currencies to take this into account.

Liquidity risk can be a serious risk management problem and substantial losses can occur due to the lack of market liquidity or liquidation costs. Typically, the costs associated with "forced" liquidation are underestimated, as market participants stand back when someone is forced into action. In the recent past, the triggering of barrier options caused much of the volatility in the currency market. This caused otherwise inexplicable gaps in the currency markets, similar to the effects created by the presence of large stop-loss or limit orders. There may also be one-way liquidity traps in many markets, where liquidity can be deceptively high upon entry to the market, only to disappear when attempting to leave.

In general, option-pricing models assume that the currency market follows Brownian motion – ie, they lack memory of historical price movement or its path. However, in the presence of liquidity "holes", these assumptions are violated, as the latest price path becomes very relevant to subsequent price movements. Attempts to deal with this issue in option pricing have led to a better understanding of transaction costs, with adjustments now being made to the implied volatility inputted into these models. Dependent on a trader's existent option book, the "augmented" volatility may be either at a mark-up or markdown relative to normal implied volatility. This results in jumps in volatility that are essentially flagging these liquidity gaps.

There is a further form of liquidity risk, which is the lack of availability of price in any particular market or product. This arises when there is insufficient activity or a dearth of market-makers, or a lack of appetite amongst those holding countervailing positions to post a price. Instances of lack of liquidity in this form include such instruments as illiquid OTC contracts. All of these forms of lack of liquidity are dealt with by market-risk limits.

REGULATORY RISK

Adverse or unacceptably large movements in a currency may result in increased control on movements in and out of that currency by governments or regulators in any country. These controls or inhibitors of movement may be as simple as direct intervention by the authorities, usually in the guise of the Central Bank, or the raising or lowering of interest rates to counteract the adverse movements. These types of regulatory involvement are covered by market and gap-risk limits.

If pressure persists in a currency beyond a certain level of dissatisfaction with governments or regulators, they have tools beside intervention which they may use to contain adverse movement. Initially, this will manifest itself in the reduction of the trading authority that each government or central bank gives to banks domiciled, or with branches, within its own borders. However, with the increased globalisation of the banking and foreign exchange industry and also the development, in some currencies, of

NDF markets, locally based regulations have become increasingly difficult to apply. Beyond these trading restrictions, the controls become considerably more arduous and generally involve restricting the movement of capital – particularly speculative capital – in and out of a currency. They may also include some constraint on local banks regarding the amount of liquidity, as expressed in FX forwards or outright forward transactions, that they may undertake with, or provide to, offshore counterparties. The most severe measures that may be introduced by governments incorporate the introduction of full capital controls, whereby any FX activity in a currency is permitted only through a regulatory mechanism that determines whether the nature of that transaction is indeed commercially based. For managers caught wrong-footed with exposures in currencies where capital controls are introduced or reintroduced, especially if this occurs suddenly or arbitrarily, it can be a painful experience.

Currencies are as different as the countries that use them. In the same way, governments and central banks have a heritage of management methods for those currencies. Knowledge of these differences is important in understanding the behaviour of currencies.

The philosophy of exchange rate parties has changed over the years. In the past, it was considered beneficial to devalue a currency under pressure, due to the presumption that this made exports more competitive and imports more expensive, thus redressing the trade balance. It was eventually found that pricing was not necessarily a major factor in export growth, while the impact of higher import prices had an immediate negative effect on inflation. A devalued currency had an unfortunate tendency to continue devaluing. As the FX world has moved towards regarding currencies from an investment rather than a trade standpoint, the economics and political advantages of currency strength and stability, both real and psychological, become apparent, because they deliver the advantage of reduced import prices thereby lowering inflation – and also facilitate inflows of capital to make financing easier. But if maintaining a strong currency is in resistance to fundamental trends, then eventually the effect of this exerts its toll, often in unforeseen ways. It is essential for a government to pursue a long-term policy and, although it is important to show responsibility in economic affairs, and to create artificial market conditions through interventions; regulations are only stop-gap solutions. At best it can buy time and correct short-term aberrations. However, in most cases it will create more problems that are often harder to cope with than the original ones.

Techniques for addressing the risk of incremental regulatory control, and especially the more severe measures, are difficult to apply scientifically, as they involve addressing what are either predominately political or fast-deteriorating economic situations. Put simply, a thorough understanding of the country in which a manager is undertaking exposures and also relationships with banks or other agencies that have good local knowledge is vital. A specific understanding of the likelihood of regulatory intervention, and of the likelihood of a point of severity in adverse currency movement causing capital constraints, is important. If there is a strong likelihood of direct regulatory action, then positions in that currency should be liquidated and mismatches in forward books should be reduced, as controls may come into effectiveness immediately or at an arbitrarily chosen future date.

The prospect of this type of constraint explains why many managers trade only fully convertible major currencies. For the rest, there is an onus of responsibility to reduce exposure when regulatory intervention of a type that may restrict capital movement becomes a real threat.

CREDIT AND DELIVERY RISK

The majority of hedge fund managers' foreign exchange activity is undertaken with major banks, broker/dealers, or on recognised futures exchanges. They generally have limited delivery risk, which is a reflection of the creditworthiness and robustness of those institutions with which they deal directly. Credit risk arises when a counterparty is either unwilling or unable to fulfill their contractual obligations. This can result in forced liquidation that can transform a paper loss into an actual loss – consequently, it is vital that managers select their counterparties carefully.

It must be recognised that sovereign risk is a type of credit risk that can occur when local regulatory authorities prevent free capital flow through the imposition of foreign exchange controls. Sovereign risk is country specific, while default risk is company specific.

There is an important distinction that needs to be made regarding credit risk associated with foreign exchange between the default of a counterparty before the delivery date, thereby creating an exchange-rate risk, and default of a counterparty on the due date, which is a far more serious problem. Failure on a delivery date creates a capital risk, as contracts to deliver one currency against another may only be honoured on one side, thus creating a risk for the full face value of the transactions. Fortunately, instances of this type of default in major market participants are rare.

It has to be recognised that apart from direct risk from failure of counterpart bank or broker/dealer, there is a risk in any particular market in the event that delivery of any of the major participants fails. This failure may have a dramatic impact upon its depth and liquidity. In some instances, when banks' exposures are driven by their hedge fund managers' activity, they may seek to recoup some part of any losses if one of their counterparts fail.

It is regrettable that, with regard to the FX product, the market in general and banks in particular have not moved further down the road of netting their exposures. A sizable proportion of FX activity, particularly the more vulnerable type between major institutional banks and, in some countries, smaller domestic onshore banks, is still not subject to a suitably comprehensive form of netting arrangement. This allows for the prospect of a delivery failure having sizable general market repercussions in the currency pair in question.

The techniques for addressing delivery risk in terms of risk management specify that managers be cautious in their choice of bank and broker dealers. In the case of activity in minor currencies, awareness of the level to which counterparty banks and broker dealers are offsetting positions with potentially more vulnerable local banks in any more market place is important. Also, from an industry perspective it is as important for managers to be involved in ongoing initiatives to reduce settlement and delivery risk by the increased use of netting and moves toward intra-day settlement of FX transactions.

DETERMINATION OF CURRENCY POSITIONS

Now that we have examined the three most important risk areas exposed to hedge fund managers, we now look at the FX exposure that ought to be undertaken – what currencies to hold and in what amounts.

The approach which we have developed and instituted over a number of years is to apply nominal limits to each of our individual currency exposures, and, then utilise VAR analysis to manage the correlation and overall portfolio risk that arises as a consequence of holding a number of currency positions at once. (We will discuss VAR later.)

Specifically, prior to the commencement of each quarter, we undertake analysis of all convertible currencies and NDFs. We initially discard a number of currencies where the absolute depth of market is too small, or the liquidity/spread/price is too wide to warrant undertaking wholesale FX positions. This group will also include a number of currencies where governmental or regulatory restrictions preclude access, without the serious risk of positions being disadvantaged by sudden changes in regulatory framework.

With this in mind, we select a number of currencies within which we are comfortable taking wholesale foreign exchange risk. Within this group we then undertake a more detailed analysis of liquidity and volatility, and a more subjective measure of predictability, to arrive at nominal limits for each currency.

With regard to liquidity, we not only analyse recent liquidity, but we also look back at more historical liquidity and our limits are therefore derived from a blend of both. As an example, a currency such as the Hungarian forint will have relatively high liquidity if we only analyse the recent past. This is because the forint has been maintained in a basket arrangement versus the US$ and euro, and solely against the euro for the last three years. This implicit stability accrues from the assumption that Hungary will accede to the European Union and eventually become affiliated to the euro within the next few years. One has to reach further back in history to include analysis of the impact on liquidity should that basket arrangement for any reason break down, and the Hungarian forint be left fully floating, in order to arrive at appropriate risk limitations.

With regard to our analysis of volatility, we take the measure of this predominately from the currency option market, but again we reach back in history for historical instances of stress in any currency (for example, the 1999 Brazilian devaluation) in order to place an additional filter on absolute positional size.

Our analysis of predictability is a more subjective measure, which looks at the general characteristics of a currency over time. Some currencies tend to advance and retreat in a reasonably logical and sequential fashion, and as such it is relatively straightforward to take advantage of themes or trends. Others act in a far more illogical fashion, swiftly retreating after an initial advance, or *vice versa*. These predictable characteristics are the result of the types of flows or transactions that drive movements in the currency. Currencies with sizable but sporadic speculative or investment flows, but with relatively few underlying commercial or trade flows to provide a cushion, will inevitably behave in a more unpredictable fashion.

The result of this analysis of liquidity, volatility and predictability provides a framework of maximum exposure for each currency pair. Given that in this portfolio approach, there is an attempt to blend exposures in major and minor currencies, the results of the analysis inevitably produce a situation whereby we undertake commensurately larger exposures in major currencies than in minors, and also that those differences can be substantial.

It is important to point out that even adopting a quarterly approach to nominal limit structure is insufficient if one-off events occur to impact specific regions or groups of currencies. As an example of this, our process substantially reduced market-risk limits for all Eastern Europe currencies as soon as the Russian crisis occurred in August 1998.

As part of the decision-making process in determining whether to undertake an exposure currency, managers tend to look for a nominal risk/reward ratio of approximately 1 to 1.75 in any given currency position. It is ambitious to expect that opportunities that deliver risk/rewards ratios of 1 to 4 or better occur in currencies with much frequency. Generally, assessing a wider range of currencies produces better risk/reward opportunities. However, many currency managers restrict their activities to the G7 currencies purely for reasons of liquidity or absolute market size, and thus are excluded from a great number of opportunities.

VALUE-AT-RISK

More recently, with the introduction of the currency options market in the early 1980s and the subsequent development of a Non-Deliverable Forwards (NDFs) market in a wider range of currencies, a more sophisticated method of assessing foreign exchange risk was required. This led to the development of VAR that can be used to quantify any of the risks mentioned. Essentially, VAR summarises, in a single number, the worst possible loss over a specific future time for a given probability level, under normal market conditions. Typical VAR statements might be: "the daily VAR of a hedge fund is £90 million at the 95% level of confidence". This means that there is a one in 20 chance that the fund could lose more than £90 million sterling over a normal day.

VAR can be calculated using three different approaches: historical, variance-covariance and Monte Carlo. The methodologies for these are very different and there are advantages and disadvantages to each.

The historical method uses historical price movements to simulate the portfolio through time to provide a return series. This series is then sorted, so that if 100 data points were to be used, then the 95% case would be the return associated with the 95th worst return. This method uses historical exchange-rate data to determine returns on a portfolio over the VAR estimate time horizon. These returns are then sorted from highest (gain) to lowest (loss). Given the level of confidence, we can obtain a VAR estimate.

A major advantage with the historical methods is their ability to handle complex instruments with asymmetric payoffs and the fact that portfolio VAR can be calculated without the need to understand the complex inter-relationships between the components of the portfolio. (There not being a requirement to understand the complex inter-relationships between the components of the portfolio.) In addition, historical methods account for the distributions of daily changes in many market variables that have fatter tails than normal distributions. Therefore, it accurately reflects the historical probability distribution of market variables. Finally, compared to other approaches, the historical method is also easy to understand and explain.

A typical criticism of this approach is the fact that historical data is used in this analysis and that a particular history may not be relevant today or in the future. For example, depending on which 100 days we use in our analysis, we could get very different results.

The variance-covariance method is an approach where the inter-relationships between the portfolio constituents and their individual volatilities form the basis of the estimation process. These parameters are often estimated by historical data analysis. However, if the returns are non-normal, as they invariably are with many instruments including options, then the estimation of correlations and volatilities becomes suspect, as these measures implicitly assume a normal distribution.

The advantage of this method is that it is convenient and simple to use.

However, the obvious disadvantage is that normal distribution is assumed to describe the behaviour of the portfolio components. The probability of the worst observed loss is under-estimated due to the use of this normal distribution.

The Monte Carlo approach requires the user to define the future distribution of the portfolio constituents and their inter-relationship. Using these inputs, the approach mathematically simulates the portfolio over time to create thousands of separate cases, which are sorted and typically handled in a fashion similar to the historical method of estimating VAR.

The advantages of this approach are that it can account for a wide range of risks such as non-linear price risk, volatility risk, and model risk. In addition, it has the ability to analyse any return distribution (unlike the variance-covariance model, it does not assume a normal distribution). Therefore, it is attractive for analysing path-dependent options.

Unfortunately, the Monte Carlo approach is highly computationally intensive and the end result can be difficult to explain intuitively. In addition, it can be subject to model risk, unless some sensitivity analysis is conducted. For example, one bad assumption can negatively affect the entire set of results.

CONCLUSION

After examining the various risks that a hedge fund manager faces, we can see the different types of risk analysis that can, and indeed ought, to be undertaken. Nominal limits and currencies can be chosen on the basis of an analysis of the currency markets, with respect to liquidity, volatility and predictability.

The different approaches to VAR are then analysed. All three methods hold both advantages and disadvantages, and choosing any particular approach depends on the hedge fund managers' own portfolio.

Most risk analysis from both a nominal and VAR perspective has been undertaken at the end-of-day or once-a-day basis. However, with recent technology improvements, we can start to see improved facilities for providing near real-time analysis, not only of nominal limits but also of VAR. As more FX transactions move to an electronic base, and execution is completed via the Internet, the opportunity exists for risk management to move closer to real-time.

Part IV

Perspectives from the Consultants

22

Incorporating Hedge Fund Risk into the Design Parameters of a Traditional Investment Programme

Mary Ann Johnson

Johnson Custom Strategies, Inc

Hedge funds are not for the uninitiated. They present a series of difficult analytical problems for those who are responsible for integrating them into a more traditional investment programme. Without a precise understanding of hedge funds' role within the total investment programme, selection is an exercise that could lead to grave disappointment. In order to achieve success, it is important to ensure that the objective of the hedge fund allocation is clearly defined at the outset, and that expectations regarding return potential and risk characteristics are both clearly understood and realistic.

CUSTOMISING AN INVESTMENT PROGRAMME
Establish objectives
The first, and most crucial, step in customising a client's investment programme is to establish its objectives, which are as singular as the clients themselves. For corporate retirement plans, the objectives are designed around actuarial assumptions. Endowments aim to exceed the rate of inflation plus an annual distribution factor. Individuals generally intend to exceed the rate of inflation plus liquidity needs, a tax hurdle rate and any other unique requirements. Specific asset classes are not referenced at this point and risk is defined as failing to meet the objectives over a given time.

Frontier modelling
Once the objectives are established, we develop an asset allocation strategy and select investment styles within the asset classes. Efficient frontier modelling, based on the average expected return, standard deviation and

covariance between the return series, is used to evaluate various asset allocation scenarios and investment styles, so that the optimal portfolio for the client can be isolated.

While efficient frontier modelling is a useful tool for viewing various asset allocation combinations, we are sceptical about its ultimate accuracy in predicting outcomes. Aside from state retirement systems and corporate pension plans that have a perpetual life and a contingent source of funding in the event of catastrophic loss, most entities and individuals possess neither the time horizon nor the patience to overcome the estimation errors that affect efficient frontier models. For instance, few investors today remember the 16-year period from 1965 to 1980 when, based on Ibbotson & Associates' data, US common stocks produced a 6.2% annualised total return, barely outperforming inflation at 5.9%. Current focus is on the 20-year period from 1979 to 1999 when US stocks compounded at 17.9% versus a 1.6% inflation rate. The result has been an increased expectation for market returns, which has climbed from 8–9% in the 1980s, to 9–10% in the 1990s and ultimately to 10–11% in the year 2000. The returns incorporated into efficient frontier models assume a much longer time span than those adopted by most investors who were, at the end of 1999, contemplating equity returns in excess of 20% *ad infinitum*.

Hedge fund allocation
Due to the imperfections of efficient frontier modelling, we remove hedge funds from the overall asset allocation process and focus instead on the alpha (or value-added) a hedge fund allocation can provide at either the total fund or asset class level. In our opinion, the purpose of a hedge fund allocation is to be additive, providing an incremental return to the existing investment programme or asset class. We do not consider the hedge fund's performance in isolation, but in relation to the benchmark it has been selected to enhance. The hedge fund allocation should be viewed as a subsector choice which complements the total investment programme or asset class, and not as an asset class of its own.

Assessing risk in relation to hedge funds is a delicate undertaking. Insufficient data and inaccurate predictions regarding returns and volatility render traditional measurements useless. The wild card in hedge fund statistics tends to be the unpredictable volatility rather than the long-term returns. Event risk, leverage, derivatives, short selling and complex financial instruments play such an important role within the hedge fund universe that volatility can rise or fall unexpectedly at any given time, even if past experience has indicated fairly consistent returns. Surprises are more commonplace in the hedge fund arena, and they tend to be fast and harsh. Although a number of superb hedge fund databases have been compiled, they cannot overcome the deficiencies of simple statistical analysis based on return and volatility. As concluded in a paper by Danielson, deVries and Jorgensen (1998):

> Our results question the assumptions embedded in popular risk management paradigms, which effectively assume much greater volatility forecastability at long horizons than appears consistent with the data, and suggest that for improving long-horizon risk management, attention is better focused elsewhere. One such area is the modelling of extreme events, the probabilistic nature of which remains poorly understood, and for which recent developments in extreme value theory hold promise.

Although this study and its conclusions relate to value-at-risk (VAR) models, which are sturdier than efficient frontier models, we believe its conclusions are applicable to both.

In addition to the questionable forecastability of hedge fund characteristics, there is an inherent mismatch between the long time horizon required for efficient frontier modelling and the short time horizons of most hedge fund strategies and investors. Although many hedge fund managers purport to have a long-term investment perspective, there is actually an intrinsic one-year horizon due to the annual incentive fees paid on all gains, whether realised or not. Managers simply cannot afford to hold unhedged positions over the long term and suffer the financial consequences of an unexpected drawdown at year-end. Financial incentives are predicated by consistent returns and the preservation of capital, which means that managers must hedge portfolios in order to limit losses. This should, by its very nature, lead to steadier results than those achieved by long-only traditional managers; however, it does not address the issue of unpredictable volatility.

Market-neutral strategies

Market-neutral strategies, popular among institutional investors who view them as safe and consistent, provide a prime example of what can happen if all variables are not considered. Market-neutral strategies include long/short equity, merger arbitrage, convertible arbitrage, fixed income arbitrage and others. The performance objective is to neutralise market risk by offsetting specific risk as equally as possible between long and short positions. Many asset allocators assume returns of 10–12%, standard deviation of 6–7%, and a low or negative correlation to equity and fixed-income asset classes. These highly favourable characteristics are devoured by efficient frontier models through which, if unconstrained and based on average return and risk assumptions for cash, US equities and fixed income and international equities could return an optimal portfolio model with an allocation of 55% to the Standard & Poor's 500 and 45% to market neutral. However, presumably "safe" strategies have been subject to significant drawdowns due to leverage, poor security selection and event risks; the more "neutral" the strategy, the more difficult it is to recoup losses without increasing the risk profile of the underlying portfolio. Traditional modelling and risk measures are incapable of estimating such events and, if relied upon, can result in faulty hedge fund allocations.

Type of hedge fund

The type of hedge fund to be implemented becomes the next focus of our strategy compilation. If there is a significant allocation to indexed equities within the structure of the underlying programme, the use of index futures with an alpha transport overlay using market-neutral portfolios would warrant consideration. We might supplement a high fixed-income allocation with fixed-income-like absolute return strategies, and use more aggressive opportunistic hedge funds to enhance the returns on a high equity allocation. If the objective of the hedge fund is to increase diversification and enrich the returns of the total investment programme, we would select multiple hedge funds with highly specific but complementary strategies, keeping in mind that over-diversification and high manager turnover ultimately detracts from, rather than improves, results.

Appropriate benchmarks

Once the purpose and type of the hedge fund allocation were fixed, we would next determine appropriate benchmarks against which to measure its overall effectiveness. The choice of whether to compare the allocation to the total fund or a specific asset class depends on the investment objectives of the complete programme and the traditional strategies that comprise it. Benchmarks are developed for each hedge fund, or, if multiple funds are packaged into a fund-of-funds, for the total hedge fund allocation. The benchmarks are specifically designed to reflect the objective of the allocation and are based upon its expected value-added. For example, a customised fund-of-funds would be expected to provide net returns in excess of the total programme's return, excluding the hedge fund allocation, over rolling three-year periods. Hedge equity could be expected to return in excess of the Standard & Poor's 500 over rolling three-year periods with less variability, or to provide net returns over those of the clients' diversified equity allocation within the same time frame. Portable alpha may be anticipated to exceed the returns of 90-Day Treasury Bills by 200, 300 or 400 basis points net annually, depending on the strategy's leverage. We would look to convertible and merger arbitrage to provide a net positive rate of return each year, regardless of market conditions, or to provide a return in excess of the client's traditional fixed-income managers (excluding cash). These are tough but realistic examples of benchmarks that are designed to reflect high expectations, available investment techniques and securities, and the incentive fee which must be overcome. These hurdle rates also reflect the higher degree of potential risk and uncertainty that will accrue to the overall portfolio if hedge funds are included in the mix.

Selection of hedge funds

The final step in the programme design is the selection of individual or multiple hedge funds. Our focus at this point is on fundamental portfolio and manager assessments in conjunction with return and statistical risk measurements.

ANALYSING RISK

Any discussion of risk is controversial because it highlights uncertainty and combines it with the possibility of loss. The critical elements required to analyse risk include the source, degree, type and timing of potential losses. Financial risk can range from catastrophic loss, such as Granite Partners, LP and others in 1994 and Long Term Capital Management in 1998, to unfortunate timing, where a losing investment that may eventually turn around must be liquidated after it has already lost a significant amount of money. Various risk measures are useful in evaluating the past, but possess little predictive power. Just as the validity of the efficient frontier and its reliance on standard deviation has come into question, other measures of "risk" move in and out of favour as investors discover their inherent lack of predictability. Backward-looking risk measures quantify the past but do not tell you the future with assurance. The difficulty in predicting both returns and risk is evident in the high degree of manager turnover by hedge fund investors. We suspect most manager turnover is due to reliance on historical data and risk measures that are assumed to be sustainable, but which have no proven forecastability.

As stated by Byron Wien of Morgan Stanley Dean Witter & Co, "Everyone agrees that risk is important, but no one can agree on how to measure or define it". Newer VAR measures focus on active decisions, but still lack "predictive" power with regard to unanticipated events. Since it is difficult to define risk in a long-only world, the complexity of measuring hedge fund risk where complex financial systems are prevalent is currently problematic.

Much of the controversy about risk centres on the effort to reduce risk measurement to a single number, ie, standard deviation. The problem with standard deviation is that it assumes all returns are symmetric. An improvement on standard deviation is semi-variance, which separates positive from negative returns when compared to a chosen benchmark or absolute return number. The assumption built into semi-variance is that bad returns constitute risk while good returns do not. While it is a better measure than standard deviation, no predictable interpretation of the outcome has been developed. The Sharpe ratio, a measure of efficiency utilising the relationship between the annualised riskless return and standard deviation, is a good measure of past efficiency, but is lacking in predictive value. By the time the Sharpe ratio declines, losses have already occurred. The most statistically robust VAR programmes measure the amount of money that can be lost over short periods of time, but VAR applications relate to active portfolio and asset allocation decision-making instead of assessing the long-term probability of loss within a particular investment or asset class.

As evidenced by the above discussion, a reliable "formula" for predicting returns and risk has yet to be developed. Therefore, we use a wide range of current measures to evaluate, to the best possible extent, past return patterns. These include standard deviation, beta, alpha, r-square, Sharpe ratio, information ratios, tracking error and others. In addition, we have incorporated less-well-known statistics into our analysis. As with more standard risk measures, each has its positive attributes and drawbacks, as described below.

Semi-variance

Proponents favour semi-variance because it focuses on undesirable outcomes, assuming that high returns are not risky. When dealing with hedge funds, however, extraordinarily high returns may be achieved by taking on additional risk at the portfolio level. Therefore, the lack of attention to extremely high returns is a concern because the risk assumed to achieve high returns may also have a high probability of producing extremely negative returns. When measuring semi-variance against equity or fixed income benchmarks, it is also important to recognise that many hedge funds do not have 10 or 15-year performance histories; therefore the use of this statistic can result in an interesting diversion with no application, because markets have been in an uptrend with few negative periods against which to measure returns. Despite these drawbacks, the most positive feature of semi-variance is that when returns are asymmetric, it measures the downside. Finally, the semi-variance calculation can be based on a target return, useful because many hedge fund strategies are expected to produce an absolute return either above zero, Treasury bills, Libor or a fixed number (eg, 12% per annum). Semi-variance adds the most insight when a fixed return is chosen as the target.

Probability of ruin

This analysis begins with the assumption that any return earned in the past can be duplicated. By establishing a number that represents "ruin" (–15%, –20% or –50%, etc) through Monte Carlo simulations, the model calculates the probability of reaching that return. This analysis is useful because it is possible for a hedge fund to have a low standard deviation, but a high probability of ruin. The most positive attribute of this analysis is that it establishes an identifiable downside, albeit based on historical returns. However, without including at least 60 data points within an environment that includes events that should have negatively impacted the strategy, the analysis is not revealing.

Net exposure

Most hedge fund investors and managers consider net exposure (long positions minus short positions) to be a good indication of portfolio "risk". Many hedge fund managers reduce "risk" by lowering their net exposure and by increasing cash. We believe a better gauge of portfolio risk is the hedge ratio (long positions divided by short positions). This ratio more accurately reflects the portfolio's sensitivity to negative returns and the level of protection offered. For instance, at 50% long and 50% short, a portfolio has a net exposure of "0", is considered "neutral", and has a hedge ratio of 1.00. Any deviation from neutral represents a change in the portfolio's exposure to long-only risk. Table 1 shows that if two portfolios are 115% long/80% short and 95% long/60% short, both have a net exposure of 35%, which is considered relatively low and indicative of a conservative profile. However, with hedge ratios of 1.44 and 1.58 respectively, both are carrying more risk than a neutral portfolio, despite their low net exposures. If the market were to decline and security selection is assumed to add value, longs (ie, good companies or securities) should decline less then shorts (ie, bad companies and/or overpriced securities). Interestingly, the portfolio with the lower hedge ratio is expected to perform better, all things equal. By monitoring the hedge ratio, the investor gets a better sense of the aggressiveness of the portfolio and how it might perform in a negative environment compared to neutral.

Table 1   Example of net exposure compared to long/short ratio

	Portfolio I	Portfolio II
Long exposure	115%	95%
Short exposure	(80)	(60)
Net exposure	35%	35%
Long/Short ratio	1.44x	1.58x
Hypothetical return if:		
Longs drop –10%	–11.5%	–9.5%
and		
Shorts drop –20%	+16.0%	+12.0%
Net return:	4.5%	2.5%

Transparency

One of the greatest difficulties investors face in hedge fund assessment is lack of access to trades, security positions and hedging techniques. In the absence of information regarding individual trades and positions, the investor cannot determine how the manager achieved results, and is consequently unable to evaluate whether past performance is repeatable. Lack of access also prohibits the use of sophisticated attribution analysis, utilised by institutional investors to identify the source of performance, quantify risk factors and monitor changes in portfolio characteristics over time. Some hedge funds with institutional partners have been forced to provide information regarding top holdings, while others provide total disclosure, but most have been reluctant to succumb to institutional reporting requirements and standards. Our goal is to subject all hedge fund portfolios to the same scrutiny as that applied to institutional separate accounts. Depending on the types of investors involved, future high profile failures might result in required disclosure.

CONCLUSION

As can easily been seen by the foregoing, hedge fund risk is complicated and does not lend itself to traditional risk measurement techniques. Complex investment techniques and securities, when combined with leverage, are prone to surprises. Secrecy and lack of transparency add substantial risks from the investor's perspective. Despite the drawbacks, their usefulness within a well-thought-out portfolio is unquestionable; however, so are the pitfalls which can occur if they are used indiscriminately. Careful analysis, assessment and, above all, planning for the perfect fit are all essential in ensuring the successful incorporation of hedge fund strategies in a well-rounded investment programme.

BIBLIOGRAPHY

Danielson, J., C. G. deVries and B. N. Jorgensen, 1998, "The Value of Value at Risk: Statistical, Financial and Regulatory Considerations", *FRBNY Economic Policy Review*, October.

23

Risk Management for Hedge Funds and CTA's: VAR Versus SPAN Margin

George Martin and Sam Y. Chung

University of Massachusetts and TRS Associates; Long Island University

The past decade has seen the explosive growth in the technology and techniques of quantitative risk assessment, usually under the rubric of value-at-risk (VAR). What is novel about VAR is that it tries to do two things:

❏ to provide an integrated methodology for the risk measurement of portfolios of diverse financial assets; and
❏ to describe that risk in probabilistic terms.

However, despite the growth of VAR as a risk measurement tool, it remains the case that the bulk of risk management is conducted using risk metrics that are neither cast in nor reducible to probabilistic quantities. Specifically, most risk management is conducted not through direct VAR constraints, but through margin constraints and other techniques that seek to limit the quantity of capital allocated to a particular position or positions. Therefore, an important issue is, therefore the relationship between these two types of constraints. Here, we investigate the relationship between generic parametric and nonparametric VAR measures and a set of futures margins well established by various derivatives exchanges. We develop a number of useful results, including some rules of thumb, that should be of value to risk managers and others responsible for managing positions in markets for various assets.

SPAN MARGIN VERSUS VAR

Let us begin with a few brief words about Standard Portfolio Analysis of Risk (SPAN). The relevant exchange's margin committee determines the appropriate "scan ranges" for the asset underlying each contract; there amount to set a set of sixteen possible stress scenarios presumed to occur over one trading day, including various changes in price and implied volatility. The factors considered include historical data, liquidity, open interest and current volatility, with the goal being to ensure the viability of the clearinghouse (index futures margins are, however, dictated by the Federal Reserve). For an individual contract, the set margin requirement is the maximum loss on a contract under one of the scan scenarios. SPAN itself is a system of determining the aggregate margin requirements for a portfolio of contracts, and is mostly devoted to giving credit for offsetting positions (eg, calendar spreads) on predetermined contract combinations.

As a rule of thumb, SPAN margins for futures contracts are set at about the 97.0–99.5% level for *absolute* changes in the futures (which means even more stringent VAR terms in actual long or short positions), though they can often be tighter, as in Bonds. For example, the current S&P500 spec initial margin is US$23,438 or about 6.7%; this move has only been exceeded (in the spot) on six of the past 5,565 days of available data, giving an unconditional empirical quantile of 99.89%.

Table 1 presents 3 sets of statistics for comparing SPAN with a generic single contract VAR, calculated according to the standard RiskMetrics methodology, using daily data from 1990–1996 (the period for which the Futures Industry Institute (FII) makes available a panel of margin rates)[1].

❏ The empirical coverage rate for SPAN (ie, the fraction of trading days in which the absolute value of the change in value in the futures contract exceeds the margin rate), the mean exceedance (where the denominator is the number of exceedances), and the maximum exceedance.
❏ The empirical coverage rate where the VAR estimate is set to be 2.58 times the RiskMetrics vol forecast (ie, the 99% level for absolute

Table 1 Weights used in margin risk assessment simulations

Contract	Vol Wts	Margin Wts	Ratio
CME – Australian $	13.13%	14.82%	88.59%
CME – UK Sterling	9.59%	10.51%	91.24%
CME – Canadian $	23.21%	23.48%	98.87%
CME – Deutschmark	9.52%	9.95%	95.67%
CME – Nikkei 225	4.69%	2.71%	173.18%
CME – Jap Yen	9.75%	10.32%	94.44%
NYM – Light Crude	2.82%	2.41%	116.71%
CMX – Copper	4.17%	4.78%	87.16%
CBT – US Tbond	11.95%	9.30%	128.44%
CBT – Soybeans	5.88%	5.61%	104.76%
CBT – Wheat	5.31%	6.11%	86.87%

Table 2   Probability that portfolio loss does not exceed various levels (assuming all positions are wrong)

		Assets			
		3	5	7	8
Portfolio loss	1.0000	99.6732%	99.8944%	99.9400%	99.9564%
	0.8333	99.1800%	99.6416%	99.8264%	99.8732%
	0.7143	98.3084%	99.1492%	99.4824%	99.6020%
	0.6250	97.1032%	98.3220%	98.9364%	99.0888%
	0.5556	95.6532%	97.1560%	97.9528%	98.2632%
	0.5000	93.7820%	95.5940%	96.5496%	96.9368%

Table 3   Probability that portfolio loss does not exceed various levels (assuming random long/short)

		Assets			
		3	5	7	8
Portfolio loss	1.0000	99.9232%	99.9812%	99.9884%	99.9932%
	0.8333	99.8012%	99.9576%	99.9724%	99.9852%
	0.7143	99.5544%	99.8756%	99.9548%	99.9712%
	0.6250	99.2252%	99.7744%	99.9016%	99.9448%
	0.5556	98.8124%	99.5624%	99.8236%	99.8872%
	0.5000	98.3132%	99.3156%	99.6884%	99.7992%

changes), as well as the corresponding exceedance measures.
❏ The number of standard deviations as a VAR input required to equate the VAR coverage ratio with the SPAN coverage ratios, as well as exceedance measures.

From the information in Table 1, one can, in fact, see that the SPAN rates are in the 97–99.8% range, or, assuming symmetry in returns, 100% – (100% – SPAN Rate)/2 for actual positions. The corresponding VAR rates are in the 3–4.5 standard deviation range, which is in the 99.8–99.999% range (assuming Normality). More interesting perhaps is the fact that when VAR levels are set to SPAN coverage ratios, mean and max exceedences for SPAN are generally less than that for RiskMetrics VAR. None of this should be terribly surprising, since one would expect a committee of market professionals to be capable of outperforming a naïve statistical method in assessing market conditions. The exponentially weighted average forecast of future volatility for the assets in question appears to have only limited forecast accuracy, particularly when it comes to forecasting extremes. Results using more developed VAR estimation results should be more favourable to VAR, but would undermine our goal of presenting results that are generic enough to be useful to a wide range of market professionals.

In Panel 1, we include some more detailed information on the relationship between SPAN margin and VAR for 11 contracts that are more important in a typical trading portfolio of an active trader of futures contracts.[1]

Of course, in the context of risk analytics for hedge funds and CTAs, contracts are held in portfolios. Since SPAN does not give credit for positions that are not directly or almost directly offsetting, SPAN margins effectively assume that inter-contract correlations are one. The figure 1 below gives the ratio VAR/SPAN for two to 20 equal-vol weighted assets, assuming the equal interasset correlation given on the x-axis and zero higher moments. (Note that the correlation matrix is not well-defined – ie, it is not positive definite – for $\rho < -1/(n-1)$, and as such there are minimum ratios of VAR/SPAN that are greater than zero.) While this is useful information to assess the consequences of not crediting a portfolio risk measure for lack of correlation in its constituent assets, it is important to see how this works in practice, both at the futures contract level, as well as in actual managed portfolios.

To investigate the actual performance of SPAN in portfolios, we form daily portfolios of 3, 5, 7 and 8 of the contracts just mentioned in our assessment of individual contract risk coverage rates. As a useful ingredient for

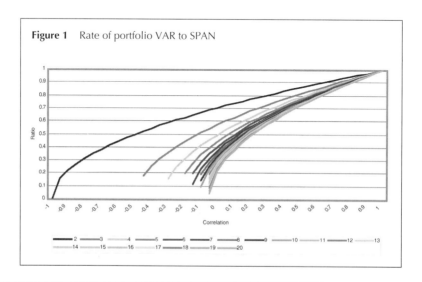

Figure 1   Rate of portfolio VAR to SPAN

the analysis, we report the correlation structure of the return series in Panel 1c: we can see that the correlations are generally very low. (To understand and manage portfolios with assets that are more highly correlated daily we can collapse the number of assets in question into the number of "independent" groupings of assets that are assumed to be, within the group, very highly correlated – eg, all contracts in a specific interest rate complex or in a specific equity complex.)

The actual analysis is conducted as a simulation. We do this by bootstrapping the historical data described above. The methodology is :

❏ a random day from the historical data is sampled (with replacement);
❏ N contracts (N = 3, 5, 7 or 8) are selected via sampling (without replacement);
❏ the quantity of each contract such that (Available Margin Dollars)/N dollars of margin are allocated to each contract is determined based on the margin requirements of that specific day, where the base case is Available Margin Dollars = 1;
❏ the portfolio loss for that day is calculated assuming that the fund is on the wrong side of every contract in the portfolio, or assuming that the fund is randomly long/short each contract, and that the fund has no stops; and
❏ empirical quantiles are then determined from 250,000 repetitions of the resampling.

To get some idea of how portfolio allocations are assigned, it is useful to see the weights implied by average margin usage, as well as by vol:

From Panel 1b we can see that T-Bond, Nikkei and Crude margin-based weights are more stringent than that for currencies or ags. The results of the bootstrapping are summarised in Panels a and b.

These may be interpreted in the following way: suppose one allocates one dollar of margin across a set of N contracts, such that the margin usage in each contract is equal to $1/N$. The probability that the loss on that portfolio (assuming either all wrong way positions or random long/shorts) on any given day is less than or equal to US$1, US$0.83, US$0.71, US$0.62, US$0.55, or US$0.50 is given in the column corresponding to N. We can see that these empirical quantiles are very stringent, even under worse-case scenarios, and are certainly more stringent that typical VAR-probability quantile levels implemented by trading institutions.

We can also look at the risk measurement properties of margin in actual manager portfolios. We have daily end-of-day data on margin/equity ratios and returns for nine diversified CTAs, and we use these as a basis for our estimation of a benchmark, empirical distribution function for margin usage/empirical VAR. From a risk management perspective, we are interested in two quantities: the relationship between margin at the close of T−1

Panel 1a   Daily Correlations (90–96)

	CME-AUS	CME-STER	CME-CAN	CME-DM	CME-NIKKEI	CME-YEN	NYM-CRUDE	CMX-COPPER	CBT-US TBOND	CBT-SOYABEANS	CBT-WHEAT
CME-AUS	1.000	0.114	0.228	-0.008	0.053	-0.090	0.052	0.029	-0.001	0.014	0.021
CME-STER	0.114	1.000	0.069	0.753	-0.021	0.430	-0.002	0.046	0.065	0.059	0.047
CME-CAN	0.228	0.069	1.000	-0.028	0.044	-0.118	0.031	-0.038	0.156	-0.018	-0.003
CME-DM	-0.008	0.753	-0.028	1.000	-0.082	0.556	-0.016	0.020	0.032	0.070	0.084
CME-NIKKEI	0.053	-0.021	0.044	-0.082	1.000	-0.097	-0.096	-0.008	-0.006	0.035	0.036
CME-YEN	-0.090	0.430	-0.118	0.556	-0.097	1.000	-0.090	-0.008	-0.138	0.002	0.034
NYM-CRUDE	0.052	-0.002	0.031	-0.016	-0.096	-0.090	1.000	-0.039	-0.091	0.047	-0.004
CMX-COPPER	0.029	0.046	-0.038	0.020	-0.008	-0.008	-0.039	1.000	0.022	-0.095	0.038
CBT-US T BOND	-0.001	0.065	0.156	0.032	0.181	-0.138	-0.091	0.022	1.000	-0.095	-0.024
CBT-SOYABEANS	0.014	0.059	-0.018	0.070	0.035	0.002	0.047	-0.095	-0.095	1.000	0.382
CBT-WHEAT	0.021	0.047	-0.003	0.084	0.036	0.034	-0.004	0.038	-0.024	0.382	1.000

Panel 1b   SPAN vs. VAR 1990–1996

SPAN Contract	Jap Yen	Nikkei	Deutschmark	Canadian $	UK Sterling	Australian $	Light Crude	Copper	US Tbond	Soybeans	Wheat
empirical quantile	1.4770%	0.2460%	1.4223%	1.3129%	1.6958%	1.3129%	0.4667%	2.4806%	0.2188%	1.4223%	2.4070%
mean exceedence	0.6348%	0.4568%	0.4188%	0.1640%	0.6213%	0.4645%	1.9595%	0.9608%	0.2713%	0.6742%	0.9601%
max exceedence	3.1310%	1.0018%	1.6139%	0.4464%	2.5391%	2.2486%	8.0000%	4.4359%	0.4974%	2.0736%	7.1187%
VAR standard devs = 2.58 empirical quantile corresponding to 99% normal											
empirical quantile	2.7192%	2.6858%	2.4417%	3.2186%	3.6626%	2.4417%	3.1361%	3.8898%	2.3862%	3.1632%	2.7192%
mean exceedence	0.6193%	0.9240%	0.4703%	0.1980%	0.4582%	0.3334%	1.8605%	1.0143%	0.3163%	0.9167%	0.6607%
max exceedence	3.5254%	3.9073%	1.4053%	0.7734%	2.6090%	2.3176%	21.3910%	4.9649%	1.6371%	2.4873%	5.1839%
VAR Coverage = SPAN Coverage stdevs	3.05	4.36	2.95	3.42	3.08	3.01	4.70	2.91	4.23	3.48	2.62
empirical quantile	1.4983%	0.2498%	1.4428%	1.3319%	1.6648%	1.3319%	0.4734%	2.4311%	0.2220%	1.4428%	2.3862%
mean exceedence	0.7497%	1.8133%	0.4903%	0.1614%	0.5498%	0.4049%	2.2968%	1.0285%	0.2831%	0.6929%	0.7040%
max exceedence	3.2802%	3.3368%	1.2638%	0.5699%	2.2697%	2.1587%	11.8519%	4.3350%	0.8660%	1.5820%	5.1236%

We do not present data on the S&P500 since the margin rates in the early 90s were set, at the Federal Reserve's direction, at 15–25% and so there were no exceedances.

and the absolute value of returns on from the close of T–1 to the close of T – a forecasting relationship, and the relationship between margin and the absolute value of returns when both are measured at the end of the current trading day. Below we present two figures which give the estimated empirical cumulative distribution functions for both the "forecast" and the "current" relationships between margin to equity and the absolute value of returns – the first is the entire range of values, and the second is a detail of just the area of 95% to 99.5%. From the data and comparison with the above results on the probability of portfolio losses, we can see that the estimated forecast and current empirical distribution functions are consistent with the construct that these CTAs have on average what amounts to a net of seven uncorrelated and randomly selected positions. We can also see from the detail that the forecast margin versus absolute value of return is more stringent than the current ("realised") ratio, and thusly indicating the appropriateness of using such a forecast.

We can develop more sophisticated, multi-factor models of risk measurement for both VAR and margin usage that go beyond merely estimating empirical distribution functions. To understand the relationship between returns and risk measures in a more systematic way, we need to examine the relationships not just at the most extreme quantiles, but over a range of quantiles. To do this in an analytical manner, we can estimate a quantile regression of relationship between observed changes in the value, V, of a portfolio and observed explanatory variables. Specifically, we want to estimate a relationship between our observed quantities x_{it} and our τ-period VAR, measured as $|R_\tau| = |(V_{t+\tau} - V_t)/V_t|$, such $VAR_{t+\tau} = \Sigma_i f_i(x_{it})$

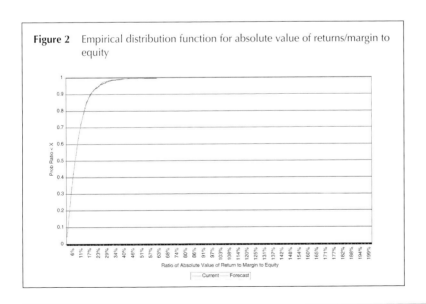

Figure 2   Empirical distribution function for absolute value of returns/margin to equity

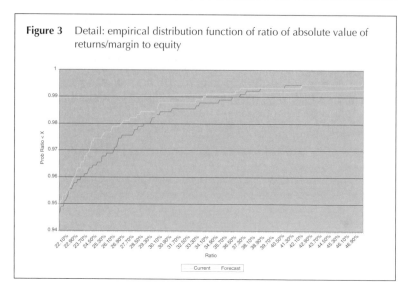

Figure 3   Detail: empirical distribution function of ratio of absolute value of returns/margin to equity

$+ \varepsilon_{t+\tau}$. Unspecified so far is the fact that associated with our VAR measurement is a confidence level, α. We can impose this constraint by requiring that Prob $(-\text{VAR}_{t+\tau} + \Sigma_i f_i(x_{it}) = \varepsilon_{t+\tau} > 0) = \alpha$ which is obviously immediately translatable into a constraint on the fraction of residuals with positive sign. To estimate the functions f_i we need to impose some constraints on them. To make the results analytically tractable, we require that for a given (α, τ), each f_i is a scalar; hereafter we always assume that $\tau = 1$ day, so that each f_i is parameterised only by α.. The L^1 loss function used requires that we minimise the sum of the absolute value of residuals, so that the results are robust to outliers. Results of this kind of analysis will be made available in future publications, but preliminary results suggest that observable quantities, like implied volatilities and the level of risk being taken, add to the ability to forecast future risk quantilies.

CONCLUSIONS

The above analysis has provided some results that market professionals should find useful in managing the risks of diversified portfolios of assets subject to exchange-based margin requirements. We show that exchange-based margin can be much more stringent than simple statistical VAR models, and that margin-based measures can be translated into non-parametric VAR-equivalent measures for actual managed portfolios. We also suggest a statistical methodology for expanding the analysis to multi-factor risk determinants. From the above analysis, we suggest that margin or other quantity-based constraints can be useful in both managing and measuring market risks.

1 The daily data is on front month futures contracts rolled on the last day that the contract is available for purchase by non-commercial entities. This is actually a somewhat pessimistic roll scenario, since specs almost always roll significantly before this date into the more liquid next out contract, and volatility tends to be greater in non-financials contracts as one approaches delivery.

2 Of course, this result is partly driven by the assumption of normality for estimating VAR quantiles. But this is less of a problem than one would expect at first glance, since that non-normality should be captured in part by increased volatility estimates, as positive kurtosis in returns biases sample-based estimates of volatility upward.

24

Enterprise Risk Management for Hedge Funds: An Applied Perspective

Murray Nash and Andy Lee*

NetRisk

The greater part of this book is dedicated to the understanding and management of individual risks as they pertain to hedge funds. In this chapter, we take a step back and concern ourselves with the higher level issues of managing risk at the entity level. We address questions about the merits and practical considerations involved when bringing together decentralised and disparate information (ie, market, credit and operational risk information from multiple management systems) in a manner that promotes a consolidated view and consistent decision-making across the entity, without unduly compromising the individual managers' accountability.

MONEY OWNERS' AND MANAGERS' RATIONALES FOR ENTERPRISE RISK MANAGEMENT

In any enterprise risk management exercise, we must begin by defining the entity we are analysing and the perspective we take. In the case of hedge funds there are at least two perspectives that must be considered: that of the money manager (hedge fund) and that of the money owner (investor). Money owners are the principals that delegate (or outsource) the management function to their agents, the money managers.[1] Managers are in the business of providing value to owners. In many cases, this entails more than simply providing positive alpha – it entails doing so in a manner consistent with the expectations of the investor and with the potential to provide information which makes this process transparent.

The owners of money have the following reasons for seeking risk information on the hedge funds they are investing in.

* The authors would like to thank Alastair James for his ideas, opinions, and help in editing. They would also like to extend their gratitude to Marta Johnson and Lara Swann for their guidance and expertise in the field of operational risk.

❑ Owners are concerned with allocating money to a group of managers that collectively offer an attractive profile of returns (in this regard, owners are akin to a fund-of-funds). This generally means that they are seeking investments that offer attractive returns without increasing risk significantly.[2] This rationale underlies the naming of the hedge fund industry in the first place. The argument is that, as an asset class, hedge funds offer returns that were largely uncorrelated with the returns of the more traditional asset classes.

❑ Money owners are also more likely to allocate money to managers that are able to offer information on their activities to facilitate transparent monitoring.

Money managers have the following reasons for producing enterprise risk information.

❑ Those managers volunteering transparency can expect to be more successful at attracting and keeping investors. This is the other side of the observation that investors are increasingly demanding this type of information and are making risk management a focus of the manager selection process.

❑ Risk information can assist the portfolio managers within the hedge funds by providing a better understanding of the sources of risk that threaten their strategies and whether or not they are being adequately compensated.

❑ The franchise value of the hedge fund is contingent on providing good (risk-adjusted) returns. Otherwise the funds under management, for both products and across the entire asset management firm, will be eroded. Enterprise risk management information is used to identify concentrations of risk across products. These concentrations will have adverse reputational effects in the event that the firm reports large losses across multiple products. Moreover, with the recent merger activity amongst asset management companies, there may be concerns regards ensuring that the risk and return attributes of each product offering are relatively distinct, ie, the individual products are not substitutes.

The economics of the fee structures paid to hedge funds and the resulting incentives further emphasise the demand for risk measurement systems. Managers are generally paid a small fixed fee plus a performance-based component. The performance component has an option feature to it, in much the same way that traders' bonuses do. The performance component has an asymmetric payout to the hedge fund, which enjoys an (increasing) share of the returns in the event of good performance, yet fails to partially "insure" the money of the investors if they lose. If the performance fee is simply a function of returns (either absolute or relative to a benchmark, then the hedge fund manager and the investors' interests are unlikely to be aligned. The manager might maximise the expected return from the performance fee by taking risks in search of higher returns.

A number of partial solutions to this problem have been developed eg, having the managers invest a large portion of their personal money in the fund, compliance monitoring aimed at limiting risk, and relying on the manager's reputation to attract funds in the future.[3] An alternative approach is to reward the managers on the basis of risk-adjusted returns, eg, nominal returns are deflated to reflect the risks, inherent in earning the returns. Enterprise risk management makes this possible, and some managers are now offering risk-adjusted, return-based fee structures.

Proprietary information
A number of hedge fund managers have proprietary strategies that depend upon continuing secrecy for the viability of their franchise. Unsurprisingly in these cases, there is a great reluctance to provide investors with details of the composition of their portfolio. This situation is not inconsistent with the framework set out above, which argues that, in general, managers have incentives to provide owners with risk information; however, funds that can demonstrate superior performance are likely to attract queues of investors willing to invest without requiring risk information. There are numerous examples of niche funds operating under veils of secrecy that are over-subscribed.

However, there will also be a large group of investors (likely to be of the institutional variety, as contrasted with High Net Worth Individuals) that will be either unwilling to accept these conditions, or only willing to invest lesser amounts than if there were more information available. Hedge funds wanting to grow assets under management are likely to be under greater pressure from the marginal investor to provide greater transparency around their strategy and risks – a strong and consistent return series will not be enough. One compromise is to provide summary level risk information as an alternative to specific holdings, as discussed below.

ENTERPRISE RISK MANAGEMENT AND THE ART OF THE INFORMED TRADE-OFF
Enterprise risk management involves the development of a strategy for managing all types of risks – ie, market, credit and operational risks – across all businesses, portfolios and operations. For a money owner with multiple managers or a relatively large hedge fund with numerous products, this issue is not trivial. Conceptually, the non-additive properties of risk – ie, portfolio effects – and the disparate nature of the various risks add to the difficulty of a meaningful aggregation. We discuss these issues in the section "The Consolidated Risk Picture" below.

The applied risk management perspective is as important as, if not more important than, the conceptual components when designing a firm-wide risk framework. From an applied risk management perspective, informed trade-offs must be made to ensure the resulting process is "right-headed". Notably, the marginal benefits exceed the marginal costs. Too often, enterprise risk management projects are overly ambitious, and are treated as an unconstrained exercise or a race for complexity. Most enterprise risk management systems that fail do so because of a reluctance to make trade-offs reconciling intellectual purity with more practical considerations. Successful firm-wide risk management necessitates the application of the 80–20 rule; the last 20% of precision incurs 80% of the total cost.

In the one extreme, the enterprise risk-management designer may aim to replicate trading desk-level analytics at the enterprise level, although hindered by the additional burdens of consolidating this information in a consistent manner. This approach can result in overly complex and costly systems that fail from the outset on basic business workflow criteria, such as providing decision-makers with the information they require within the necessary timeframe. Moreover, the project plans for such ventures are often of the "big bang" variety, failing to provide the ultimate users with interim deliverables for checking the project's direction. This creates the avoidable risk that the ultimate deliverable will fall short of user expectations.

In the other extreme, enterprise risk management never happens due to decision paralysis. Notably, there is an up-front acknowledgement that complex enterprise-wide solutions are ultimately ill-conceived, too costly and do not address the right business issues. Again the general objection is with respect to the inability of a system to deliver full accuracy and complexity. This approach may be considered more enlightened, if only because it avoids near certain and costly failures.

By using perfection as the measure of success, neither extreme is likely to result in the optimal solution. It is the authors' view that neither approach is relevant in an imperfect world.

The design of an enterprise risk-management system should be founded on a clear understanding of whichever decisions it will support, as well as how it is expected to influence behaviour. As users of enterprise level information often have different roles and perspectives to traders or portfolio managers, why start from the proposition that they require the same detailed information? The appropriate starting point ought to be the roles and uses of enterprise risk systems and the costs of incremental improvements.

To make informed trade-offs, we must look at the specifics of the situation, notably, the businesses the firm engages in, and the management processes and infrastructure that exist to support this process. We can then identify the various types of risk and begin the process of measuring and managing the material risks. To make better decisions about the appropriate enterprise risk framework, we can also look to other industries with more direct experiences for guidance, most notably the large financial institutions where it all began. However, when drawing these conclusions, we must be cautious of the very real differences between these two industries, notably operational scale, definitions of what constitutes risk and regulatory environments.

Parallels with risk systems for financial institutions

When contemplating a risk system for a hedge fund or a money owner, the analogy with the development of risk-reporting within financial institutions is worth considering. Internal measurement and reporting concerns the aggregation of risk across disparate business lines and systems. In the case of the asset management industry, the challenge is to aggregate risk from multiple asset managers with disparate investment strategies.

We can expect the evolutionary process for the asset manager industry to be similar to that which occurred within the firm, namely:

❏ reporting periods will become more frequent;
❏ risk measurement methodologies will increase in sophistication; and
❏ standalone reporting for each business entity will move to portfolio risk measurement for a combination of business entities, ie, the collection of funds that a single investor may have exposure to. For this type of aggregation to be possible, a degree of standardisation in the reporting between the various risk entities (ie, asset managers) is required.

It needs to be appreciated that these three elements are often in conflict. Greater frequency in reporting may necessitate compromising the precision of the risk methodology employed. Similarly, portfolio reporting is constrained by the lowest denominator of the various reporting entities, in terms of both the frequency of reporting and the relative sophistication of the methodologies employed.

Pitfalls and lessons learned

The more successful internal systems in complex financial institutions have not attempted to replicate the analytics at the desk level. The breadth and timeliness of information required to support strategic decision-making necessitates compromise. The challenge is to know which simplifying assumptions can be made without undermining the usefulness of the system. The objective is generally not to replace or second-guess portfolio manager decision-making, but rather to achieve a greater transparency and understanding of the risk profile. The information required by senior management and external investors is likely to be less detailed than that required in the direct management of a portfolio.

The challenge of arriving at a consistent and coherent portfolio risk measure is endemic to the majority of issues facing risk managers within large financial institutions. The conceptual breakthrough that enabled portfolio risk to be derived statistically (eg, value-at-risk) has proven to be a double-edged sword. The "devil in the detail" in implementing risk measurement across systems, business types and time zones is more difficult than a simple consideration of the mathematics would suggest.

A typical response to the challenge of portfolio risk measurement within major financial institutions has been to commit huge technology budgets, often in the order of tens of millions of dollars. A popular approach to enterprise risk management has been to build a global warehouse and place on top a comprehensive risk engine that embodied analytics as sophisticated as those found on most trading desks.

This approach, whilst being the most intellectually pure, has often resulted in disappointment because:

❏ outright failures have been quietly brushed under the carpet;
❏ unstable operating environments have resulted in frustration and challenges to the integrity of the metrics; and
❏ computational intensiveness has compromised timeliness and resulted in numbers arriving too late to impact business decision-making.

It was soon realised that throwing money at the problem did not necessarily guarantee success nor improve decision-making. With experience, risk managers opted for less ambitious solutions that gladly traded off complexity and accuracy for timeliness, breadth and cost savings. A typical depiction of this situation is shown in Figure 1.

Other considerations: reporting to institutional money owners

The connectivity opportunities created by the Internet will revolutionise the monitoring of agents by their principals, superseding the established paper-based and static reporting process. The impact will be seen in the nature of governance arrangements between firms. The Internet is an obvious delivery mechanism for the reporting of performance and risk in a timely, interactive and cost effective manner to external third parties, including shareholders and investors.

The institutional investment management market is a case in point. Institutional investors are demanding greater transparency and risk reporting from the external managers of their assets. An asset manager's ability to demonstrate superior risk process and reporting has become a differentiating factor in the management selection process. The logical next step will be the ability to aggregate risk information across asset managers to provide investors with a portfolio view. This latter point is where the real scope for the revolution will occur, as this type of analysis is only recently possible.

Figure 1 Enterprise risk management: an informed trade-off

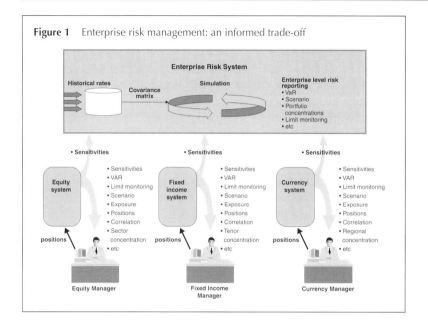

Hedge funds will need to make informed trade-offs when devising electronic external reporting strategies. First, from a cost and operations perspective, the "win-win" is to leverage the systems which have been developed for internal risk monitoring. Thankfully, the information requirements of external parties are similar, generally being some subset of that required by internal decision-makers. Alternatively, the investor might circumvent the managers directly in this process and rely on their custodians to, for instance, provide them with the risk information they require. Second, enabling external parties to consolidate their institution's risk information with other institutions' data will require data and methodology standards. Standards have the benefit of enabling comparison and aggregation, but often at the expense of relevance and accuracy. Financial institutions have been wrestling with these issues for some time, as part of developing enterprise-wide risk systems and in dealings with regulators. Standards of the type being discussed here have yet to be promulgated. However, as people come to realise the benefits, we can expect greater standardisation, either arising from a successful commercial venture or through the intervention of a third party, such as the Association for Investment Management and Research (AIMR). Third, the implications of "straight-through connectivity" on governance arrangements, which empowers third parties, needs to be understood. Further clarification of roles and responsibilities will occur, as it did within firms once enterprise-risk systems were up and running. Resulting structures and processes will need to reflect this greater transparency while protecting the delegation of authority – we all want to prevent decision paralysis from having too many "back seat" managers.

RISK MEASUREMENT IN THE ASSET MANAGEMENT INDUSTRY

The traditional approaches to risk reporting within the asset management community have been based on the observed volatility in the time series of Net Asset Values (NAV), in both absolute terms and in relation to benchmarks. NAV is the mark-to-market fund valuation that accounts for injections and withdrawals of capital and past cumulative returns. There have been considerable academic and applied efforts to extract information content out of this time series. Examples include Sharpe ratios, information ratios and Alphas. Moreover, style analysis, performance attribution and historical risk/return analysis can be derived from this type of information.

These measures have the advantage of being easy to produce and objective, and able to support portfolio analysis. However, they suffer from being backward-looking, and do not directly explain whether the volatility is explained by differences in luck, skill or risk taking (see Panel 1). There are countless examples of portfolios that earned spectacular returns with low volatility in NAV, only to blow up in stressed environments.

Sell-side firms have pioneered risk measures that can complement and address some of the shortcomings in the traditional measures. Value-at-risk (VAR) and scenario analysis are examples of approaches which can differentiate between luck and inherent risk-taking. VAR is a statistical measure of the potential loss for a given level of confidence, while scenario analysis quantifies the loss if a given set of market movements are realised. Given the context of sell-side firms, VAR analysis is usually performed for

---

PANEL 1
Backward versus forward

Forward-looking risk measures are derived on the basis of the current portfolio. Backward-looking risk measures depend on historical time series. Backward-looking risk measures are slow in accounting for changes in portfolio composition (eg, style changes) and/or sudden changes in the general market environment (eg, periods of heightened volatility). Moreover, backward-looking measures can be misleading in situations where the time series is of insufficient length to give a representative sample of the true nature of the distribution, notably low frequency/high severity events.

To illustrate this last point, we consider the following two probability distributions with the same mean (0) and standard deviation (4.5%). We draw a sample time series from each.

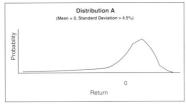

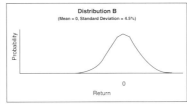

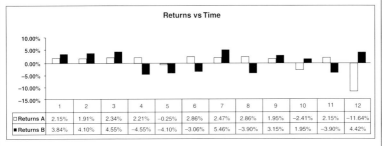

	Returns A	Returns B
Cumulative return (periods 1 to 11)	19.67%	2.72%
Standard deviation (periods 1 to 11)	1.58%	4.15%
Cumulative return (periods 1 to 12)	5.74%	7.26%
Standard deviation (periods 1 to 12)	4.12%	4.13%

Distribution A is an asymmetric distribution with considerable downside risk, as can be seen from the left tail of the distribution. This type of distribution is typical of credit portfolios and some operational risks. Distribution B is more symmetrical and is characteristic of market portfolios, which demonstrate up and down movements that are almost symmetrical (though not necessarily normally distributed).

It can be expected that the frequency of non-extreme observations will be higher in distribution A than in B. The backward-looking, risk-adjusted returns during "regular" market conditions are likely to heavily favour A. However, the probability of extreme loss is considerably higher in "stress" situations for distribution A. These results are borne out by the example. We can see from the returns of the first 11 time periods that the returns from distribution A clearly dominate distribution B. Over this period, A is able to achieve a higher cumulative return with a lower standard deviation, and therefore a more impressive risk-adjusted return. However, by introducing the 12th observation (an example of a stress environment in distribution A), the prior results are turned on their head. Forward-looking risk measures, on the other hand, are not as dependent on the actual observed distribution of returns for the period under review, and would likely lead to the conclusion that the downside risk is greater for A.

short timeframes up to two weeks. This assumption is questionable for asset management firms, but there are a number of ways to relax this assumption.

A measure of the forward-looking potential loss in a portfolio, as contrasted with the historical volatility in a fund's performance, has a number of advantages. First, the reported risk is insensitive to the manager's past performance. Another advantage of these sell-side approaches – and this is of particular interest to a new hedge fund – is that the risk profile can be derived on the basis of the current portfolio. As such, risk can be derived in the absence of an historical time series of NAVs.

Second, a change in the risk profile is instantly observed – ie, through an increase in VAR. Moreover, drill-down in the changes in the source of the VAR can be observed, perhaps indicating a change in a manager's style.

Despite these advantages, there has been reluctance from hedge funds and managers to adopt these sell-side measures. In part this has been due to questions of relevance and cost. A notable problem with these "forward looking" types of measures is that they rely on information about the current composition of the portfolio and are therefore influenced by the portfolio's sensitivity to changes in rates and prices. However, as money managers begin to invest in sell-side type systems (and custodians and data providers offer ASP-type services) then the ability to populate these models for both the managers and the owners is becoming less costly and problematic.

We dedicate the remainder of this chapter to providing an overview of the sell-side methods for measuring market, credit and operational risks that are applicable to hedge fund managers and investors. Going forward, there will be a greater reliance on these metrics within the hedge fund industry.

We are not arguing that sell-side metrics will replace the more traditional return-based measures. The two approaches each answer different questions and ultimately complement each other. As an example, an historical standard deviation in returns can be compared with a current VAR to determine whether current risk levels are consistent with past practices. VAR can also be used to define risk limits, while scenario testing enables the manager or investor to gain insight into how the portfolio might perform in adverse circumstances, thereby reducing surprises. Finally, we are not proposing the wholesale adoption of sell-side analytics. Modifications are required to reflect differences in the two environments, such as longer assumed holding periods.

TYPES OF RISKS

The enterprise is exposed to a seemingly infinite number of risks. To make this situation manageable, it is useful to classify these risks into three relatively distinct categories:

1. market;
2. credit; and
3. operational.

Market risk is the potential for loss due to adverse movements in financial and commodity prices. Credit risk is the potential loss caused by a counterparty actually failing to meet their financial obligations (ie, a default), or a perceived deterioration in the likelihood that they will make good on these obligations (ie, deterioration in credit quality). There is a growing consensus within the financial services industry on the definition of operational risk. The definition used in the 1999 BBA/ISDA/RMA Survey on Operational Risk defines it as "… the risk of loss resulting from inadequate or failed internal processes, people, systems or from external events". This definition supports the view that operational risks can be identified and are manageable, which is a significant step forward from the days when operational risk was defined as "all risks that are not market or credit".

Much work has been put into the quantification, aggregation and management of these various risk categories. From an enterprise perspective, mathematical and statistical techniques provide us with the potential to aggregate and compare disparate risks in a consistent manner, both within and across these categories.

Market risk

Market risk is the most widely understood of the three types of risks. In going from viewing risk at the individual holdings level to the enterprise level, there is an increase in the reliance and sophistication of the mathematics involved.

At the individual holdings level, statistical standard deviations have been the most widely accepted representation of risk. The magnitude of the standard deviation is the usual means for comparing the relative risk embedded in various securities. The advent of theoretical and arbitrage pricing has focused attention on the standard deviations of the independent variables (risk factors) used in pricing models rather than the security's own past. Thus, instead of measuring volatility from historical bond prices, one would concentrate on the volatilities of the underlying interest rates that are used to price the bond.

At the enterprise level, statistical correlations have made it possible to aggregate and consolidate risks derived from both the entire firm's holdings and the variety of market risks to which they are exposed (eg, interest rate, foreign exchange, equity, commodity, etc). It is this ability to aggregate risk that has made enterprise market risk management practical. The alternative aggregation method without the use of correlations would be to sum the risks across all positions, which can lead to overly conservative measures.

Much of the attention of risk management professionals has been focused on VAR. The motivation for the development of VAR was the desire to consolidate risks across the various activities of the enterprise. The VAR framework achieves the objective by quantifying risk as a single number derived from the volatilities of the risk factors and the correlations between them.

As with any quantitative model, one should be fully aware of the trade-offs and assumptions made. VAR generally relies on historical volatilities and correlations to forecast possible future outcomes. For practical modelling purposes, the correlations used are based on historical averages. It is the statistical outliers and not averages that can be the most interesting for purposes of extreme event risk measurement. It has been observed repeatedly in the past that correlations tend to break down in crisis situations. Such a breakdown occurred during the Russian debt crisis and could be explained by flight-to-quality behaviour in the markets.

These shortcomings of VAR are most often addressed by supplementing VAR analysis with deterministic stress scenario analysis. Stress scenarios need not rely on correlations and have potential to capture worst-case outcomes. It is the challenge of the prudent risk manager to create meaningful stress scenarios, as future market disasters do not occur in quite the same way as in the past.

Enterprise market risk measurement utilises statistical standard deviations and correlations. It is these same volatility and correlation measures that are used in efficient portfolio construction. Thus, in terms of market risk it is easy to see why enterprise risk management is not simply a control process, but a major ingredient for support and decision-making processes.

The VAR framework in the context of hedge funds is still valid for extended time horizons. As a forward-looking risk measure, it can be useful to money owners as a supplement to historical measures based on time series and surplus management.

Credit risk

Credit risk – the oldest form of financial risk – is the risk due to credit events such as credit rating changes and defaults related to counterparties (eg, trading counterparties, issuers, borrowers, etc). Credit risk is traditionally the main concern of banks. However, hedge funds stand to benefit from managing their credit risk.

From a management perspective, it is not enough to know only the level of credit riskiness today. Credit events are sudden and can cause extreme losses. However, the low frequency of credit events and the relative illiquidity and high transaction costs of the credit markets lend to longer horizons for credit risk analysis. The modelling of credit riskiness over time might include credit migrations with associated probabilities and default probabilities. For example, the probability of an issuer's debt credit rating being downgraded from investment grade to non-investment grade. It should be noted that credit riskiness amounts to more than just credit ratings. This includes other terms specific to the security, such as seniority and maturity.

Data requirements are the main challenge facing credit methodologies, of which there are a number. Credit events, as opposed to market events, are sudden, low-frequency occurrences, and this makes data availability limited. Data requirements are greatest for models that incorporate the migration of credit qualities and the associated losses.

The development of the measurement of credit risk has been a two-stage process. The first step was to model credit exposure, a quantification of the net value of all financial obligations due from each counterparty, both today and over the life of the instrument. The modelling of exposure should account for any mitigating agreements, such as netting agreements and collateral. Credit exposure issues are particularly complex for portfolios of derivatives where the exposures are functions of movements in the underlying risk factors.

The second development was credit VAR, a quantification of potential credit loss that is similar to a VAR framework. Credit risk can be made to conform to the VAR framework by calculating expected losses and their associated probabilities. Since distributions tend to be non-Gaussian, the probability distribution function should be calculated using a process such as Monte Carlo simulation.

Like market risk, credit VAR can be supplemented by deterministic stress scenario analysis. The most obvious scenarios are those that pertain to counterparty, issuer or country defaults and credit rating migrations.

Operational risk

When compared to market and credit risk, the measurement of operational risk is in the early stages. This is despite operational risks being of a scale and materiality as important as the other two risk types. As such, the interest in identifying, measuring and managing operational risks is gaining momentum, and advances are being made at a rapid pace.[4] The progress being made by some of the large financial institutions is setting the standard in this area, in much the same way as it did for the other two risk types. To gain some insight into how operational risk management might evolve in the hedge fund area, we use this section to summarise the state of play and directions being taken by major financial institutions.

The effort within financial institutions to understand what drives operational risks is leading to a change of emphasis from qualitative tools, including internal/external audit input and self-assessments, to more quantitative methods. Operational risk data provides the platform upon which frequency and severity distributions can be developed. The combination of these distributions results in the calculation of potential loss, similar to the VAR derived for market and credit risk.

The calibration of these operational risk models has brought into focus the need for operational loss data. Usually, examples of operational losses that are low severity and high frequency are not the problem, as the institution can look to its own past experiences to populate this part of the loss distribution. However, operational loss events in the tails of the distribution – low frequency and high severity – are more difficult to infer from one's direct experience. It is unlikely that a single firm will have enough information to capture sufficient "event" operational losses to perform a meaningful analysis. Firms have been required to look outside for other data sources that are applicable to their situation.

One response has been for firms to augment their internal operational loss information with losses that have happened to competitors and others. This approach has proved expensive to maintain. Companies specialising in building and maintaining historical loss databases have emerged to provide these services to the end-user institutions, offering lower cost data that is larger and better quality. However, even these external databases suffer from the fact that they are incomplete, as not all operational losses incurred by firms are made public, and the reported loss is often subject to "creative accounting".

The sharing of operational loss information among financial institutions, using agreed standards, would create the most complete datasheet to underlie this analysis, and would also enable benchmarking. The ability to offer incentives to participants to play the game fairly and ensure confidentiality of loss data remains a concern. However, it is one that is being overcome between the financial institutions. Data are scheduled to be exchanged among those that are members of the Multinational Operational Risk Exchange (MORE), a consortium that will aggregate event losses in a centralised database by the end of 2000.

It is too early to tell whether the approaches being explored amongst financial institutions will have traction in the hedge fund world. There are differences between the two industries, notably lesser regulatory pressure in the hedge fund industry, which to date has not provided the same impetus for the development of quantitative models. However, while regulation is an external motivator for measuring operational risk, there are other business reasons for the growth in this area. The benefits from improved management of the firm apply to hedge funds as they do to financial institutions, so we anticipate a growing interest in this amongst hedge funds. Until loss event databases are available for the asset management industry, we expect to see a continued growth in demand for the more qualitative approaches, such as self-assessment operational risk questionnaires and risk maps of process flows.

THE CONSOLIDATED RISK PICTURE

One objective of an enterprise risk management system is to provide a consolidated risk profile. This entails the aggregation of the market, credit and operational risks into a unified risk picture. At its foundation, this requires a sound understanding of the riskiness of the various individual components that constitute the universe of risks pertaining to the enterprise. As importantly, it requires an understanding of how these individual components interact with each other. A lesson from Markowitz's portfolio theory is that, in general, the total portfolio risk will be less than the sum of the constituent parts – this is known as the diversification effect. Diversification occurs both within and between the three broad risk categories. In this section, we are primarily concerned with the co-movement and interaction between the risk types (the co-movements within groups having been discussed above).

The only truly consistent approach to consolidating risk that we are aware of involves the building of a single integrated risk system. Some progress has been made in the area of integrated market and credit risk, but generally these approaches fall short of true integration. For example, whereas an integrated model might capture the change in the potential credit exposure to a Russian counterparty in the event of a rouble collapse, they do not generally capture the increased likelihood of default under these scenarios.

While we all await the arrival of the Holy Grail, the designers of enterprise risk management systems have taken a number of simplifying approaches to dealing with the interaction effects between risk categories when consolidating risks. The most simple and conservative approach is to ignore diversification entirely and take the aggregate sum of the three components (equivalent to assuming a correlation of 1). While this approach can be applauded for being conservative, it may not be the best basis for good business. Attractive risk-taking opportunities may be foregone, resulting in the under-utilisation of scarce and costly capital.

There are other simplistic yet less conservative approaches to consolidating risk. Examples include assuming that the risk categories are independent of each other, or that market and credit risks tend to be correlated with one another, while operational risk is relatively independent.[5]

Ultimately, it is more important to understand the nature of the interaction between each risk type than to gain a consolidated number that looks right. For example, assume that market risk and operational risk are independent. This assumption might be reasonable for a bank. However, it needs to be considered carefully in the context of a hedge fund. Because hedge funds manage other people's money, they take little direct market risk. However, to the extent that their funds fail to perform, then they may be taking huge operational risks in the form of legal liability and loss of business through sustained poor performance.

CONCLUSION

A well-conceived enterprise risk framework is ultimately an exercise in constrained optimisation. Having been witness to a large number of enterprise risk management projects in the financial services industry, we believe that the dominant trait distinguishing success from expensive failure is the ability for management to make the right informed trade-offs. Enterprise risk management systems should not be seen as all things to all people. Fortunately for the hedge fund industry, a lot of institutions have gone this way before, and their experiences and lessons learnt can be brought to bear here. Despite differences between hedge funds and traditional financial institutions, learning from these lessons and adopting an approach that delivers results steadily over the course of the project should significantly reduce the likelihood of failure.

Enterprise risk systems executed properly provide considerable value added for hedge funds and their investors. Hedge funds can better manage and protect their franchise value through avoiding inappropriate concentrations of risks; they are able to demonstrate sound risk process and offer appropriate degrees of transparency to investors. All of this has the potential to translate into greater fee income through growth in assets under management and stronger performance profiles.

The strong demand for risk information from institutional investors is one area that differentiates the hedge fund situation from that of the financial institutions. The role of the Internet will have increasing importance. The opportunities created by improved connectivity will change the nature of external risk reporting, and, more fundamentally, the nature of the governance relationships themselves. With the increase in the amount of information available, external parties will have greater power than ever before to challenge the compliance, decisions and ultimate performance of external managers. This transparency will place an increased premium on risk-adjusted performance and sound risk management process within hedge funds.

1   There is a large and insightful body of literature on the principal agent problem and the efficiency of contracting more generally, which is recommended to those readers interested in understanding the design of efficient contracts and monitoring arrangements. The literature emphasises problems endemic to contracting, and the institutional and contractual responses to these, which are designed to minimise transaction costs (a much wider concept than that usually implied in the finance literature) through aligning incentives, allocating property rights and addressing information asymmetry. For those interested in studying this area further, the authors recommend starting with the following three seminal pieces: Coase (1937), Jensen and Meckling (1976) and Williamson (1985).

2   Defined Benefit plans are concerned with having a portfolio of managers that provides the required returns to meet obligations to participants, without unduly putting at risk the surplus that would otherwise require an injection from the sponsor.

3   This works best in a repeat game situation with large enterprises, but is a notoriously weak incentive in an end game contracting situation with individuals.

4   A recent survey by ISDA/RMA/BBA of financial institutions showed that 25% of respondents use and 46% plan to use operational loss databases.

5   We can use historical time series of a firm's source income volatility due to market, credit and operational events to get a sense for the correlations between risk types. Obviously, there are a number of fundamental objections to extending historical correlations of this type into the future. However, we are dealing in a second-best world and often we must make do with what we have.

BIBLIOGRAPHY

Coase, R., 1937, "The Nature of the Firm", *Econometrica* (1961).

Jensen, M., and W. Meckling, 1976, "Theory of the Firm: Management Behaviour, Agency Costs and Ownership Structure", *Journal of Financial Economics* 3, pp. 305-60.

Williamson, O. E., 1985, *The Economic Institutions of Capitalism: Forms, Markets, Relational Contracting* (New York: The Free Press).

Appendix

Sound Practices for Hedge Fund Managers*†

In April 1999, the President's Working Group on Financial Markets (the PWG), comprised of the Secretary of the US Department of the Treasury and the respective chairs of the Board of Governors of the Federal Reserve System, the Securities and Exchange Commission and the Commodity Futures Trading Commission, published its report entitled "Hedge Funds, Leverage and the Lessons of Long-Term Capital Management", (the PWG Report). This report recommended that a number of measures be implemented by financial institutions, regulators and hedge funds to enhance risk management practices.‡ In the section entitled "Enhanced Private Sector Practices for Counterparty Risk Management", it stated:

A group of hedge funds should draft and publish a set of sound practices for their risk management and internal controls. Such a study should discuss market risk measurement and management, liquidity risk management, identification of concentrations, stress testing, collateral management, valuation of positions and collateral, segregation of duties and internal controls, and the assessment of capital needs from the perspective of hedge funds. In addition, the study should consider how individual hedge funds could assess their performance against the sound practices for investors and counterparties.[1]

---

† This document was produced with the participation of hedge fund managers from the following companies: Caxton Corporation; Kingdom Capital Management LLC; Moore Capital Management Inc; Soros Fund Management LLC and Tudor Investment Corporation. Counsel was provided by Sullivan & Cromwell; Consultancy by Rutter Associates.

* This document is reprinted with the permission of the authors. The authors, however, do not endorse any of the other views expressed in this volume.

‡ This document has been prepared in response to this recommendation.

OBJECTIVES OF THIS DOCUMENT
Respond to PWG Report

Following the publication of the PWG Report, a group of certain of the largest independent hedge fund managers came together to address the PWG's recommendation to develop and publish sound practices for risk management and internal controls. The views and recommendations set forth in this document reflect the input of this group. The sound practices recommendations that follow are intended to respond to the PWG Report by contributing to a continuing evolution of hedge fund manager practices. Many recommended practices have already been adopted by a number of larger hedge fund managers in recent years, as their growth has resulted in the implementation of more formalised and sophisticated management policies and structures. Other practices were initiated following the market crisis of August 1998, which created a heightened awareness among all market participants of the need for regular stress testing of market risk models and liquidity analyses. Other recommended practices are aspirational and represent goals that hedge fund managers , depending on their size and objectives, should strive to achieve. Given that the practices recommended were developed by larger hedge fund managers based on their views and business models, many may not be applicable to smaller hedge funds.

Strengthen hedge fund business practices

As part of this process and as markets continue to evolve, it is anticipated that the recommendations will be further adapted and refined. It is intended that hedge fund managers , by evaluating the recommendations and applying those that suit their particular business model, will strengthen their own businesses while contributing to market soundness by reducing the risk of their own default or failure. In this regard, this document complements the work of the Counterparty Risk Management Policy Group (the CRMPG) in its report of June 1999, which addressed many of these same issues from the perspective of a counterparty credit provider and proposed measures that seek to reduce the risk of defaults that could result in a systemic impact on financial markets.

One size does not fit all

It is important to recognise in evaluating the recommendations that the hedge fund industry is global and that the strategies, investment approaches and organisational structures of hedge fund managers vary greatly. The variations in organisational structures can be attributed partly to differences in size and partly to the different strategies used by hedge fund managers , which are distinguishable both in terms of their complexity and their product focus. The major strategies include:

❑ macro or global directional investment strategies;

❑ market-neutral or arbitrage strategies;

❑ long only, short only or long/short strategies for trading in equities;

❑ event-driven strategies that seek to profit from anticipated events, such as mergers or restructurings;

❑ regional strategies that concentrate on a particular geographic region (such as emerging markets); and

❑ sectoral strategies, which focus on a particular industry and specific asset class strategies (such as currencies).

The complexity of the strategy employed and the breadth of markets covered, combined with the amount of assets under management, will play a large part in determining the operational requirements of a hedge fund manager. For example, the infrastructure needs of a hedge fund manager managing several diversified macrofunds with several billion in net assets will be significantly greater than those of a long-only fund manager that principally trades US equities for a single fund of modest size.

The differences between Long Term Capital Management (LTCM) and most other hedge fund managers should also be acknowledged. The scale of LTCM's trading activities and the extent of leverage applied by LTCM at the time of its near collapse were unique. LTCM deployed particularly high levels of leverage in connection with its arbitrage strategies in order to profit from small discrepancies in the pricing of certain instruments. LTCM sought to leverage such narrow pricing anomalies into attractive returns for its sizable investor base by borrowing and establishing very large positions to exploit the pricing "spread" it identified. LTCM's massive use of leverage seriously compromised its ability to absorb losses when market conditions moved against it and spreads widened (rather than converging, as predicted). Its situation was further aggravated by its significant investments in illiquid instruments.

The hedge fund managers that developed the recommendations employ primarily global macro trading strategies that involve taking positions in a wide variety of largely liquid markets based on perceived broad economic trends. If a portfolio manager accurately predicts the direction of a market using this strategy, a relatively modest position can generate substantial profits without the use of excessive leverage. Although certain hedge fund managers make use of market neutral or arbitrage/convergence strategies similar to those used by LTCM, the scale of LTCM's trading using these strategies and the levels of leverage assumed by LTCM in connection with such strategies were extraordinary.

Individualised assessment and application of recommendations

The recommendations are not necessarily the only means of achieving sound practices and they should not be viewed as prescriptive requirements to be rigidly applied by all hedge fund managers. Rather, each hedge fund manager should assess the recommendations based on the size, nature and complexity of its organisation, its strategies and resources, as well as the objectives of the funds it manages, and apply them as appropriate. Certain recommendations may not be relevant or appropriate to every hedge fund manager. In evaluating the relevance of the recommendations and the ability to implement them, hedge fund managers should recognise that, while some recommendations can be implemented easily or unilaterally, others may require substantial planning and significant budgetary commitments, involve internal systems changes and infrastructure development, or negotiation with and co-operation by third parties. It should also be recognised that, while some recommendations have already been widely adopted, many are aspirational in nature or represent emerging practices that generally have not been implemented by hedge fund managers to date. Consequently, the recommendations should not be construed as definitive requirements that could serve as a basis for either auditing hedge fund managers or assessing their financial stability.

Background on hedge funds
Hedge fund defined
This document employs the PWG's general definition of a hedge fund ("hedge fund" or "fund"): a pooled investment vehicle that is privately organised, administered by a professional investment management firm (referred to herein as a hedge fund manager), and not widely available to the public. As the PWG Report observed, the term "hedge fund" is used to describe a wide range of investment vehicles, which can vary substantially in terms of size, strategy, business model and organisational structure, among other characteristics. This definition captures most of the types of investment pools that the recommendations seek to address.

The nature of hedge funds
In assessing the appropriateness of the recommendations for risk management and internal controls, it is important to distinguish the needs of hedge fund managers from those of credit providers, such as banks and other financial institutions that seek to eliminate and minimise the risks of their businesses through hedging, and other risk management methods that seek to reduce risk. Hedge fund managers are in the business of seeking and assuming calculated risks and are retained by the funds they manage to take on such risks in order to achieve the returns sought by their investors. By participating in the market as risk seekers, hedge fund managers play a unique and critical role in financial markets by providing needed liquidity and reducing systemic risk. In this sense hedge funds

often act as "risk absorbers" in markets by serving as ready counterparties to those wishing to hedge risk, even when markets are volatile, and, in doing so, reduce pressure on market prices while increasing liquidity. Additionally, hedge fund managers, through their trading based on extensive research, bring price information to the markets, which translates into market price efficiencies. Without the manager's research and commitment of capital, the markets would have potentially wider price spreads, pricing inefficiencies and illiquidity.

Perhaps, most importantly, by standing ready to lose capital, hedge funds act as a buffer for other market participants in absorbing "shocks". The managers that developed the recommendations have each been active investors and market participants for over ten years in a variety of market environments. Despite having been required to navigate difficult conditions and market crises, these firms have experienced substantial growth in assets and provided investors with attractive returns. Hedge funds also can afford investors valuable portfolio diversification, given that the performance of many hedge fund investments is uncorrelated to that of traditional investments, such as stocks and bonds. Hedge fund managers, like other large investors, are known to market regulators and supervisory authorities. In connection with their trading activities, hedge fund managers currently furnish significant information and reports to regulators (as detailed in the Additional Notes with respect to the United States).

Relationship of hedge funds and hedge fund managers
The recommendations assume that a hedge fund is governed by a board of directors, managing member, general partner, trustee or similar individual or entity with the legal authority and responsibility to direct and oversee the activities of the fund (referred to as the fund's "governing authority"). In addition, it is assumed that the assets of each fund are managed by an investment adviser or manager (the "hedge fund manager"), pursuant to an advisory or management agreement with the fund, and that the hedge fund manager is itself governed by a management committee. This committee is a group of executives or other body with the authority and responsibility to direct and oversee the hedge fund manager's trading activities on behalf of the fund ("senior management"). It is recognised, however, that the nature and structure of funds and the relationships with their managers vary substantially. In some cases, a hedge fund may have a formal board of directors, while in other cases the hedge fund manager conducts all material aspects of the hedge fund's management. In addition, the nature and structure of hedge fund managers vary substantially. Certain managers may be primarily governed by a board of directors or supervisory board, while others may be managed by their senior investment personnel. The recommendations also assume the following.

❑ A hedge fund is a separate legal entity managed under contract by the hedge fund manager. A hedge fund has an overall investment objective and may have investment restrictions that cannot be changed without notice to or approval by investors or a governing authority representing investors.

❑ Hedge fund managers may also be, and usually are, investors in the hedge funds they manage and usually are compensated in part based on the performance of the hedge fund. This structure, as well as reputational considerations, create a strong unity of interests between a hedge fund and its manager.

Risk functions of hedge fund managers

The activities of a hedge fund manager must reflect the fact that the business of a hedge fund is to seek returns by assuming commensurate levels of risk. Hedge fund managers take investment risk, in accordance with their funds' expectations, in order to earn commensurate returns. In this regard, managers must understand the sources of the returns the hedge fund is earning and identify the types and levels of risk associated with these returns. Based on this understanding, hedge fund managers should generally perform the following risk functions.

1. Consistent with its agreement with the hedge fund's governing authority and disclosure made to investors, senior management of the hedge fund manager should determine the appropriate overall level of risk for a particular fund.
2. This overall level of risk should then be allocated (among portfolio managers, strategies, asset classes, etc).
3. Once the risk allocation is determined, portfolio managers should choose the specific risks (consistent with the policies established by senior management) to be assumed, and enter into transactions in order to gain exposure to those risks.
4. The risk actually assumed by a fund must then be analysed and monitored by an independent risk analysis function, or "risk monitoring function". The resulting risk information must be disseminated to senior management and, as appropriate, portfolio managers.
5. Senior management must ensure that risk levels are acceptable and consistent with established risk policies and parameters.

In summary, senior management are responsible for setting, allocating and controlling risk (steps 1, 2 and 5); portfolio managers are responsible for putting the plan into action (step 3); and the "risk monitoring function" is responsible for monitoring and analysing the levels of risk actually assumed by the hedge fund in relation to the risk policies set by senior management, as well as reporting this information to senior management (step 4).

In the context of hedge fund managers, certain individuals may perform more than one function. For example, a portfolio manager may also be a key member of a hedge fund manager's senior management. Likewise, overlap between senior management and risk monitoring often occurs, eg, it is not uncommon for a senior manager to play an active role in the risk monitoring function. In fact, the smaller the hedge fund manager's organisation, the greater this overlap will likely be. It is critical however, that internal controls ensure the integrity of the risk monitoring function by enforcing its functional independence from the portfolio management (or trading) function.

The management and monitoring of risk is a complex and technical subject and an exhaustive treatment of the topic is beyond the scope of this document. The recommendations seek to address the risk functions of hedge fund managers in a concise manner. The Appendix, "Risk Monitoring Practices for Hedge Fund Managers", seeks to elaborate on the issues related to the recommendations made with respect to risk monitoring.

ORGANISATION OF THE RECOMMENDATIONS

The recommendations are divided into four major sections. The first addresses the responsibilities of senior management of the hedge fund manager, particularly with respect to establishing risk parameters and monitoring trading activities. The second section proposes sound practices for risk measurement and monitoring to ensure that the risk policies set by senior management are observed. The third section recommends disclosure practices to be observed when dealing with fund investors and boards of directors, counterparties and credit providers, regulatory bodies and the public. The last section proposes sound documentation practices and addresses other legal and compliance issues.

The following key points are fundamental to the recommendations.

Risk allocation and assessment are managed together
Senior management, in assigning portfolio management and trading responsibilities, should allocate capital and risk based on defined investment objectives and risk parameters, and control the allocations based on information supplied by an independent risk monitoring function. The ultimate monitoring of risk is conducted by senior management and therefore should not be divorced from decisions to allocate risk. This approach may differ from a credit provider's approach to risk management which strives for separation of these functions.

Recognise interplay of different types of risks
Hedge fund managers must recognise that market, credit and liquidity risks are interrelated, requiring the hedge fund manager to analyse the consequences of the fund's exposure to these risks in combination.

Assess liquidity during stress
Hedge fund managers should assess how funding liquidity may be compromised during periods of stress and seek to establish reliable sources of financing in order to enhance financial stability in volatile market conditions. In particular, the hedge fund manager should assess how unexpected events may cause losses that may force the liquidation of positions, and the potential "spiral" effects of such a forced liquidation on the value of the portfolios under management and sources of liquidity.

Use risk-based leverage measures
Recognising that the importance of leverage is the impact it can have on market risk, credit risk and liquidity risk, hedge fund managers should focus on measures of leverage that relate the riskiness of the portfolio to the ability of the fund to absorb that risk – "risk based leverage". Hedge fund managers should consider tracking the degree to which the fund is able to modify its risk-based leverage, by tracking the relation between the fund's market risk and actions taken. Hedge fund managers also should track traditional, accounting-based measures of leverage, because those traditional measures provide insights into the source of risk-based leverage and how that leverage could be changed.

Develop informational reports for counterparties
Each hedge fund manager should work with its counterparties to establish periodic reports that will strengthen relationship stability and, in doing so, contribute to market confidence.

Work with regulators
Hedge fund managers should work with regulators to address their specific market concerns and objectives. As significant participants in a broad array of global markets, hedge funds, like other major financial institutions and other large investors, should be prepared to co-operate with relevant regulators interested in monitoring the markets to reduce systemic risk while preserving the confidentiality of proprietary information.

Develop consensus on public disclosure
Hedge fund managers should co-ordinate with counterparties and regulators to reach a broad consensus on public disclosure which takes into account the benefits and costs to investors, creditors and the markets.

Standardise documentation and reflect collateral and default triggers in risk analysis

Each hedge fund manager should seek to standardise its approach to negotiating transaction documentation in order to achieve appropriate levels of consistency with its different counterparties and so that the legal consequences of unexpected losses or market crises (eg, collateral calls, defaults, termination events) are known and may be reflected in stress/scenario testing.

RECOMMENDATIONS
Organisational structure and internal controls

Hedge fund managers should clearly define the investment objectives and risk parameters for each fund, and the trading policies and risk limits necessary to achieve these objectives. Managers should adopt an organisational structure that ensures effective monitoring of compliance with investment and valuation policies by allocating defined supervisory responsibilities and maintaining clear reporting lines. Suitably qualified personnel should be retained and adequate systems established to produce periodic reporting that permits senior management to monitor trading activities and operations effectively. Internal procedures and periodic independent review processes should seek to ensure the enforcement of policies and identify deviations from those policies. Appropriate controls, reporting and review processes should apply to internal and external managers or traders. Third-party service providers that perform key business functions (such as NAV calculation) also should be subject to appropriate controls and review processes.

Roles and responsibilities of senior management

Senior management should approve policies and procedures commensurate with the size, nature and complexity of the manager's trading activities and consistent with the directives received from the governing authorities of the hedge funds it manages, and should review and update them when significant market events or changes in strategy occur and otherwise as appropriate.

Policies and procedures should be developed for trading activities, risk analysis, documentation, employee compliance and other key business areas, as appropriate (see specific recommendations under "Risk Monitoring" and under "Legal and Compliance").

Senior management should determine the investment and trading policies to be observed, including targeted risk profiles and parameters, based on the investment objectives of each hedge fund under management.

Senior management should allocate capital and risk based on a fund's performance objectives and targeted risk profile, taking into account the risk analysis produced by the risk monitoring function. Allocations should be re-examined and adjusted periodically (eg, at least once a year and following major market events). Senior management should have an understanding of risk analysis and undertake a rational and reasoned approach to the allocation and distribution of capital and risk among traders, strategies, asset classes and geographical regions.

Senior management should impose appropriate controls over the hedge fund manager's portfolio management and trading activities to ensure that these activities are undertaken on a basis consistent with senior management's allocated investment and trading parameters and with the investment objectives/strategies disclosed to a fund's governing authority and investors. Senior management should analyse and evaluate trading activities by regularly reviewing reports produced by the risk monitoring function. These reports should provide information regarding the risk and performance levels of the investment strategies employed and should identify deviations from trading parameters and risk limits. If the hedge fund manager changes or proposes to change its trading activities on behalf of a fund in a way that is inconsistent with the expectations of the fund's governing authority or differs materially from the disclosure contained in the fund's offering documents, it should inform the governing authority and if appropriate, investors through normal means of investor communication. Amendments should be made as deemed necessary to disclosure/offering documents to ensure that they accurately reflect the nature and risks of the fund's trading activities.

Senior management should formally approve the allocation of capital to all portfolio managers. All portfolio managers, including external portfolio managers, should be subject to controls and review processes commensurate with the amount of assets managed and form of allocation. Where capital is invested with an external portfolio manager in a managed account, applicable trading restrictions/limits, reporting requirements and termination provisions should be clearly defined in written management agreements. The performance of all portfolio managers should be monitored on a periodic basis as appropriate, depending on the form of the allocation – eg, monthly net asset value (NAV) review of a passive investment in a fund versus daily or weekly review of a significant managed account investment.

Senior management should establish formal processes for the approval, monitoring and review of the use of third-party service providers for the performance of key business functions (eg, those related to risk monitoring, valuation, prime brokerage or other administrative functions). While senior management may decide to delegate the selection of actual service providers, they should approve the process by which the selection is made. Key third-party service providers' roles, responsibilities and liability should be clearly defined in written service agreements, and their performance should be periodically reviewed.

Structure of risk monitoring function

Senior management should establish a risk monitoring function that operates independently of portfolio management functions. The risk monitoring function should be an independent source of information about and analysis of a hedge fund's performance and current risk position, the sources of its risk and resulting exposures to changes in market conditions.

The risk monitoring function should report directly to senior management and be staffed with persons having sufficient experience and knowledge to understand a fund's trading strategies and the nature and risks of its investments. Comprehensive and centralised systems for position and global exposure reporting and risk analysis should function independently of risk selection/portfolio management personnel so that trading activities and operations may be effectively supervised and compliance with trading policies and risk limits can be controlled. The risk monitoring function should produce daily risk reports that present risk measures and appropriate breakdowns by category of risk for review by appropriate members of senior management.

Valuation

Proper valuation is material both to hedge fund investors and to the risk monitoring process. Hedge fund managers should develop procedures for capturing and verifying prices for the instruments they trade and rely on external pricing sources where available. For net asset value (NAV) purposes, managers generally should value instruments at market value, making adjustments to such values in accordance with generally accepted accounting principles (GAAP) only where market conditions mandate adjustments, recognising that investors will both buy and sell shares of a fund on the basis of NAV. In contrast, hedge fund managers may determine that adjustments to market value are appropriate for risk monitoring purposes in order to enhance the accuracy of risk assessment. Policies for making such adjustments should be approved by senior management. The concepts related to valuation are explored in greater detail in the Appendix.

Hedge fund managers should have pricing policies and procedures for determining a fund's NAV on a periodic basis and for determining its value for risk monitoring purposes on a daily basis. The policies regarding NAV determination should be approved by a hedge fund's governing authority and reviewed by external auditors for compliance with applicable accounting practices. Hedge fund managers should develop procedures and/or systems for capturing pricing data for their positions from independent sources on a daily basis where possible. Procedures for periodically verifying the accuracy of pricing data should also be adopted, and material discrepancies between price sources should be investigated.

Where an instrument is not traded actively or where obtaining price information requires significant effort, weekly (or less frequent) pricing may be appropriate depending on the nature and the size of the position.

Net asset value

Senior management should determine policies for the manner and frequency of computing net asset value (NAV) based upon applicable GAAP and disclose such policies to investors. Such policies should establish valuation methods that are consistent and fair to both buyers and sellers. Financial assets and liabilities should be valued at "fair value", which is the price at which an item could be exchanged in a current transaction between willing parties, other than in a forced or liquidation sale. Consistent with GAAP, senior management should determine the valuation methods to be used where market prices are not available or are not indicative of fair value (eg, private equity investments may be valued at the lower of cost or market) and disclose such methods to a hedge fund's governing authority.

For an instrument that is actively traded, hedge fund managers should use price quotes available from reliable data vendors. The fair value of a position should be based upon the quoted price for a single trading unit in the most active market. Where price quotes are not available from data vendors, managers should attempt to obtain quotes from independent sources. For thinly traded instruments or those priced using models, hedge fund managers should document the valuation methods used and periodically subject them to independent validation. Dealer quotes and prices generated by models or other estimation methods should be regularly checked against realised prices to gauge their accuracy.

NAV valuations performed by third-party administrators should be regularly reviewed to ensure compliance with valuation policies. Valuations should be periodically validated by independent internal or external review, preferably on a monthly basis, but no less frequently than annually. The accuracy of NAV calculations should be verified by external auditors at least annually to assure compliance with GAAP.

Risk monitoring valuation
Senior management should establish policies for determining when risk monitoring valuation methods may differ from NAV for operational or risk analysis reasons. Examples where valuations different from NAV may be appropriate include situations such as those involving unusual position size, legal sale or transfer restrictions, illiquidity, control premiums or unusual hedging or transaction costs.

Independent review
A hedge fund manager's internal controls and risk monitoring processes should be subject to periodic independent reviews by either external

auditors (at least once annually) or by internal compliance or other independent personnel to ensure that management reporting is complete and accurate and to identify material deviations from internal policies and procedures.

External auditors should report their findings and any recommended actions in writing in the form of a management letter or other appropriate report; the findings of internal reviews should be similarly recorded in writing. Such findings should be relayed to senior management and other recipients to whom they may delegate for appropriate resolution and action. Review of the risk monitoring function should verify compliance with the manager's risk policies and procedures. Review of this function should also address the soundness of internal systems and the qualitative and quantitative methods used (eg, models).

Risk monitoring

Current market practice is to focus on three categories of risk that are quantifiable – market risk, credit risk and liquidity risk – and on the less quantifiable operational risk. Market risk relates to losses that could be incurred due to changes in market factors (ie, prices, volatilities and correlations). Credit risk relates to losses that could be incurred due to declines in the creditworthiness of entities in which the fund invests or with which

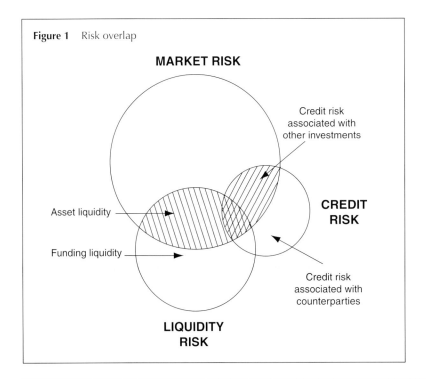

Figure 1 Risk overlap

MARKET RISK

Credit risk associated with other investments

CREDIT RISK

Asset liquidity

Funding liquidity

Credit risk associated with counterparties

LIQUIDITY RISK

the fund deals as a counterparty. Liquidity risk relates to losses that could be incurred when declines in liquidity in the market reduce the value of the investments or reduce the ability of the fund to fund its investments.

While current market practice is to treat the risks separately, it is crucial for hedge fund managers to recognise and evaluate the overlap that exists between and among market, credit and liquidity risks. This overlap is illustrated in Figure 1 (recognising that the relative sizes of the circles will be different for different strategies).

Consequently, the risk monitoring function should monitor three inter-related variants of market, liquidity and credit risks in combination:

❏ market risk – including asset liquidity and the credit risk associated with investments;
❏ funding liquidity risk; and
❏ counterparty credit risk.

In this framework, the risk sometimes referred to as sovereign risk would be included as credit risk, if the potential loss is related to the financial solvency of the sovereign, or as market risk if the potential loss is related to policy decisions made by the sovereign that change the market value of positions (eg, currency controls). The term event risk is broader and could incorporate aspects of credit risk and operational risk, as well as some elements of market risk. (For a more detailed discussion of the concepts related to the recommendations in this section, please see the Appendix.)

Market risk

This encompasses interest rate risk, foreign exchange rate risk, equity price risk and commodity price risk, as well as asset liquidity risk and the credit risk associated with investments.

Hedge fund managers should evaluate market risk, not only for each hedge fund portfolio in aggregate, but also for relevant subcomponents of a portfolio – by strategy, by asset class, by type of instruments used, by geographic region or by industry sector, as appropriate. In addition, the market risk assumed by each individual portfolio manager should be determined. Hedge fund managers should employ a value-at-risk (VAR) model or other consistent framework for measuring the risk of loss for a portfolio (and relevant subcomponents of the portfolio). While the choice of model should be left to each hedge fund manager, the manager should be aware of the structural limitations of the model selected and actively manage these limitations, including the impact of any model breakdown.

A sound market risk-monitoring process should incorporate the confidence level(s) and holding period(s) deemed appropriate depending on the markets traded and the risks assumed. The holding period(s) should reflect the time necessary to liquidate and/or neutralise positions in the portfolio. The role of the risk monitoring function is to identify the factors affecting the risk and return of the fund's investments, both within individual portfolios and across the entire range of activities of the hedge fund manager. Those factors should be incorporated into the risk monitoring process and, where appropriate, be included in the market risk model. Factors commonly incorporated in a market risk model include:

❏ level and shape of the interest rate term structure in relevant currencies;
❏ foreign exchange rates;
❏ equity prices and/or equity indices;
❏ commodity prices;
❏ credit spreads;
❏ non-linearities;
❏ volatilities; and
❏ correlation.

Hedge fund managers should consider incorporating "asset liquidity" (ie, the change in the value of an asset due to changes in the liquidity of the market in which the asset is traded) as an additional factor. Measures of asset liquidity that may be considered include:

❏ the number of days that would be required to liquidate and/or neutralise the position in question; and
❏ the value that would be lost if the asset in question were to be liquidated and/or neutralised completely within the holding period specified.

Positions managed as a separate account by external portfolio managers on behalf of the fund should be incorporated in the routine risk assessment of the overall portfolio. Passive investments in funds managed by external portfolio managers should be monitored as appropriate.

Hedge fund managers should recognise that market risk measures such as VAR do not give a complete picture of risk in that they assess the risk of "standard" market movements rather than extreme events. Hedge fund managers should actively address these limitations by conducting relevant stress tests and back-testing.

Hedge fund managers should perform "stress tests" to determine how potential changes in market conditions could impact the market risk of the portfolio. Among the potential changes in market conditions that should be considered in stress testing are:

❏ changes in prices;
❏ changes in the shape of term structures; and
❏ changes in correlations between prices.

If the portfolio contains options or instruments with options characteristics, additional changes that should be considered as part of stress testing are:

❏ changes in volatilities; and
❏ changes in non-linearities (also referred to as convexity or gamma).

Hedge fund managers also should consider including the effects of changes in the liquidity of various assets in their stress testing.

For example, hedge fund managers could examine the effects of changing the holding period. A horizon of several days may reveal strings of losses (or gains) that, while individually less than the one-day VAR, in total add up to a significant deviation from the market risk model's predicted distribution. Rather than changing the holding period to reflect the illiquidity of securities or derivatives, the hedge fund manager could gauge the impact of illiquidity by inputting changes for the appropriate market risk factors that are reflective of multiple-day market price movements (as opposed to single-day changes). If specific asset liquidity factors are incorporated in the market risk model (see above), these asset liquidity factors can be "stressed" to examine the impact of (1) changes in the value that could be lost if the position in question were to be liquidated and/or neutralised completely during the standard holding period, or (2) changes in the number of days required to liquidate and/or neutralise the position in question.

Hedge fund managers should incorporate the impact of correlated events into stress testing, where appropriate. They should also consider conducting "scenario analyses" to benchmark the risk of a fund's current portfolio against various scenarios of market behaviour (historical or prospective) that are relevant to the hedge fund manager's trading activities (eg, the October 1987 stock market event, the Asian financial crisis of 1997 or a scenario where concerns about general credit quality lead to dramatic declines in asset values combined with decreases in asset and funding liquidity).

Stress tests/scenario analyses should take into account the impact of legal and contractual relationships.

Hedge fund managers should validate their market risk models through regular back-testing. The distribution of observed changes in the value of the portfolio should be compared to the distribution of changes in value generated by a hedge fund manager's market risk model. If the frequency of changes in the value of the portfolio exceeds the frequency generated by the market risk model (a statistical expectation based on the confidence level of the market risk model), such deviation should be scrutinised to determine its source. If appropriate after investigation, the market risk model should be modified. Potential sources of deviations include:

❑ a change in the composition of the portfolio between calculation and observation;

❑ pricing models under/overstated obtainable prices;

❑ a change in the underlying market, including changes in the volatility, correlation, or liquidity of the factors used in the market risk model; and

❑ model(s) that did not adequately capture sources of risk.

Even if the frequency of changes in value in excess of that generated by the market risk model is within the expected range, if the observed change in the value of the portfolio differs significantly from the change that would be expected, given the composition of the portfolio and the observed changes in the market factors, hedge fund managers should reconcile the difference.

Funding liquidity risk

Funding liquidity is critical to a hedge fund manager's ability to continue trading in times of stress. Funding liquidity analysis should take into account the investment strategies employed, the terms governing the rights of investors to redeem their interests and the liquidity of assets (eg, all things being equal, the longer the expected period necessary to liquidate assets, the greater the potential funding requirements). Adequate funding liquidity gives a hedge fund manager the ability to continue a trading strategy without being forced to liquidate assets when losses arise.

Cash should be actively managed. Hedge fund managers should know where a fund's cash is deployed and the reason for deploying it. Managers should centralise cash management and should evaluate the costs and benefits of leaving excess cash in trading accounts (eg, margin accounts).

Hedge fund managers should employ appropriate liquidity measures in order to gauge, on an ongoing basis, whether a fund is maintaining adequate liquidity. Liquidity should be assessed relative to the size and riskiness of the fund. Possible liquidity measures include:

❑ Cash^2/Equity;

❑ VAR/(Cash + Borrowing Capacity)^3; and

❑ Worst historical drawdown/(cash + borrowing capacity).

Hedge fund managers should evaluate the stability of sources of liquidity and plan for funding needs accordingly, including a contingency plan in periods of stress. Hedge fund managers should assess their cash and borrowing capacity under the worst historical drawdown and stressed market conditions (eg, by assuming worst case haircuts on securities used to collateralise margin borrowings), taking into account potential investor redemptions and contractual arrangements that affect a fund's liquidity (eg, notice periods for reduction of credit lines by counterparties).

Hedge fund managers should periodically forecast their liquidity requirements and potential changes in liquidity measures. Hedge fund managers should perform scenario tests to determine the impact of potential changes in market conditions on a fund's liquidity. Among these scenario tests, hedge fund managers should consider including the potential response to a creditor experiencing a liquidity problem during times of market stress (eg, reluctance to release collateral). Managers should take into account in their liquidity planning redemption "windows" or other rights of investors to redeem their interests. Hedge fund managers should also take into account the relationship between a fund's performance and redemptions, and between a fund's performance and the availability of credit lines.

Counterparty credit risk

Hedge fund managers should establish policies and procedures to manage the fund's exposure to potential defaults by trading counterparties. Hedge fund managers should identify acceptable counterparties, based on a reasonable analysis of creditworthiness, and set appropriate exposure limits. Hedge fund managers should ensure that counterparties' creditworthiness is actively monitored. In addition, credit concentrations relative to exposure limits should be monitored, taking into account settlement risk as well as pre-settlement risk. Procedures should be adopted and enforced to reduce or terminate trading with counterparties whose credit quality falls below an acceptable level or where exposure exceeds set limits. Hedge fund managers should seek to establish appropriate collateral provisions or other forms of credit support in their counterparty agreements and put in place procedures for managing collateral calls between the fund and its counterparties.

Leverage

Hedge fund managers must recognise that leverage is important, not in and of itself, but because of the impact it can have on market risk, credit risk and liquidity risk – ie, leverage influences the rapidity of changes in the value of the portfolio due to changes in market risk, credit risk, or liquidity risk factors. Consequently, the most relevant measures of leverage are "risk-based" measures that relate the riskiness of a portfolio to the ability of the fund to absorb that risk. Recognising the impact that leverage can have on a portfolio's exposure to market risk, credit risk and liquidity risk, hedge fund managers should assess the degree to which a hedge fund is able to modify its risk-based leverage in periods of stress or increased market risk. Hedge fund managers should also track traditional, accounting-based measures of leverage, which can provide insights into the source of risk-based leverage and how that leverage could be adjusted.

Hedge fund managers should develop and monitor several measures of leverage, recognising that leverage, appropriately defined, can magnify the effect of changes in market, credit or liquidity risk factors on the value of the portfolio and can adversely impact a fund's liquidity.

Accounting-based leverage

Hedge fund managers should track traditional accounting-based measures of leverage. Not only are these measures routinely requested by counter-parties and credit providers, but they can also contribute to an understanding of leverage measures that incorporate risk. However, hedge fund managers should be aware of the weaknesses of these accounting-based measures, particularly as stand-alone measures of leverage. Accounting-based measures that could be tracked include traditional "balance sheet leverage measures", eg,

"gross balance sheet assets to equity" = On-balance sheet assets / Equity

and

"net balance sheet assets to equity" = (On-balance sheet assets – Matched book assets) / Equity.

Recognising that the preceding measures do not capture off-balance sheet transactions (eg, forward contracts, swaps and other derivatives), hedge fund managers may elect to track other accounting-based measures. While such measures can provide useful information if they are understood fully and interpreted correctly, hedge fund managers must recognise that accounting-based measures of leverage which attempt to include off-balance-sheet transactions are, at best, imprecise measures (eg, accounting-based measures may provide misleading information about offsetting futures positions if they do not have exactly the same expiration date).

Risk-based leverage

Hedge fund managers also should track each fund's leverage using "risk-based leverage" measures reflecting the relationship between the riskiness of a fund's portfolio and the capacity of the fund to absorb the impact of that risk. In this sense, some of the liquidity measures noted above can also be viewed as risk-based leverage measures – eg, VAR/(Cash + Borrowing Capacity). Other measures that could perform this function include the following.

❏ The simplest measure of the riskiness of the portfolio is the volatility in the value of the portfolio. This measure could be related to the fund's capital: (volatility in value of portfolio) /Equity.
❏ VAR has become a widely recognised measure of market risk; so, this measure could be related to the fund's capital: VAR/Equity.

❏ As noted above, market risk measures such as VAR are incomplete measures of market risk because they focus on "standard" market movements rather than extreme events. Consequently, the hedge fund manager should consider assessing the impact of extreme events by comparing a market risk measure derived from analysis of extreme event scenarios (or stress tests) to the fund's capital: (scenario-derived market risk measure)/Equity.

The hedge fund manager must be aware of limitations of the models used and must guard against placing too much reliance on mathematical measures of leverage alone. (As a case in point, analyses of extreme event scenarios will provide leverage information that is correct ex post only if the "right" scenarios are considered *ex ante*.) Consequently, it is essential that the hedge fund manager incorporates judgement based on business experience, in conjunction with and in addition to quantitative measures of leverage.

A crucial factor influencing the fund's ability to absorb the impact of extreme market events is the degree to which the fund can modify its risk-based leverage, especially during periods of market stress. During periods of market stress, the manager should understand its ability to reduce risk-based leverage by reducing traditional leverage resulting from either on- or off-balance sheet transactions or by reducing the level of risk that is being accepted (eg, by changing strategy or the types of assets being held in the portfolio). To track the degree to which the fund is able to modify its risk-based leverage, the hedge fund manager may wish to track variations in the fund's market risk measure (eg, VAR) over time.

Operational risk

Hedge fund managers should establish procedures to limit the fund's exposure to potential operational risks, including data entry errors, fraud, system failures and errors in valuation or risk measurement models. Hedge fund managers should consider measures to limit or mitigate operational risk, including:

❏ random spot checks of all relevant activities;
❏ effective separation between the risk selection and risk monitoring functions either by having sufficient staff to avoid overlapping activities or by providing the appropriate level of checks and balances for hedge fund managers that are too small to avoid overlapping staff;
❏ maintenance of a single, centralised position data set (to avoid the errors inherent in maintaining multiple or regionalised data sets); and
❏ establishment of an internal review function.

Hedge fund managers should establish contingency plans for responding to failure of a third party administrator, credit provider or other party that would affect the market, credit or liquidity risk of a fund. Contingency planning should address responses to a failure of a third party on a fund's ability to meet its obligation, including transfers of activity to back-up clearing systems, credit providers and other service providers and back-up providers.

DISCLOSURE/TRANSPARENCY

Investors should receive periodic performance and other information about their hedge fund investments. Hedge fund managers should also consider whether investors should receive interim updates on other matters in response to significant events. Hedge fund managers should negotiate with counterparties to determine the extent of financial and risk information that should be provided to them based on the nature of their relationship in order to increase the stability of financing and trading relationships. They should also work with regulators and counterparties to develop a consensus approach to public disclosure. Agreements and other safeguards should be established in order to protect against the unauthorised use of proprietary information furnished to outside parties.

Reporting to a fund's governing authority and investors

The investment objectives and approach plus the range of permissible investments should be clearly disclosed in a fund's offering documents. Material changes should be disclosed to a fund's governing authority and investors as appropriate.

Hedge fund managers should provide certain base-line standardised performance and other relevant information to all investors, such as:

❏ performance measures, such as quarterly or monthly net asset value calculations and periodic profit and loss;
❏ capital measures, such as total net assets under management and net changes to capital based on new subscriptions less redemptions and the effect of profit and loss;
❏ annual audited financial statements; and
❏ measures that give a view of the fund's risk, such as Sharpe ratios or VAR.

Reporting to counterparties/credit providers

Hedge fund managers should furnish periodic reports to credit providers and counterparties that extend trading lines or other forms of credit. The extent of disclosure can vary depending on the extent and nature of the relationship with the credit provider. Measures that give a view of the fund's risk and return profile, rather than specific trading positions, should be most useful to credit providers and would not sacrifice the proprietary nature of fund strategies and positions. Possible disclosures include:

❏ performance measures appropriate to the nature of the funds managed, such as periodic changes in NAV; profit and loss volatility; performance attribution by broad product classes (eg, currencies, fixed income, equities and commodities);

❏ capital measures, such as total net assets under management and net changes to capital based on new subscriptions less redemptions and the effect of profit and loss;

❏ market risk measures, such as Sharpe ratios, VAR or scenario-derived market risk measures for each relevant fund; and

❏ liquidity measures, such as cash plus borrowing capacity as a percentage of either equity or VAR.

Appropriate safeguards against a counterparty's unauthorised use of proprietary information should be adopted. Hedge fund managers should provide financial and other confidential information to a counterparty's credit department only, and not to any member of a counterparty's trading desk or department. The counterparty's credit department should confirm, preferably in a written confidentiality agreement or letter, its commitment to restrict the use of, and access to, information furnished by the hedge fund manager to the credit desk. It should also ensure such information is not shared with any trading personnel within the counterparty's organisation or any third-party without the manager's prior written consent.

Reporting to regulators

Hedge fund managers should work with appropriate governmental authorities to ensure that where large positions have a potential systemic impact, hedge fund managers along with other financial institutions and investors with significant positions comply with applicable large position reporting requirements, while preserving the confidentiality of proprietary information.

The Additional Notes detail existing large trader and large position reporting requirements, as well as other US regulatory filing requirements currently applicable to hedge fund managers depending on either their trading activity or their status as a regulated entity. Similar requirements apply in certain of the other countries where hedge fund managers do business.

Issues relating to the potential impact of public disclosure on market integrity

Hedge fund managers should co-ordinate with counterparties and regulators to develop a broad consensus approach to public disclosure, evaluating both the benefits and the costs of such disclosure to investors, creditors and the markets.

The dialogue with hedge fund managers, counterparties and regulators should assess the goals to be achieved by public disclosure. To the extent that the purpose of public disclosure is to assist creditors and investors in making informed decisions about the credit they extend or the investments they make, the benefits of the recommendations for improved risk management and internal controls by hedge fund managers and for expanded disclosure to counterparties and investors should be considered. Issues relating to the potential relationship between market integrity and public disclosure should be addressed by broad classes of market participants so that a better understanding of the benefits and costs can be achieved.

Because of the broad recognition (including recognition in the PWG Report) that disclosure of hedge fund's proprietary information on strategies or positions should not be required, any approach to public disclosure should consider what information can be collected, aggregated and disseminated without exposing sensitive strategies or positions.

LEGAL AND COMPLIANCE

A hedge fund manager's legal/compliance personnel must have the authority and resources to operate independently and effectively. This function should seek to actively manage the legal risks presented by the hedge fund manager's trading, focusing on the documentation governing trading relationships and individual transactions. In particular, hedge fund managers should pursue a consistent and methodical approach to documenting transactions so that the legal consequences of periods of market stress or performance declines may be more clearly anticipated and managed. The legal function should provide the risk monitoring function with useful input in the evaluation of a fund's projected liquidity in stressed environments, including inputs derived from the fund's transaction documentation (eg, terms regarding termination, collateral and margining).

A hedge fund manager's general counsel/senior compliance or legal officer should be recognised as a member of senior management and be granted sufficient authority to manage the legal and compliance affairs of the hedge fund manager independently and effectively.

Documentation policies

Hedge fund managers should establish transaction execution and documentation management procedures that:

❏ ensure timely execution of necessary transaction documents and enforceability of transactions; require that all trading counterparties be pre-approved prior to executing any transactions and verify counterparty authorisations;
❏ establish formal documentation requirements for all trading (including

confirmation requirements for all off-exchange trades where a master agreement has not been executed with a counterparty);

❏ ensure that appropriate security interests are created and perfected when collateral is received as part of a transaction; and

❏ where transaction documentation is performed in the operations or similar area, appropriate liaison with the legal/compliance function should be established.

Hedge fund managers should track the status of documentation and the negotiation of key provisions and terms (eg, termination events) using a database or other appropriate mechanism to ensure consistency and standardisation across funds and counterparties to the extent appropriate.

Hedge fund managers should clarify and standardise documentation on a bilateral basis with all counterparties to the extent possible in order to enhance stability during periods of market stress or declining asset levels. In particular, in its counterparty documentation, hedge fund managers generally should evaluate the appropriateness of seeking to:

❏ standardise termination and collateral events as well as events of default, cross-default clauses and the remedies available to a non-defaulting party to achieve consistency in documentation with different counterparties to the extent possible;

❏ minimise the possibility of early termination or collateral calls based upon subjective determinations by avoiding provisions that permit counterparties to terminate or make demands for collateral in their "sole discretion" (eg, avoid "material adverse change" clauses);

❏ include the decline of a counterparty's credit rating as a termination/collateral event;

❏ ensure that provisions addressing NAV declines or other performance-based triggers are structured as collateral or termination events to avoid triggering cross-default provisions under other agreements;

❏ seek grace periods in connection with performance or other termination events so that an orderly liquidation of positions may take place if necessary; and

❏ negotiate commitments from primary credit providers to ensure stability of credit facilities during temporary periods of market stress or declining assets, eg, require that credit providers give written notice within a fixed period prior to termination or reduction of a credit line or other material changes to credit terms.

Hedge fund managers should seek to negotiate bilateral collateral agreements that require each party to furnish collateral, taking into account the relative creditworthiness of the parties. In particular, managers generally should evaluate the appropriateness of seeking to:

❏ ensure satisfactory custodial arrangements are in place and that location and possible uses of collateral are clearly defined;

❏ establish collateral management procedures which permit the hedge fund manager to effectively and regularly value collateral and make calls for collateral from counterparties when permitted;

❏ negotiate thresholds that adjust with the counterparties' credit rating;

❏ ensure that the responsibilities for valuing collateral and determining the amounts of collateral to be delivered or returned are appropriately allocated between the parties to a collateral agreement (eg, by allocating such a role to the secured party or the party that is owed collateral); and

❏ negotiate provisions requiring prompt payment of collateral.

Where operational, legal or economic efficiencies would result, hedge fund managers should seek to establish "master/master" or "umbrella" cross-product netting and collateral agreements with counterparties dealing in multiple products using different agreements.

Hedge fund managers should provide input to the risk monitoring function for use in stress/scenario testing as well as liquidity analyses based on legal or contractual relationships, including:

❏ the contractual rights of counterparties to increase margin/collateral requirements, declare events of default or declare termination events in response to a fund's declining assets or other stress scenarios;

❏ the legal or contractual sales restrictions applicable to any investments;

❏ the enforceability of netting provisions in the event of a counterparty's bankruptcy; and

❏ redemption windows for investors.

Hedge fund managers should have appropriate documentation and approval processes for retaining external traders as well as administrators, prime brokers or other third-party service providers.

Compliance

Hedge fund managers should identify all actual and potential required regulatory filings and clearly allocate responsibility for such filings to appropriate personnel who will supervise and ensure timely compliance with applicable regulations and filing requirements.

Hedge fund managers should require all employees to attest in writing upon hiring and on an annual basis to their acceptance of a "code of conduct" or compliance manual, which should address, where applicable, trading rules and restrictions, confidentiality requirements, procedures to prevent the flow of non-public information from one function to another, compliance with internal policies and procedures and compliance with securities (eg, insider trading) and related laws. The compliance manual/code of conduct should be regularly updated.

CONCLUSION

In developing these recommendations, the primary goal has been to promote sound risk management and internal controls for the hedge fund industry by identifying practices that would contribute to enhancing the financial stability of large funds managed by hedge fund managers and, in turn, reduce the possibility of their failure due to unexpected market events. While the adoption of the recommendations by hedge fund managers will not reduce market volatility or eliminate the prospect of events leading to unanticipated hedge fund losses, defaults or failures, it is hoped that the adoption of these practices by the largest hedge fund managers, in combination with the implementation by their counterparties of the CRMPG recommendations, will serve to reduce the likelihood of systemic consequences resulting from a hedge fund's default or failure.

The recommendations also seek to emphasise the importance of managerial expertise and discipline to weathering market shocks and crises. While thorough and thoughtful risk measurement and analysis are critical elements of sound hedge fund management, they will not spare the hedge fund manager who refuses to take the steps necessary to preserve appropriate levels of liquidity when faced with stressed market conditions or unexpected losses. For this reason internal controls and policies for addressing stressed market conditions are at least as important as the mechanisms used to anticipate and analyse them.

While most of the recommendations contained in the first two sections may be adopted unilaterally by individual hedge fund managers, the ability to implement them may depend on the availability of qualified personnel and other resources and, consequently, their implementation may not be feasible for smaller hedge fund managers. Furthermore, many of the recommendations relating to disclosure and documentation policies will require negotiation with and acceptance by third parties, and it is hoped that the publication of this document will contribute to generating the industry support and regulatory dialogue that may be necessary to implement these recommended practices.

The recommendations were developed in the belief that the most effective form of oversight is self-evaluation combined with self-discipline. The first line of defence to market stress will always be the managers themselves, and the recommendations are intended to provide a framework of internal policies and controls that will enhance their ability to prudently address unexpected market events or losses.

APPENDIX

RISK MONITORING PRACTICES FOR HEDGE FUND MANAGERS

The objective of this Appendix is to elaborate upon the discussion of risk monitoring practices contained in the recommendations. In so doing, this Appendix describes the general array of risk management techniques and methodologies currently available, in addition to addressing the specific techniques and methodologies that should be considered as part of sound risk monitoring practices for hedge fund managers. The latter discussion includes further explanations of valuation, liquidity and leverage from the perspective of hedge fund managers. This Appendix begins by providing an overview of the risks faced by a hedge fund manager in the first section.

Valuation procedures are discussed in the following section. While not explicitly part of the risk monitoring function, proper valuation processes are crucial to effective risk monitoring.

The descriptions of the practices for monitoring market risk, funding liquidity risk and leverage form the core of this Appendix and address the following key issues.

❏ Techniques for monitoring market risk that are becoming well-accepted in financial markets – VAR, scenario analyses and stress tests, and back-testing.

❏ The importance of analysing funding liquidity risk. While the measures for monitoring funding liquidity described in this Appendix are used in other industries, hedge fund managers should focus significant attention on funding liquidity given the impact it can have on the viability of a hedge fund.

❏ Leverage in the context of hedge funds. While leverage is not unique to hedge funds, the market risk inherent in a hedge fund, coupled with the constraints imposed by funding liquidity, make the amplifying effect of leverage of particular concern to a hedge fund manager. This Appendix describes a group of static leverage measures, both accounting-based and risk-based leverage measures. Also described in this Appendix are dynamic leverage measures that can provide additional information to the hedge fund manager.

This Appendix concludes with a description of procedures for monitoring counterparty credit risk. Because hedge funds generally deal with counterparties having high credit quality, the credit risk of counterparties may be of less concern to hedge fund managers than the other sources of risk but should nonetheless by appropriately monitored.

OVERVIEW: THE RISKS FACED BY A HEDGE FUND MANAGER

Effective risk management requires that the hedge fund manager recognise and understand the source of the returns the fund is earning – ie, the risks to which the fund is exposed. Consequently, one of the primary responsibilities of the risk monitoring function is to identify and quantify the sources of risk. While observers often distinguish four broad types of risk – market risk, credit risk, liquidity risk and operational risk[4] – it is important to recognise that these risks are interrelated. Indeed, hedge fund managers should recognise that market risk incorporates elements of credit risk and liquidity risk. Defined most narrowly, market risk focuses on the impact of changes in the prices of (or rates for) securities and derivatives, the volatilities of those prices, and the correlations between pairs of prices on the value of the portfolio. However, the following elements of liquidity risk and credit risk have a similar focus.

❑ Changes in liquidity impact on the value of a security or derivative. This element of liquidity risk is sometimes referred to as asset or "market" liquidity risk.
❑ Changes in the creditworthiness of an entity impact on the value of a security or derivative issued by or indexed to that entity.

Because these three risks all focus explicitly on changes in the value of an asset or the portfolio, hedge fund managers should integrate the monitoring and management of them (ie, view them as a group, rather than individually). Hence, in the section market risk later in this Appendix, "market risk" will encompass the credit risk associated with assets held in the portfolio and asset (or market) liquidity risk, as well as the more commonly cited market risk factors: interest rate risk, foreign exchange rate risk, equity price risk and commodity price risk.

In addition to having an impact on the value of securities or derivatives held by the hedge fund, changes in funding liquidity can impact on the hedge fund managers' ability to finance its positions. Section 4 (Funding Liquidity Risk), will indicate why this risk is of greater concern to hedge fund managers than to other entities and will describe the techniques that should be used by hedge fund managers to monitor funding liquidity risk.

The hedge fund manager must also consider "leverage". However, leverage is not an independent source of risk; rather, it is a factor that influences the rapidity with which changes in market risk, credit risk or liquidity risk factors change the value of the portfolio. Indeed, it is essential to consider what leverage means – or does not mean – in the context of a hedge fund.

1. A single leverage number may not contain very much information. As will be illustrated in this Appendix, a risk-reducing transaction can increase some leverage measures while decreasing others.

2. The liquidity or price volatility of the position being leveraged is relevant to assessing effective leverage. The leverage employed by a hedge fund that holds one-year Treasury bills with ten-to-one leverage may be of less concern than that employed by a fund levered two-to-one in Russian Ministry of Finance bonds.

3. A hedge fund's capacity to absorb losses – its funding liquidity – is relevant to assessing its effective leverage. Leverage should be measured relative to a fund's capacity to absorb losses. A relatively highly leveraged fund in conventional balance sheet terms may pose a smaller risk than a less levered hedge fund with low cash positions, limited borrowing capacity, or investors that can withdraw their funds on short notice.

In Panel 1, a collection of stylised portfolios and balance sheets are used to illustrate and compare the measures of market risk, funding liquidity risk and leverage.

PANEL 1.

STYLISED PORTFOLIOS

In sections 3, 4 and 5, a collection of stylised portfolios and balance sheets are used to illustrate and compare the measures of market risk, funding liquidity risk and leverage that are discussed in the recommendations and this Appendix. As described below, these simple portfolios are composed of various combinations of three hypothetical securities (which are denoted as asset 1, asset 2 and asset 3) and two derivative contracts. Two of the securities are lower risk assets, with annualised volatility of 30% and 25%, respectively. The third asset is a higher risk asset with annual volatility of 60%. The two derivatives are simple futures contracts on the two low risk securities; therefore they have the same volatility as those securities.

Each portfolio is part of a simple balance sheet. It is assumed that US$100 of investor equity funds each strategy. To calculate all of the various risk measures, the stylised balance sheets also indicate a cash position, a futures margin position and a liability account that reflects any financing transactions. The required futures margin is 10% in cash, which is not counted as liquidity. In addition, up to 50% of assets 1, 2, or 3 can be borrowed, and 50% of the proceeds from a short sale are available to finance investments.

For each portfolio various measures of market risk, liquidity and leverage have been calculated. Note that not all the risk measures are relevant for every portfolio.

❏ Portfolios 1 and 2 illustrate positions with identical market risk but different investments to implement the strategy. Portfolio 1 is

---

an unleveraged investment in asset 1 while Portfolio 2 uses the futures contract on asset 1 to implement the same strategy.

❑ Portfolios 3 and 4 are leveraged versions of Portfolios 1 and 2. The use of balance sheet leverage (Portfolio 1) or additional derivatives contracts (Portfolio 2) has the effect of increasing the market risk of both portfolios.

❑ Like Portfolios 3 and 4, Portfolio 5 is more risky than Portfolios 1 and 2; but, instead of employing traditional leverage, the additional risk arises because the manager switches from a lower-risk strategy (invest in asset 1) to a higher-risk investment strategy (invest in asset 3).

❑ Portfolios 6 and 7 use long and short investments to illustrate the effect of a type of hedging by being long in one asset and short in another, that is positively correlated with the first. In Portfolio 6 the strategy is implemented in the cash market, while Portfolio 7 achieves identical market risk using a combination of cash and futures. As discussed later, these portfolios illustrate the complexity that can appear as the portfolio increases in size – although Portfolios 6 and 7 are generally less risky than Portfolios 3 and 4, there are conditions under which they can become significantly more risky.

Portfolios 8 and 9 are used to illustrate the effect of matched book assets – either in the futures market or the cash market – on traditional leverage and liquidity measures. Portfolios 8 and 9 represent the same net positions as Portfolios 1 and 2; but, the positions are established by combining a short position in asset 1 or futures on asset 1 (ie, –20) with long positions in the same asset (ie, 100), rather than only long positions (ie, 80).

TABLE 1
Stylized Portfolios

		Unlevered Cash versus Futures		Levered Cash versus Futures		Unlevered High Risk	Long/Short Strategy Cash versus Futures		Unlevered Strategy with Matched Book Assets	
		Cash Only	Futures Only	Levered Cash	Futures	High Risk Cash	Long/Short Cash	Long/Short Mixed	Hedged Cash	Hedged Futures
	Portfolio	*1*	*2*	*3*	*4*	*5*	*6*	*7*	*8*	*9*
Summary Balance Sheet										
Capital		100	100	100	100	100	100	100	100	100
Borrowing (outright or repo)		0	0	30				30		
Investments										
Cash Market Transactions										
Asset 1		80		120			120	120	100 . -20	
Asset 2							-60			
Asset 3						80				
Derivatives Market Transactions										
Futures on Asset 1			80		120					100 . -20
Futures on Asset 2								-60		
Cash		20	92	10	88	20	10	4	10	88
Futures Margin		0	8	0	12	0	0	6	0	12

As noted above, for hedge fund managers, changes in credit quality that affect the value of the portfolio through a change in the price of securities owned are incorporated into "market risk". However, hedge fund managers are also exposed to counterparty credit risk. Changes in the credit quality of counterparties can impose costs on the hedge fund either in the form of an increase in expected losses due to counterparty failure to perform or by forcing the hedge fund manager to find alternative counterparties.

Operational risks faced by hedge fund managers are much the same as those faced by other financial institutions – data entry errors, fraud, system failures and errors in valuation or risk measurement models. The appropriate techniques and procedures to deal with these risks are, likewise, the same techniques and procedures used by other entities. As noted in the recommendations, these include random spot checks, maintenance of a single, centralised data set, contingency plans for responding to failures in the hedge fund manager's systems or for responding to the failure of a third party service provider.

VALUATION

As noted in the recommendations, the valuation of positions serves two distinct purposes for the hedge fund manager. In addition to providing the base input to the risk monitoring process, valuation of positions is required for the calculation of NAV, which is the basis for investor subscriptions and redemptions. Hedge fund managers' valuation policies should be objective, fair, and consistent, as outlined below.

❏ Objectivity requires that hedge fund managers either calculate or verify the accuracy of prices independent of the trading/risk selection function. To that end, hedge fund managers should look to reliable price quotes from external sources wherever possible and cost effective to do so.
❏ Fairness recognises that valuation for NAV purposes will determine the prices at which investors subscribe to or redeem from the fund.
❏ Consistency can be achieved through the establishment of recognised procedures or practices. This section will provide more detail on valuation issues than was provided in the recommendations, particularly with respect to valuation for risk monitoring purposes. After restating the principles of NAV valuation, price sources and price validation will be reviewed. Then, the discussion turns to valuation for risk monitoring purposes.

Net asset valuation
Fair Value
As described in the recommendations, for NAV purposes, hedge fund managers generally should value instruments according to generally

accepted accounting principles (GAAP) for the appropriate jurisdiction, recognising that investors will both buy and sell shares of a fund on the basis of NAV and that its financial statements must reflect NAV. This generally requires the use of "fair value". For example, under FASB Statement of Financial Accounting Standards 107, the "fair value" of financial assets and liabilities under US GAAP is the amount at which the item could be exchanged in a current transaction between willing parties, other than in a forced or liquidation sale. Calculation of NAV must take into account not only the value of the financial instruments in the portfolio (sometimes referred to as "trading P&L"), but also accruals of interest, dividends and other receivables and fees, expenses and other payables.

Prices
Where market prices exist and are indicative of fair value, they should generally be used to compute NAV. For instruments that are actively traded, the fair value should be the product of the number of trading units times the quoted price for a single trading unit in the most active market, even if placing an order to sell (or buy, if short) the holding might affect the price if a market's normal one-day volume might not be sufficient to absorb the quantity held.

For instruments traded in the over-the-counter (OTC) market, hedge fund managers should, to the extent possible, attempt to obtain multiple quotes from dealers active in that market. Where appropriate, the model parameters that the dealer used in determining its valuation should be obtained and analysed. Further considerations on price data are discussed below under "Price Sources".

Senior management should establish the valuation methods to be used for NAV purposes where market prices do not exist or are not indicative of fair value. These methods should be disclosed to a hedge fund's governing authority. For investments in non-traded assets or assets that are extremely illiquid or otherwise difficult to value, hedge fund managers should document the valuation methods used and periodically subject them to independent validation. For example, because there are no objective external price references for private equity investments, hedge fund managers may determine they should be carried at historical cost.[5]

Frequency
Senior management should determine the frequency of computing NAV, which will be needed on each date for which balance sheets are prepared and each interim date on which NAV is disclosed to the governing authority or investors. Some hedge fund managers calculate a daily NAV, while others calculate NAV less frequently.

If initial end-of-day values for portfolio instruments are obtained from the hedge fund manager's trader or other front office staff, such values should be verified with a frequency determined by the materiality of the position. Significant differences between front and back office valuations should be investigated and reconciled. Alternatively, end-of-day valuation may be exclusively the role of back office staff.

Portfolio values used to calculate NAV should also be used for risk monitoring valuation, except as expressly determined otherwise by senior management due to operational or risk analysis reasons as discussed below under "Valuation for Risk Monitoring". However, valuation for risk monitoring purposes will be performed daily even though NAV may be calculated less frequently. Also, the daily expense accruals that must be reflected in NAV are generally not included in the portfolio valuation for risk monitoring purposes, which is instead based on the concept of trading P&L.

Price sources

For the following reasons, the appropriate source of price data depends on the position in question.

1. Many of the positions held by hedge funds are securities or derivatives that are listed on organised exchanges or in OTC markets for which reliable price quotes can be obtained from third-party data vendors. For those securities and derivatives, fair value can be based on the "closing" quotation or official closing price of an exchange or prices in the OTC market or other 24-hour markets as they appear on a data vendor screen (observed at the same time on each day).

2. Data vendors may also provide quotations for less actively traded instruments based on a method known as "matrix pricing". Matrix pricing uses market quotes for actively traded securities to approximate the value of a less actively traded security based on comparable characteristics, such as coupon, maturity and risk. Matrix prices can be a useful source of third-party price information, but they should be recognised as modelled prices not transaction prices.

3. Reliable quotes for certain OTC derivative instruments and structured securities may not be available from data vendors, either because the transactions are "one of a kind" or not actively traded. In many cases the only "market" for these securities is with the original counterparty to the transaction. Such instruments can be valued either by obtaining a quote from the originating counterparty or from a pricing model. While a hedge fund manager might be able to obtain quotes from other dealers not party to the original transaction (which would provide a more independent source of pricing information), such an approach may not be practical, for example because it would require disclosure of proprietary position data.

Price validation

Hedge fund managers should establish procedures for verifying the accuracy of prices obtained from data vendors, dealers, or other sources. For actively traded instruments, it may be sufficient to establish multiple feeds from data vendors in order to compare and verify their prices. In other cases, the hedge fund manager should establish procedures for verifying the inputs to models and for validating modelled prices. Modelled prices could be validated by comparing them to prices observed in the market or to prices obtained from third parties where possible. As noted in the recommendations, dealer quotes and prices generated by models or other estimation methods also should be regularly checked against realised prices to gauge their accuracy. Hedge fund managers may elect to use external auditors to verify aspects of their pricing and modelling, either as part of an annual audit or an independent review.

Valuation is typically independent of the trading function. However, for certain illiquid or hard to value investments, such as private equity investments, the valuation process may begin with a price obtained from those most familiar with a particular position, ie, the trader or analyst. However, in such situations, the hedge fund manager should take steps to independently (either internally or externally as appropriate) assess the reasonableness of that price.

Valuation for risk monitoring

The risk monitoring function typically values positions consistent with the approach taken for the NAV calculation. However, the risk monitoring function is not constrained by the requirements of GAAP. Consequently, in order to examine potential effects on the portfolio of changes in market conditions, the risk monitoring function may use alternative values or may make adjustments to the position values calculated for NAV purposes. Senior management should establish policies for determining when risk management valuation methods may differ from NAV for operational or risk analysis reasons. It would not be appropriate, however, to adjust a long position upward or a short position downward, from its fair value for risk monitoring purposes.

❑ Rather than using mid-market prices, bid prices could be used for long positions and ask prices used for short positions.
❑ Prices may be discounted to reflect the size of a position relative to the market, eg, by using "exit values" rather than fair value. Exit value reflects the likely impact on the market price where the position must be liquidated quickly, such as where the position is significantly larger than historical trading volume during the assumed required exit period.
❑ For an actively traded security held in a large enough quantity and/or involving sufficient indicia of control that a Schedule 13D or similar pub-

lic disclosure has been made of the position, and therefore where a sale of a portion could not be made anonymously, a downward adjustment from market value may be appropriate.

❏ For instruments subject to legal restrictions on sale or where the market is illiquid or has become disorderly, it may be appropriate to make a downward adjustment from the fair value.

❏ In volatile markets, prices may be discounted if the risk monitoring function does not believe that quoted bids or offers are prices at which a trade could actually be done.

❏ For a less actively traded instrument representing only a small position, and where obtaining price information requires significant effort, weekly (or even less frequent) pricing may be appropriate.

MARKET RISK

This encompasses the credit risk associated with securities and derivatives in the portfolio and asset liquidity risk, as well as interest rate risk, foreign exchange rate risk, equity price risk, and commodity price risk.

In order that senior management are able to oversee the risks that the hedge fund faces, the risk monitoring function needs to provide them with some useful measure of risk. Measuring the degree to which the portfolio is diversified (eg, the percentages of the portfolio allocated to different asset classes or to different geographical regions) may be useful; however, it is important for the hedge fund manager to recognise and understand the correlations between positions. For complex portfolios, many summary measures of market risk do not reflect such correlations. VAR is a tool which is intended to provide a summary market risk measure which incorporates correlations between positions. VAR measures the maximum change in the value of the portfolio that would be expected at a specified confidence level over a specified holding period. For example, if the 95% confidence level, one-day VAR for a portfolio is US$500,000, one would expect to gain or lose more than US$500,000 in only five of every 100 trading days on average.[6]

Since first being discussed in the Group of 30 Report in 1993,[7] VAR has become a widely-used risk measurement tool among virtually all commercial banks and investment banks.[8] Other market participants are increasingly using the VAR measure as well. A 1998 survey of pension, endowments, and foundations reported that 23% of "large" institutional investors used VAR.[9] Use of VAR by hedge funds is believed to be substantial, if not universal among the larger funds.

Parameter selection

In order to calculate a VAR measure, a numbers of parameters must be input; these parameters describe the positions in the portfolio and the underlying markets. For a given portfolio, the parameters most likely to have a significant impact on the VAR value are the time horizon or holding period (the period of time that would be necessary for the portfolio to be liquidated or neutralised), the confidence level (the probability that the change in the value of the portfolio would exceed the VAR), and the variance-covariance data (which reflects the volatility of the individual market factors and the correlation between pairs of factors). These parameters are explained further below.

❏ The time horizon or holding period used in the VAR calculation is intended to reflect the time period necessary to liquidate (or neutralise) the positions in the portfolio. In practice, if the hedge fund has positions in thinly traded or illiquid instruments, it is difficult to determine the correct liquidation/neutralisation period for the portfolio. Consequently, good practice is to use standard holding periods – eg, one day, three days, five days and 10 days in the base-case VAR calculation and then employ stress tests to determine the degree of holding period risk in the portfolio.

❏ The appropriate confidence level is defined by no mathematical formula; the appropriate confidence level is determined by the business circumstances of the entity. Different types of businesses should and do use different confidence levels. The appropriate confidence level for a specific hedge fund will be a business decision that is determined by the specific circumstances of the fund; and senior management of the hedge fund manager should be actively involved in this determination.

❏ Variance-covariance data are another significant parameter. While the measure of the riskiness of individual market factors (ie, the variances of the market factors) is important, the question of the degree of correlation (ie, covariance) between pairs of market factors is critical, because correlation has such a large impact on the VAR calculation. A number of VAR models use historic correlations. However, since historic correlations are unstable (especially during periods of market stress), the hedge fund manager should employ scenario analyses and stress testing (see below) to ascertain the impact of inaccurate correlation assumptions.

Beyond a single VAR number
Scenario analysis, stress testing and back testing
Hedge fund managers must recognise that a single VAR number is not sufficient to capture all risks faced by the hedge fund and that successful risk management requires the risk monitoring function to analyse both the sensitivity of the VAR to alternative market conditions and the reliability of the VAR calculations.

Scenario analysis

By their nature, VAR calculations are based on "typical" market days. Periods of market stress or crisis – the very times of greatest concern – will not be well represented in the data for a typical period; so the resulting VAR number will underestimate the risks of severe markets. To address this limitation, the hedge fund manager should perform scenario analyses regularly, to assess the VAR for the current portfolio in periods of market stress.

In creating scenario analyses, a hedge fund manager should use both historical stress periods – eg, 19 October, 1987, when the equity markets crashed; 4 February, 1994, when the US Federal Reserve changed direction and started increasing US interest rates; 20 December, 1994, when the Mexican peso was devalued – as well as hypothetical periods, designed perhaps to put the most pressure on the current portfolio.

Stress testing

Hedge fund managers should stress test the VAR number by changing the parameters of the VAR model. Stress tests permit the hedge fund manager to see what will happen to the VAR number if the actual values of market factors (ie, prices, rates, volatilities, etc) differ from the values used as inputs in the base-case VAR calculation. Of particular concern to hedge fund managers are "breakdowns" in the correlations reflected in current market data. In times of market crisis the correlations between asset prices or rates can change dramatically and unexpectedly, with the result that positions that were thought to be diversifying – or even hedging – end up compounding risk. While it remains difficult to hedge correlation risk, stress tests to evaluate the impact of correlation changes permit the hedge fund manager to help ensure that, when the hedge fund manager selects the assets to be included in the portfolio, the fund is accepting the desired level of correlation risk (and is being compensated for bearing that risk).

Panel 2 contains several illustrative VAR measures for each of the nine stylised portfolios introduced in Panel 1.

PANEL 2

ILLUSTRATIVE VAR MEASURES FOR EACH OF THE NINE STYLISED PORTFOLIOS INTRODUCED IN PANEL 1.

Standard VAR

A 95% one-day VAR is calculated using the historical volatilities for the assets and assuming the correlation between assets is 0.3.

Stressed VAR 1

The 95% one-day VAR is re-calculated increasing the volatility of each asset by 50% (ie, to 45% for asset 1, to 37.5% for asset 2 and to

---

90% for asset 3) and increasing the correlation between all assets to 0.9.

Stressed VAR 2

The 95% one-day VAR is recalculated again increasing the volatilities by 50% as above, but decreasing the correlation between assets to zero.

Table 2 provides confirmation of the following general propositions regarding the VAR measures.

TABLE 2
Markets of Market Risk

	Unlevered Cash versus Futures		Levered Cash versus Futures		Unlevered High Risk	Long/Short Strategy Cash versus Futures		Unlevered Strategy with Matched Book Assets	
	Cash Only	Futures Only	Levered Cash	Futures	High Risk Cash	Long/Short Cash	Long/Short Mixed	Hedged Cash	Hedged Futures
Portfolio	1	2	3	4	5	6	7	8	9
Summary Balance Sheet									
Capital	100	100	100	100	100	100	100	100	100
Borrowing (outright or repo)	0	0	30				30		
Investments									
Cash Market Transactions									
Asset 1	80		120			120	120	100, -20	
Asset 2						-80			
Asset 3					80				
Derivatives Market Transactions									
Futures on Asset 1		80		120					100, -20
Futures on Asset 2							-60		
Cash	20	92	10	88	20	10	4	10	88
Futures Margin	0	8	0	12	0	0	6	0	12
Risk Measures									
Standard VAR (asset Correlation =0.3)	2.50	2.50	3.76	3.76	5.01	3.61	3.61	2.50	2.50
Stressed VAR 1 (Vol+50%; Asset Correlation = .90)	3.76	3.76	5.64	5.64	7.51	3.67	3.67	3.76	3.76
Stressed VAR 2 (Vol +50%; Asset Correlation = 0)	3.76	3.76	5.64	5.64	7.51	6.10	6.10	3.76	3.76
Sharpe Ratio	1.05	1.05	1.05	1.05	1.32	0.69	0.69	1.05	1.05

❑ Identical positions have the same VAR regardless of whether they are implemented in the cash market (eg, Portfolio 1) or the futures market (eg, Portfolio 2). Identical in this case refers to the fact that the cash and futures positions represent the price risk associated with the same asset and in the same amount. (As discussed below, other risk measures, such as liquidity, are not identical.)

❑ VAR can be increased via traditional balance sheet leverage or the use of additional derivatives contracts. Portfolios 3 and 4 illustrate the effect of leverage on the first two portfolios.

❑ VAR can be increased by choosing higher risk assets, regardless of leverage, as illustrated in Portfolio 5.

❑ A hedge is not always a hedge. The "hedge" established via Portfolios 6 and 7 presumes that Assets 1 and 2 are positively correlated. Under normal conditions (ie, when correlation equals 0.3 in this example) the tendency of asset 1 and asset 2 to move together results in the VAR of Portfolio 6 being similar to the VAR of Portfolio 3 even though the total position size is larger. When the correlation gets more positive (Stressed VAR 1), the hedge is better, and VAR stays relatively unchanged even though overall

volatility in the market has increased by 50%. But, when the correlation gets less positive (Stressed VAR 2), the hedge is much less
effective and the combined effect of higher volatility and lower
correlation results in a significantly larger VAR. As was the case
with the earlier portfolios, the use of futures or cash market investments does not change the market risk measure, as evidenced by
the identical VAR of Portfolios 6 and 7.

Back testing

Possibly even more important than analysing the sensitivity of the VAR
number is back testing the VAR to see how it performed. By comparing
actual changes in the value of the portfolio to the changes generated by the
VAR calculation, the hedge fund manager can gain insight into whether
the VAR model is accurately measuring a fund's risk.

In back testing, one expects that the portfolio will lose more than the
VAR from time to time. For example, a 95% one-day VAR should be
exceeded five days in every 100 trading days on average. When the actual
changes in the value of the portfolio exceed VAR, the hedge fund manager
should determine the source of the discrepancy – ie, whether the VAR measure is flawed or whether this loss is simply one which was expected given
the confidence level employed or is attributable to a change in the composition of the portfolio or the market.

Relating earnings and risk

It was noted at the outset that effective risk management requires the
hedge fund manager to recognise and understand the risks the fund faces.
That, in turn, requires the hedge fund manager to understand the various
sources of the fund's earnings, both the size of the earnings and their
volatility.

One way that hedge fund managers can accomplish this attribution is by
decomposing the daily value changes by market factors. The objective is to
determine if the actual changes were what would have been predicted,
given the now known changes in the market factors. If the observed
change in the value of the portfolio differs significantly from the change
that would be expected, given the composition of the portfolio and the
observed changes in the market factors, the differences should be reconciled.

Such a source-of-return and source-of-risk attribution process sets the
stage for linking performance measurement with risk measurement. The
Sharpe ratio is widely used by investors to measure a portfolio's risk-
adjusted performance over a specific period.[10] The numerator of the Sharpe
ratio is a measure of portfolio return during the period; the denominator is

a measure of the risk incurred in achieving the return. (For example, over the past decade the Sharpe ratio for the S&P 500 has been approximately 1.2.) Investors prefer high Sharpe ratios to low, since a higher Sharpe ratio indicates that the portfolio earned superior returns relative to the level of risk incurred. There are a number of ways in which return and risk could be calculated. Below is the Sharpe ratio for some arbitrary portfolio – designated as Portfolio j – calculated using the most common conventions for measuring return and risk. The numerator is the return earned on the portfolio (Rj) in excess of the risk-free rate of return (Rf) – ie, the interest rate earned on risk-free securities such as US Treasury securities – over the same period. The denominator – the risk incurred – is measured as the standard deviation of the portfolio's daily return (σj).

$$(\text{Sharpe Ratio})_j = \frac{R_j - R_f}{\sigma_j}$$

While VAR and the Sharpe ratio contain some similar information, the two measures are different tools, designed for different purposes. VAR is primarily a risk measurement tool. The Sharpe ratio is a summary measure, combining both risk and return information. Moreover, while VAR is a risk measure and the denominator of the Sharpe ratio contains a risk measure, these two risk measures are quite different. The risk measure used in the denominator of the Sharpe ratio is a historical measure; it characterises the actual volatility of the return over some historical period. In contrast, VAR is intended to be a prospective measure of risk.

FUNDING LIQUIDITY RISK
While other entities face funding liquidity risk, this risk is a more central concern to hedge fund managers than others, because funding liquidity problems can rapidly increase a hedge fund's risk of failure. As is described below, a lack of funding liquidity can contribute to a crisis situation for the hedge fund.

Liquidity crisis cycle
Hedge fund managers should be concerned about a confluence of risks – ie, market or credit risk events affecting illiquid positions that are leveraged. Such a confluence of events could require the hedge fund to liquidate positions into a market that cascades in price because of a high volume of liquidation orders. Such a situation could be decomposed into the following three stages.

1. A loss that acts as the triggering event.
2. A need to liquidate positions to raise cash, because of this loss. The liquidation may be required either because the fund must post margin with its counterparties or because of redemptions by investors due to the loss.

3. A further drop in the fund's NAV as the market reacts to actions by the fund. Obviously, attempts by the fund to sell in too great a quantity or too quickly for the market liquidity to bear can cause a further drop in prices, precipitating a further decline in the fund's net asset value, and leading in turn to yet a further need to liquidate to satisfy margin calls or redemptions. This downward spiral can be exacerbated if other market participants have information about the fund's positions.

The point of no return comes when the effect of liquidation has a greater impact on the value of the remaining fund position than the amount of cash raised from the liquidation. If this happens, the fund is caught in an accelerating, downward spiral; eventually, it will not be able to satisfy the demands of its creditors or investors. Once the losses move beyond a critical point, it becomes a self-sustaining crisis that feeds off of the need for liquidity, a need imposed by the demands of the fund's creditors and investors. Because of its importance, hedge fund managers should focus significant attention and resources on measuring and managing funding liquidity risk. There exist a range of measures hedge fund managers can use to track funding liquidity risk. Hedge fund managers should monitor the liquidity available in the fund by tracking its cash position (ie, cash and short-term securities issued by high credit-quality entities) and its borrowing capacity (eg, access to borrowings under margin rules or credit lines).

Beyond measures of available liquidity, hedge fund managers should also monitor measures of relative liquidity. Hedge fund managers should relate the measures of liquidity – cash or cash + borrowing capacity – to the need for that liquidity. The following measures are indicators of a fund's potential need for liquidity.

Equity or NAV
Generally, a larger fund will require greater levels of liquidity. However, a fund's need for liquidity during periods of market stress is determined not only by the size of the portfolio but also by the characteristics of the assets it holds. Consequently, hedge fund managers need to have measures of potential liquidity needs that reflect the riskiness of the portfolio.

Worst historical drawdown
This indicator provides a measure of risk and of the amount of liquidity the fund has required in the past. This measure is, however, a backward-looking measure of risk and may not be indicative of the fund's current exposure.

VAR
As has been argued earlier, VAR is currently the most widely used prospective measure of market risk. Consequently, tracking the ratio of

cash (or cash + borrowing capacity) to VAR provides the hedge fund manager with an indication of whether the fund's liquidity relative to its need for liquidity is rising or falling.

Illustrative liquidity measures

Panel 3 contains the results of calculating five of the liquidity measures discussed in this section for each of the nine stylised portfolios.

PANEL 3
ILLUSTRATIVE LIQUIDITY MEASURES

Available liquidity is measured by cash that is not committed as margin, and by cash plus the "borrowing capacity" of the assets. For the three cash market assets, it is assumed that 50% of the value of a long position can be borrowed (ie, assume current Regulation T margin requirements if the three assets were equities). For simplicity, short positions in the assets are assumed to have a 50% margin requirement, in effect, allowing 50% of short trades to be used to fund long positions, or for cash.

Several features of funding liquidity risk measurement are evidenced by the stylised portfolios.

❏ Other things equal, futures (and derivatives in general) require the hedge fund manager to use significantly less cash (at origination) than would an equivalent position established via a cash market transaction. This is evidenced by Portfolios 1 and 2. (However, not reflected in these numbers is the interrelation of market risk, funding liquidity risk and leveraging. While the cash position uses more cash at origination than does the futures position, if the value of the underlying asset were to change dramatically, the resulting margin call on the futures position could have a significant impact on the fund's cash position.)

❏ For the same amount of initial capital, the use of leverage (eg, Portfolios 3 and 4) both consumes borrowing capacity and increases VAR; so, measures of available liquidity and relative measures indicate that liquidity declines.

❏ Use of leverage in the cash market decreases available cash faster than the identical strategy implemented with futures. The increase in traditional balance sheet leverage (ie, use of margin to buy assets) in Portfolio 3 sharply reduces both absolute and relative measures of liquidity since either cash or borrowing capacity is consumed in the process. The identical economic leverage is obtained using futures in Portfolio 4, but the decrease in liquidity

---

is less pronounced. (The caveat about future cash requirements for futures positions that was raised in the first point applies here as well.)

❑ Use of a relative liquidity measure – eg, VAR/(cash +borrowing capacity) – captures the impact of investing in higher risk assets while holding the amount invested constant. Portfolio 5 shows that while absolute liquidity is the same as for Portfolio 1, liquidity relative to VAR has decreased (ie, VAR is a higher percentage of available cash).

❑ Portfolios 6 and 7 illustrate once again that identical market risk portfolios present different funding liquidity risk profiles. Portfolio 7, which uses futures to short asset 2 while borrowing against asset 1 is less liquid than Portfolio 6 which shorts asset 2 in the cash market. The difference is simply that short positions in futures (and derivatives in general) do not generate cash.

TABLE 3
Measures of Liquidity

		Unlevered Cash versus Futures		Levered Cash versus Futures		Unlevered High Risk	Long/Short Strategy Cash versus Futures		Unlevered Strategy with Matched Book Assets	
		Cash Only	Futures Only	Levered Cash	Futures	High Risk Cash	Long/Short Cash	Long/Short Mixed	Hedged Cash	Hedged Futures
	Portfolio	1	2	3	4	5	6	7	8	9
Summary Balance Sheet										
Capital		100	100	100	100	100	100	100	100	100
Borrowing (outright or repo)		0	0	30				30		
Investments										
Cash Market Transactions										
Asset 1		80		120			120	120	100 , -20	
Asset 2							-60			
Asset 3						80				
Derivatives Market Transactions										
Futures on Asset 1			80		120					100 , -20
Futures on Asset 2								-60		
Cash		20	92	10	88	20	10	4	10	88
Futures Margin		0	8	0	12	0	0	6	0	12
Standard VAR (asset correlation =0.3)		2.50	2.50	3.76	3.76	5.01	3.61	3.61	2.50	2.50
Liquidity Measures										
Measures of Available Liquidity										
Cash		20	92	10	88	20	10	4	10	88
Cash + Borrowing Capacity		60	92	40	88	60	70	34	60	88
Relative Measures										
Cash/Equity		20%	92%	10%	88%	20%	10%	4%	10%	88%
(Cash + Borrowing Capacity)/Equity		60%	92%	40%	88%	60%	70%	34%	60%	88%
VAR/(Cash + Borrowing Capacity)		4.2%	2.7%	9.4%	4.3%	8.3%	9.0%	10.6%	4.2%	2.8%

Additional insight about funding liquidity can be gained by looking at the variability in the relative liquidity measure over time. A relative liquidity measure that varies over time is evidence consistent with "effective liquidity" – ie, the assets are liquid and the manager is willing to take advantage of that liquidity.

Beyond simply monitoring liquidity, hedge fund managers should manage liquidity in several dimensions. Foremost is the use of the hedge fund manager's experience and judgement to maintain liquidity levels that are adequate given the risk of loss and/or the likelihood of investor redemptions. Also, hedge fund managers should strengthen lines of communication with their credit providers, providing them with summary measures of the fund's risk and liquidity consistent with the nature of the relationship. Hedge fund managers should actively manage (or monitor) the cash in margin accounts. Similarly, managers should negotiate haircuts and two-way collateral agreements, where appropriate, to further reduce the likelihood of running out of liquidity.

LEVERAGE

As the recommendations made clear, leverage is not a concept that can be uniquely defined, nor is it an independently useful measure of risk. Nevertheless, leverage is important to hedge fund managers because of the impact it can have on the three major quantifiable sources of risk: market risk, credit risk and liquidity risk.

That leverage is not a uniquely defined concept is evidenced by the variety of "leverage" measures used in banking and finance. These measures, that are described in more detail below, may be accounting-based (also referred to as "asset-based") or risk-based. The accounting-based measures attempt to capture the traditional notion of leverage as "investing borrowed funds". Using borrowed money (or its equivalent) enables an investor to increase the assets controlled for a given level of equity capital. Accounting-based measures of leverage relate some measure of asset value to equity. Both returns and risk, relative to equity, are magnified through the use of traditional, accounting-based leverage. The risk-based measures of leverage capture another aspect associated with leverage, namely, the risk of insolvency due to changes in the value of the portfolio. The risk-based measures relate a measure of a fund's market risk to its equity (or liquidity). Although useful in this capacity, as described below, risk-based leverage measures do not convey any information about the role borrowed money plays in the risk of insolvency.

No single measure captures all of the elements that market participants, regulators, or market observers attribute to the concept of leverage. Indeed, examples will be presented in which a risk-reducing transaction increases some leverage measures while decreasing others. This leads to the observation that leverage is not an independently useful concept, but must be evaluated in the context of the quantifiable exposures of market, credit and liquidity.

While continuing to track and use accounting-based measures of leverage, hedge fund managers should focus their attention on measures of leverage that relate the riskiness of the portfolio to the capacity of the fund to absorb that risk – ie, the measures must include elements of market risk (including the credit risk associated with assets in the portfolio) and funding liquidity risk. Hedge fund managers should focus on such measures because traditional accounting-based leverage by itself does not necessarily convey risk of insolvency. To say that one fund is levered two-to-one, while another is unlevered does not necessarily mean that the levered fund is more risky or more likely to encounter liquidity problems. If the levered fund is invested in government securities while the unlevered fund is invested in equities, accounting-based leverage would lead to erroneous conclusions about the riskiness of the two funds. In this sense, accounting-based measures of leverage are arguably deficient since they convey the least information about the nature and risk of the assets in a portfolio.

Risk-based measures (see below) present a measure of market risk (usually VAR) relative to a measure of the resources available to absorb risk (cash or equity). However, in doing so, risk based measures effectively condense several dimensions of risk into a single number. The result of this compression is that some of the detail is lost; the specific effect of leverage is intertwined with dimensions of market, credit and liquidity risk. To illustrate, consider two funds with identical risk-based leverage. One fund employs two-to-one accounting leverage while investing in "low risk" strategies (eg, long/short strategies) using borrowed funds, while the other fund uses no accounting leverage but employs "high risk" strategies (eg, macro-directional) and large cash reserves. One is "high risk" and "high cash" and the other is "low risk" and "low cash/high borrowing", yet each achieves the same risk-based leverage. This comparison highlights the second reason why leverage measures are not independently useful: more comprehensive measures blend the effect of multiple risk dimensions. To assess the contribution of leverage requires additional information.

Accounting-based leverage measures

There exist a number of accounting-based measures of leverage. In addition to the pragmatic recognition that counterparties and credit providers routinely request these measures, a more compelling rationale for calculating these measures is that they can contribute to an understanding of leverage measures that incorporate risk. This is particularly true when accounting and risk-based leverage are tracked over time.

Certain accounting measures can also provide information regarding how much direct or indirect credit in the form of repurchase agreements, short sales, or derivatives are employed by a fund. However, it must be recognised that even these accounting-based measures have serious weaknesses, discussed below, particularly as stand-alone measures of leverage.

The most widely used and generally accepted accounting-based measures of leverage are those that relate items from a fund's balance sheet:

"Gross balance sheet assets to equity": on-balance-sheet assets/equity
This straightforward measure is easily calculated from published financial statements; however, it fails to incorporate two important elements of a fund's effective leverage.

1. The risk-reducing effect of on-balance-sheet hedges is not recognised. Adding a hedge to the balance sheet increases assets and thereby increases this leverage measure, even though the transaction may substantially offset the risk of another asset.
2. Derivative instruments, which have historically been carried off-balance-sheet, are not captured.[11] To the extent derivatives are used to hedge on-balance-sheet assets, this measure will overstate the fund's effective leverage. By the same token, if a fund's derivatives are used to take outright positions – ie, not as hedges – this measure will understate the fund's effective leverage.

"Net balance sheet assets to equity": (on-balance-sheet assets – matched book assets)/equity
While this measure requires more detailed information about the positions in a fund's portfolio, it does provide a partial solution to the shortcomings of the gross-balance-sheet assets to equity measure by including offsets and direct hedges as reflected in "matched book assets". However, two important elements of the fund's effective leverage are still not incorporated.

1. This measure does not reflect portfolio correlation or less direct hedges that fall outside the definition of matched book assets.
2. This measure does not incorporate off-balance-sheet instruments.

Other accounting-based measures have been proposed to capture off-balance-sheet transactions (eg, forward contracts, swaps and other derivatives). Among those measures are the following:

"Gross accounting leverage": (on-balance-sheet assets + on-balance-sheet liabilities + gross off-balance-sheet notional)/equity
Gross accounting leverage incorporates the gross amount of off-balance-sheet derivatives. Such a measure cannot reliably indicate the effective amount of leverage obtained from off-balance sheet transactions because that type of offsetting exposures are not netted. An active derivative user that uses offsetting transactions rather than closeouts to reduce or eliminate positions will accumulate a substantial notional amount of derivatives even though the risk of the position and its effective leverage are quite low.

"net accounting leverage": ((on-balance-sheet assets – matched book assets) + (on-balance-sheet liabilities – matched book liabilities) + (gross off-balance-sheet notional principal – notional principal of off-balance-sheet transactions used to hedge on-balance-sheet assets or liabilities))/equity
Net accounting leverage requires still more detail to calculate. Although it reflects matched book assets (liabilities) and off-balance-sheet hedges of balance sheet assets, it still misses off-balance sheet hedges and correlation.

Risk-based leverage measures

Risk-based leverage measures reflect the relation between the riskiness of a fund's portfolio and the capacity of the fund to absorb the impact of that risk. While not the only measure that could be used, the hedge fund's equity provides a useful measure of "capacity". There are, however, different measures of market risk that could be used as the "riskiness" measure.

(Volatility in value of portfolio)/equity

This is a measure of actual performance volatility over a given horizon relative to equity. While useful, it is subject to criticism. Since it is a retrospective measure, it is less useful if the composition of the portfolio changes or if future market conditions are not like historical conditions. Moreover, it does not isolate the effect of financing on the risk of the fund since it includes financed assets.

VAR/equity

This measure gives a picture of the fund's capacity to absorb "typical" market movements. The criticism of such a measure is that it does not reflect the risk of the fund's portfolio in extreme markets.

(Scenario-derived market risk measure)/equity

To assess the impact of extreme events, the leverage measure could be calculated using a market risk measure derived from analysis of extreme event scenarios (or stress tests). This measure gives senior management information about the hedge fund's ability to absorb extreme market events.

Panel 4 contains the results of calculating all of the accounting-based

---

PANEL 4
ILLUSTRATIVE LEVERAGE MEASURES

Table 4 contains the results of calculating all of the accounting-based leverage measures and two of the risk-based leverage measures discussed in this section. Note that "net balance sheet leverage" and "net accounting leverage" are only relevant for Portfolios 8 and 9, because these portfolios are the only ones in which the long and short positions can be netted under accounting rules.

Leverage can be interpreted in several ways: as the use of borrowed money to fund larger asset positions than would otherwise be achievable, and as the use of economic leverage to increase effect of a given change in market prices on the value of fund's equity.

The illustrative portfolios demonstrate several common features of accounting-based and risk-based leverage.

❏ The most common leverage measure, gross balance sheet leverage (or assets/equity) is not indicative of the types of assets employed or the amount of risk assumed. In the illustration, gross balance sheet leverage is the same in Portfolios 1, 2, 4, 5 and 9 even though the risk and investment strategy differ significantly across portfolios. Similarly, while the amount of risk assumed in Portfolio 8 is identical to the risk assumed in Portfolio 1, the levels of gross balance sheet leverage differ.

❏ The purpose of the net balance sheet leverage measure is to adjust for matched book assets. Comparison of net balance sheet leverage with gross balance sheet leverage for Portfolio 8 shows an instance where this occurs.

❏ Gross accounting leverage, which sums assets, liabilities, and futures is not informative about investment strategy (cash versus futures) or the market risk of the portfolio. Note that the riskiest portfolio as measured by VAR – Portfolio 5 – has the lowest accounting leverage. Similarly, Portfolios 1 and 2 are low risk, yet gross accounting leverage varies by 80% between them.

❏ That net accounting leverage adjusts for matched book assets and derivatives that hedge on-balance-sheet positions is seen by comparing gross accounting leverage with net accounting leverage for Portfolios 8 and 9. Note that this measure does not capture the use of a futures position to offset an identical futures position, ie, the matched futures in Portfolio 9. The risk-based leverage measures come closer to capturing the nature of the risks as reflected in the specific strategies. (Note Portfolios 1, 2, 8 and 9.) However, they too miss certain aspects of the risk picture. For example, Portfolios

TABLE 4
Measures of Leverage

		Unlevered Cash versus Futures		Levered Cash versus Futures		Unlevered High Risk	Long/Short Strategy Cash versus Futures		Unlevered Strategy with Matched Book Assets	
		Cash Only	Futures Only	Levered Cash	Futures	High Risk Cash	Long/Short Cash	Long/Short Mixed	Hedged Cash	Hedged Futures
	Portfolio	1	2	3	4	5	6	7	8	9
Summary Balance Sheet										
Capital		100	100	100	100	100	100	100	100	100
Borrowing (outright or repo)		0	0	30				30		
Investments										
Cash Market Transactions										
Asset 1		80		120			120	120	100 , -20	
Asset 2							-60			
Asset 3						80				
Derivatives Market Transactions										
Futures on Asset 1			80		120					100 , -20
Futures on Asset 2								-60		
Cash		20	92	10	88	20	10	4	10	88
Futures Margin		0	8	0	12	0	0	6	0	12
Standard VAR (asset Correlation =0.3)		2.50	2.50	3.76	3.76	5.01	3.61	3.61	2.50	2.50
Leverage Measures										
Accounting-Based Measures										
Gross Balance Sheet Leverage		1	1	1.3	1	1	1.6	1.3	1.2	1
Net Balance Sheet Leverage									1	1
Gross Accounting Leverage		1	1.8	1.6	2.2	1	2.2	1	1.4	2.2
Net Accounting Leverage									1.2	2.2
Risk-Based Measures										
VAR/Capital		2.50%	2.50%	3.76%	3.76%	5.01%	3.61%	3.61%	2.50%	2.50%
Stress 1 VAR/Capital		3.76%	3.76%	5.64%	5.64%	7.51%	3.67%	3.67%	3.76%	3.76%
Stress 2 VAR/Capital		3.76%	3.76%	5.64%	5.64%	7.51%	6.10%	6.10%	3.76%	3.76%

3 and 4 have the same VAR/Equity, but the cash market strategy employed in Portfolio 3 uses more cash and borrowing capacity, and is therefore riskier from a liquidity standpoint (VAR is 9.4% of liquidity in Portfolio 3 compared to only 4.3% of liquidity in Portfolio 4).

❏ Stress and scenario analysis are essential elements of liquidity and leverage analyses. The long/short strategy employed in Portfolios 6 and 7 is similar in risk-based leverage to Portfolios 3 and 4 until one looks at the stress scenarios. Because of the reliance on correlation, the leverage of Portfolios 6 and 7 is potentially much larger in a period of market stress.

leverage measures and two of the risk-based leverage measures discussed in this section.

While the preceding leverage measures are the ones most commonly used by hedge fund managers, other measures may be used to analyse leverage. Indeed, because of the interrelation between market risk, funding liquidity risk and leverage, measures of funding liquidity risk described in this section – particularly cash + borrowing capacity relative to VAR – also provide the hedge fund manager with insights about a fund's leverage.

Dynamic measures of leverage

A crucial factor influencing a fund's ability to absorb the impact of extreme market events is the degree to which a fund can modify its risk-based leverage, especially during periods of market stress.

Treating equity as constant, there are two ways a hedge fund manager could reduce risk-based leverage.

1. If a hedge fund manager wishes to continue an existing investment strategy, risk-based leverage could be reduced by reducing traditional leverage resulting from either on- or off-balance-sheet transactions.
2. A hedge fund manager could reduce risk-based leverage by reducing the level of risk that is being accepted (eg, by changing strategy or the types of assets being held in the portfolio). To track the degree to which the fund is able to modify its risk-based leverage, the hedge fund manager should track variations in the fund's market risk measure (eg, VAR) over time.

The following two measures could be used to track the relationship over time between measures of market risk and actions taken by the hedge fund manager to adjust leverage. Both of these measures consider a short time interval (one or two days – one week); both assume that equity is constant.

Changes in portfolio market risk
A decline in a portfolio's market risk measure (eg, VAR) in a period following an increase in that market risk measure in the preceding period, could be evidence of the hedge fund manager's ability to de-lever the portfolio during a period of market stress. (The market risk measure could be VAR or the observed volatility of the value of the portfolio during the relevant period.)

Relationship between a change in market risk and a subsequent change in cash + borrowing capacity
All other things equal, if a hedge fund manager is able to reduce the portfolio's accounting-based leverage, the result would be an increase in cash or in borrowing capacity. Therefore, an increase in cash + borrowing capacity in a period following an increase in the market risk measure for the portfolio (eg, VAR) could be evidence of the hedge fund manager's reacting to market stress by reducing leverage.

COUNTERPARTY CREDIT RISK
Hedge fund managers enter into transactions with a variety of counterparties including banks, securities firms, exchanges and other financial institutions. The risk of loss to the fund as a result of the failure of a counterparty to perform as expected, constitutes counterparty credit risk.

Credit risk is present to some extent in almost any dealing with a third party, including the settlement of securities and derivatives transactions, repurchase agreements, collateral arrangements and margin accounts. It is also present in open derivatives positions where the exposure of one counterparty to another will change over the life of the contract as the contract's value fluctuates. Hedge fund managers should be aware of, and track, concentrations of credit risk with particular counterparties, and where applicable, different regions of the world. The willingness of the manager to enter into a transaction with a specific counterparty should depend on the loss the hedge fund would suffer were the counterparty to default. That, in turn, depends on the magnitude of the fund's exposure to the counterparty and the likelihood of default, ie, the counterparty's creditworthiness.

An assessment of exposure to a particular counterparty should include analysis of the following elements of exposure.

❑ Current replacement cost. The amount the fund would lose if its counterparty were to become insolvent immediately and the hedge fund manager had to replace the contract in the market.
❑ Potential exposure. A probabilistic assessment of the additional exposure that could result if the counterparty does not default immediately but instead defaults at some date in the future. Potential exposure is particu-

larly applicable to derivatives transactions where exposure is reciprocal and likely to change substantially before the contract expires.

❑ The probability of loss. The likelihood of a default by the counterparty over the relevant time horizon. This is a function of the counterparty's current credit quality, the length of the transaction, and possibly the nature of the transaction itself.

❑ Risk mitigation and documentation. The extent to which collateral, netting provisions or other credit enhancement reduces the magnitude of the exposure to a counterparty. Hedge fund managers can greatly reduce their credit exposure to counterparties by negotiating bilateral netting and collateral provisions in their documentation and establishing document management processes to ensure transactions are documented consistently and in a timely manner.

ADDITIONAL NOTES

US REGULATORY FILINGS BY HEDGE FUND MANAGERS

Listed below are regulatory filings (excluding tax-related and state "blue sky" filings) that hedge fund managers may be required to make in the United States depending on either their trading activity or their status as a regulated entity. The filings made to regulators by individual managers will vary depending on the type and volume of trading in which they engage, their business model and the jurisdictions in which they operate. For example, like other market participants and institutional investors, managers are required to make certain filings in the United States if the size of the positions they hold in certain markets reaches "reportable" levels. In addition, some managers are regulated entities in the US or are otherwise subject to a regulatory regime, and, like other similarly situated entities, are required to make certain filings in that capacity. This Appendix lists filings required in the United States where the above circumstances apply to a manager. Hedge fund managers may also be subject to regulatory reporting and filing requirements in the foreign jurisdictions in which they conduct their business.

Federal reserve – treasury securities position and foreign exchange transaction reporting

Large position reporting

❑ Report of positions in specific Treasury security issues that exceed the large position threshold specified by the US Treasury Department (minimum US$2 billion).

❑ Reports are filed in response to notices issued by the US Department of the Treasury if such a threshold is met.

❑ Reports are filed with the Federal Reserve Bank of New York and are not public.

Form FC-1

❑ Report of weekly, consolidated data on the foreign exchange contracts and positions of major market participants.

❑ Reports to be filed throughout the calendar year by each foreign exchange market participant which had more than US$50 billion equivalent in foreign exchange contracts on the last business day of any calendar quarter during the previous year.

❑ The report is filed with the appropriate Federal Reserve Bank acting as agent for the US Department of the Treasury and is confidential.

Form FC-2

❑ Report of monthly, consolidated data on the foreign exchange contracts and foreign currency denominated assets and liabilities of major market participants.

❑ Reports to be filed throughout the calendar year by each foreign exchange market participant which had more than US$50 billion equivalent in foreign exchange contracts on the last business day of any calendar quarter during the previous year.

❑ The report is filed with the appropriate Federal Reserve Bank acting as agent for the US Department of the Treasury and is confidential.

Form FC-3

❑ Report of quarterly, consolidated data on the foreign exchange contracts and foreign currency denominated assets and liabilities of major market participants.

❑ Reports to be filed throughout the calendar year by each foreign exchange market participant which had more than US$5 billion equivalent in foreign exchange contracts on the last business day of any calendar quarter during the previous year and which does not file Form FC-2.

❑ The report is filed with the appropriate Federal Reserve Bank acting as agent for the US Department of the Treasury and is confidential.

Treasury auction filings
Treasury auction

❑ Treasury security reports filed as necessary. Confirmations must be filed by any customer who is awarded more than US$500 million of US government securities in a Treasury auction. The confirmation must include its reportable net long position, if any.

❑ The confirmation is filed with the Federal Reserve Bank to which the bid was submitted and is not public.

Treasury international capital forms

Forms CM, CQ-1 and CQ-2

❑ Forms filed by US persons who have claims on, or financial liabilities to unaffiliated foreigners, have balances on deposit with foreign banks (in the US or abroad) or otherwise engage in transactions in securities or other financial assets with foreigners. Forms CQ-1 ("financial liabilities to, and claims on, unaffiliated foreigners") and CQ-2 ("commercial liabilities to, and claims on, unaffiliated foreigners") are quarterly reports, which collect data on financial and commercial liabilities to, and claims on, unaffiliated foreigners held by non-banking enterprises in the US, which must be filed when the consolidated total of such liabilities are US$10 million or more during that period. Form CM ("dollar deposit and certificate of deposit claims on banks abroad") is a monthly report whereby non-banking enterprises in the US report their total dollar deposit and certificate of deposit claims on foreign banks, which must be filed when the consolidated total of such claims are US$10 million or more during that period.

❑ The forms are filed with the Federal Reserve Bank of New York and are non-public except for aggregate information.

Form S

❑ Form filed by any US person who purchases or sells US$2 million or more of long-term marketable domestic and foreign securities in a month in direct transactions with foreign persons.

❑ The form is filed with the Federal Reserve Bank of New York and is non-public except as to aggregate information.

Securities and Exchange Commission (SEC)

Sale of securities by an issuer exempt from registration under Reg D or 4(6)

Form D

❑ Notice of sale filed after securities, such as interests in a private hedge fund, are sold in reliance on a Regulation D private placement exemption or a Section 4(6) exemption from the registration provisions of the 1933 Act. The form is filed with the SEC and relevant states and is publicly available.

Secondary sale of restricted and control securities under Rule 144

Form 144

❑ Form filed as notice of the proposed sale of restricted securities or securities held by an affiliate of the issuer in reliance on Rule 144 when the amount to be sold during any three month period exceeds 500 shares or units or has an aggregate sales price in excess of US$10,000. The form is filed with the SEC and the principal national securities exchange, if any, on which such security is traded and is publicly available.

Ownership of equity securities publicly traded in the United States
Schedule 13D
❏ Disclosure report for any investor, including a hedge fund and its fund manager, who is considered beneficially to own more than 5% of a class of equity securities publicly traded in the US. The report identifies the source and amount of the funds used for the acquisition and the purpose of the acquisition.
❏ This reporting requirement is triggered by direct or indirect acquisition of more than 5% of beneficial ownership of a class of equity securities publicly traded in the US Amendments must be filed promptly for material ownership changes. Some investors may instead report on short-form Schedule 13G if they are eligible (see Schedule 13G).
❏ The report is filed with the SEC and is publicly available.

Schedule 13G
❏ Short form disclosure report for any passive investor, including a hedge fund and its fund manager, who would otherwise have to file a Schedule 13D but who owns less than 20% of the subject securities (or is in certain US regulated investment businesses) and has not been purchased for the purpose of influencing control.
❏ This reporting requirement is triggered by direct or indirect acquisition of beneficial ownership of more than 5% of a class of equity securities publicly traded in the US Amendments must be filed annually if there are any changes, and either monthly (for US regulated investment businesses) or promptly (for other passive investors) if ownership changes by more than 5% of the class.
❏ The report is filed with the SEC and is publicly available.

Forms 3, 4 and 5
❏ Every director, officer or owner of more than 10% of a class of equity securities of a domestic public company must file a statement of ownership. The initial filing is on Form 3 and changes are reported on Form 4. The Annual Statement of beneficial ownership of securities is on Form 5. The statements contain information on the reporting person's relationship to the company and on purchases and sales of the equity securities.
❏ Form 3 reporting is triggered by acquisition of more than 10% of the equity securities of a domestic public company, the reporting person becoming a director or officer, or the equity securities becoming publicly traded, as the case may be. Form 4 reporting is triggered by any open market purchase, sale, or an exercise of options of those reporting under Form 3. Form 5 reporting is required annually for those insiders who

have had exempt transactions and have not reported them previously on a Form 4.
❏ The statements are filed with the SEC and are publicly available.

Registered and unregistered institutional investment managers
Form 13F
❏ Quarterly position report for registered and unregistered institutional investment managers (ie, any person, other than a natural person, investing in or buying and selling securities for its own account, and any person exercising investment discretion with respect to the account of any other person) with investment discretion over US$100 million or more in equity securities publicly traded in the United States. Reports contain position information about the equity securities under the discretion of the fund manager, and the type of voting authority exercised by the fund manager.
❏ The reporting requirement is triggered by an institutional investment manager holding equity securities having an aggregate fair market value of at least US$100 million on the last trading day of a calendar year and require a report as of the end of that year and each of the next three quarters.
❏ The reports are filed with the SEC and are publicly available.

Material associated persons of registered broker-dealers
Form 17-H
❏ Material Associated Persons (MAP) reports, filed by registered broker-dealers. Some hedge fund managers are affiliated with registered broker-dealers. MAPs generally include material affiliates and parents and may therefore include an affiliated hedge fund manager or the related hedge fund. Broker-dealers must report (1) organisational chart of the broker-dealer, (2) risk management policies of the broker-dealer, (3) material legal proceedings, and (4) additional financial information including aggregate positions, borrowing and off-balance sheet risk for each MAP.
❏ The reporting requirement is triggered by status as broker or dealer registered under Section 15 of the Exchange Act.
❏ This report is filed with the SEC quarterly and cumulatively at year-end and is not public.
❏ There are also a variety of filings with the SEC and the securities self-regulatory organisations that must be made by registered broker-dealers and their employees who are associated persons.

Commodity Futures Trading Commission (CFTC) and National Futures Association (NFA), registered commodity trading advisors (CTAs) and commodity pool operators (CPOs)

Commodity pool operator and commodity trading advisor registration

❏ An individual or entity that operates or solicits funds for a commodity pool is generally required to register as a commodity pool operator. As a result, a hedge fund manager may be required to register as a commodity pool operator if the hedge fund trades futures or options on futures and the hedge fund manager operates the fund.

❏ An individual or entity that, for compensation or profit, advises others as to the value of or advisability of buying or selling futures contracts or options on futures must generally register as a commodity trading advisor unless it has provided advice to 15 or fewer persons (including each person in an advised fund or pool) in the past 12 months and does not generally hold itself out to the public as a CTA. Providing advice indirectly includes exercising trading authority over a fund or account. A hedge fund manager, therefore, may also be required to register as a CTA if the related hedge fund trades futures or options on futures.

❏ The documents required for registration as a commodity pool operator or commodity trading advisor are: a completed Form 7-R (which provides CPO or CTA information), a completed Form 8-R (which provides biographical data) and fingerprint card, for each principal (defined to include executive officers, directors and 10% owners), branch office manager and associated person (defined to include persons soliciting fund interests or accounts or supervising persons so engaged), and proof of passage of the Series 3 exam for each associated person and proof of passage of the Series 3 and futures branch office manager exams for each branch office manager.

❏ Applications for registration are filed with and approved by the NFA under authority granted to it by the CFTC and the registration documents are generally public except for fingerprint cards, although confidentiality may be requested for certain information relating to the principals.

Form 3-R amend. 7-R

❏ Form used to report any changes to information contained in the basic registration Form 7-R.

❏ The requirement to file this form is triggered by changes in the information provided in Form 7-R.

❏ The form is filed with the NFA and is public, though confidentiality may be requested for certain information relating to the principals.

Form 8-T associated person termination
❏ Form that must be filed within 20 days of the termination of an associated person, principal or branch manager. The form is filed with the NFA and is generally public.

Ethics examination for all registered persons
❏ Ethics training is required under CFTC Reg §3.34 for all associated persons and any individual registered as a CPO or CTA. In connection with the annual registration update, each NFA member will receive a report indicating ethics training due or overdue for its associated persons. The member is responsible for providing proof of ethics training to the NFA, and the NFA will confirm this information to the public.

Annual report
❏ Annual report of a fund that must be filed pursuant to Reg §4.22(c) by that fund's CPO. The annual report must contain certain information, such as actual performance information and fees, and must be distributed to each participant in the fund. The annual report must be filed by a registered CPO with the CFTC within 60 days of the fund's fiscal year-end and is generally publicly available; however, the CFTC is prohibited from disclosing information that would separately disclose the business transactions or market positions of any person or trade secrets or names of any investors.

CPO/CTA questionnaire
❏ Annual compliance questionnaire concerning its business activities for applicants registered as CPOs or CTAs. The questionnaire is filed with the NFA and is not public.

NFA self-audits
❏ In order to satisfy their continuing supervisory responsibilities, NFA members must review their operations on an annual basis using a self-examination checklist. The checklist focuses on a member's regulatory responsibilities and solicits information on whether the member's internal procedures are adequate for meeting those responsibilities.
❏ Registered CPOs and CTAs as members of the NFA are required to conduct such self-audit annually.
❏ A written attestation is then signed and dated by the supervisory personnel that they have reviewed the operations in light of the checklist. This attestation is retained by the member and not forwarded to the NFA and as such is not public.

Claims for exemption

❏ Filings made pursuant to Reg §4.12(b)(3) (notice of claim for exemption from certain requirements by a CPO that complies with the Securities Act and manages a fund with limited trading in commodity futures and options), Reg §4.7(a)(3) (notice of claim for exemption by a CPO with "qualified eligible participants" as investors), and Reg §4.7(b)(3) (notice of claim for exemption by a CTA advising "qualified eligible clients"). Reg §4.7 provides exemptions for qualifying CPO/CTO applicants from most disclosure and other requirements of CPOs and CTAs.

❏ These statements are filed with the CFTC and NFA and are public.

Disclosure document

❏ CPOs and CTAs are generally required to prepare detailed Disclosure documents containing specified information. Such documents are filed with the CFTC and NFA and provided to investors but are not publicly available.

❏ CPOs and CTAs operating under Reg §4.7, however, are exempt from the disclosure document requirement and are required only to provide all material disclosures. In addition, under the exemption provided in Reg §4.8, funds (which would otherwise be treated as commodity pools) with exemptions under Reg §4.12(b) (compliance with the requirements of the Securities Act and certain limits on the trading of commodity futures and options) or which sell interests solely to "accredited investors" and rely on the safe harbour provisions of Rule 506 or 507 of Regulation D under the Securities Act may begin soliciting, accepting and receiving money upon providing the CFTC and the participants with disclosure documents for the fund, which requirement may be satisfied by a private placement memorandum.

Year-end financial reports for §4.7 funds

❏ Annual Report requirements for §4.7 funds (ie, funds, which by having only qualified eligible participants, are exempt from the normal disclosure requirements applicable to commodity pools). The form must contain a Statement of Financial Condition, a Statement of Income (Loss), appropriate footnote disclosure and other material information and a legend as to any claim made for exemption.

❏ The annual report is filed with the CFTC, NFA and distributed to each investor, and the report is not public.

Position reports

Form 40

❏ "Statement of Reporting Trader" for persons who own or control reportable positions in futures. A hedge fund and/or hedge fund manager will be required to file a Form 40 if it holds reportable positions. The

form must be filed within ten business days following the day that a hedge fund's and/or its managers' position equals or exceeds specified levels. Such specified levels are set separately for each type of contract. For example, the reportable level for S&P 500 futures is 600 contracts. The Form 40 requires the disclosure of information about ownership and control of futures and option positions held by the reporting trader as well as the trader's use of the markets for hedging. Hedging exemptions from speculative position limits must be reported.
❏ The form is filed with the CFTC and is not publicly available.

Form 102
❏ Form filed by clearing members, futures commission merchants (FCMs), and foreign brokers, which identifies persons, including hedge funds, having financial interest in, or trading control of, special accounts in futures and options, informs the CFTC of the type of account that is being reported and gives preliminary information regarding whether positions and transactions are commercial or non-commercial in nature. The form must be filed when the account first becomes "reportable" (ie, when it first contains reportable futures or options positions), and updated when information concerning financial interest in, or control of, the special account changes. In addition, the form is used by exchanges to identify accounts reported through their large trader reporting systems for both futures and options.
❏ The form is filed with the CFTC and is non-public.

Selected stock and futures exchange reports
Application for exemption from speculative position limits

Speculative position limit exemption
❏ Application filed for exemption from speculative position limits. Exchanges generally have speculative position limits for physical commodities and stock index contracts, and the CFTC has speculative position limits for agricultural commodities. Exemptions from such limits are generally available for hedging transactions. Financial contracts, such as interest rate contracts, do not have such position limits.
❏ For example, under Rule 543 of the Chicago Mercantile Exchange (CME), persons intending to exceed speculative position limits on S&P 500 contracts must either file the required exemption application and receive approval prior to exceeding such limits or receive verbal approval prior to exceeding such limits and, if approved, file the required application promptly thereafter. Generally, an application for any speculative position limit exemption must show that such position is a bona fide hedging, risk management, arbitrage or spread position.
❏ The filing is made with the appropriate exchange in the case of physical

commodities and stock index contracts and with the CFTC in the case of agricultural commodities.

Federal Trade Commission (FTC)
Filings Made Prior to Mergers and Acquisitions

Hart-Scott-Rodino notice
❏ Notice filed prior to the consummation of certain mergers, acquisitions and joint ventures. After notice is filed there is a waiting period while the FTC and Department of Justice review the competitive effects of the transaction. The notice includes information about the transaction and the participants in the transaction.
❏ The notice and waiting period requirement are generally triggered by the following tests: either the acquiring person or the acquired person must be engaged in US commerce or an activity affecting US commerce, a person with total assets or net sales of US$100 million or more is acquiring voting securities or assets of a person with total assets of US$10 million or more, and as a result of the transaction, the acquiring person will hold 15% or more of the voting securities or assets of the acquired person or an aggregate of US$15 million or more of assets and voting securities of the acquired person. A notice would generally have to be filed for an over US$15 million purchase by a hedge fund with US$100 million in assets if an exemption were not available. Acquisitions of voting securities are exempt from filing if they are made "solely for the purpose of investment" and if, as a result of the acquisition, the securities held do not exceed 10% of the outstanding voting securities of the issuer. Securities are acquired "solely for investment purposes" if the person acquiring the securities has no intention of participating in the formulation, determination, or direction of the basic business decisions of the issuer.
❏ The notice is filed with the FTC and the Department of Justice and is confidential.
❏ This document is reprinted with the permission of the authors. The authors, however, do not endorse any of the other views expressed in this volume.

1   PWG Report, p37.
2   "Cash" refers to cash plus cash equivalents (short-term, high-quality investments).
3   "Cash + Borrowing Capacity" = cash plus access to borrowings, eg, under margin rules or credit lines.
4   As was noted in the recommendations, "sovereign risk" may be viewed either as "credit risk", if the potential loss is related to the financial solvency of the sovereign, or as "market risk", if the potential loss is related to policy decisions made by the sovereign that change the market value of positions (eg, currency controls). "Legal risk", other than those covered by the preceding discussion of "sovereign risk", would be included as "operational risk".

5   Since illiquid instruments with long holding periods will generally not be included in the daily risk monitoring model, valuing these instruments on a daily basis for risk monitoring is not necessary.

6   For a discussion of VAR and VAR calculation techniques, see Philippe Jorion, *Value at Risk: The New Benchmark for Controlling Market Risk* (McGraw-Hill, 1997).

7   "Derivatives: Practices and Practices", Group of Thirty Global Derivatives Study Group, July 1993.

8   Since 1995, the Basle Committee on Banking Supervision and an IOSCO technical committee have been examining the risk management procedures and disclosures of leading banks and securities firms in the industrialised world. The latest survey, released in December 1999, indicated that virtually all banks and securities firms covered by the survey used VAR techniques to measure market risk.

9   "1998 Survey of Derivative and Risk Management Practices by U.S. Institutional Investors", Risk, August, 1999.

10 The Sharpe ratio is attributed to William F. Sharpe, who described a measure of "return to variability" for use in comparing investment performance.

11 Derivative instruments will be required to be carried on balance sheet under Financial Accounting Standard 133, which was scheduled to become effective in 2000.

Findings on Disclosure for Institutional Investors in Hedge Funds

The Investor Risk Committee (IRC) was launched by the International Association of Financial Engineers (IAFE) in January, 2000. To date the IRC of the IAFE has held two working sessions on the topic "What is the right level of disclosure by alternative asset managers?". Members of the IRC soon focused their discussions on investments in hedge funds by institutional investors.

The IRC consists of individuals from hedge fund investment managers (herein referred to as "managers" and from a variety of institutional investors including pension funds, endowments, foundations, insurance companies, fund of funds and others (herein referred to as "investors").

The work of the IRC has come at the right time – it is estimated that investors now make up about 20% of all hedge fund assets and that this will continue to grow – investors observe that hedge funds will help in meeting liability and growth targets.

The IRC's work has resulted in a set of findings that can be used by investors and managers to benchmark their practices in comparison to their peers. After very lively initial debate, members of the IRC soon reached consensus on a number of critical issues. This document sets forth the IRC's findings. It is a starting point that the IRC hopes will encourage greater participation from investors in this rapidly growing area.

For the purposes of this document, the IRC adopts the definition of a hedge fund used in *Sound Practices for Hedge Fund Managers*[1] a pooled investment vehicle that is privately organized, administered by a professional investment management firm . . . and not widely available to the public.

As such, a wide variety of investment vehicles are included in this definition – small and large (in assets or staff), operating in one market or many, following a single, simple strategy or a combination of complex strategies, operating on-shore or off-shore under various organisational structures, etc.

IRC FINDINGS

1. Investors have three primary objectives in seeking disclosure from managers:

   ❏ *Risk monitoring*: ensuring that managers are not taking on risks beyond represented levels in terms of allowable investments, exposures, leverage, etc;
   ❏ *Risk aggregation*: ensuring the investors' ability to aggregate risks across their entire investment programme in order to understand portfolio level implications; and
   ❏ *Strategy drift monitoring*: ensuring the investors' ability to determine whether a manager is adhering to the stated investment strategy or style.

2. IRC members agreed that full position disclosure by managers does not always allow them to achieve their monitoring objectives, and may compromise a hedge fund's ability to execute its investment strategy.

   Despite the fact that many investors receive full position disclosure for many of their investments, the 80 members of the IRC who have participated in the meetings to date have agreed that full position disclosure by managers is not the solution. Managers have expressed significant concerns over the harm that full position disclosure could cause for many common hedge fund strategies (for example macro and risk arbitrage). Investors agreed they did not wish to force disclosure that would be adverse to the manager, and therefore to their investment. In addition, many investors expressed concern over the operational difficulties associated with processing such vast quantities of diverse data.

3. IRC members agreed that the reporting of summary risk, return and position information can be sufficient as an alternative to full position disclosure. Such summary information should be evaluated on four dimensions: content, granularity, frequency, and delay.

   ❏ *Content*: describes the quality and sufficiency of coverage of the manager's activities. This dimension covers information about the risk, return and positions on an actual, as well as on a stress-tested, basis.

❏ *Granularity*: describes the level of detail. Examples are Net Asset Value (NAV) disclosure, disclosure of risk factors (APT[2], VAR[3], etc), disclosure of tracking error or other risk and return measures at the portfolio level, by region, by asset class, by duration, and by significant holdings, etc.

❏ *Frequency*: describes how often the disclosure is made. High turnover trading strategies may require more frequent disclosure (for example, daily) than private or distressed-debt investment funds where monthly or quarterly disclosure is more appropriate.

❏ *Delay*: describes how much of a time lag occurs between when the fund is in a certain condition and when that fact is disclosed to investors. A fund might agree to either full or summary position disclosure, but only after the positions are no longer held.

4. IRC members have agreed that usability of any alternative disclosure depends upon sufficient understanding of the definitions, calculation methodologies, assumptions and data employed by the manager. This may be accomplished in a variety of fashions including: discussions between investors and managers; by the manager providing for adequate transparency of their process; or via independent verification.

5. IRC members should benchmark their practices in relation to their peers. IRC members agreed that a major challenge to peer group performance and risk comparisons, as well as aggregation across managers, is the use of a variety of calculation methodologies, assumptions and data that is employed in the market place. IRC members do not, however, feel that "one size fits all". Multiple peer groups may be relevant, depending on the nature of the investor, as well as the strategies employed by the manager. Investors and managers believe that an industry effort should be made to improve the ability to conduct comparisons of managers as well as multi-manager portfolio analysis.

6. IRC members have agreed that detailed reporting is not a substitute for initial and ongoing due diligence reviews, on-site visits and appropriate dialogue between investors and managers.

7. IRC members agree that market, credit, leverage, liquidity and operational risks are interrelated. Accordingly, members believe that exposure to these risks in combination should be included in the dialogue between investors and managers.

CONCLUSION

The IRC's goal is to provide the consensus of opinion from substantial groups of managers and investors in response to the question "What is the right level of disclosure by hedge funds?". The IRC invites all managers, investors and other interested parties to comment and assist this industry group in the evolution of the document. The IRC, through the IAFE, plans additional forums on related topics and seeks your input regarding items of interest to you and on the IRC's work during 2001. Topics suggested at the time of writing include:

❏ developing an industry consensus on a "generally accepted technique" for mapping position data into risk factors, and/or methodologies for calculation of risk statistics;

❏ developing a questionnaire to be filled out by managers that will generate a "scatter plot" of current practices;

❏ developing a questionnaire to be filled out by investors that will address minimum standards for the evaluation of alternative asset managers; and

❏ developing sample templates for disclosure within various strategy types, including sample methods for bucketing managers into various strategy types, and how to handle the "other" category of managers.

1   Reprinted as the first part of the appendix.
2   APT refers to the Arbitrage Pricing Theory, but we consider any models that use a linear combination of risk factors that can be combined to explain the risk of a particular holding or portfolio of holdings.
3   VAR refers to Value-at-Risk, a probabilistic statement about the estimated capital at risk of loss within a given confidence interval over a period of time.

What is the Optimal Portfolio Risk Measurement? A Review of Value-at-Risk

Sam Y. Chung

Long Island University

Value-at-risk (VAR), a primary tool for financial risk assessment, has become as commonly used a term in corporate and investment analysis as the Capital Asset Pricing Model (CAPM) or Markowitz portfolio theory. While a variety of VAR definitions exists, VAR is generally defined as an amount lost on a portfolio with a given small probability over a fixed number of days. The major challenge in implementing VAR analysis is the specification of the probability distribution of extreme returns used in the calculation of the VAR estimate. Since VAR estimation is, by its nature, highly dependent on good predictions of uncommon events, or catastrophic risk, any statistical method used for VAR estimation has to have the prediction of tail events as its primary goal.

The concept and the use of VAR is fairly recent. VAR was first deployed by major financial firms in the late 1980s and its use has exploded since that time. Consequently, numerous VAR-related academic literatures have been published in various journals (Table 1 shows a summary and main results of a selected bibliography). VAR can be used for a variety of purposes, such as monitoring managers, tracking portfolio exposures, tracking formal models of risk exposure (eg, guaranteed funds), as well as numerous other applications including optimal hedging.[1] However, statistical techniques and rules of thumb that have proven useful in the prediction of an intra-day and day-to-day risk, are not necessarily appropriate for VAR analysis (see Duffie and Pan, (1997) and Jorion (1997)).

The development of techniques to evaluate and forecast the risk of uncommon events has moved at a rapid rate. These method fall into three main classes:[2]

1. parametric prediction of conditional volatilities, of which JP Morgan's *RiskMetrics* is the best known;

2. non-parametric prediction of unconditional volatilities such as techniques based on historical simulation or stress-testing methods; and[3]
3. semi-parametric method for VAR estimation which is a mixture of the first two approaches, where it combines non-parametric historical simulation with parametric estimation of the tail of the return distribution.

In the following sections these three major categories of VAR modelling and their advantages, disadvantages and appropriate usage are discussed.

Definition of value-at-risk

Value-at-risk (VAR) is a single statistical measure of maximum possible portfolio losses. Specifically, it is a measure of losses due to "normal" market movements. Losses greater than the VAR are suffered only with a specified small probability. VAR aggregates all of the risk in a portfolio into a single number suitable for use in the boardroom, reporting to a regulator, or disclosure in an annual report.

Mathematically, VAR is defined as: the expected loss of a portfolio that will occur (1) with probability α, (2) over some time interval, t. VAR is the $(1-\alpha)$ quantitile of the profit & loss distribution, ie, it satisfies the relation:

$$Pr(v(w) \leq VAR) = 1-\alpha$$

where we assume that the profit-loss distribution is a continuous and strictly monotone function.

In order to compute VAR, we need to identify the basic market rates and prices that affect the value of the portfolio. These basic market rates and prices are the "market factors". It is necessary to identify a limited number of basic market factors simply because otherwise the complexity of trying to come up with a portfolio level quantitative measure of market risk explodes.

NON-PARAMETRIC APPROACH
Historical simulation

Historical simulation (HS) is a simple, theoretical approach that requires relatively few assumptions about the statistical distributions of the underlying market factors. Instead of making distributional assumptions about returns, past returns are used to predict future returns. As shown in Table 3, the advantage of HS is that few assumptions are required and the method is easy to implement. The primary assumption is that the distribution of the returns in the portfolio is constant over the sample period. Historical simulation has been shown to compare well with other methods (Mahoney 1996), however past extreme returns can be a poor predictor of extreme events, and as a result HS should be used with care. The reason is

Table 1 Summary of selected research regarding value-at-risk methodology

Bibliography	Title	Topic	Major Results
Ait-Sahalia, Yacine and Lo, Andrew, NBER (1997)	"Non-parametric Risk Measurement and Implied Risk Aversion"	A nonparametric VAR measure that incorporates economic valuation according to the state price density associated with the underlying price process.	▪ The state-price density yields VAR values that are adjusted for risk aversion, time preferences, and other variation in economic valuation.
Jones,M. and Schaefer S, London School of Economics (1997)	"Non-linear Value at Risk"	An alternative approach which uses a quadratic approximation to the relation between asset values and the risk factors.	▪ The quadratic approximation VAR is more accurate for non-linear assets and less computationally intensive then the linear method.
Danielsson, J. and de Vries, C., Risk 11 (1998)	"Value at Risk and Extreme Returns"	A VAR which involves modelling the tails of financial returns explicitly with a tail kernel estimator.	▪ For a sample of US stock returns, the estimates from applying the tail kernel are more accurate in the VAR prediction than those from JP Morgan's RiskMetrics.
Garman, Mark, Risk 9 (1997)	"Improving VaR"	VAR from two basic calculations;(a) the total, diversified VAR for a portfolio and (b) the undiversified VAR for some portfolio subset.	▪ Component VAR may be based upon the VAR-Delta concept and the relationship of the VAR-Delta to the VAR is analogous to the relationship between the option delta and the option price.
Longin, Francois M., Journal of Banking and Finance (1999)	"From VaR to Stress Testing: The Extreme Value Approach"	Extreme value theory and its application to the computation of the VAR of a position .	▪ An approach based on extreme values allows quantification of behaviour of extreme movements in prices and rates.

Table 1 Continued

Lucas, A. and Klaasen, P., *Journal of Portfolio Management* 25 (1998)	"Extreme Returns, Downside Risk, and Optimal Asset Allocation"	A discrepancy between the tail fatness of the true distribution of asset returns and that of the distribution used by investment managers.	■ Minimising the absolute mismatch between the normal and actual or true VAR leads to the choice of a Gaussian maximum quasi-likelihood estimator.
Duffie, D. and Jun Pan, *Journal of Derivatives* 4 (1997)	"An Overview of Value at Risk"	A broad overview of models of VAR emphasising the role of price jumps and of stochastic volatility in determining the tail fatness.	● Overview methods for approximating VAR of derivatives based on delta and gamma and introduce an extensive numerical example illustrates the accuracy of various methods.
Hall, John and A. White, *Journal of Derivatives* 5 (1998)	"Value at Risk when Daily Changes in Market Variables Are Not Normally Distributed"	A simple approach for dealing with the tail characteristics of actual returns distributions, by mapping between the percentiles of the actual returns distribution and the normal.	■ The alternative allows both a simulation of normal variates to produce returns distributed according to the actual distribution and estimates of correlations from JP Morgan's *RiskMetrics*.
Butler J.S. and Barry Schachter, *Review of Derivatives Research* 1 (1998)	"Estimating Value at Risk with a Precision Measure by Combining Kernel Estimation With Historical Simulation"	A new VAR estimator that uses a Gaussian kernel and Gaussian quadrature in estimating moments of the pdf of the p-th percentile of the return distribution.	■ This estimator offers an improvement over the historical simulation because, unlike the usual approach, it produces a standard error which can be used to gauge the precision of the estimated VAR.

that by its nature, HS has nothing to say about the probability outcomes which are worse than the sample minimum return. However, HS does not give very accurate probability estimates for the borderline of the sample return and the choice of the sample size can have a large impact on the value it predicts. In addition, the simplicity of HS makes it difficult to conduct sensitivity experiments, where a VAR is evaluated under a number of scenarios.

A major problem with HS is the discreteness of extreme returns. In the interior, the empirical sampling distribution is very dense, with the adjacent observations very close to each other. As a result, the sampling distribution is very smooth in the interior. The closer one gets to the extreme, the longer the interval between adjacent returns becomes (see Danielsson and de Vries, 1997). Extreme observations are typically the most important for VAR analysis. However since these values are clearly discrete, the VAR will also be discrete, and hence be either under-predicted or over-predicted.[4] As a result, VAR estimates that are dependent on the tails will be measured discretely with a high variance, making HS in many cases a poor predictor of the VAR.

Butler and Schachter (1996) proposed a variation of HS by use of "a kernel smoother" to estimate the distribution of returns. This type of methodology has both advantages and drawbacks. The advantage is that a properly constructed kernel distribution provides a smooth sampling distribution. Hence sensitive experiments can be readily constructed, and variable insight can be gained about the return process. Additionally, such distribution may not be as sensitive to the sample length as HS is. Note that these advantages are dependent on a properly constructed kernel distribution. In kernel estimation, the specific choice of a kernel and window length is extremely important. While kernel estimation will provide good estimates for the interior, there is no reason to believe that even the most careful kernel estimator will describe the tails adequately.[5]

Aït-Sahalia and Lo's method

In their article, (1998) Aït-Sahalia and Lo propose an alternative to statistical VAR, which incorporates many other aspects of market risk that are central to the practice of risk management. The idea is based on the seminal idea of Arrow (1964) and Debreu (1959), the Arrow-Debreu security which is recognised as the fundamental building block of all modern financial asset pricing theories, including the CAPM, and the Black and Scholes (1973) and Merton (1973) option-pricing models.

By construction, Arrow-Debreu prices[6] have a probability-like interpretation; they are non-negative and sum to unity. However, since they are market prices determined in equilibrium by supply and demand, they contain much more information than statistical models of prices. Also, under some conditions, Arrow-Debreu prices reduce the sample probabilities on which statistical VAR measures are based, hence *the standard measures of VAR are special cases of the Arrow-Debreu framework*.

The fact that the market prices of the Arrow-Debreu securities need not be equal across states implies that a one-dollar gain need not be worth the same in every state of nature. The worth of one dollar in a given state is precisely the Arrow-Debreu price of that security. Therefore, we can use Arrow-Debreu securities to measure an alternative VAR (economic-VAR). Furthermore, the economic-VAR incorporates and reflects the combined effects of aggregate risk preferences, supply and demand, and probabilities. Additionally, if aggregate preferences were risk natural, economic-VAR reduces to a special case, hence no information is lost in using economic-VAR as a starting point for the risk management process. Economic-VAR is, however, computationally complex.

Butler and Schachter's method

Butler and Schachter (1996) used a Gaussian kernel and Gaussian quadrature in estimating moments of the probability density functions (PDF) of the distribution of the return on a trading portfolio. They offer this estimator as an improvement over the usual approach to historical simulation VAR because it provides a standard error which can be used to estimate more precise VAR.

Thus, their kernel attaches a normal PDF to each data point[7] and the smoothing is accomplished by centring each PDF on the data point with a standard deviation.[8] They derive the PDF of the order statistic and calculate its mean and variance, then the mean of that PDF is the estimate of VAR. They employ Gaussian quadrature to calculate both the mean of the PDF of the percentile (for the estimate of the VAR) and the variance of the PDF (for the standard error of the estimate).

PARAMETRIC APPROACH

In parametric forecasting, the predicted future volatility of an asset is an explicit function of past returns, and the estimated model parameters. The most common models are the unconditional normal with frequently updated variance estimate, or explicit models for conditional heteroscedasticity like the GARCH model, with normal innovations.

JP Morgan's *RiskMetrics*

This model is basically a non-stationary Garch (1, 1) model. The normal Garch (1, 1) model is a generalisation of the Arch model introduced by Engle (1982) with a more parsimonious parameterisation and better convergence properties.

The simple GARCH (1, 1) model is:

$$R_t = C + \varepsilon_t$$

$$\sigma_t^2 = w + \alpha\varepsilon_{t-1}^2 + \beta\sigma_{t-1}^2$$

where R_t denotes the daily return, and

σ_t^2 is the conditional variance of the ε_t, for t = 1, . . ., T.

In this basic Garch model, the conditional variance is assumed to be normal with mean zero. Non-negativity constraints on the parameters are necessary to ensure that the conditional variance estimates are always positive, and parameters are estimated using constrained maximum likelihood.

Garch models with normal innovations have been proved valuable in forecasting common volatilities, however they perform poorly in predicting extreme observations or spikes in returns. The normality assumption is primarily a matter of conversions and a Garch model with normal innovations can easily be estimated, with the most common specification being the Student-t distribution.

The advantage of the Student-t innovations is that they are thick-tailed and hence will, in general, provide better predictive densities; note that the Student-t contains Gaussian error as a special case. The disadvantages of non-normal innovations are several; eg, multivariate versions of such models are typically hard to estimate and recursive forecasts of future volatilities are difficult for most distributions, since they are typically not self-additive.

Variance-covariance approach (analytic approach)

The variance-covariance approach is based on the assumption that the underlying market factors have a multivariate normal distribution. In using this assumption, it is possible to determine the distribution of mark-to-market portfolio profits and losses, which is also normal. Once the distribution of possible portfolio profits and losses has been obtained, standard mathematical properties of normal distributions are used to determine the loss that will be equalled or exceeded x% of the time.

There are also various multivariate volatility models which can be used for VAR calculations (Risk Conference, 1998). Some of the multivariate Garch (MGarch) model are introduced and compared in the following section.

Between univariate and multivariate Garch models, the issue is how to parameterise the elements of the covariance matrix. In a univariate Garch model, the variance depends on the information set:

$$\sigma_t = f(\varepsilon_{t-1}, \varepsilon_{t-2}, K) \quad \text{where } \sigma_t \text{ and } \varepsilon_{t-1} \text{ are scalars.}$$

In the multivariate Garch model, however, the covariance matrix depends on the information set:

$$\Omega_t = f(\varepsilon_{t-1}, \varepsilon_{t-2}, K)$$
$$= E_{t-1}(R_t - \mu_t)(R_t - \mu_t)$$

where ε_{t-1} is a N vector and Ω_t is an N $\times$ N conditional covariance matrix, given all information available at time t–1.

Various types of multivariate Garch models are compared in Table 2.

Table 2
Multivariate GARCH Model

Model name	**VECH (Bollerslev, Engle and Woolridge, 1988)**
Basic concept	Each element of covariance process follows its own independent vector-ARMA pro
Scalar notation	$\sigma_{ij,t} = w_{ij} + a_{ij}\varepsilon_{i,t-1} + b_{ij}\sigma_{ij,t-1}$
Matrix notation	$vech(\Omega_t) = W + A \cdot vech(\varepsilon_{t-1}\varepsilon'_{t-1}) + B \cdot vech(\Omega_{t-1})$
Pro	Flexible/easy interpretation of parameters/simple hypothesis tests
Con	Diagonality restrictions imposed/ only positive definite by chance
Study-application	Time-varying betas/time-varying hedge ratios(futures hedge ratio)
Model name	**BEKK (Engle and Kroner, 1995)**
Basic concept	N different portfolios derive the covariance matrix
Scalar notation	$\sigma_{ij,t} = w_{ij} + \lambda_i\lambda_j\varepsilon_{p,t-1} + \lambda_i\lambda_j\sigma_{rs,t-1}$
Matrix notation	$\Omega_t = \Omega_o + A'\varepsilon_{t-1}\varepsilon'_{t-1}A + B'\Omega_{t-1}B$
Pro	Positive definite/ flexible and general
Con	Large number of parameters/ estimation can be difficult
Study-application	Risk premium in currency forward market/ uncovered interest rate parity analysis
Model name	**F-ARCH (Factor ARCH, Engle, 1987)**
Basic concept	Limited number of portfolios derive the covariance matrix
Scalar notation	$\sigma_{ij,t} = w_{ij} + \lambda_i\lambda_j\varepsilon^2_{p,t-1} + \lambda_i\lambda_j\sigma_{p,t-1}$
Matrix notation	$\Omega_t = \Omega_0 + \lambda\lambda'(w'\varepsilon_{t-1}\varepsilon'_{t-1}w) + \lambda\lambda'(w'\Omega_{t-1}w)$
Pro	Can be estimated on bigger systems/ guaranteed positive definite/ useful interpreta
Con	Restrictive/ correlations almost constant
Study-application	Modelling term structure dynamics/ modelling stock price dynamics
Model name	**CCORR (Constant Correlations, Bollerslev, 1990)**
Basic concept	Keep correlations fixed and let covariance dynamics be driven by the variance dyna
Scalar notation	$\sigma_{ij,t} = \rho_{ij}\sqrt{\sigma_{ii,t}\sigma_{jj,t}}$,where $\sigma_{kk,t} = GARCH$
Matrix notation	$\Omega_t = \Lambda_t R \Lambda_t$, where $\Lambda_t = diagonal \{\sigma_{11,t}, \Lambda, \sigma_{NN,t}\}$ and $R = \{\rho_{ij}\}$
Pro	Easy to estimate even for large system/ positive definite if R is positive definite
Con	Correlations are constant, making forecasts less useful/very similar to stacked univariate GARCH models
Study-application	EMU currency volatility/dynamic hedge ratios

---

SEMI-PARAMETRIC APPROACH

Economic analysis often depends on assessment of the probability of extreme quantiles (see Danielsson and De Vries (1997)). For example, insurance companies focus on the probability of ruin, and commercial banks use the VAR methodology to calculate the loss that can be incurred with a given low probability on their trading portfolio. Accurate estimation of the borderline in sample and out of sample combinations is essential for these problems. The tail characteristics are also important for econometric issues such as the convergence rate of regression estimators and selection of appropriate test statistics.

Danielsson and de Vries (1997) proposed the semi-parametric model in their Extreme Value Theory, comparing with HS and JP Morgan's *RiskMetrics* on a portfolio of stock returns and derivatives. For predictions of low probability worst outcomes, *RiskMetrics* analysis underpredicts the VAR while HS overpredicts the VAR. However, the estimates obtained from applying the semi-parametric method are more accurate in the VAR prediction. This value can be estimated by bootstrapping.

WHICH METHOD IS BEST?

With three methods from which to choose, the obvious question is: *does the optimal VAR method exist? And if so, which method of VAR is the best?* Unfortunately, there is no easy answer. The methods differ in their ability to capture the risk of non-linear instruments, ease of implementation, ease of explanation to senior management, flexibility in analysing the effect of changes in the assumptions, and reliability of the results. The best method will therefore be determined by which dimensions the risk manager finds most important. Table 3 summarises how the three methods differ.

Table 3
Comparison of Main VAR Categories

	Approach (method)		
	Non-parametric (Historical Simulation)	Parametric (Variance-Covariance)	Semiparametric (Monte Carlo)
Calculation involved	Historical data set Simulate portfolio using historical returns as actual return distribution	Volatility and correlation matrix Matrix algebra to arrive at VAR	Volatility and correlation matrix Monte Carlo simulation to generate portfolio return distribution
Pros	Naturally address the "fat cells" problem Performs well under backtesting Capture non-linear risk	Easy to understand Least computationally intensive Industry standard	Accommodates any statistical assumptions about risk factors. Capture non-linear risk
Cons	Relies on history Computationally intensive data intensive	May mis-state non-linear risks "Fat-tail" problem	May have sampling error
Appropriate for	Both Linear and Non-linear instruments	Only Linear instruments	Both Linear and Non-linear instruments

Estimating parameters of the wrong distribution typically implies incorrect extreme estimations, both because of mis-specification and because the data in the centre of the empirical distribution have too much influence over the parameter estimates of the wrong model. However, if only the tails are modelled, this influence is absent. The semi-parametric model may be superior to a non-parametric model because the latter is difficult to use for constructing out-of-sample estimates. Historical simulation performs better in predicting the VAR, but suffers from a high variance and discrete sampling far out in the tails. Moreover, HS is unable to address losses which are outside the sample. The performance of the extreme value estimator method performs better than both plain-vanilla *RiskMetrics* and HS in the rail. If one is only interested in the extreme combinations, one should rely on the asymptotic form of the tail distribution instead of having to model the whole distribution. However, the area of extreme value methods has not been well-developed yet, compared to other risk measurement areas. There is no single, completely dominant extreme-value risk measurement model in the area, although there exists several applications of the tail estimators.

CONCLUSION

In value-at-risk (VAR), as in many other areas of investment theory or financial engineering, the conceptual or theoretical foundation of the risk management principals are well known. In application, however, many of the modelling approaches used to apply these principals contains potential model risk or implementation risk. VAR is not a new concept. Estimation of portfolio risk and measurement of the probability of potential loss has always been a central part of investment and risk management. What is new is that both regulatory and technological advances have added many refinements to the process. Moreover, since there is no fundamental theory deriving the modelling process, one can never obtain an "optimal risk management" model but only prove that other models or approaches are wrong or not suitable for certain pricing processes. Put simply, one must continually keep testing the various approaches in as many different ways as possible to see when they work and when they do not. Investment and risk managers can at least have the comfort of knowing that if their present approaches are not "too right", at the same time they may, at least, not be "too wrong".

1   Research on the application of various VAR approaches to the existing portfolio has been reported by authors like Culp, Mensink, and Neves (1998); Marshall and Siegel (1996).

2   Given the extent of the literature on various approaches to VAR estimation and the extent of potential model risk or systems risk (application risk of the model), this chapter limits its review to three main categories of VAR models.

3   Marshall and Siegel (1996) tested the Risk Metrics in application by giving the same portfolio to a number of risk management vendors. Each vendor used his or her own inputs to value the securities and the portfolio with the same VAR system (*RiskMetrics*). Not surprisingly, as financial instruments increased in complexity, wide variations in output resulted. The article also reported greater variation in the *RiskMetrics* based VAR results than encountered in various non-parametric results. The authors concluded that both model risk and application risk (systems risk) may result in requiring an independent body to determine a single approach to VAR risk measurement and pricing processes if VAR results are to attain industry standards.

4   In the empirical study (Danielsson and de Vries, 1997), this effect is somewhat more pronounced for the individual asset than for the market portfolio S&P500, due to diversification. Furthermore, the variance of the extreme order statistics is very high.

5   For example, to the degree that financial data are, in general, thick tailed with high excess kurtosis, a Gaussial kernel, which assumes that the estimated distribution has the same shape as the normal, is unsuitable for financial data.

6   Arrow-Debreu prices are determined by the combination of investors' preferences, budget

dynamics, information structure, and the imposition of market-clearing conditions; ie, general equilibrium conditions.

7   Note that the use of a normal (Gaussian) kernel estimator does not make the ultimate estimation of parametric VAR.

8   Bandwidth, here, they used US0.9\sigma$n$^{-0.2}$, where σ is the standard deviation of the data estimated from the available observation and n is the sample size. This bandwidth is based on Silverman (1986).

BIBLIOGRAPHY

Aït-Sahalia, Y., and A. Lo, 1998, "Nonparametric Risk Management and Implied Risk Aversion", Working Paper.

Alexander, C., and C. Leigh, 1997, "On the Covariance Matrices Used In VAR Models", *Journal of Derivatives* 4, pp. 50–62.

Bahar, R., M. Gold, T. Kitto and C. Polizu, 1997, "Making the Best of the Worst", *Risk* 10, pp. 100–3.

Baldoni, R. J., and G. J. Yeager, 1996, "Value-At-Risk Can and Should Be Used By Corporates", *Treasury Management International,* October, pp. 24–33.

Beckstrom, R., 1995, "VAR, the Next Generation", *Derivatives Strategy,* October, pp. 37–46.

Beder, T., 1995, "VAR: Seductive But Dangerous", *Financial Analysts Journal,* September/October, pp. 12–24.

Blanco, C., and M. B. Garman, 1998, *New Advances in Value at Risk: Applications of VAR Delta, VAR Beta, and Component VAR.*

Butler, J. S., and B. Schachter, 1998, "Estimating Value at Risk With a Precision Measure By Combining Kernel Estimation With Historical Simulation", *Review of Derivatives Research* 1, pp. 371–90.

Culp, C. L., R. Mensink and A. Neves, 1998, "Value at Risk for Asset Managers", *Derivatives Quarterly* 5(2), pp. 21–33.

Danielsson, J., P. Hartmann and C. G. de Vries, 1998, "The Cost of Conservatism: Extreme Returns, Value-at-Risk, and the Basle Multiplication Factor", *Risk* 11(1), pp. 101–03.

Danielsson, J., and C. G. de Vries, 1997, "Value at Risk and Extreme Returns", Working Paper.

Duarte, A. M., 1998, "Optimal Value at Risk Hedge Using Simulation Methods", *Derivatives Quarterly* 5(2), pp. 67–75.

Duffie, D., and J. Pan, 1997, "An Overview of Value at Risk", *Journal of Derivatives* 4, pp. 7–49.

Garman, M. B., 1996a, "Improving on VAR", *Risk* 9(5), pp. 61–3.

Garman, M. B., 1996b, "Making VAR More Flexible", *Derivatives Strategy,* 1–5, April, pp. 52–3.

Ho, T., M. Chen and F. Eng, 1996, "VAR Analytics: Portfolio Structure, Key Rate Convexities and VAR Betas", *Journal of Portfolio Management* 23, pp. 89–98.

Hull, J., and A. White, 1998, "Value at Risk When Daily Changes in Market Variables Are Not Normally Distributed", *Journal of Derivatives* 5, pp. 9–19.

Jorion, P., 1996a, "Value at Risk: The New Benchmark for Controlling Market Risk", *Irwin Professional.*

Jorion, P., 1996b, "Risk 2: Measuring the Risk in Value-At-Risk", *Financial Analysts Journal* 52, pp. 14–24.

Jorion, P., 1997, "In Defense of VAR", *Derivatives Strategy* 2, pp. 20–3.

Marshall, C., and M. Siegel, 1997, "Value at Risk: Implementing A Risk Management Standard", *Journal of Derivatives* 4, pp. 11–20.

McCarthy, M., 1999, "Value at Risk in an Investment Management Business: Enhancing the Control Framework", *Bank Accounting & Finance* 10, pp. 17–21.

Schachter, B., 1997, "The Lay Person's Introduction to Value at Risk", *Financial Engineering News* 1, pp. 5–9.

Schachter, B., 1998, "The Value of Stress Testing in Market Risk Management", in T. Haight (ed), *Derivatives Risk Management Service.*

The Risk of Hedge Funds

Alexander M. Ineichen

UBS Warburg

Probably every disclaimer by a financial wholesaler or intermediary contains some sort of warning that past performance is no guarantee for future performance – hedging the firm against the abstinence of common sense. The following anecdote best describes this issue with past performance of hedge funds. At a 1995 seminar on hedge fund selection, a European institutional investor stood up:[1]

> History and statistics are worth nothing! You just can't tell how a hedge fund
> will perform, from its past performance!

A later conversation with this individual revealed that his institutional hedge fund portfolio had been invested heavily in macro funds. This touches two aspects of performance analysis of hedge fund returns: diversification and outliers. The investor was not diversified since many styles had positive returns in 1994. Furthermore, macro funds, as a group, have been extremely successful during the 1990s, with 1994 being an exception (outlier).

This said, there is no guarantee that future hedge fund performance will be equal to past risk/return characteristics. However, as Winston Churchill once put it: "The further backward you look, the further forward you can see."

This chapter is designed to understand the main risk/return as well as correlation characteristics in the past. The understanding of a strategy's concept plus knowledge of how the strategy performed in the past will allow us to make educated estimates of how these strategies will perform in the future. We believe that, over time, some of the hedge fund return and risk characteristics should remain fairly stable.

All returns shown in this chapter were on a US$ and total return basis net of fees.[2] Our main focus was on standard risk and return performance characteristics (Sharpe ratio), higher moment risk factors (outliers in the return distribution) and downside correlation.

HEDGE FUND STRATEGIES
The beta of hedge funds can differ widely

We believe that one of the most important issues from an investor's perspective in terms of investing in hedge funds is the knowledge about the different investment styles in the hedge fund industry. Equity investors are typically familiar with the fact that the equity market has different sectors and styles to invest in and that the different styles have different return, risk and correlation characteristics. The same is true for hedge funds. There is a vast amount of different strategies available. The style differences of hedge funds differ widely in one respect with styles and sectors in the equity arena. In equities, all sector and style indices have a beta (exposure) to the market of around one. The beta of the different hedge fund styles varies from minus a multiple of one (short seller using leverage) to a multiple of plus one (long-biased fund using leverage).

Figure 1 segments some hedge fund strategies into styles and sub-styles. The classification is subjective. As with equities, there are different style classification systems in the market. In this chapter we focused on exposure (and therefore correlation) to the underlying market of the different strategies.

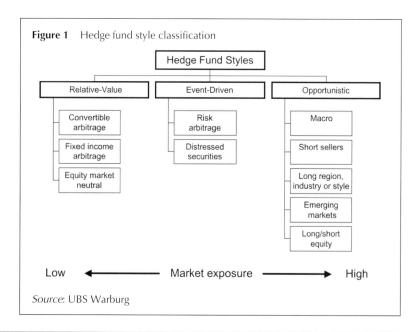

Figure 1 Hedge fund style classification

Source: UBS Warburg

One of the main differences between hedge funds and other money managers is their heterogeneity and the fact that hedge funds are less regulated. This means categorising hedge funds is difficult and the above classification is therefore subjective, inconsistent with some hedge fund data vendors and incomplete. Any classification of hedge funds is an attempt at fitting something into a box. However, some hedge fund strategies do not fit into a box. There are many hedge funds, which do not fit into this classification and/or are hybrids of the above structure.

Correlation with equity market as main classifier

At the first level we distinguish between relative-value, event-driven and 'the rest' which we called 'opportunistic' in Figure 1. The main reason for this distinction is that relative-value had historically very little exposure/correlation to the overall market, whereas event-driven had little exposure/correlation and all other styles have variable degrees of exposure to the market.

We believe the main bone of contention in Figure 1 is probably the classification of long/short equity as opportunistic.[3] Long/short equity is the largest style in terms of number of managers pursuing the strategy. However, the managers in this group are not homogeneous. Some have long biases, others are market-neutral or short or vary over time. The

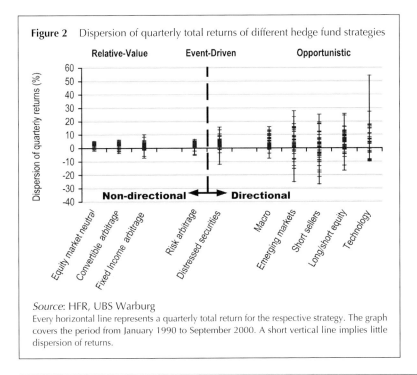

Figure 2 Dispersion of quarterly total returns of different hedge fund strategies

Source: HFR, UBS Warburg

Every horizontal line represents a quarterly total return for the respective strategy. The graph covers the period from January 1990 to September 2000. A short vertical line implies little dispersion of returns.

managers in the long/short equity sub-style, who are close to market-neutral are effectively pursuing a relative-value strategy and therefore are closer to the 'equity market neutral' camp. However, we justify the classification of long/short equity style as opportunistic because most managers have historically made the bulk of their gains on the long side, and, partly as a consequence, maintain net long exposure.

Other classification systems distinguish between directional and non-directional at the first level instead of relative-value, event-driven and opportunistic. With such a classification, risk arbitrage (aka merger arbitrage) would be defined as non-directional, whereas distressed securities as directional. Figure 2 would justify such a classification system as the dispersion of returns of risk arbitrage are much lower than for distressed securities which have a strong directional bias.

RISKS OF RELATIVE-VALUE STRATEGIES
Convertible Arbitrage
❏ The HFRI Convertible Arbitrage index has performed in line with the MSCI World over the past 10.5 years. However, volatility was much lower. The index underperformed MSCI Europe and the S&P 500 index.
❏ The smoothness of the wealth creation is worth pointing out. The wealth profile was flat on two occasions and slightly negative on one occasion. In 1990 convertible arbitrage added little value due to global recession

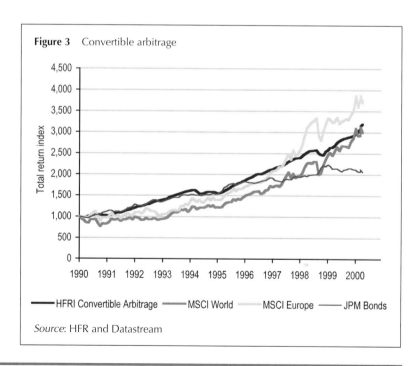

Figure 3   Convertible arbitrage

Source: HFR and Datastream

and in 1994 due to US interest rate rises. The fall in autumn 1998 was due to widening of most arbitrage spreads and redemptions from the industry due to LTCM.

Table 1 Convertible arbitrage risk and return characteristics

	# of monthly returns*	Annual return (%)	Volatility (%)	Sharpe ratio**	Worst 1-month return (%)	Negative months (%)	Worst 1-year return (%)
S&P 500 (Total return)	124	18.3	13.7	0.97	−14.5	32	−3.1
MSCI World (Total return)	124	11.7	14.1	0.48	−13.3	36	−16.5
MSCI Europe (Total return)	124	13.5	14.7	0.58	−12.6	34	−12.1
HFRI Convertible Arbitrage Index	124	11.9	3.5	1.96	−3.2	13	−3.8
Hennessee HF Index – Conv Arb	88	10.1	3.7	1.36	−3.3	14	−7.1
CSFB/Tremont Convertible Arbitrage	76	9.3	5.2	0.83	−4.7	18	−9.0

Source: HFR, Hennessee, CSFB/Tremont, Datastream, UBS Warburg calculations
* ending April 2000; ** based on risk free rate of 5%

❏ Annual returns were around 11% achieved with a volatility of around 3.5%. The high year of the HFRI Convertible Arbitrage Index was in 1995 at 19.9%, and the low year was 1994 at -3.7%. As of July 2000, the strategy performed by 12.4%.
❏ Convertible arbitrage has one of the lowest volatility averages of all strategies analysed in this report. Annual volatility was around 3–4%. Only equity-market-neutral strategies had a lower volatility.
❏ Convertible arbitrage was among the top three strategies based on the worst monthly loss and number of negative months as a percentage of the total. It is mid-range in terms of high Sharpe ratio, worst one-year cumulative return and low correlation to equity markets.

The first of the following two graphs shows the returns of various hedge fund indices with some equity and bond indices. The second graph compares monthly total MSCI World returns with HFRI Convertible Arbitrage Index returns.

❏ Figure 4 illustrates the attractiveness of convertible arbitrage. The returns are positive and consistent across different data vendors and time periods. The volatility is lower than the volatility in bonds and the returns average around 11%, which is higher than long-term equity returns.
❏ Figure 5 shows that the returns are derived from convertible arbitrage and not by taking on equity market risk. The intercept (alpha) of the HFRI Convertible Arbitrage index to the MSCI World is 0.86. The slope

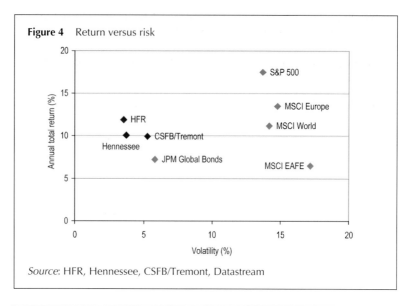

Figure 4 Return versus risk

Source: HFR, Hennessee, CSFB/Tremont, Datastream

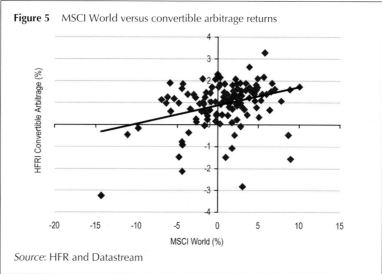

Figure 5 MSCI World versus convertible arbitrage returns

Source: HFR and Datastream

(beta) measuring the exposure to the equity market is very low, around 0.08.

❑ Convertible arbitrage strategies can yield positive returns in equity bull markets despite their short stock positions. In Q4 99, for example, convertible arbitrage had positive returns despite world equity markets rising 17% during the quarter. Losses in short equity positions were balanced by an increase in equity volatility and because certain pockets, like investing in new issues and positive developments in a 'busted' or low credit quality convertible, provided a source of returns.

The following table shows some further statistics of convertible arbitrage.

Table 2 Statistical analysis of convertible arbitrage returns

	Alpha to MSCI World	Beta to MSCI World	Skew	Excess kurtosis	Correlation on MSCI World	Correlation on JPM Global Bonds
HFRI Convertible Arbitrage Index	0.86	0.08	−1.52	3.54	0.330	−0.004
Hennessee HF Index – Conv Arb	0.68	0.09	−1.23	3.17	0.308	−0.058
CSFB/Tremont Convertible Arbitrage	0.71	0.06	−1.66	4.08	0.146	−0.252
EACM Relative-value – Convertible Hedge	0.82	0.04	−1.56	4.46	0.183	−0.457

Source: HFR, Hennessee, CSFB/Tremont, Evaluation Associates, Datastream, UBS Warburg calculations

❏ All convertible arbitrage indices have positive alpha and extremely low beta against the MSCI World. The low beta indicates that returns are generated without getting exposed to the equity market as a whole. In other words, the source of returns in convertible arbitrage is not derived from capturing the equity risk premium such as in long equity funds. The returns are derived to a large extent from exploiting market inefficiencies.

❏ The distribution of returns is slightly negatively skewed (to the left with a long tail to the left) and leptokurtic (narrow distribution with outliers). Figure 8 on p. 387 will show that the negative outliers are small. Overall, we regard the non-normality of the return distribution of convertible arbitrage as minor.

❏ Correlation to equities was around 0.30 over a longer period of time and around 0.16 in recent history. The correlation coefficients are statistically significant.

❏ The correlation with bonds is negative, but statistically not significant. Intuitively we would have assumed a positive and statistically significant correlation to bonds, ie, a negative correlation to changes in interest rates. Convertible arbitrageurs are normally simultaneously long the convertible securities and short the underlying securities of the same issuer, thereby working the spread between the two types of securities. Returns result from the difference between cash flows collected through coupon payments and short interest rebates and cash paid out to cover dividend payments on the short equity positions. Returns also result from the convergence of valuations between the two securities. Positions are designed to generate profits from the fixed income security as well as the short sale of stock, while protecting principal from market moves. The worst case scenario, therefore, is rising interest rates (losses on the bonds) and rising equity markets (losses on the short equity position), widening credit spreads (losses on the bonds) and falling stock implied volatility. The fact that correlation to bonds is not significant is an indication that the convertible arbitrageurs tend to hedge duration risk.

The following two graphs show the performance of convertible arbitrage in different market environments and average quarterly returns in down-markets versus average quarterly returns in friendly markets.

❑ 1994 was the worst year based on the HFRI Convertible Arbitrage Index, which was down by 3.7% during 1994. The year was characterised by rising US interest rates. Convertible arbitrage behaved orderly during the Asian crisis in 1997. All hedge fund strategies except short sellers suffered during the Russian crisis in 1998 due to the collapse of LTCM. However, convertible arbitrage, equity market neutral and risk arbitrage suffered least.

❑ Theoretically, falling interest rates is good for convertible arbitrageurs because of the long position in the convertible, which reacts inversely to moves in interest rates due to its bond characteristics. However, declining interest rates in 1992, 1993 and 1995 encouraged many companies to call convertible issues and lower their cost of capital, thus adding to the

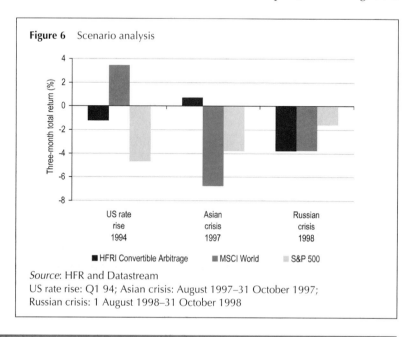

Figure 6   Scenario analysis

Source: HFR and Datastream
US rate rise: Q1 94; Asian crisis: August 1997–31 October 1997;
Russian crisis: 1 August 1998–31 October 1998

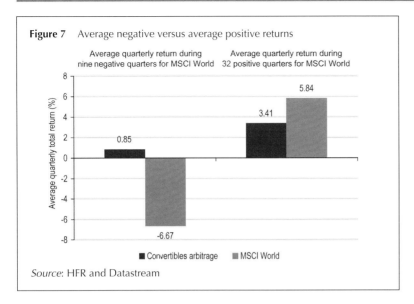

Figure 7   Average negative versus average positive returns

Source: HFR and Datastream

hedging difficulties as investors prematurely lost their conversion premiums and accrued interest. The sudden rise in interest rates in 1994
caused additional problems as investment floors dropped dramatically.

❑ When the Dow dropped 554 points on 27 October 1997 and when similar
volatility occurred later in the quarter in Japan, convertible arbitrage
strategies performed well as the stock positions dropped more swiftly
than the related convertible bonds. Thus, the managers earned more on
their short stock positions than losses incurred on the long convertible
positions. However, there were a few exceptions who lost money with
Japanese resettables due to the lack of opportunity to sell short or the
instruments did not behave in the market as the pricing models suggested they would.

❑ Q4 98 sent equity-linked markets in Japan into a tailspin due to the introduction of new short-selling rules. The uproar's inception was founded
in the Ministry of Finance's (MOF) initiative to curb 'rumour mongering'
and other speculative attacks on Japanese stocks. The MOF promulgated
securities legislation modelled after the US regulation on short-selling
(the 'uptick' rule). Unfortunately, they created mass confusion among
custodians, stock lenders and stock borrowers by not clearly stating
under what conditions and to whom the rule's draconian penalties
would apply. Large-scale and immediate retrenchment of stock lending
activity resulted from the MOF's obfuscation of the new rules. Many
convertible and warrant hedgers were forced to liquidate positions at
distressed prices for fear of being caught naked-long without the offsetting short hedge. Ultimately, the MOF issued clarification of the rules the
day they became effective averting further deterioration in the market.

Nonetheless, some losses were incurred. This example illustrates the exposure of the strategy to regulatory issues.

❑ Convertible arbitrage also experienced difficulties during the LTCM collapse in autumn 1998. In the US, the flight to quality and liquidity led investors to shun smaller and lower credit quality convertible issues leading to price deterioration and a significant widening in bid-ask spreads. Liquidations by hedge funds and proprietary trading desks in an already liquidity hampered market further exacerbated the tone of the market.

❑ 1999 was a difficult year for the convertible arbitrage industry, as the year was characterised by rising interest rates, mostly rising equity markets and falling stock volatility (except for the last quarter). US convertibles, which tend to be of lower credit quality, suffered when the Federal Reserve started to raise interest rates. There was even less activity than normal during summer from proprietary trading desks that did not want to take positions ahead of the enormous supply scheduled to the market in autumn. Potential illiquidity surrounding Y2K also discouraged participants. The main reason for the year ending profitably was the fact that issuance was extremely cheap making the arbitrage profitable despite rising rates and equities and falling volatilities.

❑ We regard the outperformance of convertible bond arbitrage in equity bear markets as worth pointing out (Figure 7 on p. 385). Between January 1990 and March 2000 there were nine quarters in which MSCI World reported a negative return. During these quarters convertible arbitrage showed an average return of 0.85% that compares with –6.67 in the case of the MSCI World. During the 32 quarters where MSCI World ended in positive territory, convertible arbitrage performed by 3.4% per quarter against 5.84 for the MSCI World.

❑ The above examples illustrate that convertible arbitrage can perform well in bear markets, primarily due to short stock position in the arbitrage. In other words, exposure to convertible arbitrage is attractive to bearish or neutral investors in search of instruments with positive expected return but low correlation to equities.

The next graph shows how returns have been distributed in the past and compares the historic return distribution with a normal distribution of convertible arbitrage and a normal distribution of historical MSCI World returns both based on historic mean return and standard deviation of returns. For Figure 9, we have sorted the convertible arbitrage returns and compared them with the corresponding market returns. This allows us to see in which market environment the extreme positive and negative returns were achieved.

❑ Figure 8 shows how narrowly around the mean the monthly returns were distributed, especially compared with the market. The outliers are

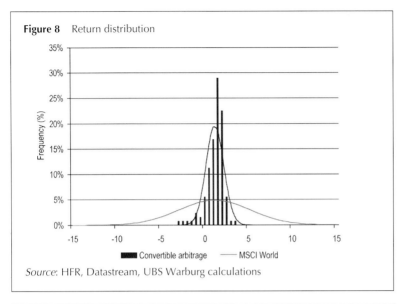

Figure 8   Return distribution

Source: HFR, Datastream, UBS Warburg calculations

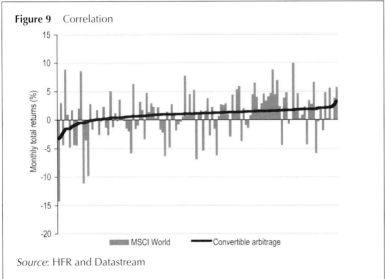

Figure 9   Correlation

Source: HFR and Datastream

minor. Six returns were below the 95% range and one above. None of the returns were outside the 99% range.

❑ Figure 9 shows that negative convertible arbitrage returns were not con-centrated during equity market declines. The figure shows that convertible arbitrage returns tend to have low variability compared to equity returns and that there is little relation between the two sets of returns.

Conclusion and outlook

We regard convertible arbitrage as an attractive hedge fund strategy. Stable returns of around 11% were achieved with very low volatility and low correlation to equities. The returns are achieved with little exposure to the equity market. Convertible arbitrages are not necessarily negative in equity market downturns. Downside risk is limited. No significant correlation to bonds suggests limited duration risk. We do not believe that these characteristics will change materially going forward.

However, there are capacity constraints to convertible arbitrage. One of the main drivers of recent returns in convertible arbitrage are derived from issuance of new paper. Convertible arbitrageurs play a dominant role in the issuance of paper. Future performance is, therefore, to some extent dependent on future issuance. A further constraint is the ability to borrow stock and sell short.

From a convertibles issuance perspective, the 1990s can be described as boom years. Convertible bonds became an asset class of their own. To some investors, convertibles are the best of both worlds: convertible bonds pay income plus provide upside to equity. Bond investors bought convertible bonds because of the 'equity-kicker' in a low interest rates environment. Equity investors used convertible bonds to add some downside protection to ever-rising stock markets. Corporates like the 'cheap' financing through low coupon, locking in low interest rates and reducing the costs of debt. Given the pending corporate restructuring in Europe and Asia we expect supply and demand of convertible bonds to increase hand in hand. With this increase, the opportunities for convertible arbitrageurs increase as well.

FIXED INCOME ARBITRAGE

❑ Based on HFR indices, the fixed income arbitrage hedge fund style has not done extremely well. Since 1990, it has only marginally outperformed the JPM Global Bonds Index with a similar degree of volatility.

❑ Performance analysis would look more attractive if we excluded H2 98. From January 1990 to June 1998, the HFRI Fixed Income Arbitrage indexed yielded 11.9% a year, which compares with only 8.5% for the JPM Global Bonds Index. The best year was 1992 when the HFRI Fixed Income Arbitrage Index gained 22.1%. The worst year was 1995 where the hedge fund index increased by 'only' 6.1%.

❑ The HFRI Fixed Income Arbitrage index has yielded a return of 8.9% with a volatility of 5% from 1990 to April 2000. Returns were slightly higher than bonds and volatility slightly lower. In other words, fixed income arbitrage did slightly better than a long-only bonds strategy. The higher risk-adjusted returns of the hedge fund strategy was confirmed when we compared the CSFB/Tremont relative-value bond hedge index with the corresponding bond returns for the same time period.

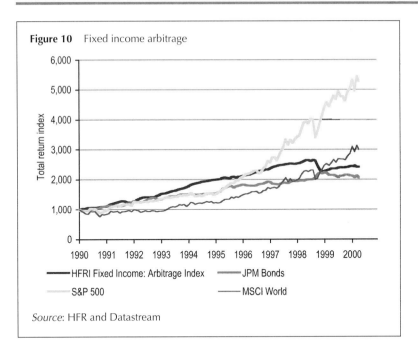

Figure 10 Fixed income arbitrage

Source: HFR and Datastream

Table 3 Fixed income arbitrage risk and return characteristics

	# of monthly returns*	Annual return (%)	Volatility (%)	Sharpe ratio**	Worst one-month return (%)	Negative months (%)	Worst one-year return (%)
S&P 500 (Total return)	124	18.3	13.7	0.97	−14.5	32	−3.1
MSCI World (Total return)	124	11.7	14.1	0.48	−13.3	36	−16.5
JPM Global Bond Index (Total return)	124	7.4	5.8	0.41	−3.3	39	−6.2
HFRI Fixed Income: Arbitrage Index	124	8.9	5.0	0.79	−6.45	19	−10.6
CSFB/Tremont Fixed Income Arbitrage	76	6.5	4.6	0.32	−6.96	22	−10.1

Source: HFR, CSFB/Tremont, Evaluation Associates, Datastream, UBS Warburg calculations
* ending April 2000, ** based on risk free rate of 5%

The first of the following two graphs shows the returns of various hedge fund indices with some equity and bond indices. The second graph compares monthly total JPM Global Bond returns with the HFRI Fixed Income Arbitrage index.

❏ Figure 12 shows that the returns were derived from fixed income arbitrage and not by taking on interest rate risk. As a matter of fact, fixed income arbitrage is about exploiting market inefficiencies between

389

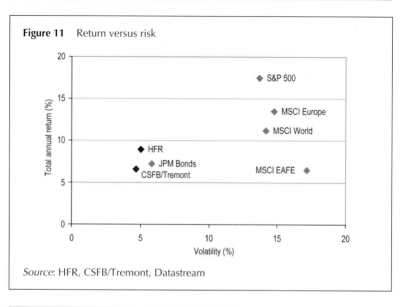

Figure 11 Return versus risk

Source: HFR, CSFB/Tremont, Datastream

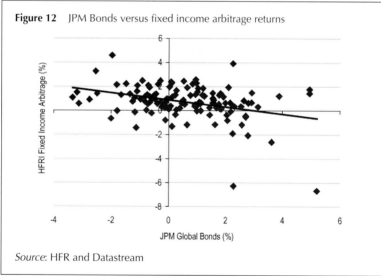

Figure 12 JPM Bonds versus fixed income arbitrage returns

Source: HFR and Datastream

related interest rate instruments and hedging away interest rate risk. The intercept (alpha) of the HFRI Fixed Income Arbitrage index to the JPM Global Bonds index was 0.89. The slope (beta) measuring the exposure to the bond market is negative and relatively low, in this case, around –0.30.

The following table shows some further statistics of fixed income arbitrage. Note that we compare the fixed income arbitrage indices with the JPM Global Bond Index.

❏ The distribution of returns is slightly negatively skewed (to the left with a long tail to the left) and extremely leptokurtic (narrow distribution with outliers). Figure 16 on p. 394 shows that the negative outliers are relatively small in absolute terms but represent a strong deviation from normality of returns.

Table 4   Statistical analysis of fixed income arbitrage returns

	Alpha to JPM Bonds	Beta to JPM Bonds	Skew	Excess kurtosis	Correlation on MSCI World	Correlation on JPM Global Bonds
HFRI Fixed Income: Arbitrage Index	0.89	−0.30	−1.92	9.07	−0.043	−0.345
CSFB/Tremont Fixed Income Arbitrage	0.64	−0.26	−3.28	15.19	0.064	−0.319

Source: HFR, CSFB/Tremont, Datastream, UBS Warburg calculations

❏ The two outliers occurred in September and October 1998 – a period that will probably not go down in history as the happiest of times for fixed income arbitrageurs (widening of credit spreads). Fixed income arbitrageurs are often long an instrument that is liquid and of high credit quality and short a less liquid instrument of lower credit quality. If credit spreads widen, the arbitrageur can potentially, if credit is unhedged,

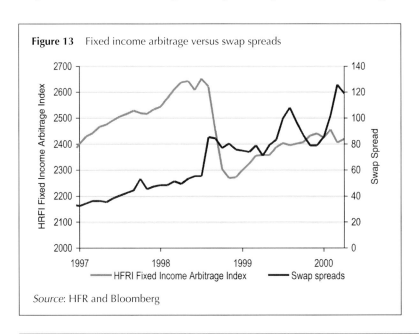

Figure 13   Fixed income arbitrage versus swap spreads

Source: HFR and Bloomberg

suffer a loss. From an investors' perspective, fixed income arbitrageurs are short a disaster insurance policy because they usually are short the credit spread. In an economic disaster, credit spreads widen and investors that short the spread lose money. Additionally, liquidity dries up, worsening the situations. The result is few, but high standard deviation negative returns. In other words, as with any other short put option position, the investors receive the premium in calm markets but loses money in market turmoil, as the put option moves in-the-money. For long-term investors, like insurance companies, selling put options (insurance policies) can be attractive.

❏ Excluding these two outliers from 1998 results in a reduction of skew and an excess kurtosis to nearly zero. Figure 13 shows the rise in swap spreads due to the Russian default and the subsequent fall in fixed income arbitrage returns. An increase in swap spreads arises when there is a flight-to-quality situation. Such situations occur when a large number of investors seek the safety and stability of government securities to escape from turmoil in international stock and bond markets. The resultant buying of government securities generally causes the credit spread to widen.

❏ The correlation between fixed income arbitrage and global equities is around zero but not statistically significant. The correlation with global bonds is around –0.4. This negative correlation to bonds implies positive correlation to changes in interest rates: if interest rates rise, bonds fall and fixed income arbitrage returns rise.

The following two graphs show the performance of the HFRI Fixed Income Arbitrage Index in different market environments and average quarterly returns in down-markets versus average quarterly returns in friendly markets.

❏ In October 1998, the bond markets went into a tailspin because a vast network of participants had essentially closed their trading doors, freezing the otherwise highly liquid and tightly traded bond markets. In a flight to quality and liquidity, all assets have been severely and negatively re-priced. This included swaps, investment grade corporate bonds, high yield bonds, mortgage-backed securities, municipal bonds and emerging-market bonds. The violence and velocity of these movements have been of historic proportions.

❏ Fixed Income Arbitrage has been subject to negative press and regulatory scrutiny in the wake of LTCM 1998 catastrophe. Many investors departed from the strategy. Investors who acknowledged that the well-documented problems were not a result of an inherently flawed strategy, but were instead attributable to manager specific factors such as over-leverage, investments outside of core competency, and too large of a

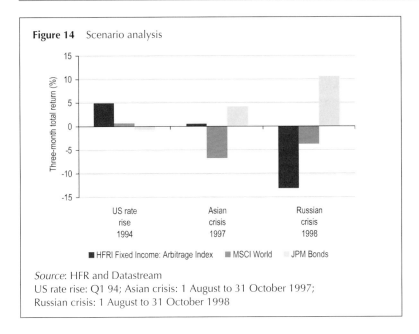

Figure 14 Scenario analysis

Source: HFR and Datastream
US rate rise: Q1 94; Asian crisis: 1 August to 31 October 1997;
Russian crisis: 1 August to 31 October 1998

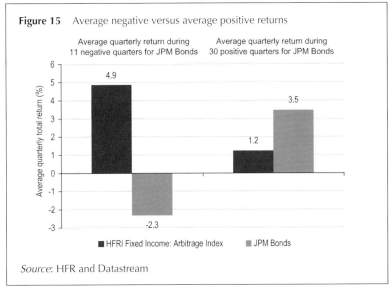

Figure 15 Average negative versus average positive returns

Source: HFR and Datastream

balance sheet were rewarded in 1999. The HFRI Fixed Income Arbitrage
Index increased by 7.4% in the year after LTCM despite swap spreads
widening beyond the post-LTCM level.
❑ Figure 15 shows in which market environments fixed income arbitrageurs make money. In the quarters where global bonds fell by an

average of 2.3% fixed income arbitrage yielded 4.9%. In the quarters where global bonds increased by an average of 3.5%, fixed income arbitrage yielded only 1.2%.

The graph below shows how returns have been distributed in the past and compares the historic return distribution with a normal distribution of fixed income arbitrage and a normal distribution of historical JPM Global Bond returns both based on historic mean return and standard deviation of returns. In Figure 17, we have sorted the fixed income arbitrage returns and compared them to the corresponding market returns. This allows us to see in which market environment the extreme positive and negative returns were achieved.

❏ Figure 16 highlights the deviation of the historic return distribution from normality. There were four returns below the 95% range and none above this range. Two returns were below the 99% range. The experience in September and October 1998, where the HRFI Fixed Income Arbitrage Index lost 6.5% and 6.1% respectively, was a six standard deviation event for this discipline. To put this into perspective, the largest monthly loss prior to autumn 1998 was only 2.6%.

❏ Fung and Hsieh (1999) provide three explanations why fixed income arbitrage provides equity-like returns with bond-like volatility:[4]

(1) Fixed income arbitrage funds are capturing true mispricings.

(2) They are acting as market makers providing liquidity.

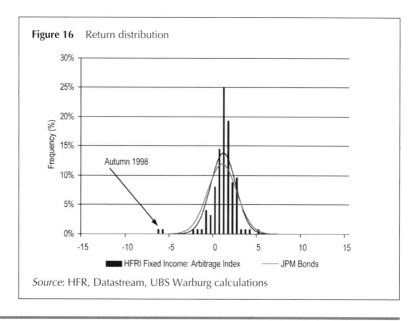

Figure 16 Return distribution

Source: HFR, Datastream, UBS Warburg calculations

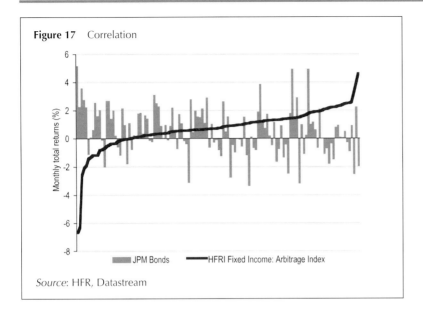

Figure 17   Correlation

Source: HFR, Datastream

(3) They sell economic disaster insurance – where the low historical return volatility is consistent with a period over which the gathering of insurance premium has yet to be tested by a disaster payout.

The third point can explain the outliers since insurers are essentially 'short volatility.' They perform best in calm markets and worst in volatile markets.

❏ Figure 17 shows that large negative returns in fixed income arbitrage are concentrated when bonds rise, ie, when interest rates fall. The most extreme positive returns from fixed income arbitrage occur both in rising and falling bond markets.

Conclusion and Outlook

The reputation of fixed income arbitrage as a relative-value strategy has suffered because of the LTCM debacle. However, LTCM is likely to go down in financial history as a mismanaged company where leverage was excessive. Most trades would have been profitable if funding had been managed appropriately and carried to the end.

We believe that inefficiencies in fixed income markets will continue to exist. The skill and the determination (read funding) for these inefficiencies to be exploited will not disappear because of LTCM. Fixed income arbitrage represents a sound alternative to allocating funds in bonds. This is especially the case in an environment of rising interest rates and inflation uncertainty since fixed income arbitrage shows negative correlation with bond markets. When bonds did poorly in the past (interest rates rise), returns in fixed income arbitrage were higher.

EQUITY MARKET NEUTRAL

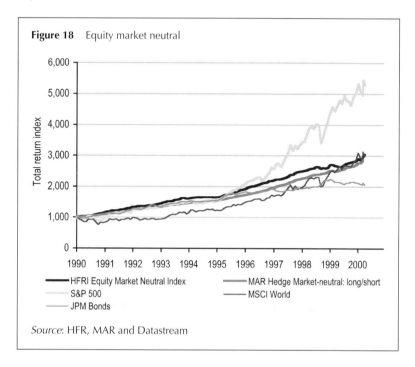

Figure 18   Equity market neutral

Total return index

6,000 — 5,000 — 4,000 — 3,000 — 2,000 — 1,000 — 0

1990 1991 1992 1993 1994 1995 1996 1997 1998 1999 2000

— HFRI Equity Market Neutral Index   — MAR Hedge Market-neutral: long/short
— S&P 500   — MSCI World
— JPM Bonds

Source: HFR, MAR and Datastream

❏ Both equity market neutral indices performed in line with MSCI World with less volatility. The indices were flat in 1994 and showed some degree of volatility in 1998.
❏ As with other relative-value strategies the smoothness of the wealth creation is worth pointing out.
❏ Returns in equity market neutral have been around 11% in the past. Equity market neutral had the lowest volatility of around 2.8%, highest Sharpe ratio of around 2.4, highest 'worst month' and 'worst year' of around –1.3% and –1.5% respectively.

Figure 19 shows the return of various hedge fund indices with some equity and bond indices. Figure 20 compares monthly total MSCI World returns with the HFRI Market Neutral index returns.

❏ Equity market neutral is the purest form of alpha generation in the equity arena. The average 11% return shown in Figure 19 is nearly pure

Table 5 Equity market neutral risk and return characteristics

	# of monthly returns*	Annual return (%)	Volatility (%)	Sharpe ratio**	Worst one-month return (%)	Negative months (%)	Worst one-year return (%)
S&P 500 (Total return)	124	18.3	13.7	0.97	−14.5	32	−3.1
MSCI World (Total return)	124	11.7	14.1	0.48	−13.3	36	−16.5
MSCI Europe (Total return)	124	13.5	14.7	0.58	−12.6	34	−12.1
HFRI Equity Market Neutral Index	124	11.4	3.2	2.00	−1.67	15	1.6
MAR Hedge Market–neutral: long/short	123	10.8	1.7	3.44	−1.03	2	4.9
CSFB/Tremont Equity Market Neutral	76	11.5	3.5	1.84	−1.15	18	−2.0

Source: HFR, MAR, CSFB/Tremont, Datastream, UBS Warburg calculations
* ending April 2000 (except MAR: ending March 2000); ** based on risk free rate of 5%

Figure 19 Return versus risk

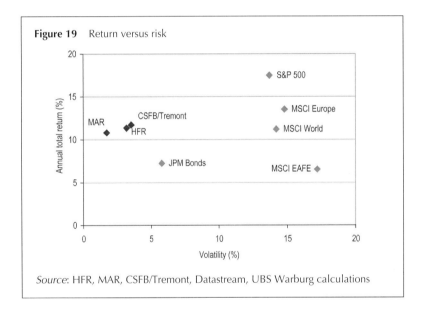

Source: HFR, MAR, CSFB/Tremont, Datastream, UBS Warburg calculations

alpha. In our view there is hardly any market risk, as shown in Figure 20. Most of the risk is stock-specific where the information is highest.

❏ In other words, an investor who in the beginning of 1990 decided to swap the risk free rate with, for example, the MSCI World index total return and invested the principal in a fund of equity market neutral funds would have paid, say 200bp for the equity index returns and have ended up with an annual return of around 16% (12% from the equity index, plus 11% from the fund of equity market neutral funds, minus

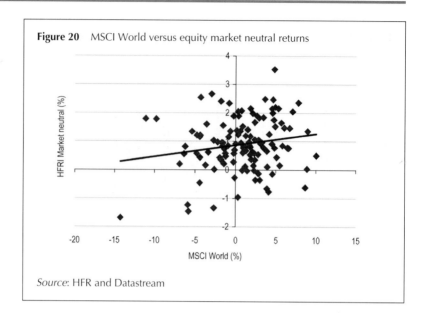

Figure 20 MSCI World versus equity market neutral returns

Source: HFR and Datastream

200bp cost from the swap transaction, minus the risk free rate).[5] The following chart shows the breakdown of such a strategy by year. Had the
strategy been done with MSCI World Index, the total annual return
would have been around 16.0%, which compares with around 11% for
the MSCI World Total Return Index.

❑ The strategy would have outperformed MSCI World in all years except
1994 and 1999.

❑ We believe that the concept of portable alpha (or alpha transport) is ideally suitable in connection with hedge fund investing once risk to single
hedge funds is diversified. Figure 21 shows the annual returns of such a
strategy compared with MSCI World total returns. The (hypothetical)
manager running such a strategy would have outperformed index funds
most of the time and the majority of active managed funds nearly all of
the time.

Table 6 shows some further statistics of equity market neutral strategies.

❑ As already mentioned, the alpha of the strategy is positive and the exposure to the market negligible. The return distribution is fairly normal, ie,
returns seem neither skewed nor kurtotic. Correlation with equities is
low, ie, around 0.2 and statistically significant at the 95% level.
Correlation with global bonds is positive but not significant.

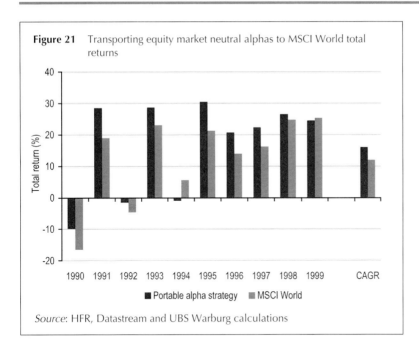

Figure 21 Transporting equity market neutral alphas to MSCI World total returns

Source: HFR, Datastream and UBS Warburg calculations

Table 6 Statistical analysis of equity market neutral returns

	Alpha to MSCI World	Beta to MSCI World	Skew	Excess kurtosis	Correlation on MSCI World	Correlation on JPM Global Bonds
HFRI Equity Market Neutral Index	0.86	0.04	−0.18	0.41	0.174	0.150
MAR Hedge Market-neutral: long/short	0.83	0.03	0.30	2.62	0.254	0.206
CSFB/Tremont Equity Market Neutral	0.77	0.12	−0.03	−0.28	0.450	0.022

Source: HFR, MAR, CSFB/Tremont, Datastream, UBS Warburg calculations

The following two graphs show the performance of the HFRI Equity Market Neutral Index in different market environments and average quarterly returns in down-markets versus average quarterly returns in friendly markets.

❏ The HFRI Equity Market Neutral Index was up both during the US rate rise of 1994 as well as the Asian crisis in 1997. Since the Russian crisis coincided with the default of LTCM and the associated early redemptions, fear of early redemptions, and the (forced) reduction of leverage in

399

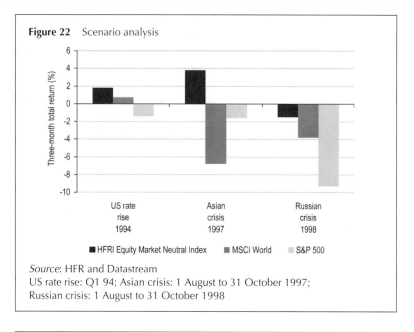

Figure 22   Scenario analysis

Source: HFR and Datastream
US rate rise: Q1 94; Asian crisis: 1 August to 31 October 1997;
Russian crisis: 1 August to 31 October 1998

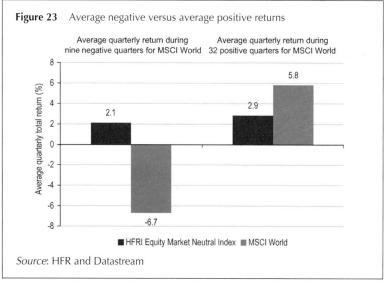

Figure 23   Average negative versus average positive returns

Source: HFR and Datastream

difficult market conditions, even equity market neutral funds reported, on average, small losses.

❏ Since January 1990, there were nine quarters where MSCI World reported a negative return. During these quarters, relative-value equity market neutral showed an average return of 2.1%, which compares with

–6.7% in the case of the MSCI World. During the 32 quarters where MSCI World ended in positive territory, the relative-value arbitrage index gained 2.9% per quarter against 5.8% for the MSCI World. In other words, quarterly returns are between 2–3% regardless of equities going up or down.

❏ These two comparisons, as well as the analysis done on other relative-value strategies, highlight the robustness of the relative-value sector in general and its ability to perform well in down-markets in particular.

Figure 24 shows how returns have been distributed in the past and compares the historic return distribution with a normal distribution of equity market neutral and a normal distribution of historical MSCI World returns, both based on historic mean return and standard deviation of returns. For Figure 25, we have sorted the equity market neutral returns and compared them with the corresponding market returns. This allows us to see in which market environment the extreme positive and negative returns were achieved.

❏ Figure 24 shows how narrowly around the mean the monthly returns were distributed, especially compared with the equity market. There are no outliers of significance. Five returns were below the 95% range and one return above. Note that only 18 of the 124 monthly returns were below zero. This compares with 40 for the S&P 500, and 45 for the MSCI World Index.

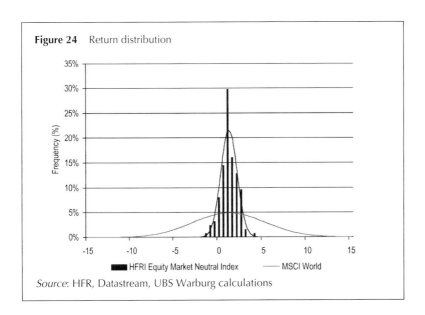

Figure 24 Return distribution

Source: HFR, Datastream, UBS Warburg calculations

401

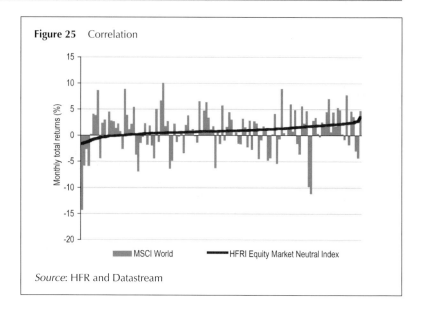

Figure 25 Correlation

Source: HFR and Datastream

Conclusion and outlook

We regard equity market neutral as one of the most attractive strategies. The sector has proven that it is an alpha-generator par excellence and not a beta-merchant at all. Our analysis leads us to believe that the risk/return as well as the correlation characteristics of equity market neutral strategies are fairly stable and therefore, to some degree, can be extrapolated into the future. Capacity constraints are an issue. However, as long as there will be violations to the law of one price there will be market participants making money on the conversion.

This concludes our analysis of relative-value strategies. The following section takes a closer look at two event-driven strategies, ie, risk arbitrage and distressed securities.

RISK OF EVENT-DRIVEN STRATEGIES
Risk arbitrage
❑ The HFRI Merger Arbitrage Index has outperformed nearly all equity indices over the past 10 years. This was the case when sentiment was friendly for equities.
❑ Risk arbitrage is another example of sustainable, smooth, stable, positive returns.
❑ Absolute returns in risk arbitrage have been around 13–14% in the past with volatility of less than 5% resulting in a relatively high Sharpe ratio of c1.8.
❑ The worst monthly losses are higher than, for example, equity market neutral. However, the worst annual return is around zero in the long run

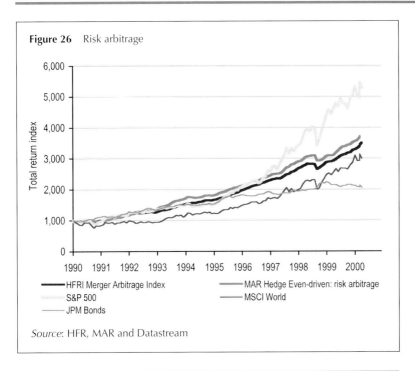

Figure 26 Risk arbitrage

HFRI Merger Arbitrage Index
MAR Hedge Even-driven: risk arbitrage
S&P 500
MSCI World
JPM Bonds

Source: HFR, MAR and Datastream

Table 7 Risk arbitrage risk and return characteristics

	# of monthly returns*	Annual return (%)	Volatility (%)	Sharpe ratio**	Worst one-month return (%)	Negative months (%)	Worst one-year return (%)
S&P 500 (Total return)	124	18.3	13.7	0.97	−14.5	32	−3.1
MSCI World (Total return)	124	11.7	14.1	0.48	−13.3	36	−16.5
MSCI Europe (Total return)	124	13.5	14.7	0.58	−12.6	34	−12.1
HFRI Merger Arbitrage Index	124	12.9	4.6	1.70	−6.46	10	0.4
MAR Hedge Event-driven: risk arbitrage	123	13.6	4.6	1.89	−5.61	9	−1.7
Hennessee HF Index – Merger Arb	88	14.3	3.5	2.66	−4.97	9	5.6

Source: HFR, MAR, Hennessee, Datastream, UBS Warburg calculations
* ending April 2000 (except MAR: ending March 2000); ** based on risk free rate of 5%

and around 5% in recent history. The number of negative months has been extremely low at around 10%.

The first of the following two graphs show the return of the various hedge fund indices with some equity and bond indices. The second graph compares monthly total MSCI World returns with the HFRI Merger Arbitrage Index.

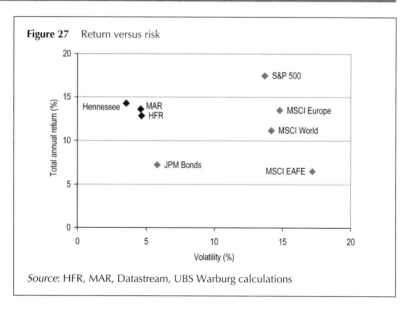

Figure 27   Return versus risk

Source: HFR, MAR, Datastream, UBS Warburg calculations

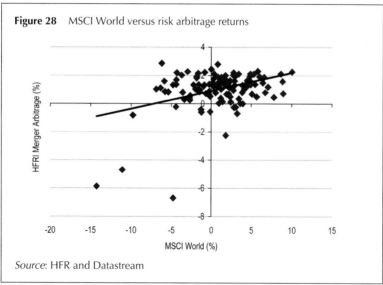

Figure 28   MSCI World versus risk arbitrage returns

Source: HFR and Datastream

❏ Figure 27 puts the attractive risk return characteristics described above into perspective. Risk arbitrage had very high returns with volatility lower than global bonds. However, Figure 28 reveals some outliers in down markets.

The following table shows some further statistics of risk arbitrage.

Table 8   Statistical analysis of risk arbitrage returns

	Alpha to MSCI World	Beta to MSCI World	Skew	Excess kurtosis	Correlation on MSCI World	Correlation on JPM Global Bonds
HFRI Merger Arbitrage Index	0.88	0.13	–3.38	15.44	0.376	0.017
MAR Hedge Event-driven: risk arbitrage	0.95	0.13	–1.69	7.96	0.376	–0.078
Hennessee HF Index – Merger Arb	0.91	0.14	–2.66	15.66	0.443	–0.086

Source: HFR, MAR, Datastream, UBS Warburg calculations

❏ The exposure to the market is higher than in equity market neutral, but still very low at around 0.13. The distribution of returns were negatively skewed and strongly leptokurtic, indicating the presence of outliers. The correlation to the equity market was around 0.4 and statistically significant at the 99% level. Correlation to bonds was not significant.

Figures 29 and 30 show the performance of the HFRI Merger Arbitrage index in different market environments and average quarterly

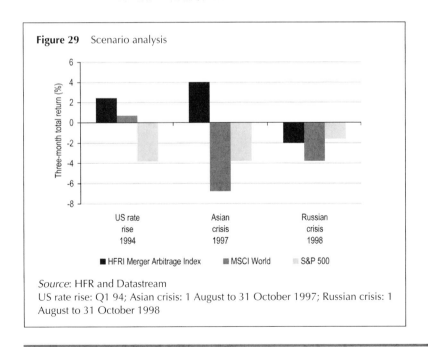

Figure 29   Scenario analysis

Source: HFR and Datastream
US rate rise: Q1 94; Asian crisis: 1 August to 31 October 1997; Russian crisis: 1 August to 31 October 1998

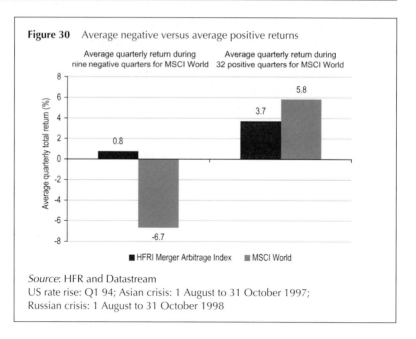

Figure 30 Average negative versus average positive returns

Average quarterly return during
nine negative quarters for MSCI World

Average quarterly return during
32 positive quarters for MSCI World

Source: HFR and Datastream
US rate rise: Q1 94; Asian crisis: 1 August to 31 October 1997;
Russian crisis: 1 August to 31 October 1998

returns in down-markets versus average quarterly returns in friendly markets.

❏ Neither the US rate rise in 1994 nor the Asian crisis in 1997 did negatively affect risk arbitrage. Normally, increases in downside volatility has no impact on the long-term profitability of risk arbitrageurs as the spreads, eventually, converge despite the markets' volatility. However, short-term volatility can have an impact on the spread of longer-duration deals. A market disruption can diminish the risk appetite for longer-duration deals of several months to completion. The spread of the deals which are expected to complete within a couple of weeks are normally not affected by short-term volatility.

❏ The reason for the negative outliers in risk arbitrage is more micro than macro. There are only a limited number of transactions available to this category and most managers employing this strategy have similar trades put on, ie, long the stock of a company being acquired in a merger, leveraged buyout, or takeover and simultaneously short in the stock of the acquiring company. The opportunities are limited to deals where the acquiring company is a large, listed and liquid traded stock where it is possible to borrow stock for shorting.

❏ Risk arbitrage offers some degree of protection, although less than some relative-value strategies discussed above. To some extent, risk arbitrage is short equity market delta because a trade is normally transacted on a deal-ratio basis as opposed to a cash-neutral basis. Since January 1990, there were nine quarters where MSCI World reported a negative return. During these quarters, relative-value arbitrage showed an average return of 0.8% which compares to -6.7% in the case of the MSCI World. During the 32 quarters where MSCI World ended in positive territory, the relative-value arbitrage index gained 3.7% per quarter against 5.8% for the MSCI World.

The figure below shows how returns have been distributed in the past and compares the historic return distribution with a normal distribution of risk arbitrage and a normal distribution of historical MSCI World returns, both based on historic mean return and standard deviation of returns. For Figure 32, we have sorted the risk arbitrage returns and compared them to the corresponding market returns. This allows us to see in which market environment the extreme positive and negative returns were achieved.

❏ Figure 31 shows the leptokurtic features of the distribution very well. The historic return distribution has been narrow with more outliers than normality would suggest. Note that the outliers are on the downside and not on the upside. Four returns were outside the two-standard deviation range. The negative outliers occur in dislocating market conditions. When equity markets fall rapidly, all spreads in the portfolio widen at the same time. Diversification across many deals does not prevent these negative outliers. In other words, there are limited outliers on the upside, but outliers on the downside are in the nature of the strategy. We

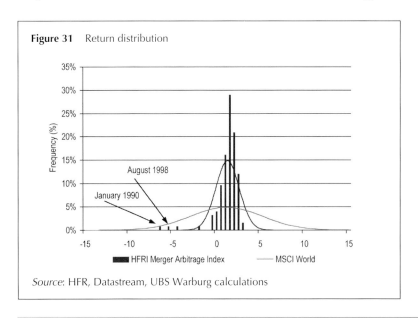

Figure 31 Return distribution

Source: HFR, Datastream, UBS Warburg calculations

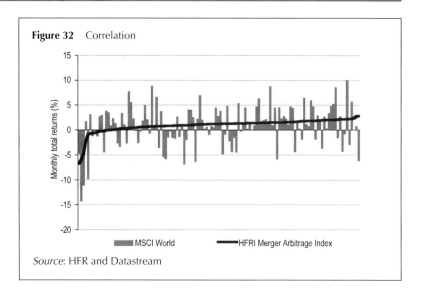

Figure 32 Correlation

MSCI World   HFRI Merger Arbitrage Index

Source: HFR and Datastream

therefore expect the return distribution characteristics to remain similar going forward.

❏ Figure 32 shows that most negative risk arbitrage returns occurred in down-markets, whereas the extreme positive returns are not dependent on the direction of the market.

❏ Risk arbitrage occasionally faces some challenges with respect to anti-trust issues. The Federal Trade Commission (FTC), one of the US agencies charged with enforcing antitrust regulations, continues to 'rethink' existing merger-review standards. This changing attitude stems from the FTC's view that a number of mergers that relied on negotiated divestitures have failed to protect competition. Thus, the FTC has taken the stance that they will simply opine on whether the proposed merger would inhibit competition and thereby refrain from participating in more protracted settlement negotiations. When the FTC has communicated this position, a number of deals have experienced difficulties as evidenced by the break of Royal Ahold/Pathmark, the delayed approval of Exxon/Mobil and the derailment of Abbott Labs/Alza.

❏ In the case of the BP Amoco/Arco acquisition, the FTC was effectively forced to take legal action if they persisted to oppose the merger. As illustrated in Figure 33, the FTC's opposition and potential legal challenge to the BP Amoco/Arco merger had shaken investors' confidence in the deal, causing the spread to widen dramatically. Likewise, other merger deals with regulatory concerns have experienced similar effects.

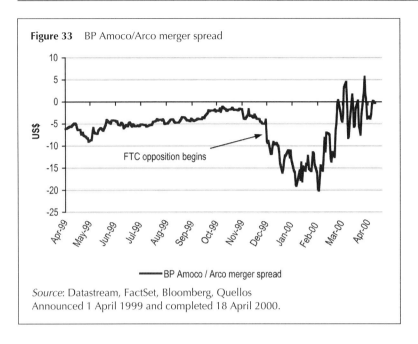

Figure 33 BP Amoco/Arco merger spread

Source: Datastream, FactSet, Bloomberg, Quellos
Announced 1 April 1999 and completed 18 April 2000.

Conclusion and outlook

We regard risk arbitrage as an attractive hedge fund strategy despite higher correlation to equity returns and limited downside protection features. The risks to merger arbitrage are, to a large extent, of a legal/regulatory nature, which is uncorrelated to returns in capital markets. Future profitability of risk arbitrage is determined by the amount of capital involved and to some extent is constraint by the number of opportunities and the ability to sell short.

We expect future corporate activity to remain strong, fuelled by continued consolidation in several global styles and a rapid expansion of M&A activity in Europe and Asia, facilitated by booming equity markets and high valuations. The M&A value as a percent of market capitalisation is still well below that of the 1980s. In particular, we expect the number and size of European and cross-border deals to increase significantly, driven by the single currency, disappearing commercial barriers among the EU nations and globalisation. The changes in the law, government regulation and business practices in Europe and Asia could substantially change the investment landscape in these regions. For risk arbitrageurs, 'change' equals 'opportunity'. We expect the overall growth in value in M&A globally to outpace the growth of risk arbitrage capital. This should result in sustaining attractive spreads and risk-adjusted return potential going forward.

The late 1990s has already seen the beginnings of change in Europe manifested in the rise in size and number of cross-border corporate transactions. Despite the EU's sluggishness in forging uniform merger rules, it now appears imminent that the EU will adopt British-style takeover regulations.[6] Such rules would still have to be enacted at the national level, however, EU adoption coupled with market forces such as the Mannesmann/Vodafone transaction should pressure national governments to reform their laws. Additional impetus for change in Europe stems from Germany's tax reform approved by the Upper House on 14 July 2000. Tax efficient portfolio re-allocations from 2002 are expected to pave the way for in-market and cross-border mergers in the old economy sectors, and the realisation of cost synergies through rationalisation and economies of scale. Simultaneously, it will probably facilitate balance sheet optimisation of financials and the re-allocation of funds towards more profitable investment areas.

Through less concrete measures, Japan has also officially sanctioned the unwinding of the cross-holdings that have long been a feature of the keiretsu system. We are seeing the revitalisation of the moribund equity-linked market as corporations issue exchangeable securities to monetise their cross-holdings. The elimination of cross-holdings would have the secondary effect of spurring corporate takeover activity as the barriers to corporate mergers are lowered. While Europe is farther along in the process, the harmonisation of takeover rules and elimination of tax barriers will likely provide a strong catalyst for change.

With this increasing merger-and-acquisition activity, including the trend of consolidation presently taking place in Europe and Asia, and a growing number of investors looking for reprieve from volatile equity markets, merger arbitrage is a hedge fund strategy likely to grow in importance in portfolios seeking absolute returns and diversification opportunities.

DISTRESSED SECURITIES
❏ Distressed securities, as the next graph implies, has performed well in the past. When risk is defined as standard deviation of returns, distressed securities has outperformed equity in the long run.
❏ Volatility is slightly higher than with relative-value strategies or with bonds but substantially lower than with equities. The dispersion of returns has also been higher with distressed securities than with other event-driven strategies such as risk arbitrage. Unlike risk arbitrage, distressed securities have a long bias. The annualised standard deviation has been around 7%. This results in a Sharpe ratio of approximately 1.5.
❏ Around 20% of the returns were below zero. Distressed securities provide much less downside protection than some relative-value strategies discussed previously. However, the discipline is less erratic on the downside than equities.

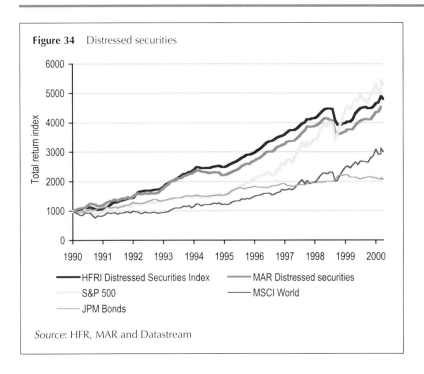

Figure 34 Distressed securities

Source: HFR, MAR and Datastream

Table 9 Distressed securities risk and return characteristics

	# of monthly returns*	Annual return (%)	Volatility (%)	Sharpe ratio**	Worst one-month return (%)	Negative months (%)	Worst one-year return (%)
S&P 500 (Total return)	124	18.3	13.7	0.97	−14.5	32	−3.1
MSCI World (Total return)	124	11.7	14.1	0.48	−13.3	36	−16.5
MSCI Europe (Total return)	124	13.5	14.7	0.58	−12.6	34	−12.1
HFRI Distressed Securities Index	124	16.4	6.6	1.73	−8.5	16	−6.4
MAR Hedge Event-driven: Distressed securities	123	15.9	7.6	1.44	−9.2	22	−7.6
Hennessee HF Index – Distressed	88	15.0	7.1	1.40	−8.9	18	−8.6

Source: HFR, MAR, Hennessee, Datastream, UBS Warburg calculation
* ending April 2000 (except MAR: ending March 2000); ** based on risk free rate of 5%

The first of the following two graphs shows the returns of various hedge fund indices with some equity and bond indices. The second graph compares monthly total MSCI World returns with the HFRI Distressed Securities Index.

411

❏ The three distressed securities indices are from three different sources covering two different periods. The fact that they result in nearly the same risk/return profile is an indication that the characteristics are robust and could be stable going forward.[7] However, there are some viable reservations regarding the quality of the data for distressed

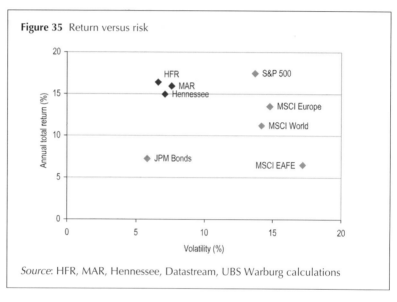

Figure 35 Return versus risk

Source: HFR, MAR, Hennessee, Datastream, UBS Warburg calculations

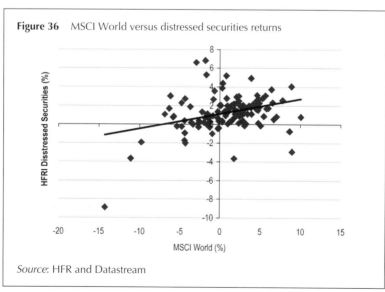

Figure 36 MSCI World versus distressed securities returns

Source: HFR and Datastream

securities. Given the nature of the strategy, managers often hold illiquid positions for which there is no market which makes calculating net asset values at the end of a month rather challenging.

❏ Figure 36 points to some negative outliers that occur in both positive as well as negative markets.

The following table shows some further statistics of distressed securities.

Table 10   Statistical analysis of distressed securities returns

	Alpha to MSCI World	Beta to MSCI World	Skew	Excess kurtosis	Correlation on MSCI World	Correlation on JPM Global Bonds
HFRI Distressed Securities Index	1.15	0.15	−1.08	7.38	0.326	−0.174
MAR Hedge Event-driven: Distressed securities	1.02	0.23	−1.16	4.55	0.419	−0.045
Hennessee HF Index – Distressed	0.85	0.24	−1.18	9.34	0.427	−0.173

Source: HFR, MAR, Datastream, UBS Warburg calculations

❏ The intercept between returns from distressed securities and MSCI World is relatively high, indicating that there are returns not explained by market risk.

❏ The beta to the MSCI is around 0.2, which is slightly higher than with some relative-value strategies discussed above.

❏ Historical returns were slightly negatively skewed (to the left with a long tail to the left) and leptokurtic (narrow distribution with outliers).

❏ Correlation to equities was around 0.4, the same as for risk arbitrage, the other event-driven strategy discussed in this chapter. The correlation is statistically significant at the 99% level. The correlation to bonds is not statistically significant. Note that relative-value strategies in equities have a correlation with the market of around 0.25–0.30 whereas event-driven strategies have a correlation coefficient of around 0.40.

The following two graphs show the performance of the HFRI Distressed Securities Index in different market environments and average quarterly returns in down-markets versus average quarterly returns in friendly markets.

❏ Intuitively, we would not expect distressed securities to lose money during a global crisis since the positions in distressed securities are more micro than macro. Distressed securities showed nearly the same returns

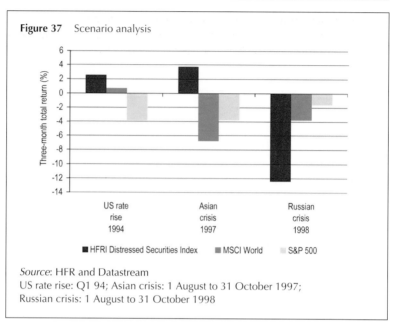

Figure 37   Scenario analysis

Source: HFR and Datastream
US rate rise: Q1 94; Asian crisis: 1 August to 31 October 1997;
Russian crisis: 1 August to 31 October 1998

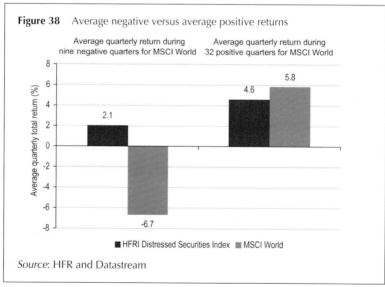

Figure 38   Average negative versus average positive returns

Source: HFR and Datastream

as risk arbitrage during the US rate rise in 1994 and the Asian crisis in 1997. However, the strategy was one of the worst performers during the Russian crisis (or credit crisis) in 1998. Only emerging markets and fixed income arbitrage suffered larger losses during autumn 1998. The nature of the strategy is to be long low investment grade credit. A widening of credit spreads is bad for the strategy as the following graph illustrates. 1998 was the worst year since 1990 where the HFRI Distressed Securities Index lost 4.2%.

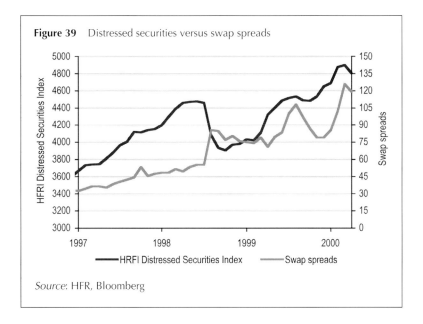

Figure 39   Distressed securities versus swap spreads

Source: HFR, Bloomberg

❏ Distressed securities strategies perform poorly in recessions. 1990 and 1994 saw returns of 6.4% and 3.8% respectively. However, the recessions led to a number of well established companies running into financial difficulties, which meant that there were good opportunities in this segment in the years that followed recession years. In the years 1991 and 1995, distressed securities yielded returns of 35.7% and 19.7% respectively.

❏ The 1999 calendar year witnessed 144 publicly traded US companies with total assets of US$58.6bn filing for Chapter 11 bankruptcy. This was the greatest number of defaults in any year since 1986 and the greatest asset total in any year since 1992, when US$64.2bn went into Chapter 11. Calendar returns of the HRFI Distressed Securities index in 1992 and 1999 were 25.2% and 16.9% respectively.

❏ In average down-quarters distressed securities yields a positive absolute return as Figure 38 shows. However, the strategy does better in equity-friendly markets. As fixed income arbitrage and, to a lesser extent, convertible arbitrage, investors invested in distressed securities are short a disaster put option. If disaster strikes, credit spreads widen, and the net asset values of distressed securities falls.

The first graph of the following pair shows how returns have been distributed in the past and compares the historic return distribution with a normal distribution of distressed securities and a normal distribution of historical MSCI World returns both based on historic mean return and standard deviation of returns. For Figure 41, we have sorted the distressed securities returns and compared them with the corresponding market returns. This allows us to see in which market environment the extreme positive and negative returns were achieved.

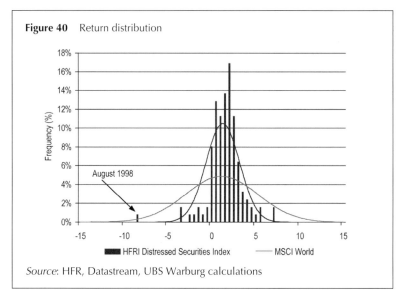

Figure 40   Return distribution

Source: HFR, Datastream, UBS Warburg calculations

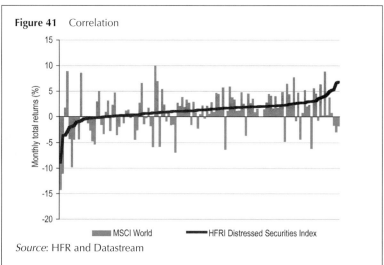

Figure 41   Correlation

Source: HFR and Datastream

❏ Figure 40 shows the positive kurtosis (narrow distribution with outliers) of the historical return distribution when compared with the normal distribution. Note that 20 from the 124 monthly returns were below zero which compares with 40 in the S&P 500 total return index and 45 in the case of the MSCI World total return index. There were eight observations outside the 95% range, four on the upside and four on the left-hand side of the mean return. We believe the nature of the strategy dictates the presence of outliers going forward since, to some extent, investors in distressed securities are short a disaster put option.

❏ Negative returns from distressed securities were moderately concentrated in down markets. Note that the highest returns were achieved in down-markets too.

Conclusion and outlook

Based on risk considerations, distressed securities represent the average hedge fund discipline: not the most conservative and not the most aggressive strategy. For the long-term investors distressed securities are attractive because of high returns with medium risk and the sustainability and predictability of this relationship.

As long as companies blow up, we expect managers of distressed securities to make money. The strategy is a good example of regulatory arbitrage. Most investors must sell securities of troubled companies. Policy restrictions and regulatory constraints do not allow them to own securities with very low credit ratings. As a result, a pricing discount occurs that reflects both these structural anomalies as well as uncertainty about the outcome of the event. For the attractive risk/return combinations in distressed securities to disappear, in our opinion, investment policies and financial regulation would have to change dramatically.

This concludes our performance analysis for event-driven strategies. In the following section, we take a closer look at some strategies we branded 'opportunistic'.

RISKS OF OPPORTUNISTIC HEDGE FUND STRATEGIES

In some hedge fund universes, 'opportunistic' is defined as a sub-category with short-term investment horizon. Note that in this chapter we use the term to classify hedge funds which are not relative-value (ie, market neutral) or event-driven. Except short sellers, hedge funds in this category are long or have a long bias.

Macro

❏ Macro funds, as a group, have performed well in the past. However, their returns have been falling over time.

❏ There are large differences between the different hedge fund databases we used for this chapter. One return characteristic seems to be that the

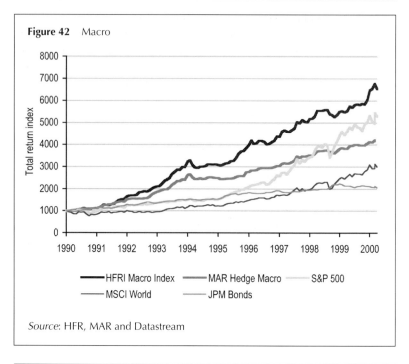

Figure 42 Macro

Source: HFR, MAR and Datastream

Table 11 Macro risk and return characteristics

	# of monthly returns*	Annual return (%)	Volatility (%)	Sharpe ratio**	Worst one-month return (%)	Negative months (%)	Worst one-year return (%)
S&P 500 (Total return)	124	18.3	13.7	0.97	−14.5	32	−3.1
MSCI World (Total return)	124	11.7	14.1	0.48	−13.3	36	−16.5
MSCI Europe (Total return)	124	13.5	14.7	0.58	−12.6	34	−12.1
HFRI Macro Index	124	19.9	9.1	1.64	−6.40	29	−7.1
MAR Hedge Macro	123	15.1	7.1	1.41	−5.36	28	−7.9
Hennessee HF Index – Macro	88	10.6	9.6	0.58	−7.52	40	−13.8
CSFB/Tremont Global Macro	76	12.8	14.8	0.53	−11.55	39	−22.2

Source: HFR, MAR, Hennessee, CSFB/Tremont, Datastream, UBS Warburg calculations
* ending April 2000 (except MAR: ending March 2000); ** based on risk free rate of 5%

longer the data series used, the better the performance is, both absolute and on a risk-adjusted basis.
❏ Risk-adjusted returns seem high when measured over the past ten years. However, the Sharpe ratio derived from the CSFB/Tremont macro index indicates that the heyday of macro funds are over, ie, the index performed in line with MSCI World total return index. The CSFB/Tremont macro index starts in 1994. The annual returns from

HFR, MAR and Hennessee for the period of January 1994 to April 2000 (MAR until March) fall to 11.8%, 7.9% and 6.9% respectively. The Sharpe ratios fall to 0.78, 0.44 and 0.20. In other words, macro funds have become less attractive to investors over time. Currently, we do not see the catalyst for this trend to reverse. The HFRI Macro Index fell by 1% from January to July 2000, despite opportunities in form of interest rates rises in the US, the Euro in free-fall, and the rising oil prices.

The first of the following two graphs shows the returns of various hedge fund indices with some equity and bond indices. Figure 44 compares monthly total MSCI World returns with the HFRI Macro index.

❏ Figure 43 reveals that macro funds are difficult reviewed as a group. The group in itself is strongly heterogeneous. The dispersion among single fund returns is extraordinary. In addition, as we have pointed out, hedge fund data in general is not perfect. It seems that macro fund data from different data vendors is heavily biased towards selection and mean returns and historical standard deviations strongly period dependent.
❏ Figure 44 shows the negative outliers occurring in down markets. This suggests that downside correlation to other asset markets is high.

Table 12 shows some further statistics on macro returns.

❏ The statistics vary across data vendors and across different time periods.

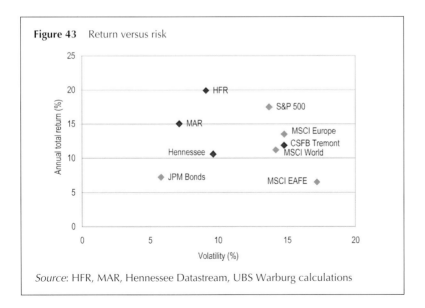

Figure 43   Return versus risk

Source: HFR, MAR, Hennessee Datastream, UBS Warburg calculations

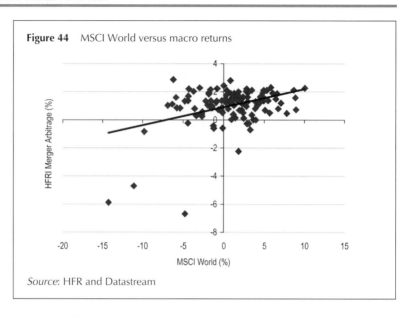

Figure 44   MSCI World versus macro returns

Source: HFR and Datastream

Table 12   Statistical analysis of macro returns

	Alpha to MSCI World	Beta to MSCI World	Skew	Excess kurtosis	Correlation on MSCI World	Correlation on JPM Global Bonds
HFRI Macro Index	1.26	0.29	0.05	0.17	0.451	0.071
MAR Hedge Macro	0.99	0.19	0.69	2.02	0.369	−0.017
Hennessee HF Index – Macro	0.31	0.41	−0.18	0.88	0.533	−0.025
CSFB/Tremont Global Macro	0.52	0.34	−0.09	0.60	0.297	−0.209

Source: HFR, MAR, Hennessee, CSFB/Tremont, Datastream, UBSW calculations.

This is an indication of diminishing investment opportunities in this discipline. The distribution of historical returns is hardly skewed and only shows a minimal degree of positive excess kurtosis. The correlation to equities ranges from 0.3 to 0.55.

The following two graphs show the performance of the HFRI Macro index in different market environments and average quarterly returns in down-markets versus average quarterly returns in friendly markets. Note that we changed the time period in Figure 46. We have reduced the period to January 1994 through March 2000 period to take into account that macro yielded higher returns in the distant past than they did in the recent past. Figure 46, therefore, is based on 25 quarterly returns.

❏ Macro funds were hit hard during the US rate rise in Q1 94 and during

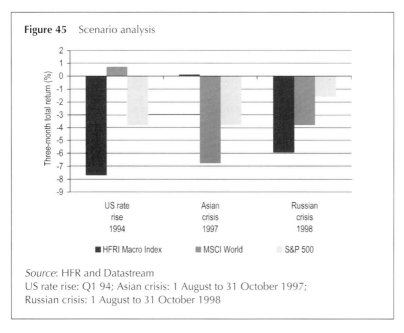

Figure 45   Scenario analysis

Source: HFR and Datastream
US rate rise: Q1 94; Asian crisis: 1 August to 31 October 1997;
Russian crisis: 1 August to 31 October 1998

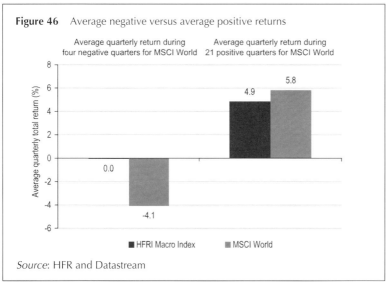

Figure 46   Average negative versus average positive returns

Source: HFR and Datastream

the Russian credit crisis in 1998. Macro funds, overall, were flat during the Asian crisis in 1997.

❑ The Asian crisis was much reminiscent of the ERM Crisis of 1992. Substantial amounts of 'carry trades' were involved in the build-up of both crises. These carry trades allowed Thai corporations and banks to borrow in foreign currencies, which had a lower interest rate than the domestic currency. As long as the domestic currency did not depreciate, the foreign currency loans represented a cheap source of funding. In the end, the carry trade led to an unsustainable equilibrium. By fixing the exchange rate, the Thai central bank was indirectly paying a risk premium to foreign investors to support domestic funding needs. However, when these foreign lenders are themselves highly leveraged institutions such as proprietary desks from investment banks (and occasionally leveraged domestic corporations), the resultant equilibrium is at best tenuous. In July 1997, for whatever reason, some foreign lenders decided to unwind their carry trades in Thailand. They sold baht and bought dollars in the spot market, putting tremendous pressure on the baht.

❏ Figure 46 shows that since 1994, macro funds provided some downside protection but underperformed equities during bull phases. Since 1990, the HFRI Macro index showed a positive average quarterly return of 1.4%, while the MSCI World total return index fell by an average of 6.7%. The macro index increased by 5.9% in quarters where the MSCI index increase by 5.8% on average. This underlines the observation that terms are deteriorating.

The next figure shows how returns have been distributed in the past and compares the historic return distribution with a normal distribution of macro and a normal distribution of historical MSCI World returns both based on historic mean return and standard deviation of returns. For Figure 48, we have sorted the macro returns and compared them with the

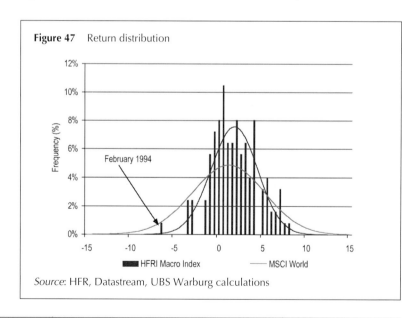

Figure 47　Return distribution

Source: HFR, Datastream, UBS Warburg calculations

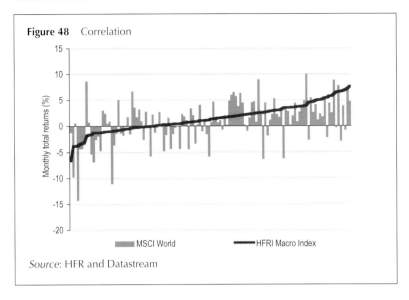

Figure 48   Correlation

Source: HFR and Datastream

corresponding market returns. This allows us to see in which market environment the extreme positive and negative returns were achieved.

❏ There were four outliers lower than two standard deviations from the mean and three returns higher than two standard deviations above the mean. The February 1994 return is outside the 99% range (three standard deviation from mean).

❏ Figure 48 shows that the negative macro returns occurred in negative markets whereas the extremely positive returns were primarily achieved during strong equity markets. This suggests that there is a high correlation to equities both in falling as well as in rising markets.

Conclusion and outlook

We regard macro funds as one of the least attractive strategies in the hedge fund universe of strategies. The (prior April 2000) 300-fold performance of George Soros Quantum fund is not representative for the discipline as a whole. Macro funds are the least focused, and their investment philosophy most vague.

However, there will probably always be macro fund managers that will deliver returns of 30–40% to their partners. As Louis Moore Bacon put it:

> At the end of the day, the overall viability of the . . . [macro] funds continues to rest on my abilities to call the markets and manage risk.[8]

We expect the popular press to continue to pick macro managers and promote them to "icons of finance". Our reservations for macro funds derives from the belief that these icons can be identified ex-post but not ex-ante. In 1969 it was difficult to foresee that a dollar given to a Mr Soros would grow to US$300 within three decades.

SHORT SELLERS

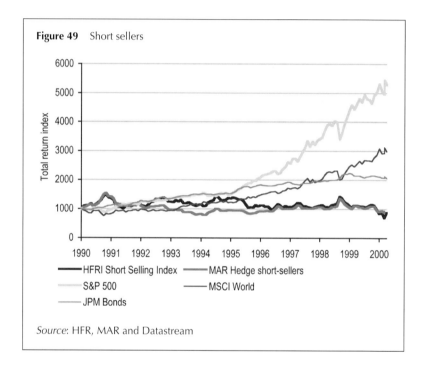

Figure 49   Short sellers

Total return index

HFRI Short Selling Index   MAR Hedge short-sellers
S&P 500   MSCI World
JPM Bonds

Source: HFR, MAR and Datastream

❏ Given the long bull market, hedge funds dedicated to a short bias have not done extremely well in the past.

❏ All short selling indices reported negative annual returns over the period available. Volatility was substantially higher than in equities in general.

❏ The worst one-month return varies between –9% and –22%, respectively. The worst one-year cumulative return varies between –25% and –29%, respectively.

❏ More than 50% of the returns were below zero due to the extended length of the 1990s bull market.

Figure 50 shows the returns of various hedge fund indices with some equity and bond indices. Figure 51 compares monthly total MSCI World returns with the HFRI Short Selling index.

Table 13 Short sellers risk and return characteristics

	# of monthly returns*	Annual return (%)	Volatility (%)	Sharpe ratio**	Worst one-month return (%)	Negative months (%)	Worst one-year return (%)
S&P 500 (Total return)	124	18.3	13.7	0.97	−14.5	32	−3.1
MSCI World (Total return)	124	11.7	14.1	0.48	−13.3	36	−16.5
MSCI Europe (Total return)	124	13.5	14.7	0.58	−12.6	34	−12.1
HFRI Short Selling Index	124	−1.1	22.2	−0.28	−21.7	52	−25.4
MAR Hedge short-sellers	123	−0.7	17.2	−0.33	−12.1	50	−27.8
Hennessee HF Index – Short Only	88	−7.7	21.1	−0.60	−13.8	57	−29.3
CSFB/Tremont Dedicated Short Bias	76	−4.9	17.7	−0.56	−8.7	55	−28.0

Source: HFR, MAR, Hennessee, CSFB/Tremont, Datastream, UBSW calculations.
*Ending April 2000 (except MAR: ending March 2000). **based on risk free rate of 5%

Figure 50 Return versus risk

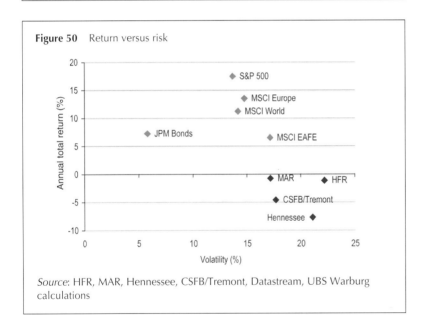

Source: HFR, MAR, Hennessee, CSFB/Tremont, Datastream, UBS Warburg calculations

❏ Figure 51 shows the negative correlation of short selling to equities. Note that the y-axis is of larger scale than the x-axis and the slope is around −1.

Table 14 shows some further statistics of short selling.

❏ The exposure to the market as a whole is around −1. The distribution of returns seems slightly positively skewed when the HFR index is ignored. Returns were also slightly leptokurtic. Correlation to MSCI World is

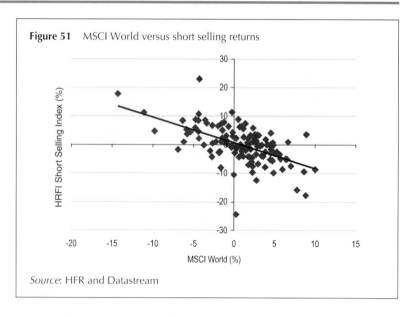

Figure 51   MSCI World versus short selling returns

Source: HFR and Datastream

Table 14   Statistical analysis of short selling returns

	Alpha to MSCI World	Beta to MSCI World	Skew	Excess kurtosis	Correlation on MSCI World	Correlation on JPM Global Bonds
HFRI Short Selling Index	0.70	−0.90	−0.13	2.46	−0.580	−0.070
MAR Hedge short-sellers	0.62	−0.74	0.37	1.91	−0.610	−0.007
Hennessee HF Index – Short Only	0.85	−1.16	0.88	4.48	−0.708	−0.094
CSFB/Tremont Dedicated Short Bias	0.83	−0.98	0.91	2.49	−0.730	−0.009

Source: HFR, MAR, Hennessee, CSFB/Tremont, Datastream, UBSW calculations.

around −0.7 and statistically significant. Correlation to bonds is not significant.

The following two graphs show the performance of the HFRI Short Selling index in different market environments and average quarterly returns in down-markets versus average quarterly returns in friendly markets.

❑ Short sellers were the only category reporting positive returns in autumn 1998. Short sellers outperformed the other strategies analysed in this report in Q1 94 but not during the Asian crisis 1997. Long/short equity performed best during the Asian crisis.

Figure 52 Scenario analysis

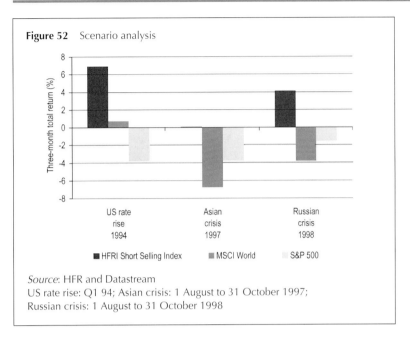

Source: HFR and Datastream
US rate rise: Q1 94; Asian crisis: 1 August to 31 October 1997;
Russian crisis: 1 August to 31 October 1998

Figure 53 Average negative versus average positive returns

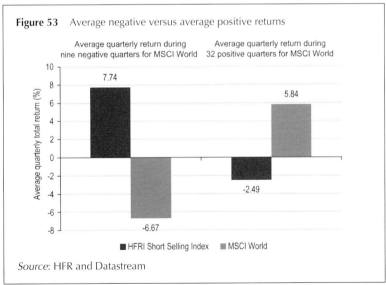

Source: HFR and Datastream

❏ When markets fall by x%, short sellers earn 1.16x on average. However,
if markets rise by x%, short sellers lose only around 0.42x on average.
This asymmetry suggests that short sellers could perform well in flat
markets.

❏ We described fixed income arbitrage and distressed securities being short a disaster put option because of its negative correlation with credit spreads and its erratic and negative returns when markets tumble. Short selling has some elements of a long disaster put option position. Returns are negatively correlated with equity markets. This negative correlation features seem to hold during market crises, ie, if history is any guide, short sellers do well when nearly everyone else in the industry does not.

Figure 52 shows how returns have been distributed in the past and compares the historic return distribution with a normal distribution of short sellers and a normal distribution of historical MSCI World returns, both based on historic mean return and standard deviation of returns. In Figure 53, we have sorted the short sellers' returns and compared them to the corresponding market returns. This allows us to see in which market environment the extreme positive and negative returns were achieved.

❏ The frequency distribution of historical returns looks fairly normal with a few outliers. There were five outliers outside the 95% range, three on the downside and two on the upside. There were two outliers outside the three standard deviation range, one on each side. The most extreme positive return was achieved in April 2000 when TMT corrected.
❏ Figure 55 shows the reverse relationship between market returns and returns from short selling. Note that the extreme returns from short selling are much more erratic than the corresponding market returns.

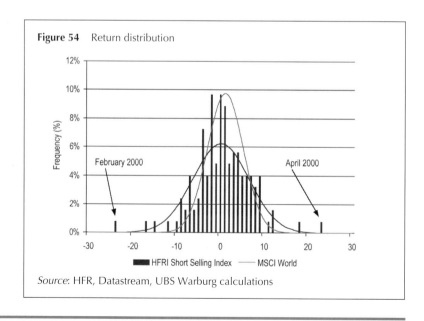

Figure 54   Return distribution

Source: HFR, Datastream, UBS Warburg calculations

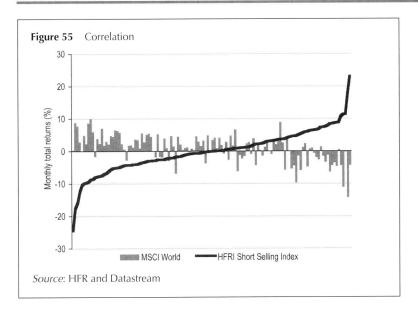

Figure 55 Correlation

Source: HFR and Datastream

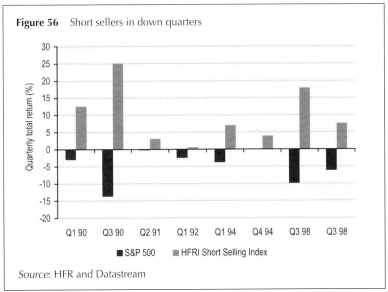

Figure 56 Short sellers in down quarters

Source: HFR and Datastream

This is due to profits from two different sources, the (possibly leveraged) short equity position and the short interest rebate.

❏ From eight negative quarters in the S&P 500 (from Q1 90 until Q1 00), short sellers reported positive returns in all cases implying correlation of –0.90 and a beta of –1.6 (Figure 56).

Conclusion and outlook

The main advantage of short sellers is their negative correlation with equities. If the equity markets go down one can expect hedge funds with a short bias to make money. In a portfolio context, exposure to short sellers, therefore, can be seen as a partial hedge.

According to Tremont (1999) estimates, only around 0.4% of assets under management are in the short selling discipline. We do not believe this to change significantly over time. However, the analysable history of hedge funds has never witnessed an extensive bear market. It is possible that many long/short equity funds employ a short bias during a bear market.

SECTOR HEDGE FUNDS[9]

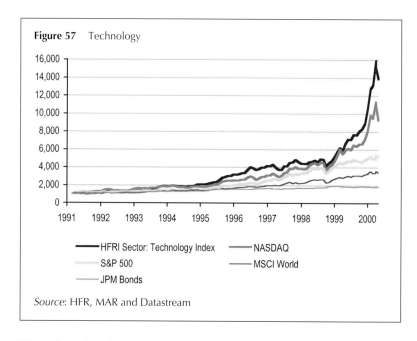

Figure 57 Technology

HFRI Sector: Technology Index — NASDAQ
S&P 500 — MSCI World
JPM Bonds

Source: HFR, MAR and Datastream

❏ Based on data from HFR, hedge funds in technology outperformed the NASDAQ index substantially, especially since Q1 99.
❏ Returns in the technology sector have been between 33% and 41%, to some extent capturing the equity risk premium of the sector. In 1999, the HFRI Technology Index increased by 124.3% and by 0.9% in 2000 (as of October).
❏ Volatility has been around 18%, which is slightly lower than a comparable index such as the NASDAQ Composite. The low volatility figure is to some extent surprising. Hedge fund portfolios are often strongly concentrated and certainly not as broad as the NASDAQ Composite with

Table 15   Technology risk and return characteristics

	# of monthly returns*	Annual return (%)	Volatility (%)	Sharpe ratio**	Worst one-month return (%)	Negative months (%)	Worst one-year return (%)
NASDAQ Composite	111	27.3	20.9	1.07	−22.2	32	−5.7
S&P 500 (Total return)	111	18.7	13.1	1.04	−14.5	30	0.5
MSCI World (Total return)	111	13.3	12.8	0.48	−13.3	33	−4.7
MSCI Europe (Total return)	111	14.2	13.9	0.58	−12.6	32	−12.1
HFRI Sector: Technology Index	111	32.9	18.8	1.48	−15.2	32	−8.9
Hennessee HF Index – Technology	52	41.0	18.3	1.96	−10.4	29	4.4

Source: HFR, Hennessee, Datastream, UBS Warburg calculations
*Ending April 2000. **Based on risk free rate of 5%

more than 4,500 members. The low volatility is an indication that the hedge fund managers do not participate fully in the swings of the sector, ie, hedging early or taking profits early. A further explanation is the low correlation among the various Technology hedge funds. Where one would expect traditional Technology funds to have similar portfolios, portfolios of alternative managers might vary substantially in terms of stock selection, net economic leverage and ratio between long and short positions.
❏ The worst monthly loss was around 15% in August 1998, which compares with a corresponding fall in the NASDAQ of 22%.

The first of the following two graphs (Figure 74) shows the returns of various hedge fund indices with some equity and bond indices. The second graph compares monthly total MSCI World returns with the HFRI Technology index.

The following table shows some further statistics of Technology hedge funds.

Table 16   Statistical analysis of technology returns

	Alpha to NASDAQ World	Beta to NASDAQ World	Skew	Excess kurtosis	Correlation on NASDAQ World	Correlation on JPM Global Bonds
HFRI Sector: Technology Index	0.76	0.80	0.20	1.75	0.887	−0.016
Hennessee HF Index – Technology	1.27	0.64	0.13	0.56	0.915	−0.034

Source: HFR, Hennessee, Datastream, UBS Warburg calculations

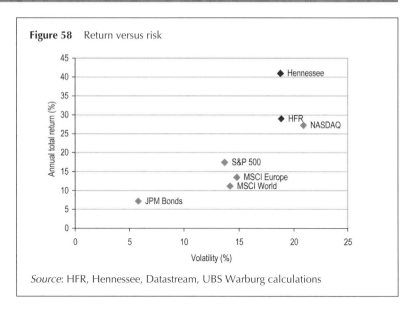

Figure 58   Return versus risk

Source: HFR, Hennessee, Datastream, UBS Warburg calculations

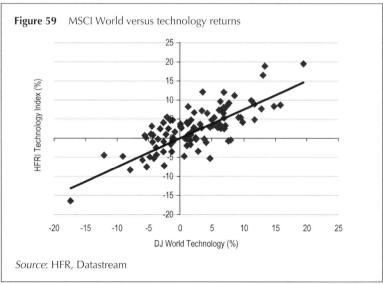

Figure 59   MSCI World versus technology returns

Source: HFR, Datastream

❏ Beta to market is high. In other words, a typical characteristic of sector funds is that they get their returns to a large extent from being long, ie, capturing the equity risk premium. The distribution of historic return measured traces of positive skew and positive kurtosis. Correlation with NASDAQ is high, ie, around 0.90.

The following two graphs show the performance of the HFRI Technology index in different market environments and average quarterly returns in down-markets versus average quarterly returns in friendly markets.

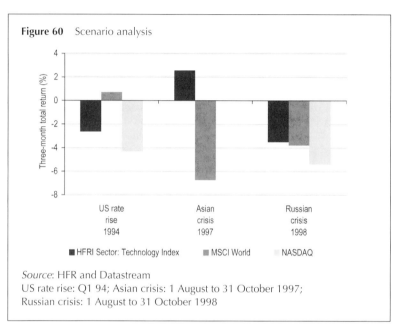

Figure 60   Scenario analysis

Source: HFR and Datastream
US rate rise: Q1 94; Asian crisis: 1 August to 31 October 1997;
Russian crisis: 1 August to 31 October 1998

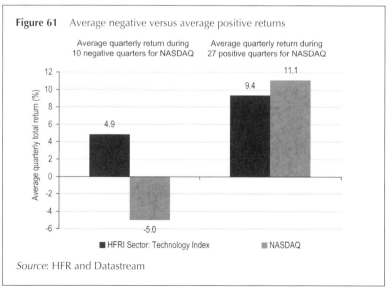

Figure 61   Average negative versus average positive returns

Source: HFR and Datastream

433

❑ Technology hedge funds have outperformed the NASDAQ during the US rate rise in 1994, the Asian crisis and even in autumn 1998.

❑ Technology hedge funds substantially outperform the market when markets fall. On average, hedge funds in the Technology sector have out-performed the NASDAQ by nearly 10% in down-quarters by underperforming the index by around 2% in up-quarters.

Figure 62 shows how returns have been distributed in the past and com-pares the historic return distribution with a normal distribution of hedge funds in the Technology sector and a normal distribution of historical NASDAQ returns, both based on historic mean return and standard devia-tion of returns. In Figure 63, we have sorted the hedge funds returns and compared them with the corresponding market returns. This allows us to see in which market environment the extreme positive and negative returns were achieved.

❑ The frequency distribution has some resemblance with a normal distrib-ution. The normal distribution derived from Technology sector hedge fund returns has a higher historical mean return with slightly lower volatility than the NASDAQ equivalent normal distribution. There were four returns outside the 95% range from the HFRI Sector Technology Index, three of them positive. A total of three returns were outside the 99% range, two of them positive.

❑ Figure 63 reveals where this hedge fund style derives its returns. As

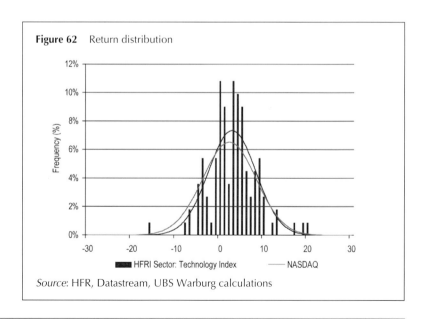

Figure 62   Return distribution

Source: HFR, Datastream, UBS Warburg calculations

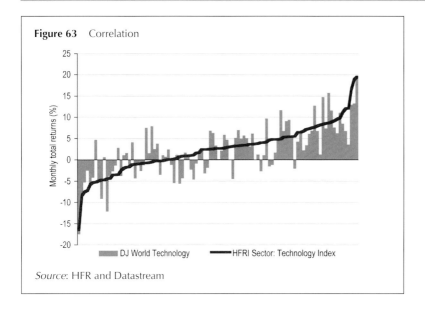

Figure 63   Correlation

Source: HFR and Datastream

already mentioned, the primary source of return of sector funds is the return of the underlying sector.

Conclusion and outlook

Sector funds are a combination of beta and alpha. In that sense they are similar to traditional funds. Sector hedge funds have some advantages. One is that they have outperformed traditional funds in the past. Given the regulatory flexibility and principal-aligned incentive structures of hedge funds, there is a sound probability that the outperformance against traditional funds will subsist in the future.

The next opportunistic absolute return strategy is emerging markets. In this chapter we treat emerging markets as a separate opportunistic hedge fund strategy. One could argue that it should be classified as a long-only hedge fund strategy where the focus is regional. One reason why we separated emerging markets into a separate category is because hedge fund investing often involves exploiting market inefficiencies as opposed to capturing the risk premium of the underlying asset class. Inefficiencies in emerging markets are substantially higher than in developed markets. Hedge funds should be doing well. In addition, hedge funds are not always simply long the asset class in the emerging market.

EMERGING MARKETS

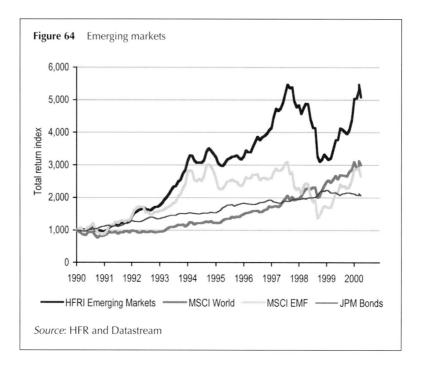

Figure 64   Emerging markets

Source: HFR and Datastream

❑ HFRI Emerging markets has outperformed MSCI EMF by a wide margin over the past ten years.

❑ Over a period longer than ten years, hedge funds in emerging markets have performed around 16% annually which compares with 10% for the MSCI Emerging Markets Free index. Over shorter periods, emerging market returns have been lower due to market turbulence essentially everywhere (Asia, South America, Russia). Note that the MSCI EMF moved a lot in the second half of the 1990s but ended the half-decade more or less unchanged.

❑ Volatility was substantially lower than with the MSCI EMF index. Volatility of emerging markets hedge fund returns was around 17%, which compares with 24% in the case of the MSCI EMF. Hence, hedge funds in this segment have produced superior risk-adjusted returns. The lower volatility from the four emerging markets hedge fund indices is derived from the fact that the different hedge funds can run different strategies. Since these strategies are weakly correlated with each other, volatility of the hedge fund index or a portfolio containing different emerging market hedge funds is low. Volatility is most likely lower than

Table 17   Emerging markets risk and return characteristics

	# of monthly returns*	Annual return (%)	Volatility (%)	Sharpe ratio**	Worst one-month return (%)	Negative months (%)	Worst one-year return (%)
S&P 500 (Total return)	124	18.3	13.7	0.97	−14.5	32	−3.1
MSCI World (Total return)	124	11.7	14.1	0.48	−13.3	36	−16.5
MSCI Europe (Total return)	124	13.5	14.7	0.58	−12.6	34	−12.1
MSCI EMF (Total return)***	124	9.9	24.4	0.20	−34.1	36	−49.6
HFRI Emerging Markets (Total) Index	124	17.1	16.6	0.72	−21.0	33	−42.5
MAR Hedge Global Emerging Markets	123	15.4	17.8	0.58	−26.7	29	−45.1
Hennessee HF Index – Emerging M.	88	10.5	16.0	0.34	−20.1	40	−39.9
CSFB/Tremont Emerging Markets	76	7.1	21.4	0.10	−23.0	43	−44.2

Source: HFR, MAR, Hennessee, CSFB/Tremont, Datastream, UBS Warburg calculations
*Ending April 2000 (except MAR: ending March 2000), **Based on risk free rate of 5%. ***Emerging Markets Free

comparing a portfolio of traditional emerging market funds, because traditional equity funds are simply long the asset class.

❑ The worst monthly and worst annual returns were slightly higher in the case of the hedge funds than with the MSCI EMF. This implies that the hedge fund industry invested in this segment has the ability to cut losses short or hedge. However, hedging in emerging markets is difficult or impossible because of market restrictions to sell short either directly or synthetically. Emerging markets, therefore, use lower leverage than hedge funds in developed markets. The lack of hedging possibilities and low use of leverage make emerging markets hedge funds look similar to traditional long-only funds. However, emerging markets have greater flexibility than traditional funds. They are not necessarily long the asset class.

The first of the following two graphs shows the returns of various hedge fund indices with some equity and bond indices. The second graph compares monthly total MSCI EMF returns with the HFRI Emerging markets index.

❑ Figure 65 shows different risk/return characteristics for different hedge fund indices. This is because we mixed different time periods and the second half of the 1990s was significantly worse than the first half. We therefore suggest comparing the HFR and MAR indices with MSCI EMF since it covers the full decade. The figure illustrates that the industry

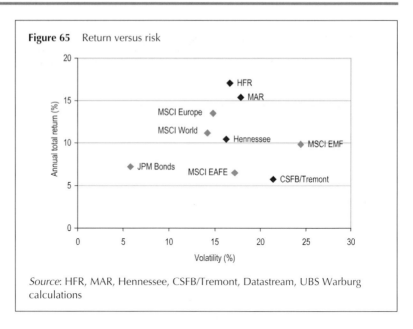

Figure 65 Return versus risk

Source: HFR, MAR, Hennessee, CSFB/Tremont, Datastream, UBS Warburg calculations

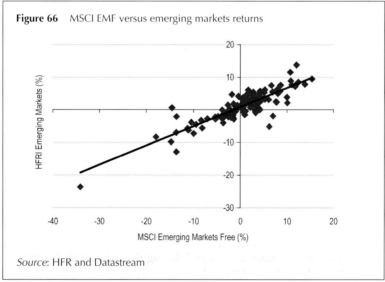

Figure 66 MSCI EMF versus emerging markets returns

Source: HFR and Datastream

performs significantly better than the index on an absolute as well as risk-adjusted basis.

❏ Figure 66 shows that correlation between hedge fund returns and MSCI EMF index returns is high. The outliers are close to the slope.

❏ Exposure to the region is the main explanatory factor of the emerging markets hedge fund returns. The beta is around 0.6. This is less than with

---

Table 18   Statistical analysis of emerging markets returns

	Alpha to MSCI EMF	Beta to MSCI EMF	Skew	Excess kurtosis	Correlation on MSCI EMF	Correlation on JPM Global Bonds
MSCI EMF (Total return)	0.00	1.00	−1.31	4.42	1.000	−0.055
HFRI Emerging Markets (Total) Index	0.85	0.59	−1.27	5.54	0.865	−0.057
MAR Hedge Global Emerging markets	0.71	0.55	−1.93	12.72	0.755	−0.071
Hennessee HF Index – Emerg Mkts	0.50	0.57	−1.32	6.30	0.823	−0.227
CSFB/Tremont Emerging Markets	0.52	0.69	−0.91	3.72	0.871	−0.272

Source: HFR, Hennessee, Datastream, UBS Warburg calculations

---

other long biased hedge fund strategies. The reason is that emerging market hedge fund managers do not necessarily exploit inefficiencies in the equity markets only. For example, emerging market hedge funds were not in equities at all during the Peso Crisis of 1994. Hedge funds exploited market inefficiencies in Brady bonds by hedging currency risk. This resulted in significant outperformance of mutual funds which, essentially, were just long equities, the currency unhedged. This flexibility to allocate funds where the opportunities are results in a beta that is significantly lower than one.

❏ Emerging market hedge fund returns have been negatively skewed and leptokurtic in the past, as have been returns on the MSCI EMF.
❏ Correlation with the MSCI EMF is high at around 0.8.

The following two graphs show the performance of the HFRI Emerging Markets index in different market environments and average quarterly returns in down-markets versus average quarterly returns in friendly markets.

❏ Hedge funds in emerging markets outperformed the MSCI EMF during rising US interest rates in 1994 and during the Asian crisis in 1997, but heavily underperformed the index during the Russian credit crisis.
❏ On average, however, hedge funds outperform MSCI EMF by 6% during down-quarters and underperformed the index by only 2% during up-quarters. This pattern lets us assume that hedge funds in this segment hedge so they are not exposed to the full fall and re-enter once the trend has reversed, missing out on some of the early gains of a rebound.

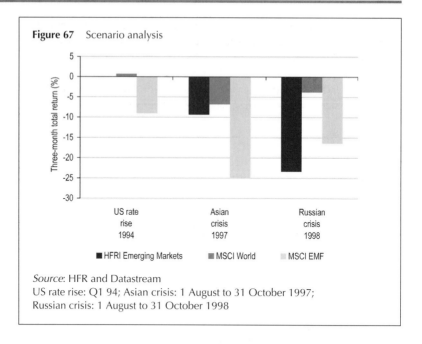

Figure 67 Scenario analysis

Source: HFR and Datastream
US rate rise: Q1 94; Asian crisis: 1 August to 31 October 1997;
Russian crisis: 1 August to 31 October 1998

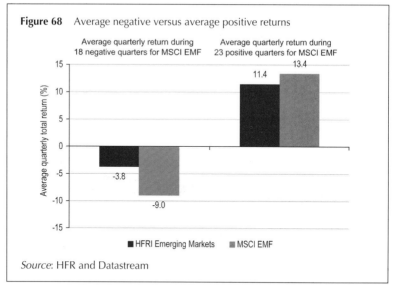

Figure 68 Average negative versus average positive returns

Source: HFR and Datastream

Figure 69 shows how returns have been distributed in the past and compares the historic return distribution with a normal distribution of hedge funds in the emerging market sector and a normal distribution of historical MSCI EMF returns, both based on historic mean return and standard deviation of returns. In Figure 70 we have sorted the hedge funds returns and compared them to the corresponding market returns. This allows us to see in which market environment the extreme positive and negative returns were achieved.

❏ The frequency distribution has some resemblance with a normal distribution. However, excess kurtosis was high. There were six returns outside

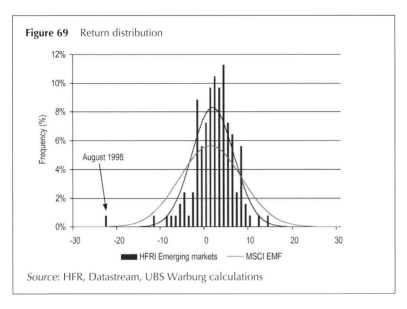

Figure 69 Return distribution

Source: HFR, Datastream, UBS Warburg calculations

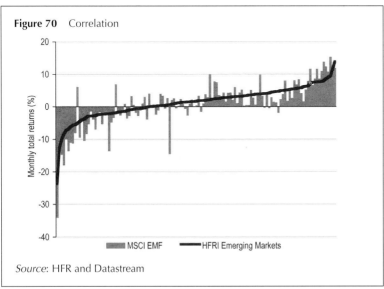

Figure 70 Correlation

Source: HFR and Datastream

the 95% range, two of them were positive. August 1998 was the only monthly return outside the 99% range.

❏ Figure 68 reveals that negative returns are concentrated in negative market environments and positive hedge fund returns in positive market environments. The graph also shows that hedge fund managers miss some but not all of the falls in the underlying markets. This means hedge fund managers occasionally are hedged, ie, manage to avoid loss of principal. Missing only a few of the corrections increases the performance substantially. Ian Wace of Marshall Wace Asset Management thinks along these lines. Wace used the term negative compounding:

> This business [hedge funds] has nothing to do with positive compounding; it has to do with avoiding negative compounding. . . The P&L is the only moderator of hubris. You are not given money to lose it.[10]

Conclusion and outlook

Emerging market hedge funds have some appeal. Emerging markets are inefficient in many ways. The inefficiencies in these markets are full of opportunities for skill-based strategies apart from simply capturing the risk premium of the equity asset class. We believe that exploiting inefficiencies by simultaneously controlling market risk is probably more profitable than in developed markets because there are more inefficiencies. This was true in the past and, in our view, should hold in the future. However, if history is any guide, emerging market hedge fund returns are volatile.

LONG/SHORT EQUITY

❏ Long/short equity was one of the most profitable hedge fund strategies in the past. The HFRI Equity Non-Hedge Index, our proxy for this market segment, outperformed even the S&P 500. Long/short equity is not

Table 19   Long/short equity risk and return characteristics

	# of monthly returns*	Annual return (%)	Volatility (%)	Sharpe ratio**	Worst one-month return (%)	Negative months (%)	Worst one-year return (%)
S&P 500 (Total return)	124	18.3	13.7	0.97	−14.5	32	−3.1
MSCI World (Total return)	124	11.7	14.1	0.48	−13.3	36	−16.5
MSCI Europe (Total return)	124	13.5	14.7	0.58	−12.6	34	−12.1
HFRI Equity Non-Hedge Index	124	21.7	13.8	1.21	−13.3	31	−9.7
CSFB/Tremont Long / Short Equity	76	18.8	12.5	1.10	−11.4	29	−9.9

Source: HFR, CSFB/Tremont, Datastream, UBS Warburg calculations
*Ending April 2000. **Based on risk free rate of 5%

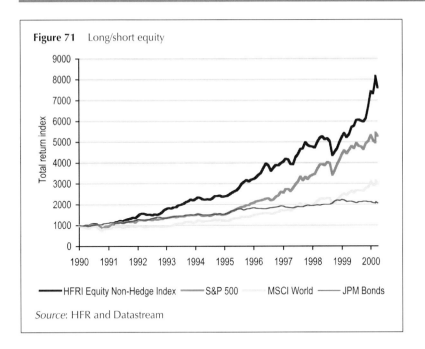

Figure 71 Long/short equity

Source: HFR and Datastream

only one of the most profitable, it is also the largest segment with c30% market share.
❏ The main characteristic of this category is high historical performance. Based on the two indices used, historical total returns were around 20% outperforming most equity indices. The main focus of this category is to make money and less to control risk. However, the heterogeneity within this category is large.
❏ The volatility of the returns is about the same as with equities in general, ie, around 13% when measured based on monthly returns. Outperformance and equal risk results in higher risk-adjusted returns.

The first of the following two graphs shows the returns of various hedge fund indices with some equity and bond indices. The second graph compares monthly total MSCI World returns with the HFRI Equity non-hedge index.

❏ In the past, long/short equities had high returns with similar volatility to equities in general. As a matter of fact, the category had the highest returns from the eleven strategies analysed apart from Technology, which we used as an example for sector/theme based strategies. Had we used value biased strategies as an example, long/short equity would top the annual return table.

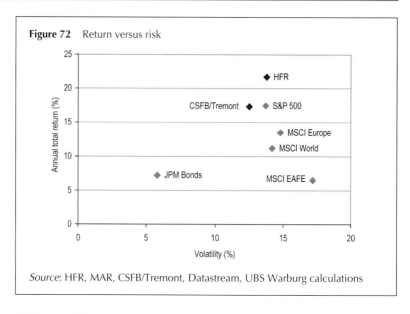

Figure 72   Return versus risk

Source: HFR, MAR, CSFB/Tremont, Datastream, UBS Warburg calculations

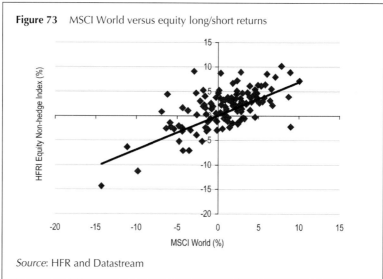

Figure 73   MSCI World versus equity long/short returns

Source: HFR and Datastream

❏ Skew and kurtosis of returns were minor. The exposure to the market was high in general but varies strongly among different hedge funds. The correlation with the equity market was high as a result. We do not believe this will change since we defined this category as strategies with a long bias (as opposed to equity market neutral). At the end of October

Table 20   Statistical analysis of long/short equity returns

	Alpha to MSCI World	Beta to MSCI World	Skew	Excess kurtosis	Correlation on MSCI World	Correlation on JPM Global Bonds
HFRI Equity Non-Hedge Index	1.07	0.64	−0.78	1.92	0.644	0.034
CSFB/Tremont Long / Short Equity	0.56	0.62	−0.29	2.91	0.641	0.000

Source: HFR, CSFB/Tremont, Datastream, UBS Warburg calculations

the one-year correlation between the HFRI Equity Non-Hedge index and the NASDAQ Composite Index was 0.967 and statistically significant at the 99% level.

The following two graphs show the performance of the HFRI Equity Non-Hedge index in different market environments and average quarterly returns in down-markets versus average quarterly returns in friendly markets.

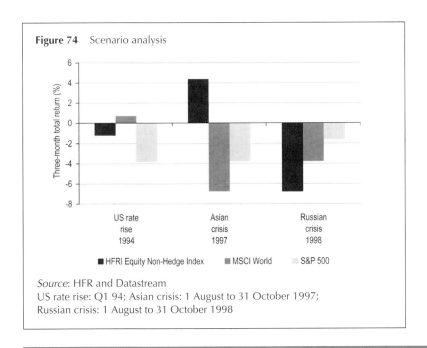

Figure 74   Scenario analysis

Source: HFR and Datastream
US rate rise: Q1 94; Asian crisis: 1 August to 31 October 1997;
Russian crisis: 1 August to 31 October 1998

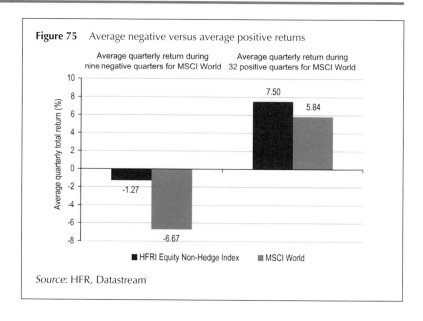

Figure 75   Average negative versus average positive returns

Source: HFR, Datastream

❏ Long/short equity has underperformed equities during the Russian crisis. As mentioned before this is primarily due to LTCM and hedge funds in general. Long/short equity performed well during the Asian crisis.

❏ We believe downside protection with long/short equity is limited. However, Figure 75 shows that, on average, long/short equity outperforms equities both in down as well as up markets. Note that the outperformance in down quarters was 540bp, which compares to 166bp outperformance in up quarters. This suggests some sort of payoff, which is similar to that of a call option position (positive delta, long gamma): if the markets rise, one has some leveraged return (as with a long call option) and the exposure to equities rises (as with a long gamma position). If the market falls, the value of the position falls as well, but to a smaller extent than the underlying market.

Figure 76 shows how returns have been distributed in the past and compares the historic return distribution with a normal distribution of hedge funds in the long/short equity sector and a normal distribution of historical MSCI World returns both based on historic mean return and standard deviation of returns. In Figure 77 we have sorted the hedge funds returns and compared them to the corresponding market returns. This allows us to see in which market environment the extreme positive and negative returns were achieved.

❏ Figure 76 shows that the normal distribution derived from historical returns and volatility is nearly equal to that of the MSCI World but with a higher mean return. Out of the 124 returns, six were outside the 95% range, of which five were on the downside. One negative return was outside the 99% range. The frequency distribution shows some

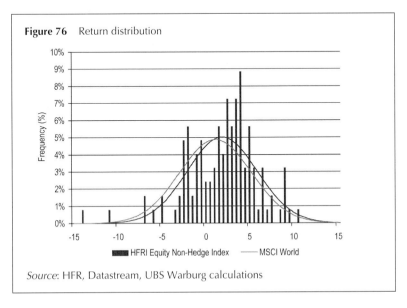

Figure 76 Return distribution

Source: HFR, Datastream, UBS Warburg calculations

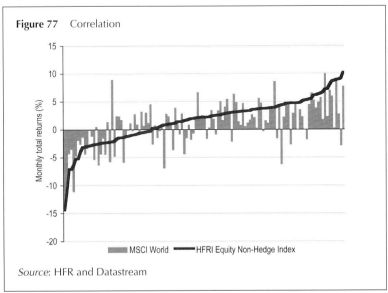

Figure 77 Correlation

Source: HFR and Datastream

concentration around –2% as well as +3%. Note that 39 of the 124 returns were negative which compares with 40 in the case of the S&P 500 and 45 with the MSCI World.

❑ Figure 77 illustrates where the high correlation to the equity market is derived. The extreme negative returns are achieved during down-markets whereas extreme positive returns were associated with positive market environments.

Equity portfolio risk reduction potential with long/short equity strategies

We believe that long/short equity strategies are ideal for equity investors trying to reduce risk without heavily sacrificing expected returns. Figure 78 shows the efficient frontier for a global investor using historical risk, return and correlation figures. An investor moving funds from equity to bonds will move down along the efficient frontier, reducing risk as well as expected returns. However, an investor moving into both bonds as well as long/short equity strategies potentially can reduce risk with keeping expected returns stable. The reason for this is not because of low correlation between equities and long/short equity strategies but because of high returns from long/short equity strategies. Correlation between equities and long/short strategies does not support the case. Figure 77 demonstrated that long/short strategies perform poorly when equity markets fall. However, Figure 75 showed that long/short equity strategies outperformed equity by 5.4 percentage points in the quarters where MSCI World yielded a negative return. This is substantially more than the 1.7% outperformance of long/short equity strategies in rising equity markets. Because long/short equity strategies outperform equities more in falling markets than in rising markets, we believe that allocating funds to long/short equity strategies reduces risk in equity-friendly as well as unfriendly markets. However, for this to be true in the future, long/short equity managers will have to continue producing 20% annual returns. We believe this is an uncertainty.

Conclusion and outlook

To some, long/short equity is the archetype of a hedge fund. Long/short equity, in the past, had high returns, high volatility and high correlation with equities. We believe that these return and risk characteristics will not change significantly. However, the dispersion between different long/short equity mangers is wide and we do not expect this dispersion to narrow.

A case could be drawn that outperformance will not be as high in the future as it was in the past. The average outperformance against the MSCI World total return index in the first five years of the 1990s was 15.7% but only 5.6% in the second half. This suggests that there will still be outperformance (alpha derived from skill) but that the alpha is deteriorating to

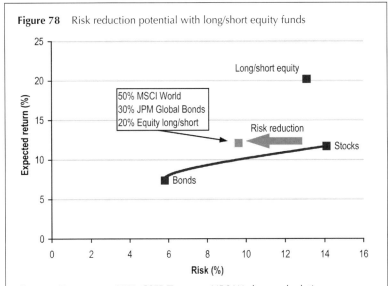

Figure 78   Risk reduction potential with long/short equity funds

Sources: Datastream, HFR, CSFB/Tremont, UBS Warburg calculations.
Based on monthly US$ total returns net of fees between January 1990 and April 2000.
Long/short equity: risk and returns are an equally weighted average from HFR and CSFB/Tremont data. Correlation to equity and bond indices are based from HFR Equity Non-hedge index.
MSCI World total return: 11.7%, volatility: 14.1%; JPM Global Bonds: 7.4% / 5.8%; Long/short equity: 20.2% / 13.1%. Correlation MSCI World/JPM Global Bonds: 0.345; MSCI World/Long/short equity: 0.654; JPM Global Bonds/Long/short equity: 0.036.

some extent. We suspect this is due to the fact that in the recent past, more long-only managers have joined the discipline. We believe that risk managers have an edge over long-biased managers in the long/short discipline with respect to managing long/short positions in general and to selling short in particular.

CONCLUSIONS

Some hedge fund strategies are designed to generate pure alpha by hedging the primary risk (eg, stock market and interest rate risk) that drive returns in the traditional asset classes. These strategies seek to exploit mispricings and inefficiencies in global capital markets by accepting idiosyncratic risk in return for generating high, risk-adjusted ratios of return with low correlation to traditional assets.

Some hedge fund strategies have returned Sharpe ratios of around 2.0 and are likely to do so in the future. Some absolute-return strategies yielded high returns, which were only weakly correlated with returns in other capital markets and weakly or negatively correlated among them-selves. We believe that these correlation characteristics are unlikely to disappear as the risk factors of the strategies are of a different nature than traditional investment strategies.

Some strategies perform better than others when equity markets fall. We believe that high downside protection is, to a large extent, predictable. Understanding the different investment philosophies is becoming increas-ingly important as more and more beta merchants camouflaged as hedge funds reach out for institutional dollars. In the case of a bear market, hedge funds without an edge in the discipline of exploiting market inefficiencies and without serious risk management capabilities are likely to tumble as did most copy-cat hedge funds in the early 1970s when markets reversed.

If there is a single most important attribute of the hedge fund industry, it is heterogeneity. The various investment strategies are conceptually differ-ent. Traditional funds are normally long an asset class and unleveraged. Hedge funds can range from leveraged short to leveraged long. However, it is the middle section – the zero-beta strategies – which, in our view, deserve the most attention.

We conclude that, in the quest for alpha, investing in hedge funds is irrefutably wise. Any investor who is not restricted to invest in hedge funds, in our view, should reach the same conclusion. Where risk, return and correlation to traditional asset classes matter, the advantages of invest-ing in absolute-return strategies should outbalance the disadvantages by a wide margin.

1   From VAN Hedge Fund Advisors (1999).
2   Except returns from Hennessee, which are gross of fees.
3   For example, Schneeweis and Pescatore (1999) distinguish between five sectors (based on Evaluation Associates Capital Markets): relative value; event-driven; equity hedge; global asset allocators; and short selling. Long/short equity is a sub-sector of the relative value sector. It defines the equity hedge sector as long and short securities with varying degrees of exposure and leverage, such as domestic long equity (long undervalued US equities, short selling is used sparingly), domestic opportunistic equity (long and short US equities with ability to be net short overall), and global international (long undervalued global equities, short selling used opportunistically). We prefer our classification system because it allows us to distinguish strategies with zero beta from the long-biased strategies.
4   Note that prior to LTCM, fixed income arbitrage had equity-like returns with bond-like volatility (around 12% a year). Figure 11 on page 390 shows the period that includes autumn 1998.
5   Calculations simplified.
6   The EC Council of Ministers has agreed a common position on takeovers in June 2000. The directive still needs to be approved by the European Parliament but this is unlikely to present further difficulties.
7   Note that there is a strong overlap between the different databases. Surely some hedge funds are in all databases.
8   From Institutional Investor (2000).
9   The characteristics of the chosen sector – Technology – cannot be representative for all sector hedge funds.

10 "Hedge funds in Europe", speech at the 2000 Hedge Fund Symposium (EIM/EuroHedge/SFI), "Can Institutions Afford to Ignore Hedge Funds?", 27 April 2000, London.

BIBLIOGRAPHY

Fung, W., and D. A. Hsieh, 1999, "A Primer on Hedge Funds", *Journal of Empirical Finance* 6, pp. 309–31.

Institutional Investor, 2000, Europe edition, 15 July.

Schneeweis, T. and J. F. Pescatore, 1999, "Alternative Asset Returns: Theoretical Bases and Empirical Evidence", in *The Handbook of Alternative Investment Strategies* (New York: Institutional Investor Inc).

Tremont Partners Inc. and TASS Investment Research, 1999, "The Case For Hedge Funds".

VAN Hedge Fund Advisors, 1999, "Quantitative analysis of hedge funds return/risk characteristics" http://www.vanhedge.com/quantit.htm.

Index

Other Titles by Risk Books

Risk Budgeting: A New Approach to Investing
Edited by Leslie Rahl, Capital Market Risk Advisors
ISBN 1 899 332 944

Options: Classic Approaches to Pricing and Modelling
Edited by Lane Hughston, King's College, London
ISBN 1 899 332 669

Rubinstein on Derivatives
By Mark Rubinstein, University of California
ISBN 1 899 332 537

Crude Oil Hedging: Benchmarking Price Protection Strategies
By Energy Security Analysis, Inc USA
ISBN 1 899 332 316

Classic Futures: Lessons from the Past for the Electronic Age
Edited by Lester G. Telser, University of Chicago
ISBN 1 899 332 928

The Telecoms Trading Revolution
With leading expert insights from the trading telecoms industry
ISBN 1 899 332 642

Derivatives: The Tools that Changed Finance
By Dr. Phelim P. Boyle and Feidhilm Boyle
ISBN 1 899 332 88X

Extremes and Integrated Risk Management
Published in association with UBS Warburg
Edited by Paul Embrechts, Federal Institute of Technology (ETH), Zurich
ISBN 1 899 332 74X

For more information on these titles, as well as the full range of titles
published by Risk Books, please visit the on-line bookstore at
www.riskbooks.com. Alternatively, phone +44 (0)20 7484 9757 or fax
+44(0)20 7484 9758 and request the latest book catalogue.